PLANETARY:

WARREN ELLIS – Writer

JOHN CASSADAY – Artist

LAURA MARTIN – Colorist

COMICRAFT – Letterer

JIM LEE	Editorial Director
HANK KANALZ	VP – General Manager
SCOTT DUNBIER & BEN ABERNATHY	Editors – Original Series
KRISTY QUINN	Editor
ED ROEDER	Art Director
PAUL LEVITZ	President & Publisher
RICHARD BRUNING	SVP – Creative Director
PATRICK CALDON	EVP – Finance & Operations
AMY GENKINS	SVP – Business & Legal Affairs
GREGORY NOVECK	SVP – Creative Affairs
STEVE ROTTERDAM	SVP – Sales & Marketing
CHERYL RUBIN	SVP – Brand Management

SPACETIME ARCHAEOLOGY

Covers by John Cassaday

PLANETARY CREATED BY WARREN ELLIS AND JOHN CASSADAY

SUSTAINABLE FORESTRY INITIATIVE
Certified Chain of Custody
Promoting Sustainable Forest Management
www.sfiprogram.org

Fiber used in this product line meets the sourcing requirements of the SFI program.
www.sfiprogram.org
NSF-SFICOC-C0001801.

planetary
mystery
in space

A COMIC BY WARREN ELLIS
JOHN CASSADAY

ADDITIONAL CONTRIBUTIONS BY
LAURA DEPUY MARTIN
and **RICHARD STARKINGS**

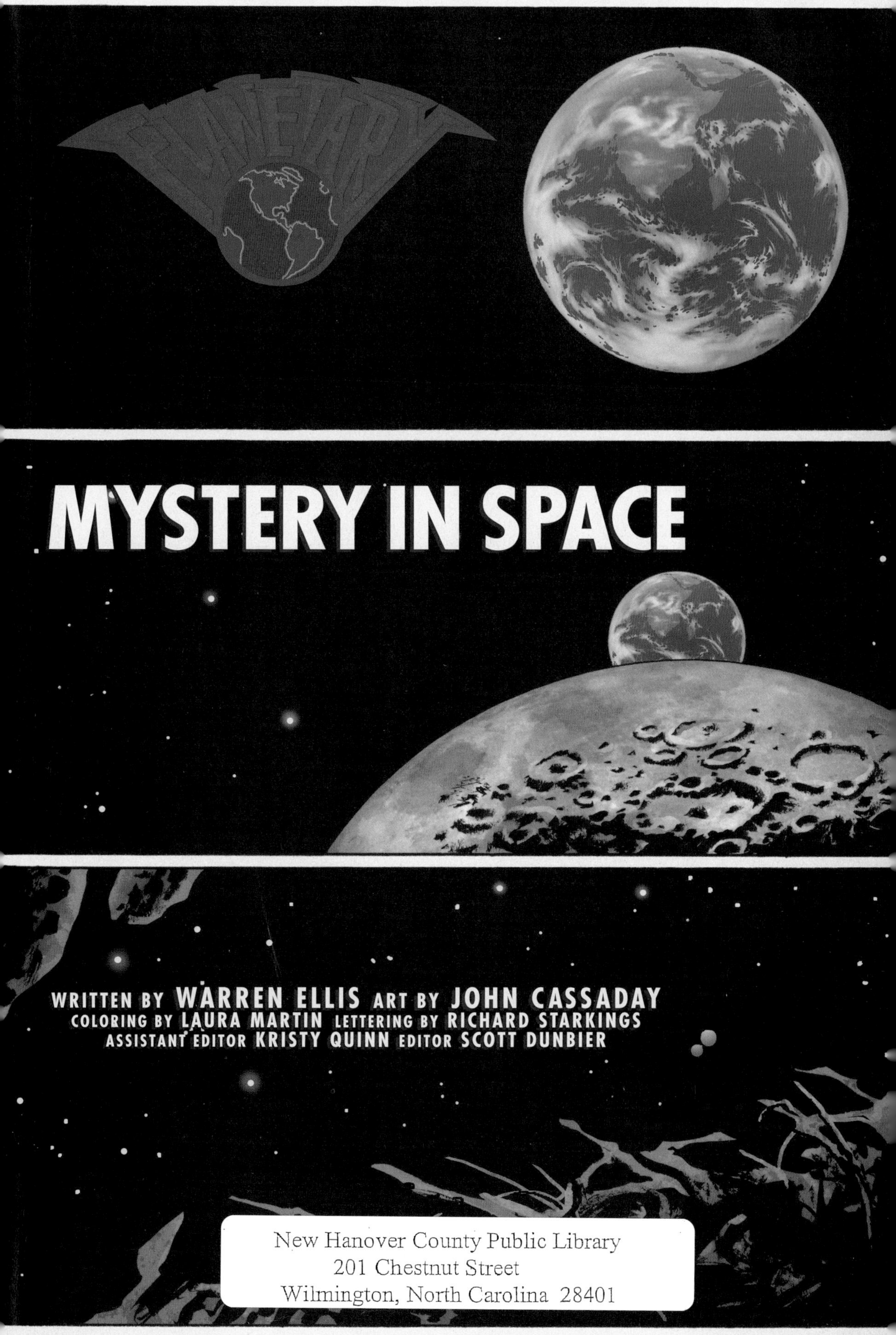
MYSTERY IN SPACE
WRITTEN BY WARREN ELLIS ART BY JOHN CASSADAY
COLORING BY LAURA MARTIN LETTERING BY RICHARD STARKINGS
ASSISTANT EDITOR KRISTY QUINN EDITOR SCOTT DUNBIER

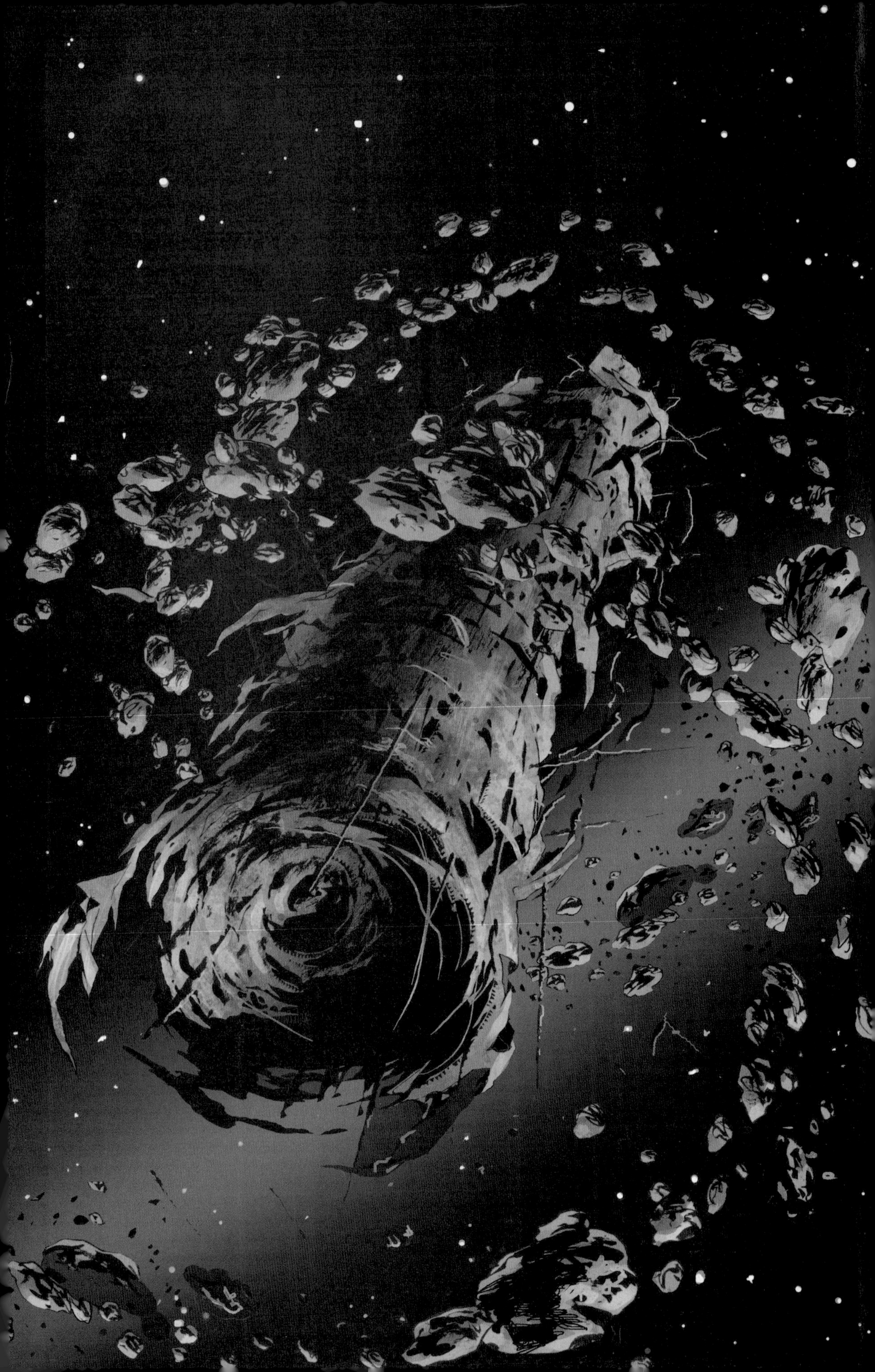

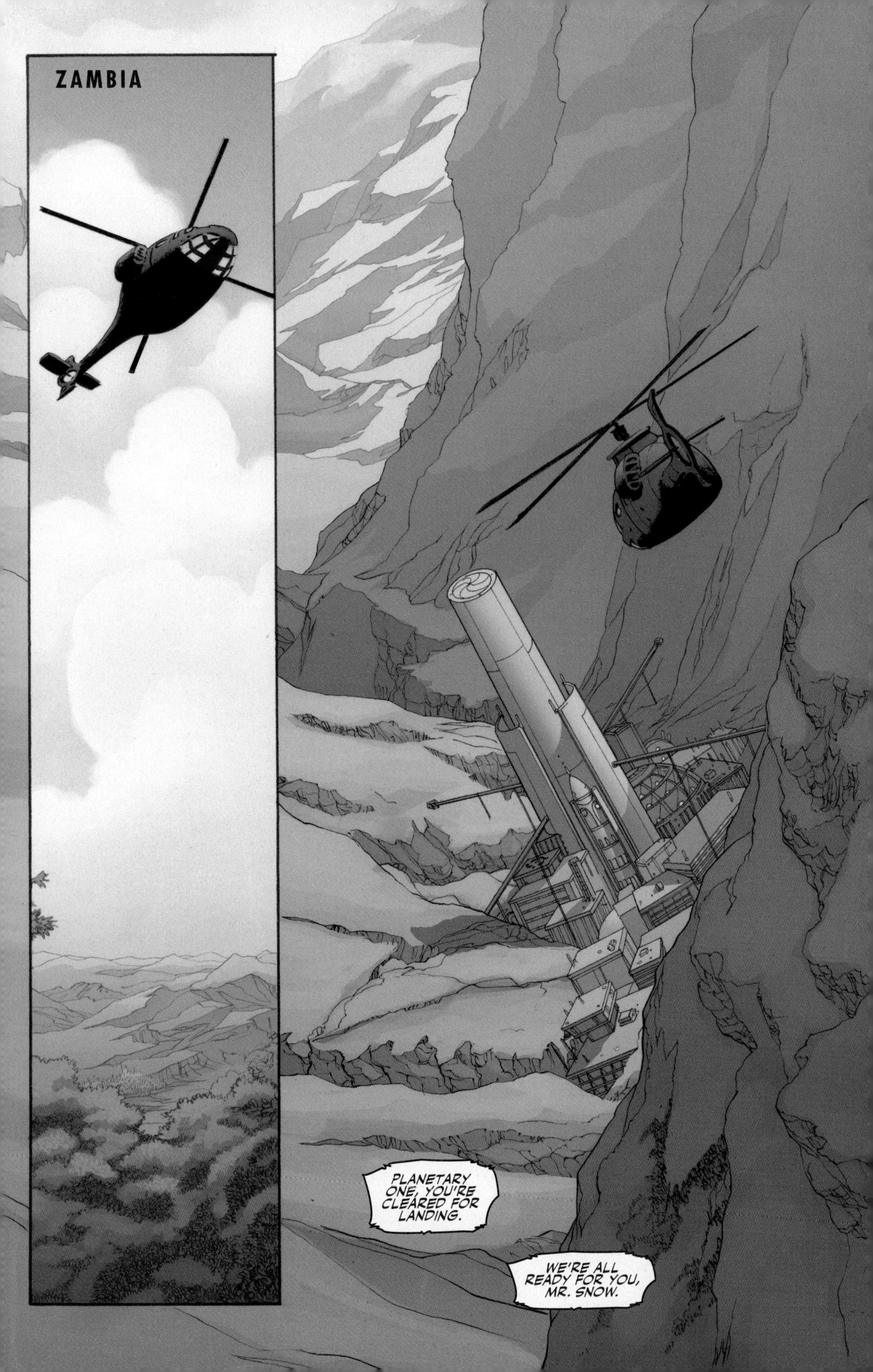
ZAMBIA
PLANETARY ONE, YOU'RE CLEARED FOR LANDING.
WE'RE ALL READY FOR YOU, MR. SNOW.

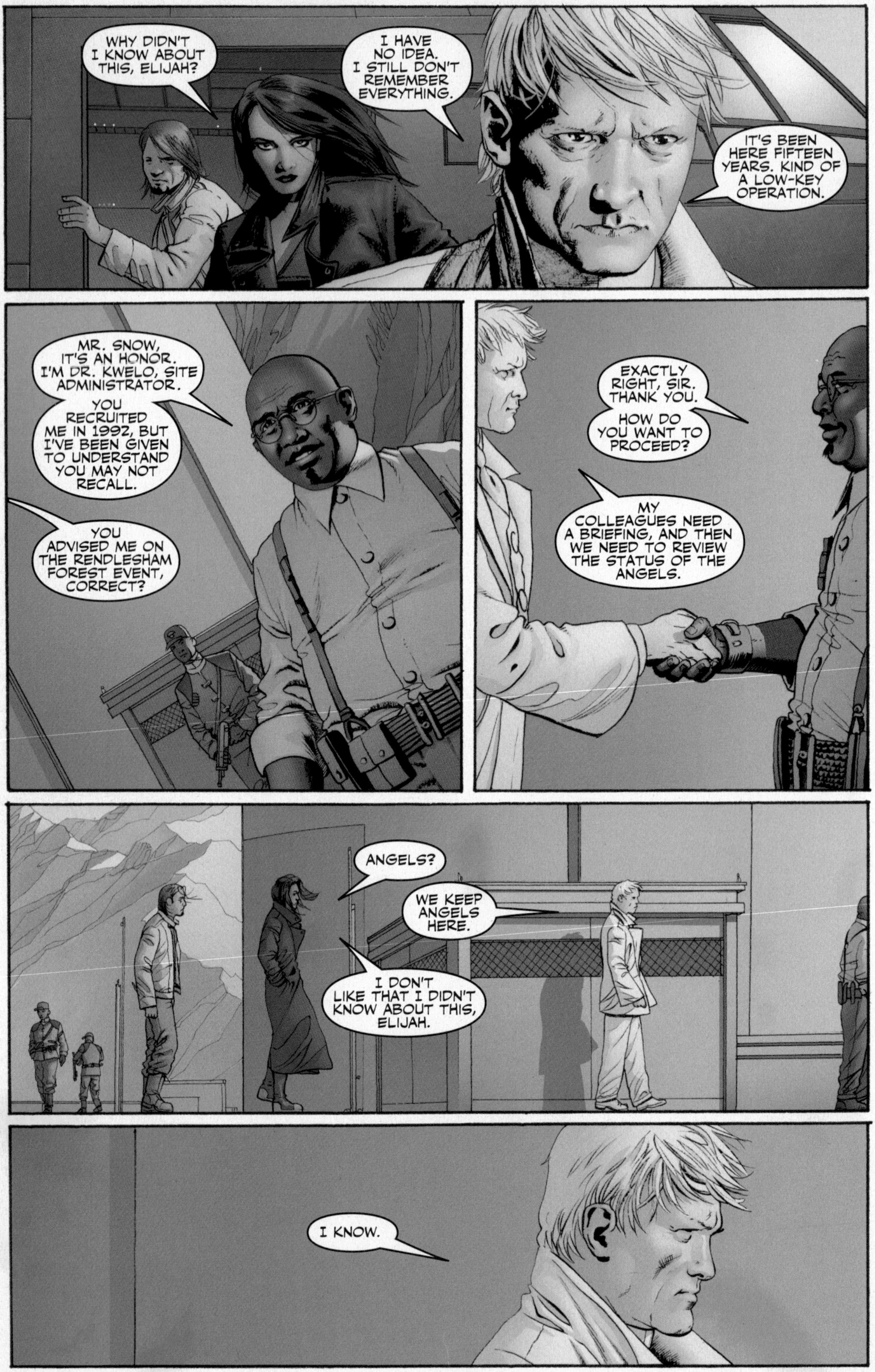
WHY DIDN'T I KNOW ABOUT THIS, ELIJAH?
I HAVE NO IDEA. I STILL DON'T REMEMBER EVERYTHING.
IT'S BEEN HERE FIFTEEN YEARS. KIND OF A LOW-KEY OPERATION.
MR. SNOW, IT'S AN HONOR. I'M DR. KWELO, SITE ADMINISTRATOR.
YOU RECRUITED ME IN 1992, BUT I'VE BEEN GIVEN TO UNDERSTAND YOU MAY NOT RECALL.
YOU ADVISED ME ON THE RENDLESHAM FOREST EVENT, CORRECT?
EXACTLY RIGHT, SIR. THANK YOU.
HOW DO YOU WANT TO PROCEED?
MY COLLEAGUES NEED A BRIEFING, AND THEN WE NEED TO REVIEW THE STATUS OF THE ANGELS.
ANGELS?
WE KEEP ANGELS HERE.
I DON'T LIKE THAT I DIDN'T KNOW ABOUT THIS, ELIJAH.
I KNOW.

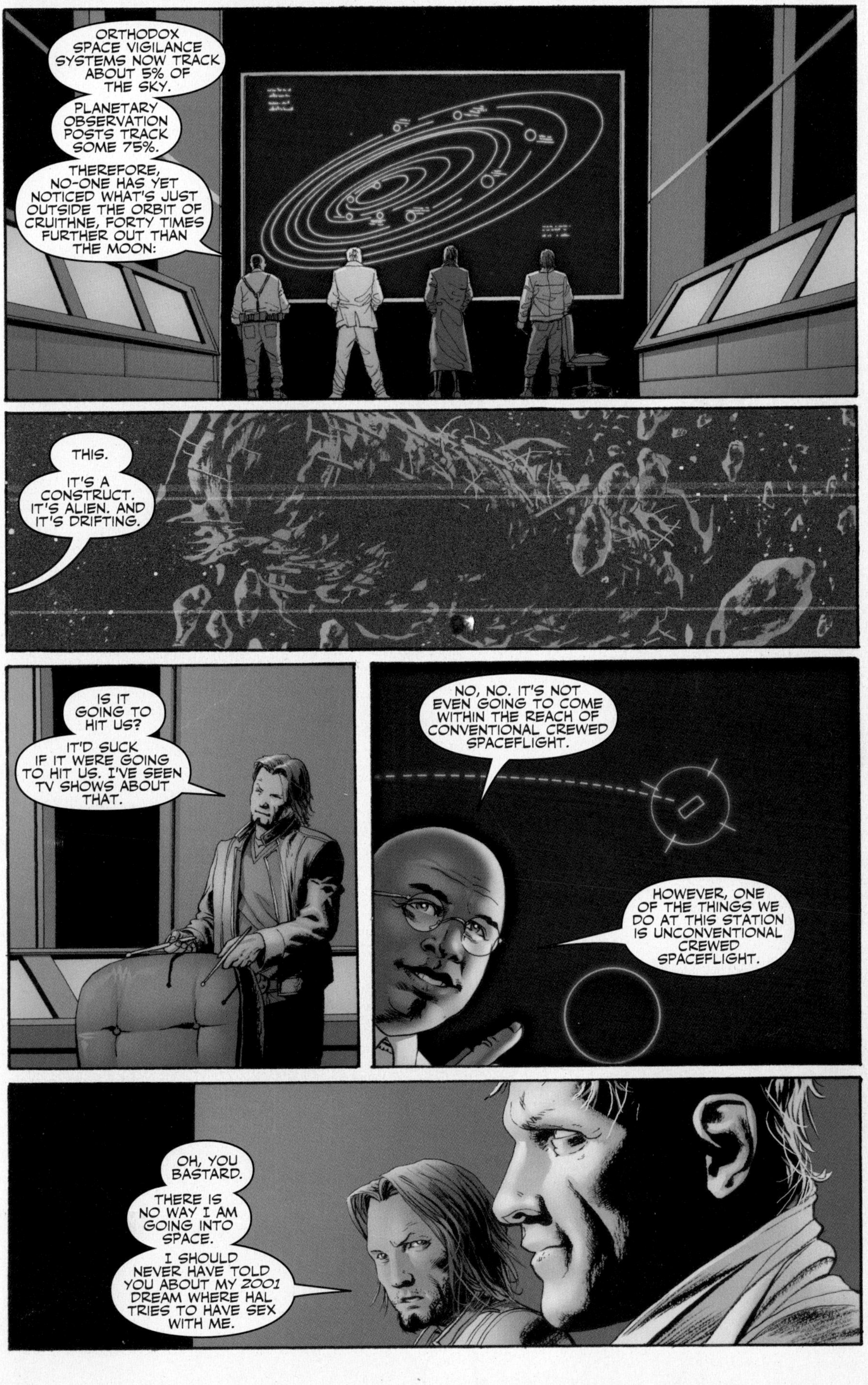
ORTHODOX SPACE VIGILANCE SYSTEMS NOW TRACK ABOUT 5% OF THE SKY.
PLANETARY OBSERVATION POSTS TRACK SOME 75%.
THEREFORE, NO-ONE HAS YET NOTICED WHAT'S JUST OUTSIDE THE ORBIT OF CRUITHNE, FORTY TIMES FURTHER OUT THAN THE MOON:
THIS.
IT'S A CONSTRUCT. IT'S ALIEN. AND IT'S DRIFTING.
IS IT GOING TO HIT US?
IT'D SUCK IF IT WERE GOING TO HIT US. I'VE SEEN TV SHOWS ABOUT THAT.
NO, NO. IT'S NOT EVEN GOING TO COME WITHIN THE REACH OF CONVENTIONAL CREWED SPACEFLIGHT.
HOWEVER, ONE OF THE THINGS WE DO AT THIS STATION IS UNCONVENTIONAL CREWED SPACEFLIGHT.
OH, YOU BASTARD.
THERE IS NO WAY I AM GOING INTO SPACE.
I SHOULD NEVER HAVE TOLD YOU ABOUT MY *2001* DREAM WHERE HAL TRIES TO HAVE SEX WITH ME.

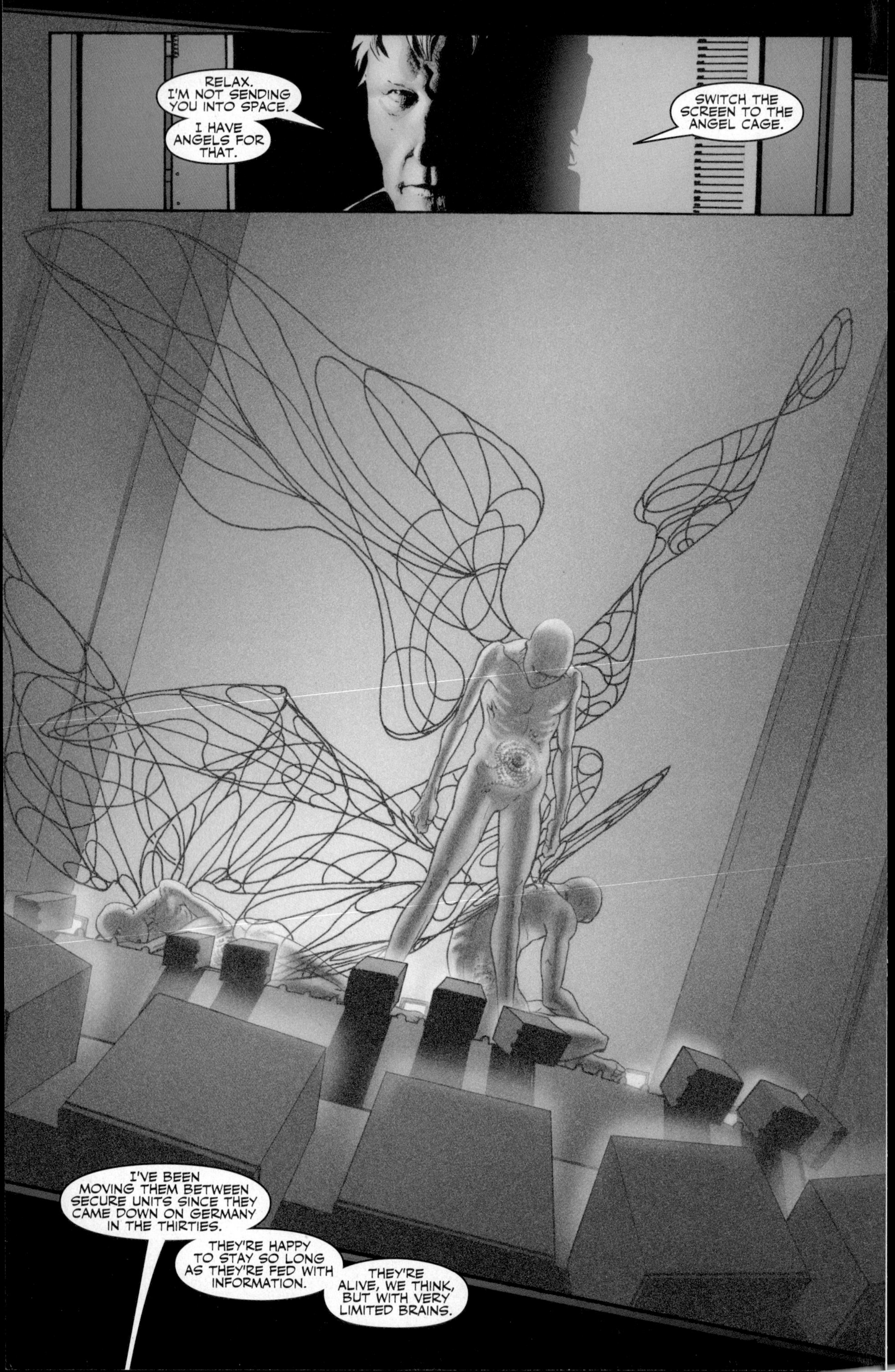
RELAX. I'M NOT SENDING YOU INTO SPACE.
I HAVE ANGELS FOR THAT.
SWITCH THE SCREEN TO THE ANGEL CAGE.
I'VE BEEN MOVING THEM BETWEEN SECURE UNITS SINCE THEY CAME DOWN ON GERMANY IN THE THIRTIES.
THEY'RE HAPPY TO STAY SO LONG AS THEY'RE FED WITH INFORMATION.
THEY'RE ALIVE, WE THINK, BUT WITH VERY LIMITED BRAINS.

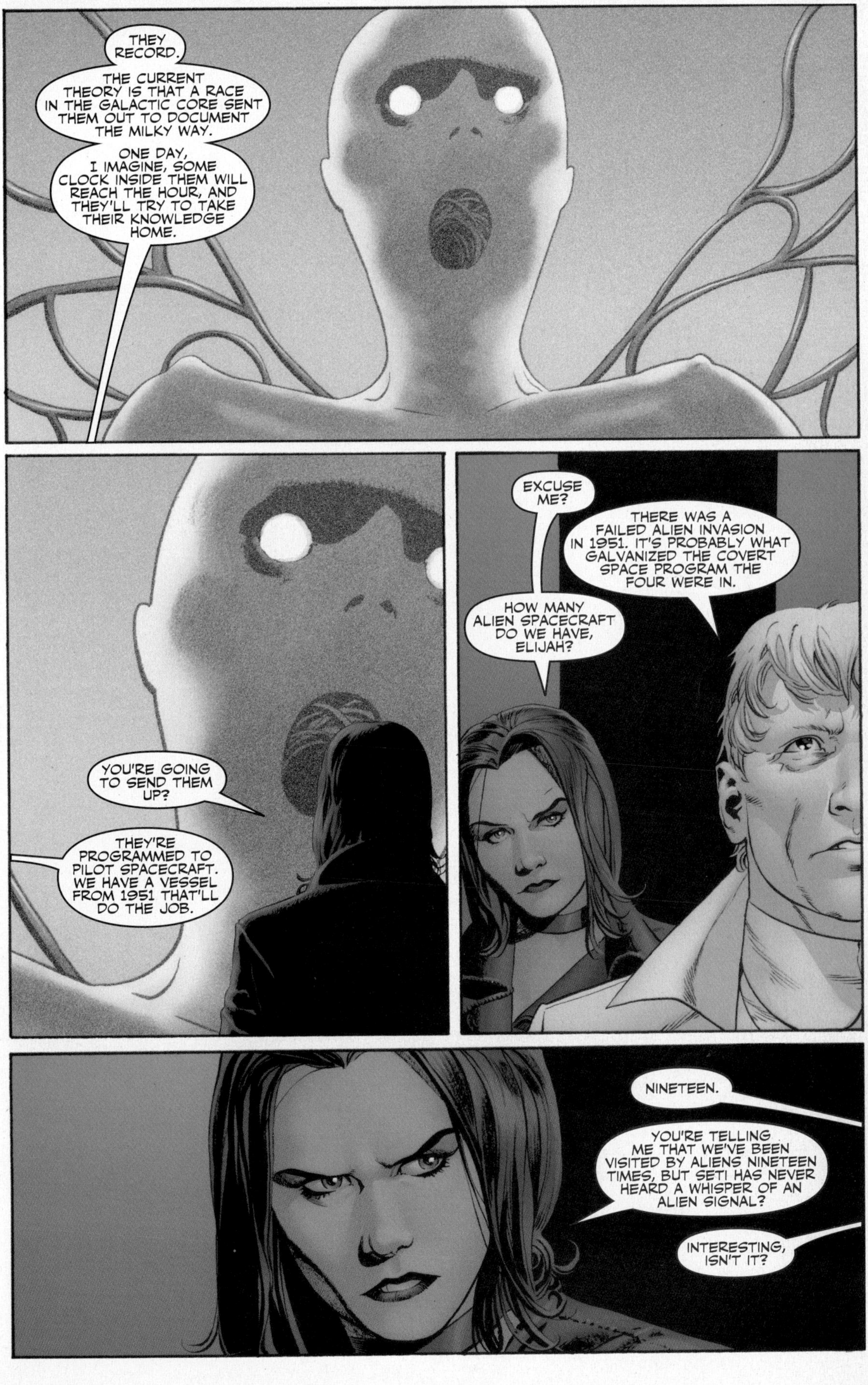
THEY RECORD.
THE CURRENT THEORY IS THAT A RACE IN THE GALACTIC CORE SENT THEM OUT TO DOCUMENT THE MILKY WAY.
ONE DAY, I IMAGINE, SOME CLOCK INSIDE THEM WILL REACH THE HOUR, AND THEY'LL TRY TO TAKE THEIR KNOWLEDGE HOME.
YOU'RE GOING TO SEND THEM UP?
THEY'RE PROGRAMMED TO PILOT SPACECRAFT. WE HAVE A VESSEL FROM 1951 THAT'LL DO THE JOB.
EXCUSE ME?
THERE WAS A FAILED ALIEN INVASION IN 1951. IT'S PROBABLY WHAT GALVANIZED THE COVERT SPACE PROGRAM THE FOUR WERE IN.
HOW MANY ALIEN SPACECRAFT DO WE HAVE, ELIJAH?
NINETEEN.
YOU'RE TELLING ME THAT WE'VE BEEN VISITED BY ALIENS NINETEEN TIMES, BUT SETI HAS NEVER HEARD A WHISPER OF AN ALIEN SIGNAL?
INTERESTING, ISN'T IT?

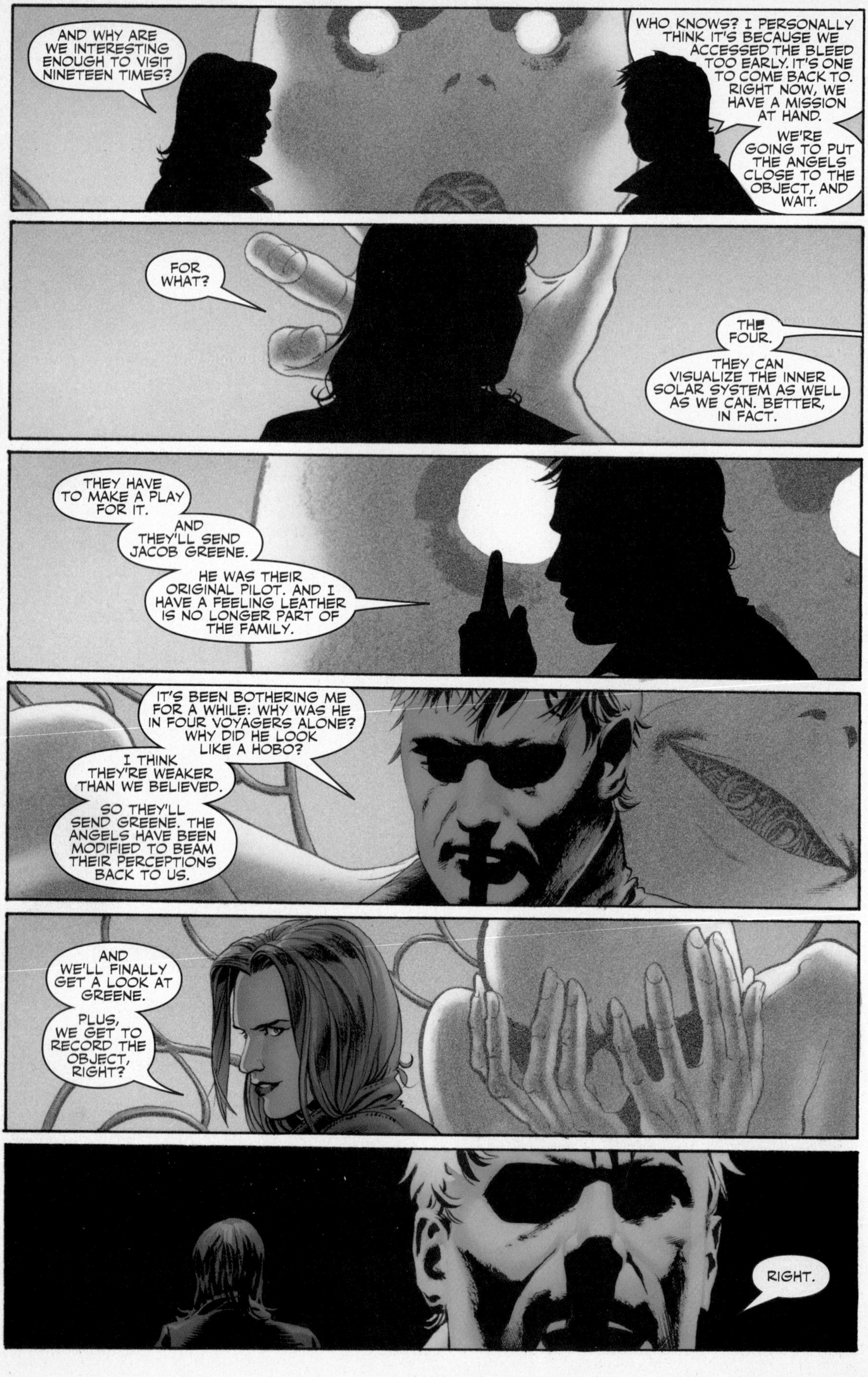
AND WHY ARE WE INTERESTING ENOUGH TO VISIT NINETEEN TIMES?
WHO KNOWS? I PERSONALLY THINK IT'S BECAUSE WE ACCESSED THE BLEED TOO EARLY. IT'S ONE TO COME BACK TO. RIGHT NOW, WE HAVE A MISSION AT HAND.
WE'RE GOING TO PUT THE ANGELS CLOSE TO THE OBJECT, AND WAIT.
FOR WHAT?
THE FOUR.
THEY CAN VISUALIZE THE INNER SOLAR SYSTEM AS WELL AS WE CAN. BETTER, IN FACT.
THEY HAVE TO MAKE A PLAY FOR IT.
AND THEY'LL SEND JACOB GREENE.
HE WAS THEIR ORIGINAL PILOT. AND I HAVE A FEELING LEATHER IS NO LONGER PART OF THE FAMILY.
IT'S BEEN BOTHERING ME FOR A WHILE: WHY WAS HE IN FOUR VOYAGERS ALONE? WHY DID HE LOOK LIKE A HOBO?
I THINK THEY'RE WEAKER THAN WE BELIEVED.
SO THEY'LL SEND GREENE. THE ANGELS HAVE BEEN MODIFIED TO BEAM THEIR PERCEPTIONS BACK TO US.
AND WE'LL FINALLY GET A LOOK AT GREENE.
PLUS, WE GET TO RECORD THE OBJECT, RIGHT?
RIGHT.

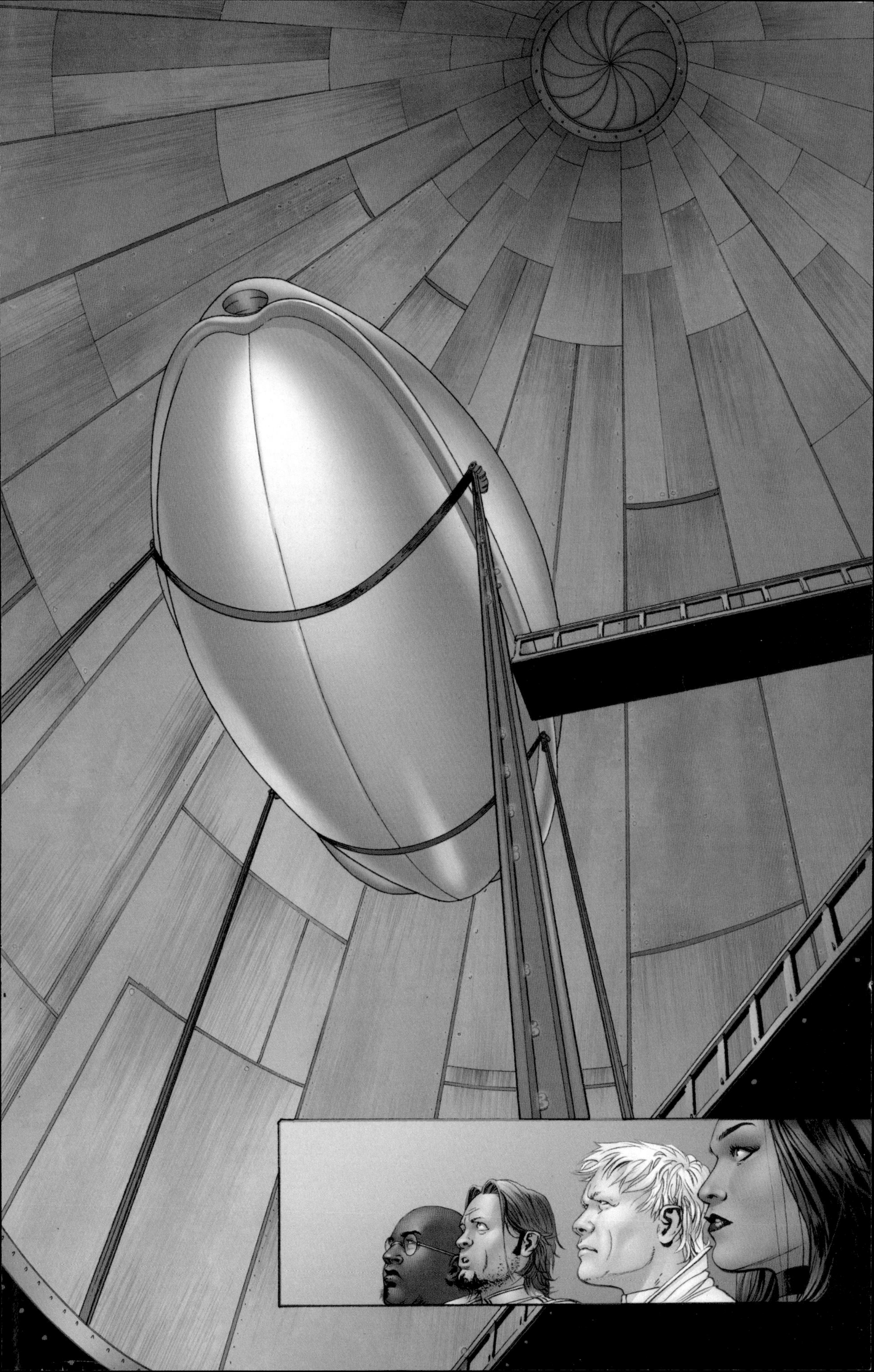

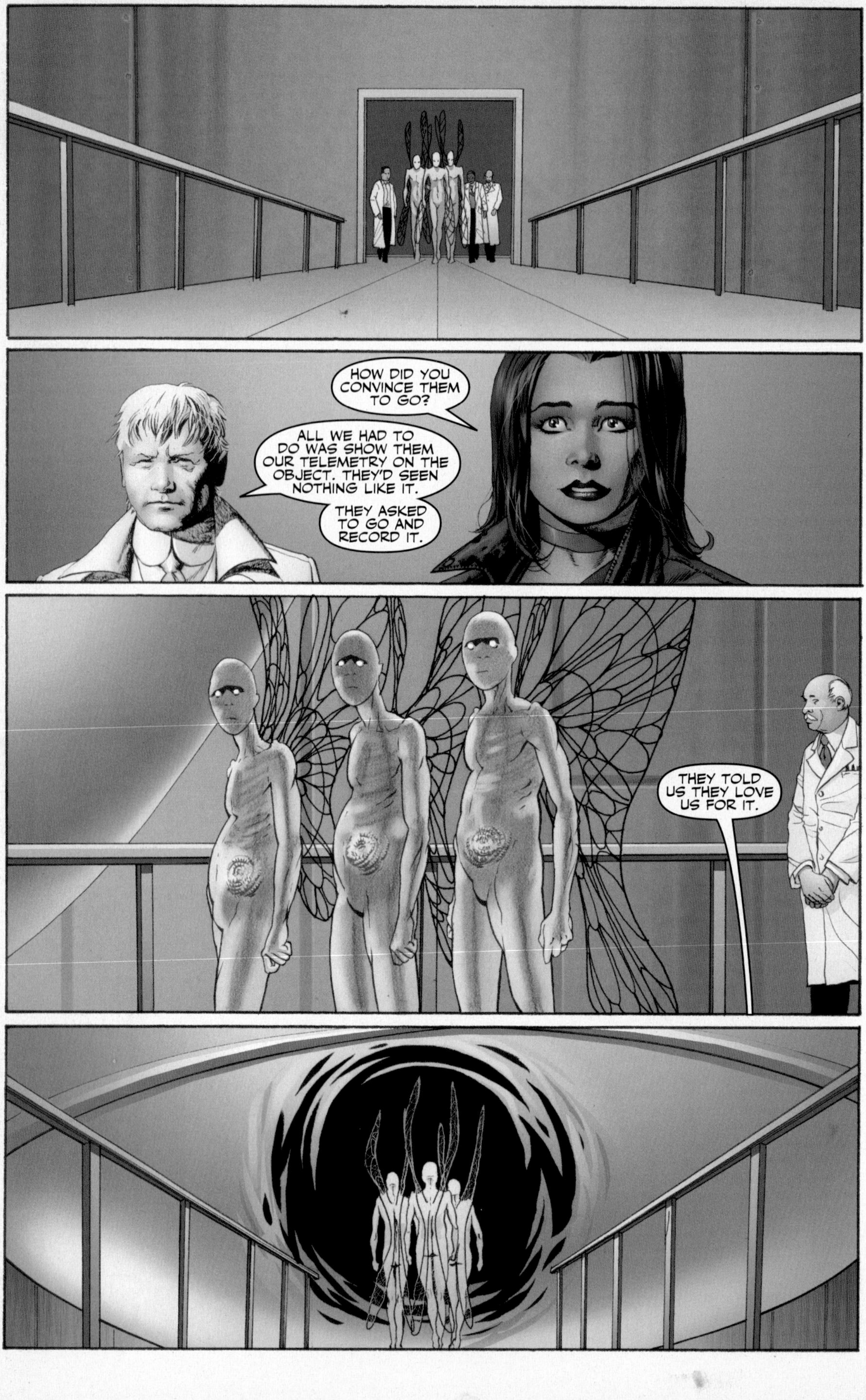
HOW DID YOU CONVINCE THEM TO GO?
ALL WE HAD TO DO WAS SHOW THEM OUR TELEMETRY ON THE OBJECT. THEY'D SEEN NOTHING LIKE IT.
THEY ASKED TO GO AND RECORD IT.
THEY TOLD US THEY LOVE US FOR IT.

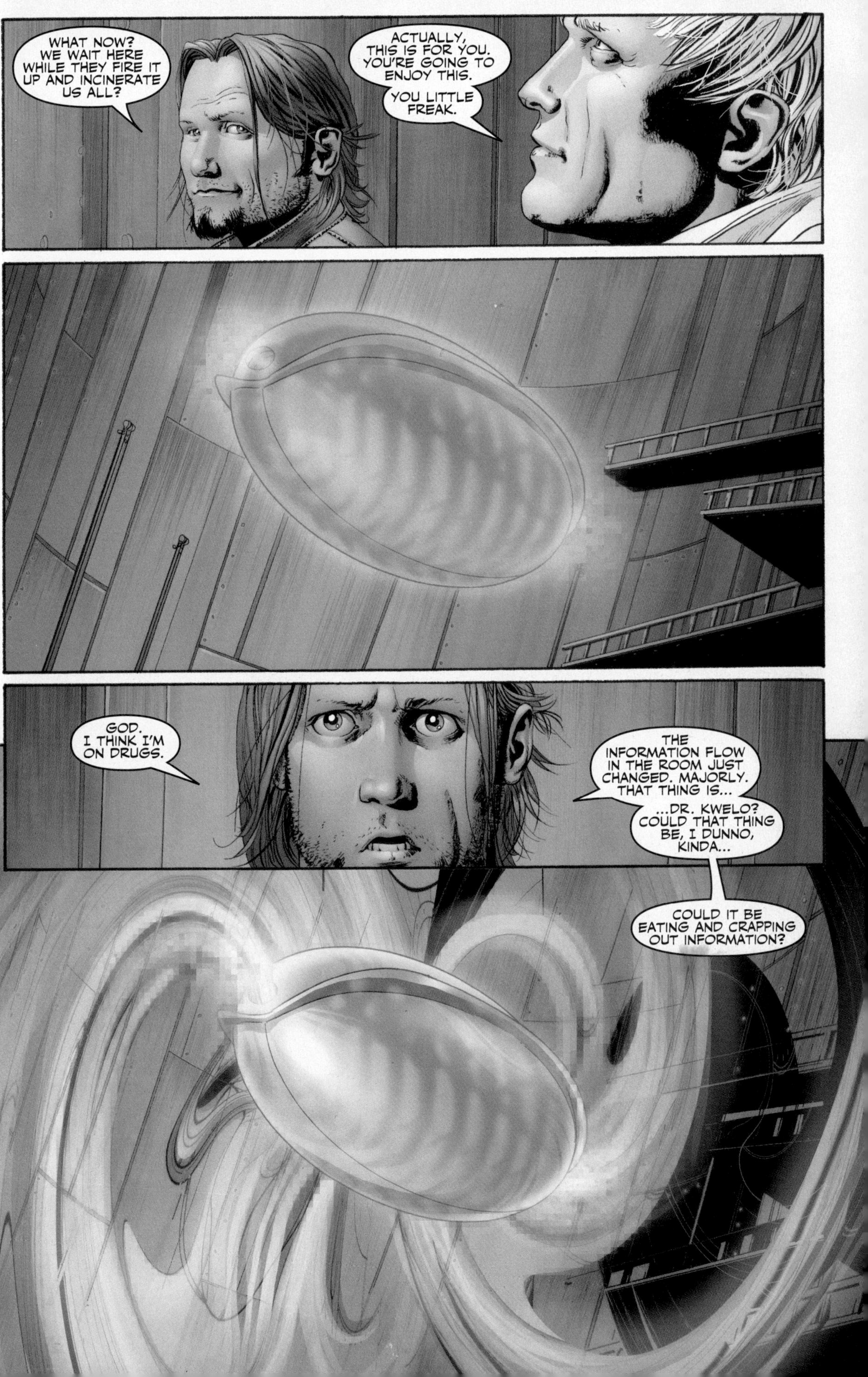

WHAT NOW? WE WAIT HERE WHILE THEY FIRE IT UP AND INCINERATE US ALL?
ACTUALLY, THIS IS FOR YOU. YOU'RE GOING TO ENJOY THIS.
YOU LITTLE FREAK.
GOD. I THINK I'M ON DRUGS.
THE INFORMATION FLOW IN THE ROOM JUST CHANGED. MAJORLY. THAT THING IS...
...DR. KWELO? COULD THAT THING BE, I DUNNO, KINDA...
COULD IT BE EATING AND CRAPPING OUT INFORMATION?

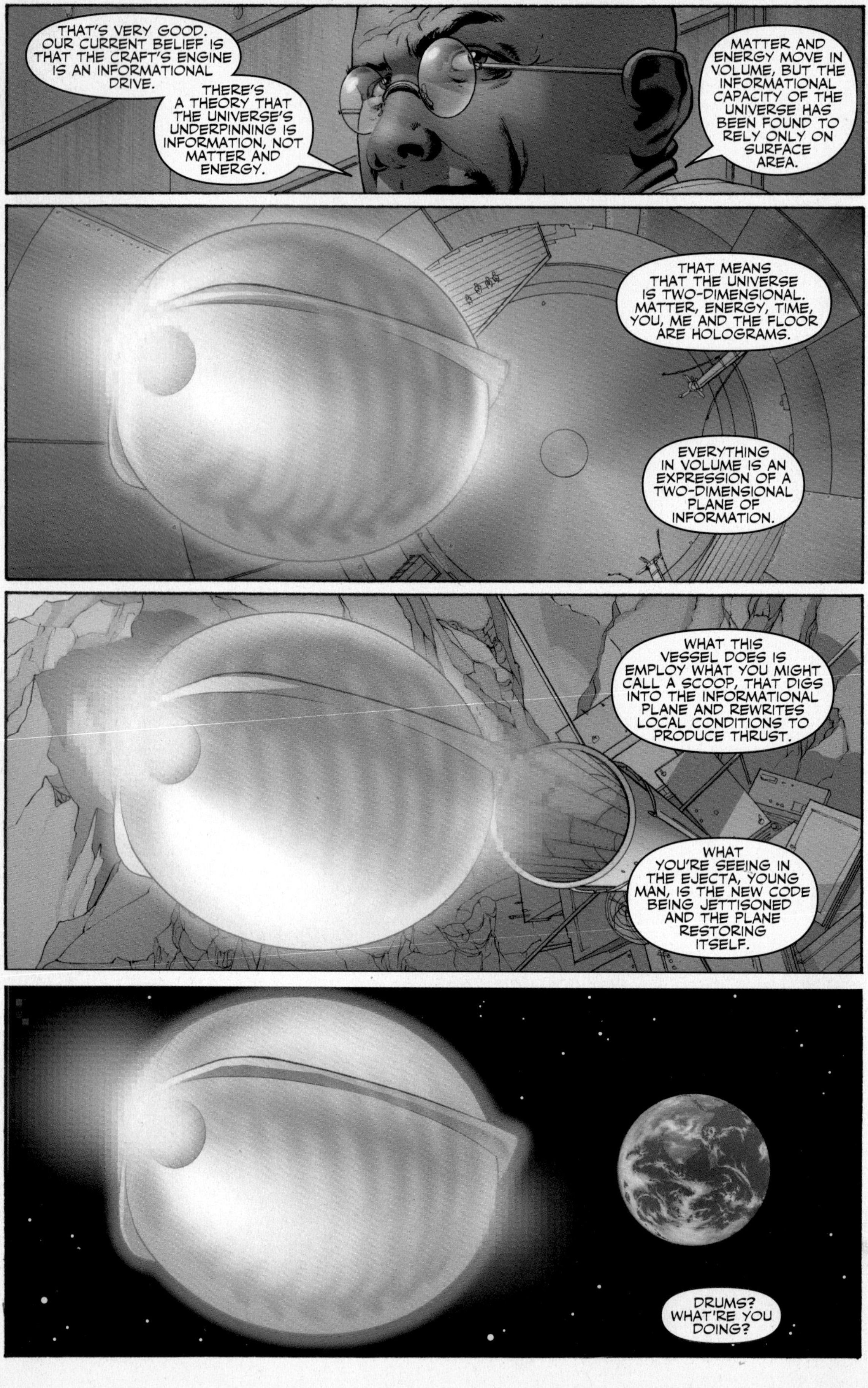
THAT'S VERY GOOD. OUR CURRENT BELIEF IS THAT THE CRAFT'S ENGINE IS AN INFORMATIONAL DRIVE.
THERE'S A THEORY THAT THE UNIVERSE'S UNDERPINNING IS INFORMATION, NOT MATTER AND ENERGY.
MATTER AND ENERGY MOVE IN VOLUME, BUT THE INFORMATIONAL CAPACITY OF THE UNIVERSE HAS BEEN FOUND TO RELY ONLY ON SURFACE AREA.
THAT MEANS THAT THE UNIVERSE IS TWO-DIMENSIONAL. MATTER, ENERGY, TIME, YOU, ME AND THE FLOOR ARE HOLOGRAMS.
EVERYTHING IN VOLUME IS AN EXPRESSION OF A TWO-DIMENSIONAL PLANE OF INFORMATION.
WHAT THIS VESSEL DOES IS EMPLOY WHAT YOU MIGHT CALL A SCOOP, THAT DIGS INTO THE INFORMATIONAL PLANE AND REWRITES LOCAL CONDITIONS TO PRODUCE THRUST.
WHAT YOU'RE SEEING IN THE EJECTA, YOUNG MAN, IS THE NEW CODE BEING JETTISONED AND THE PLANE RESTORING ITSELF.
DRUMS? WHAT'RE YOU DOING?

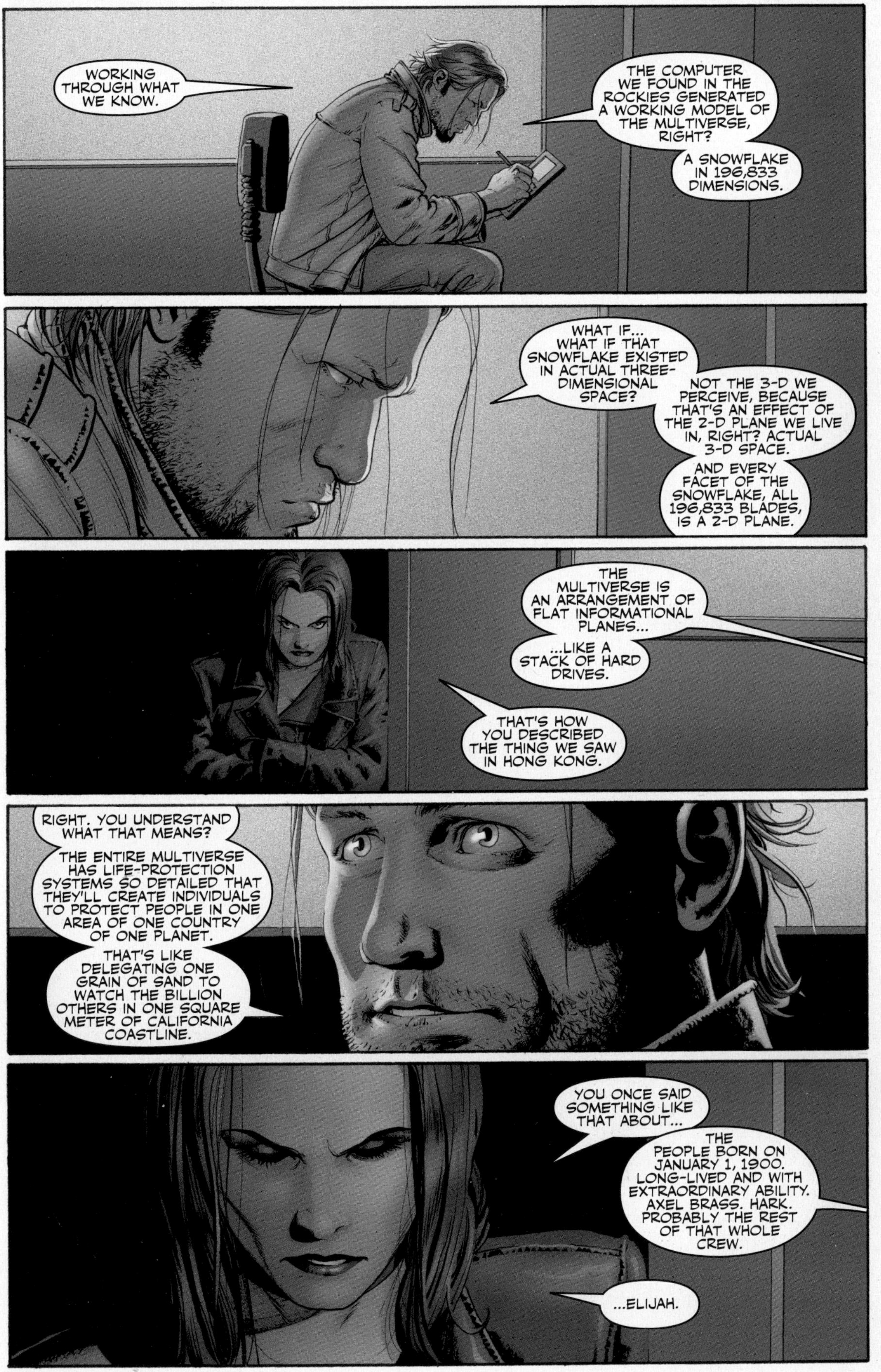
WORKING THROUGH WHAT WE KNOW.
THE COMPUTER WE FOUND IN THE ROCKIES GENERATED A WORKING MODEL OF THE MULTIVERSE, RIGHT?
A SNOWFLAKE IN 196,833 DIMENSIONS.
WHAT IF... WHAT IF THAT SNOWFLAKE EXISTED IN ACTUAL THREE-DIMENSIONAL SPACE?
NOT THE 3-D WE PERCEIVE, BECAUSE THAT'S AN EFFECT OF THE 2-D PLANE WE LIVE IN, RIGHT? ACTUAL 3-D SPACE.
AND EVERY FACET OF THE SNOWFLAKE, ALL 196,833 BLADES, IS A 2-D PLANE.
THE MULTIVERSE IS AN ARRANGEMENT OF FLAT INFORMATIONAL PLANES...
...LIKE A STACK OF HARD DRIVES.
THAT'S HOW YOU DESCRIBED THE THING WE SAW IN HONG KONG.
RIGHT. YOU UNDERSTAND WHAT THAT MEANS?
THE ENTIRE MULTIVERSE HAS LIFE-PROTECTION SYSTEMS SO DETAILED THAT THEY'LL CREATE INDIVIDUALS TO PROTECT PEOPLE IN ONE AREA OF ONE COUNTRY OF ONE PLANET.
THAT'S LIKE DELEGATING ONE GRAIN OF SAND TO WATCH THE BILLION OTHERS IN ONE SQUARE METER OF CALIFORNIA COASTLINE.
YOU ONCE SAID SOMETHING LIKE THAT ABOUT...
THE PEOPLE BORN ON JANUARY 1, 1900. LONG-LIVED AND WITH EXTRAORDINARY ABILITY. AXEL BRASS. HARK. PROBABLY THE REST OF THAT WHOLE CREW.
...ELIJAH.

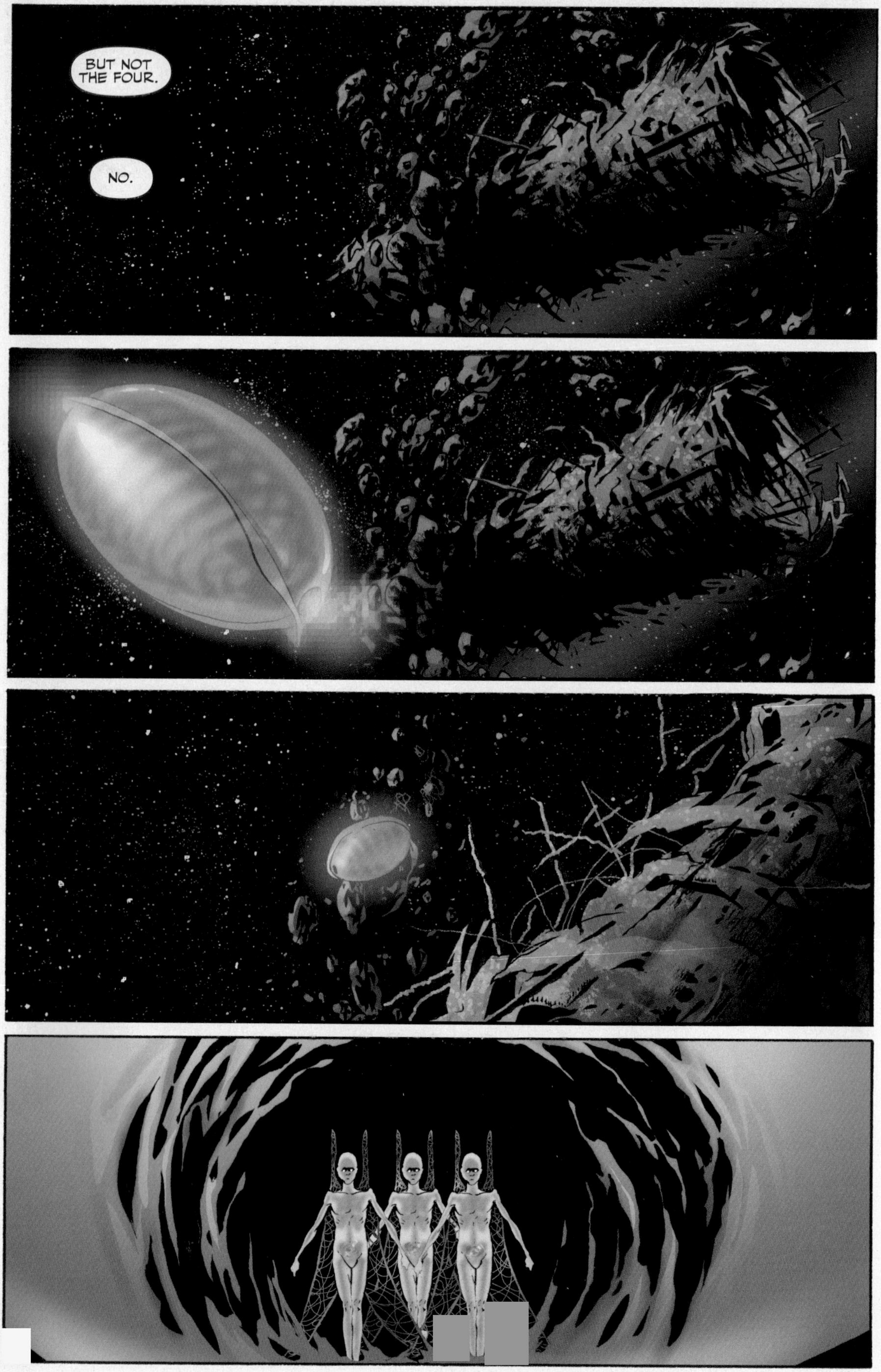
BUT NOT THE FOUR.
NO.

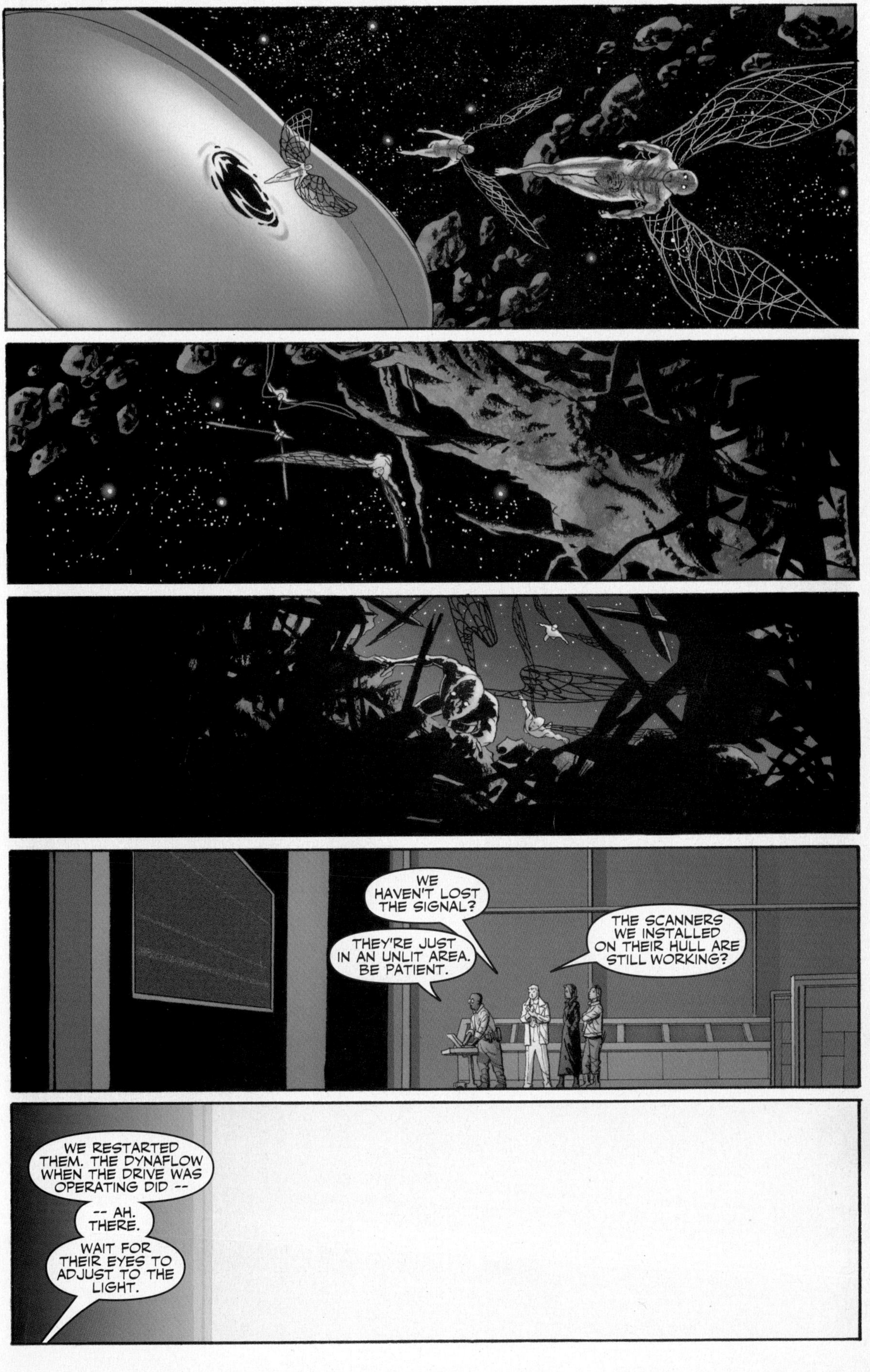
WE HAVEN'T LOST THE SIGNAL?
THEY'RE JUST IN AN UNLIT AREA. BE PATIENT.
THE SCANNERS WE INSTALLED ON THEIR HULL ARE STILL WORKING?
WE RESTARTED THEM. THE DYNAFLOW WHEN THE DRIVE WAS OPERATING DID --
-- AH. THERE.
WAIT FOR THEIR EYES TO ADJUST TO THE LIGHT.

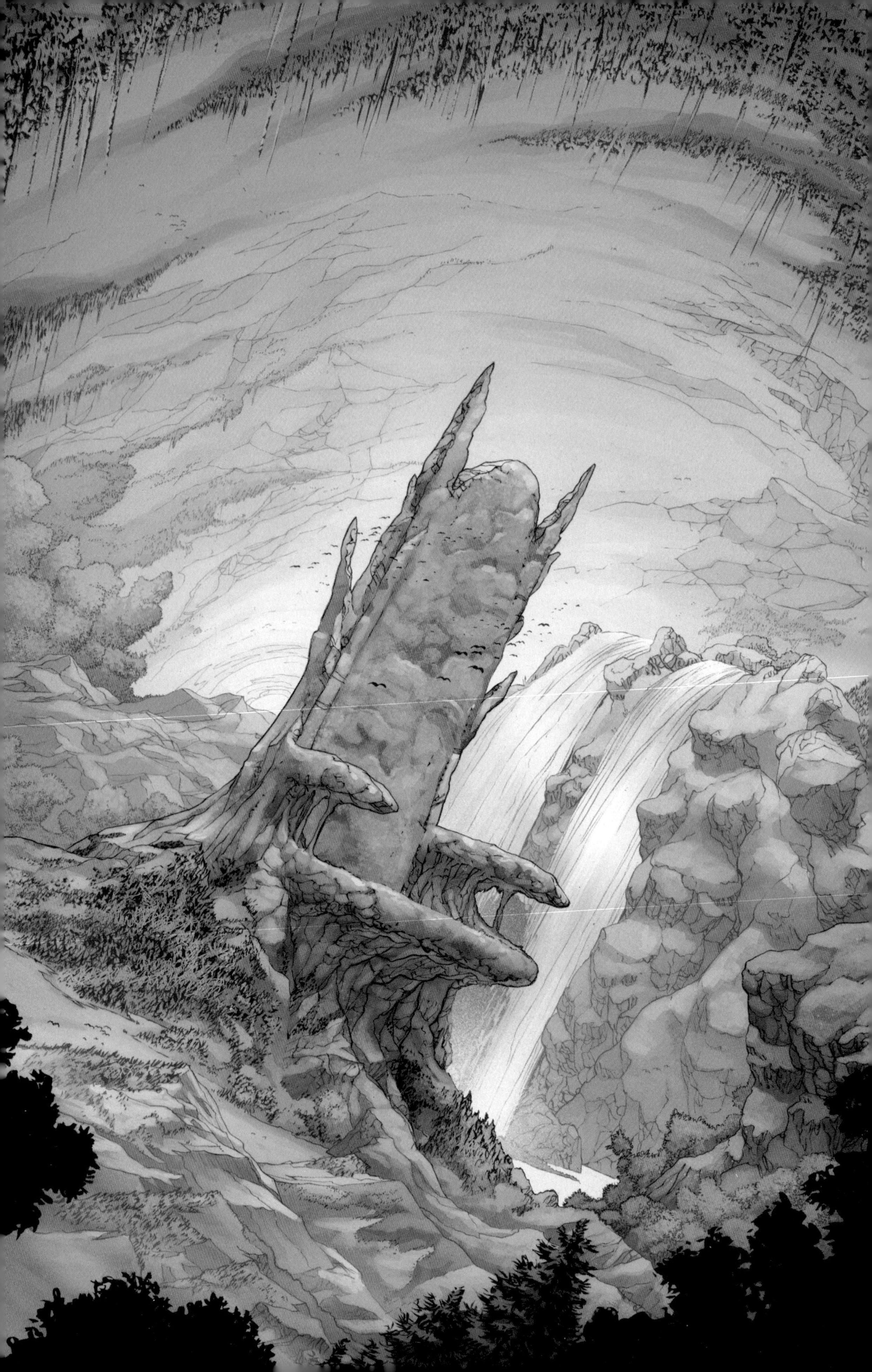

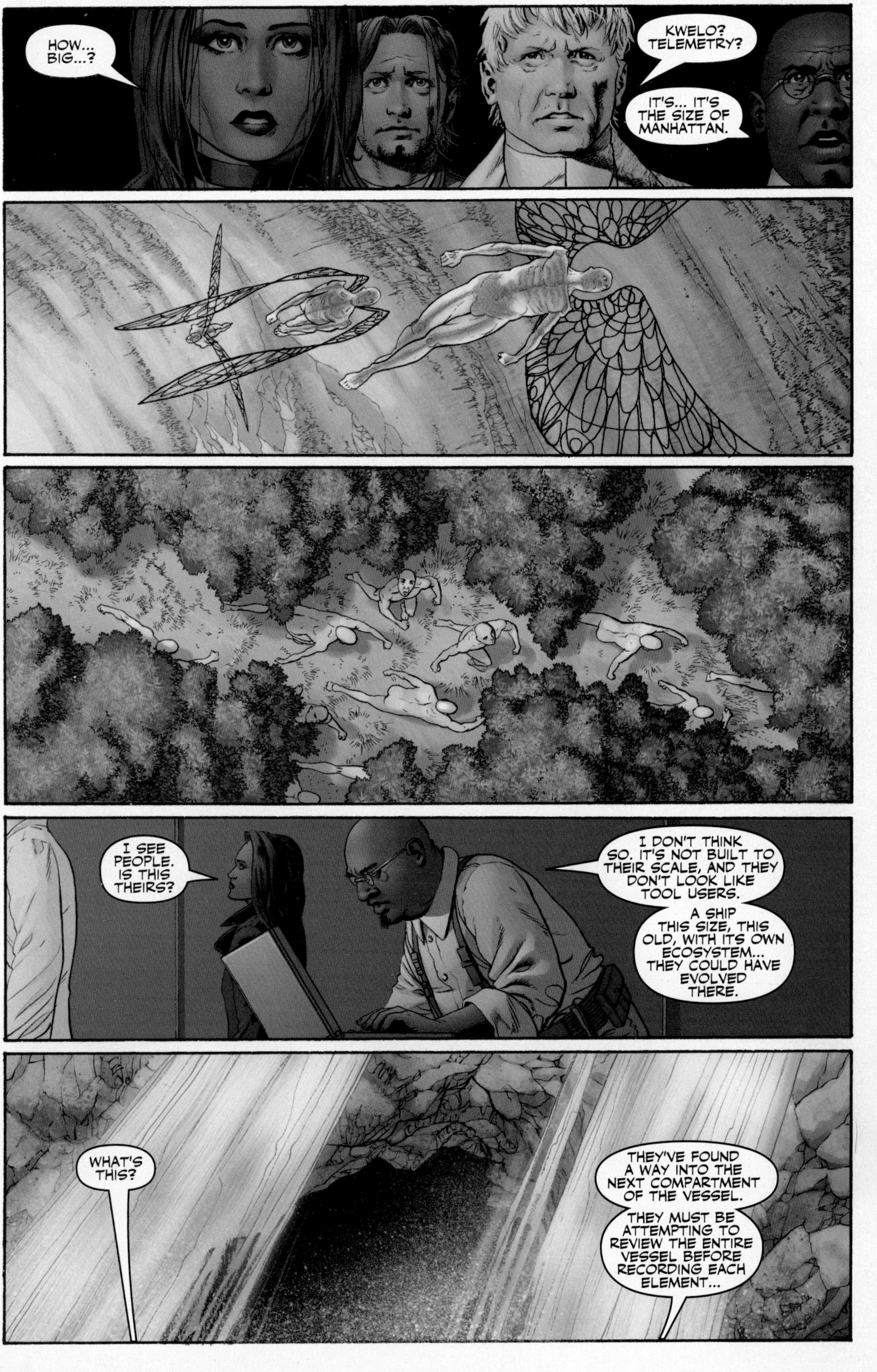
HOW... BIG...?
KWELO? TELEMETRY?
IT'S... IT'S THE SIZE OF MANHATTAN.
I SEE PEOPLE. IS THIS THEIRS?
I DON'T THINK SO. IT'S NOT BUILT TO THEIR SCALE, AND THEY DON'T LOOK LIKE TOOL USERS.
A SHIP THIS SIZE, THIS OLD, WITH ITS OWN ECOSYSTEM... THEY COULD HAVE EVOLVED THERE.
WHAT'S THIS?
THEY'VE FOUND A WAY INTO THE NEXT COMPARTMENT OF THE VESSEL.
THEY MUST BE ATTEMPTING TO REVIEW THE ENTIRE VESSEL BEFORE RECORDING EACH ELEMENT...

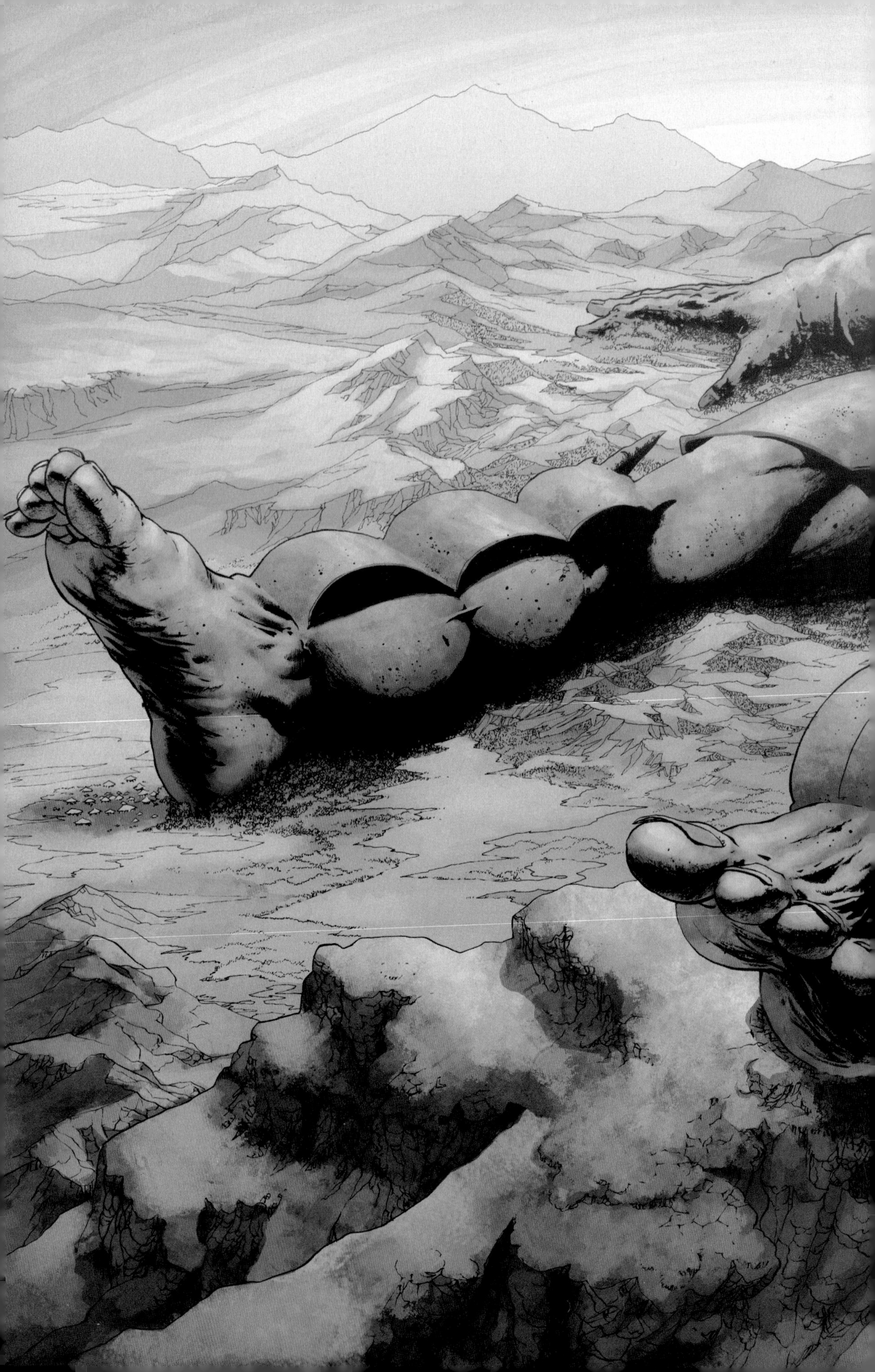

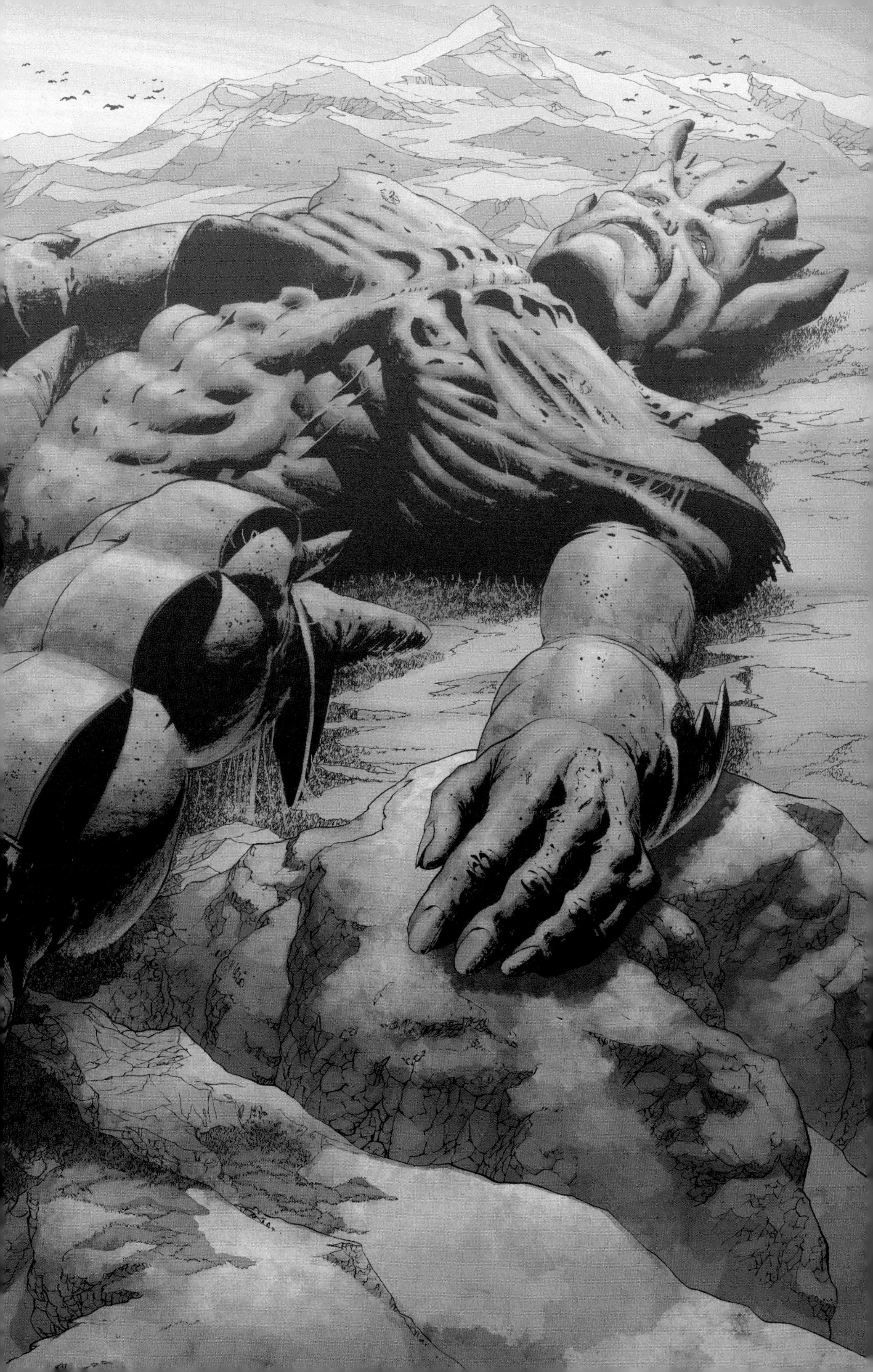

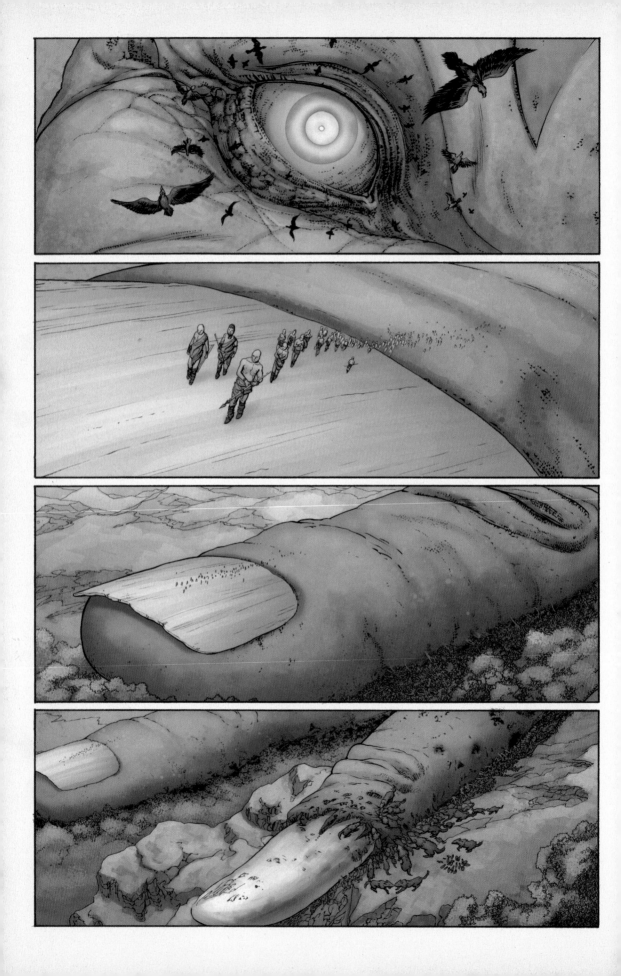

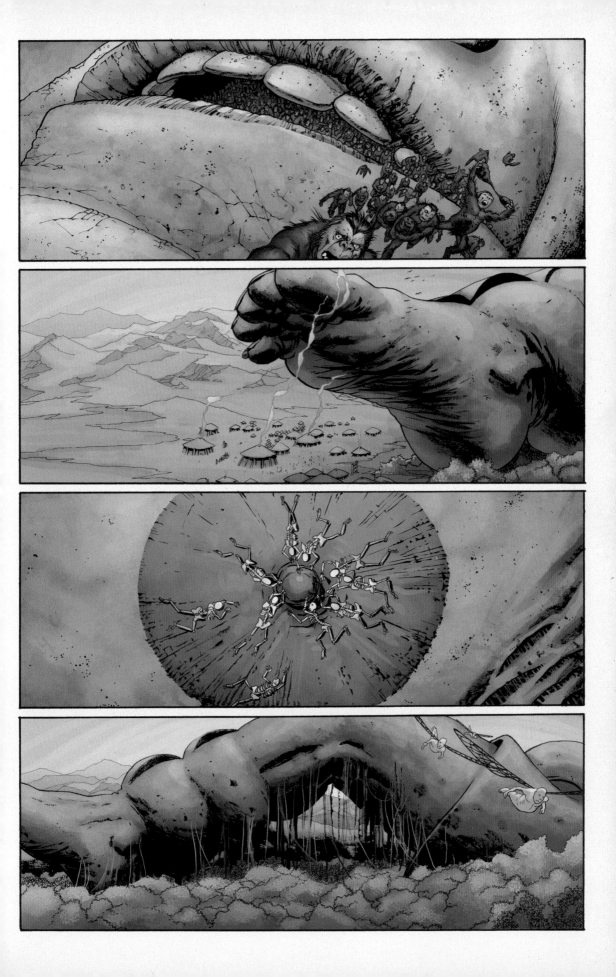

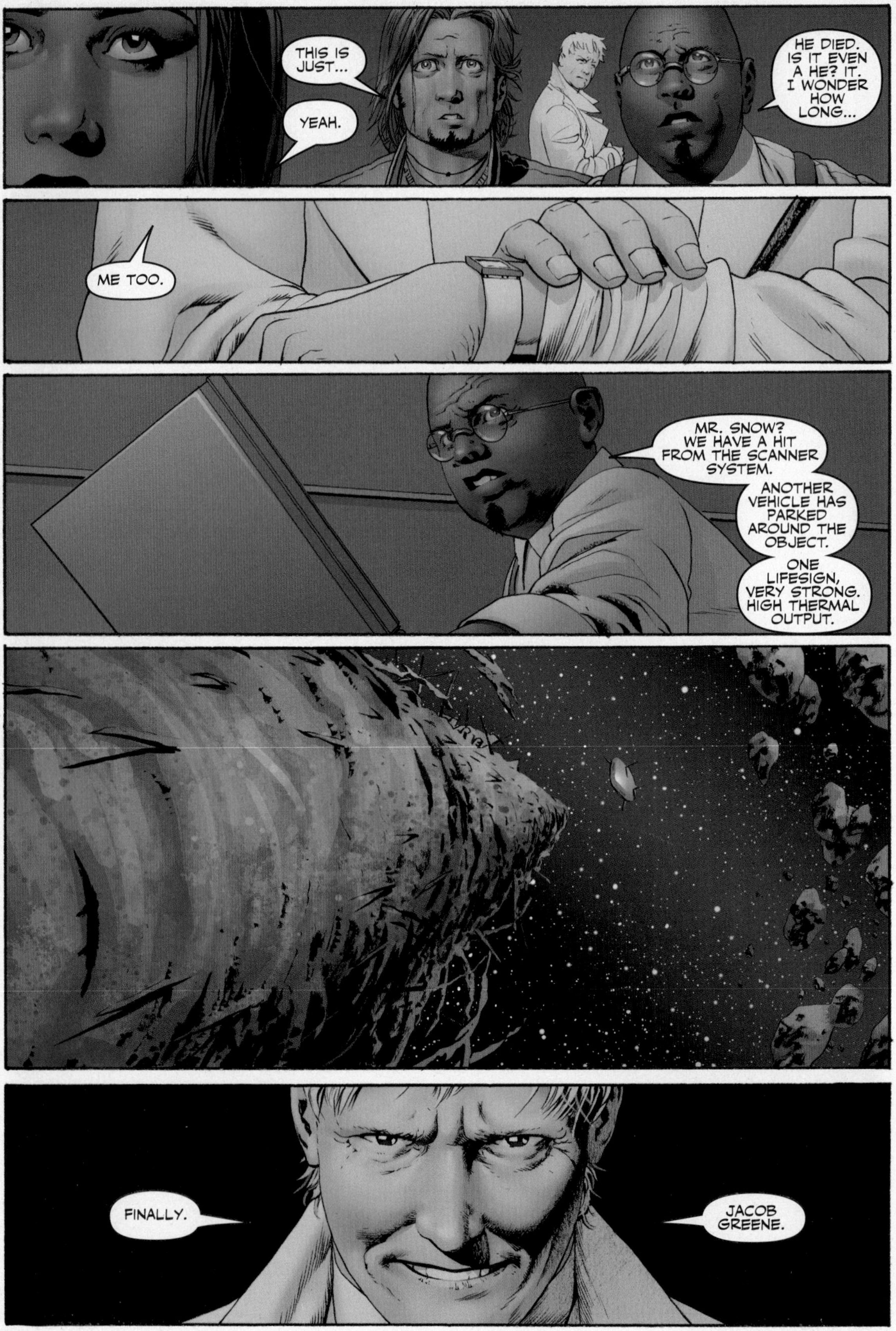
THIS IS JUST...
YEAH.
HE DIED. IS IT EVEN A HE? IT. I WONDER HOW LONG...
ME TOO.
MR. SNOW? WE HAVE A HIT FROM THE SCANNER SYSTEM.
ANOTHER VEHICLE HAS PARKED AROUND THE OBJECT.
ONE LIFESIGN, VERY STRONG. HIGH THERMAL OUTPUT.
FINALLY.
JACOB GREENE.

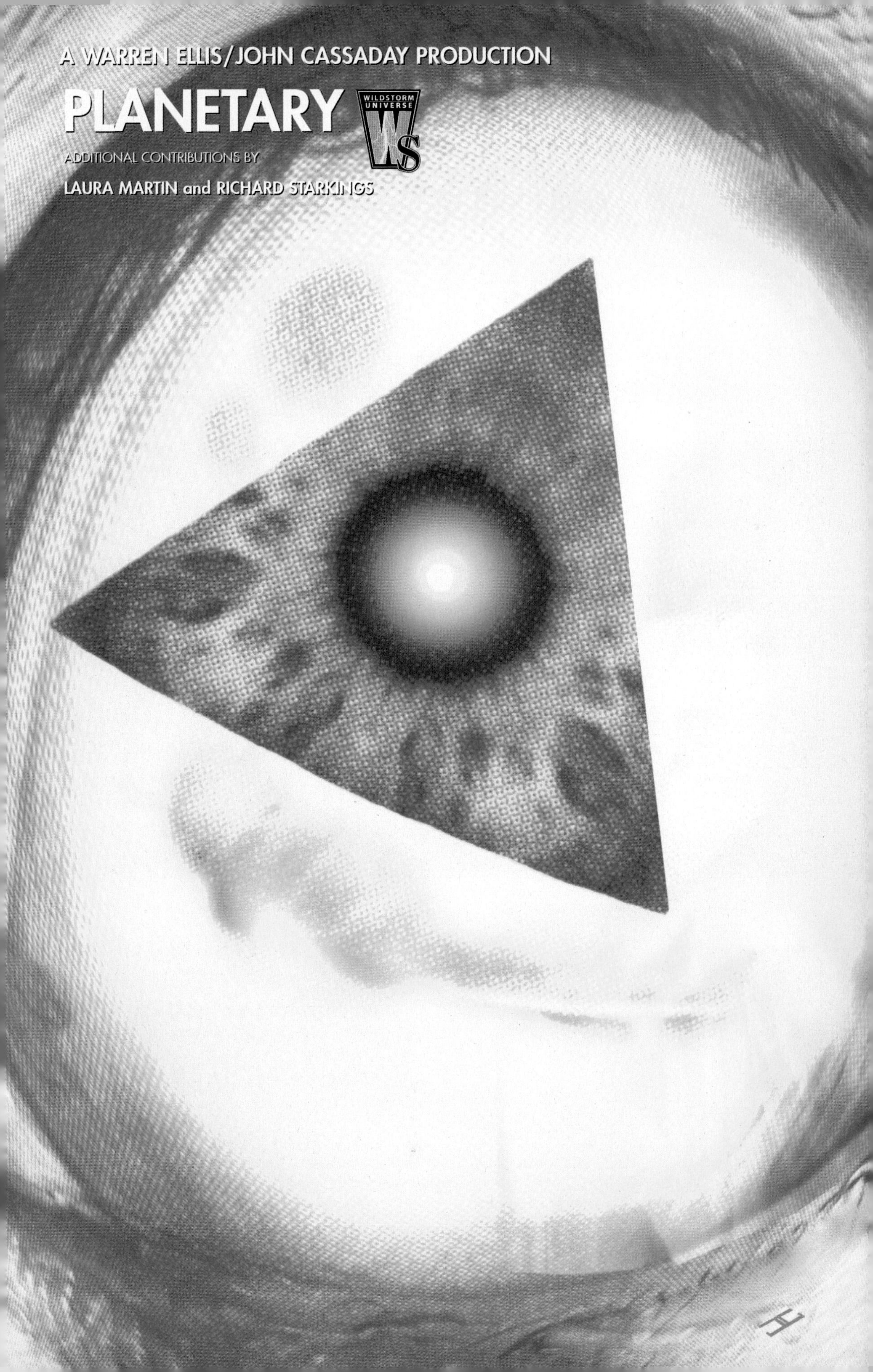
A WARREN ELLIS/JOHN CASSADAY PRODUCTION
PLANETARY
ADDITIONAL CONTRIBUTIONS BY
LAURA MARTIN and RICHARD STARKINGS

RENDEZVOUS

WRITTEN BY **WARREN ELLIS** ART BY **JOHN CASSADAY**

COLORING BY **LAURA MARTIN**

LETTERING BY **RICHARD STARKINGS**

ASSISTANT EDITOR **KRISTY QUINN**

EDITOR **SCOTT DUNBIER**

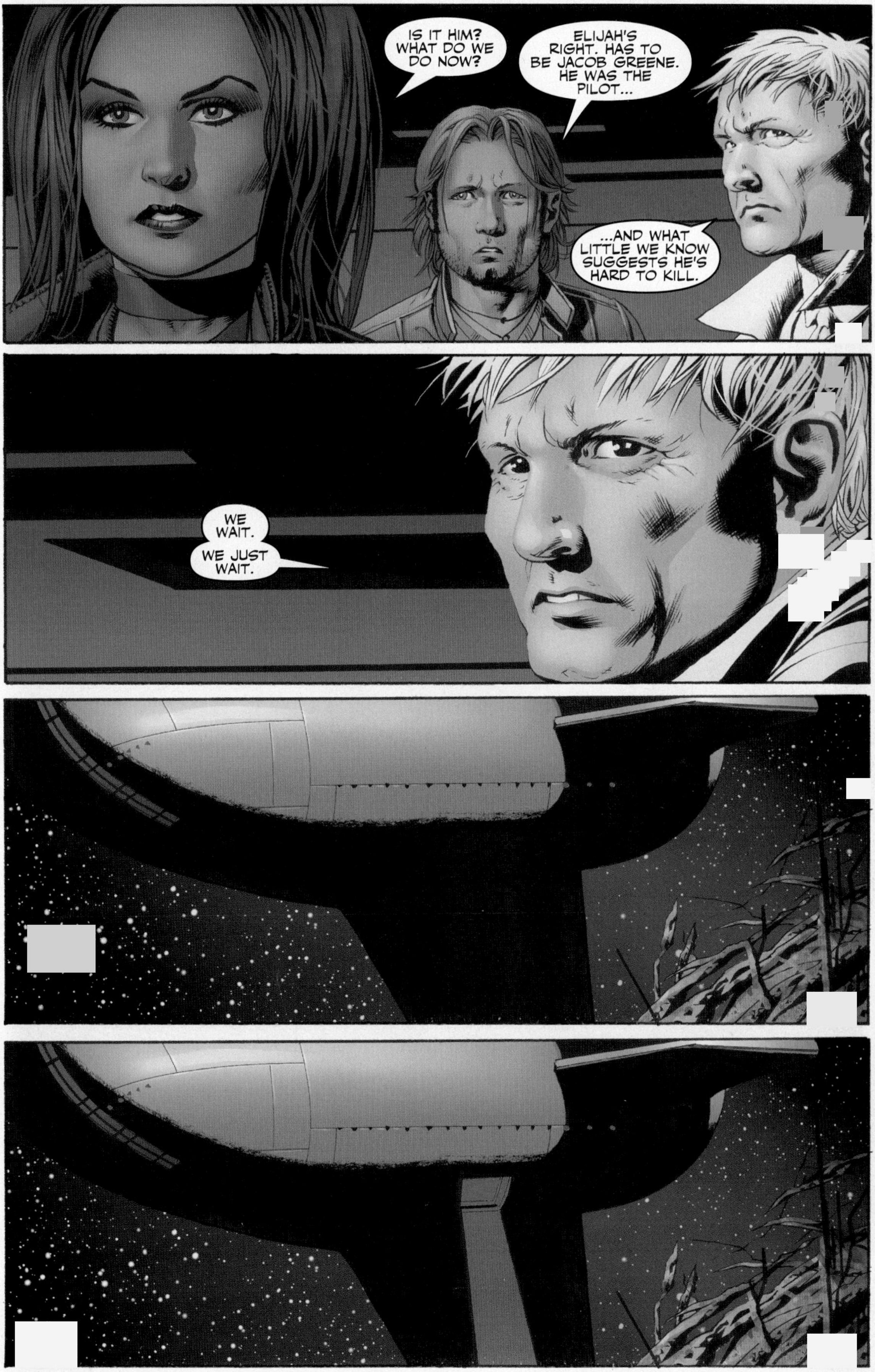
IS IT HIM? WHAT DO WE DO NOW?
ELIJAH'S RIGHT. HAS TO BE JACOB GREENE. HE WAS THE PILOT...
...AND WHAT LITTLE WE KNOW SUGGESTS HE'S HARD TO KILL.
WE WAIT.
WE JUST WAIT.

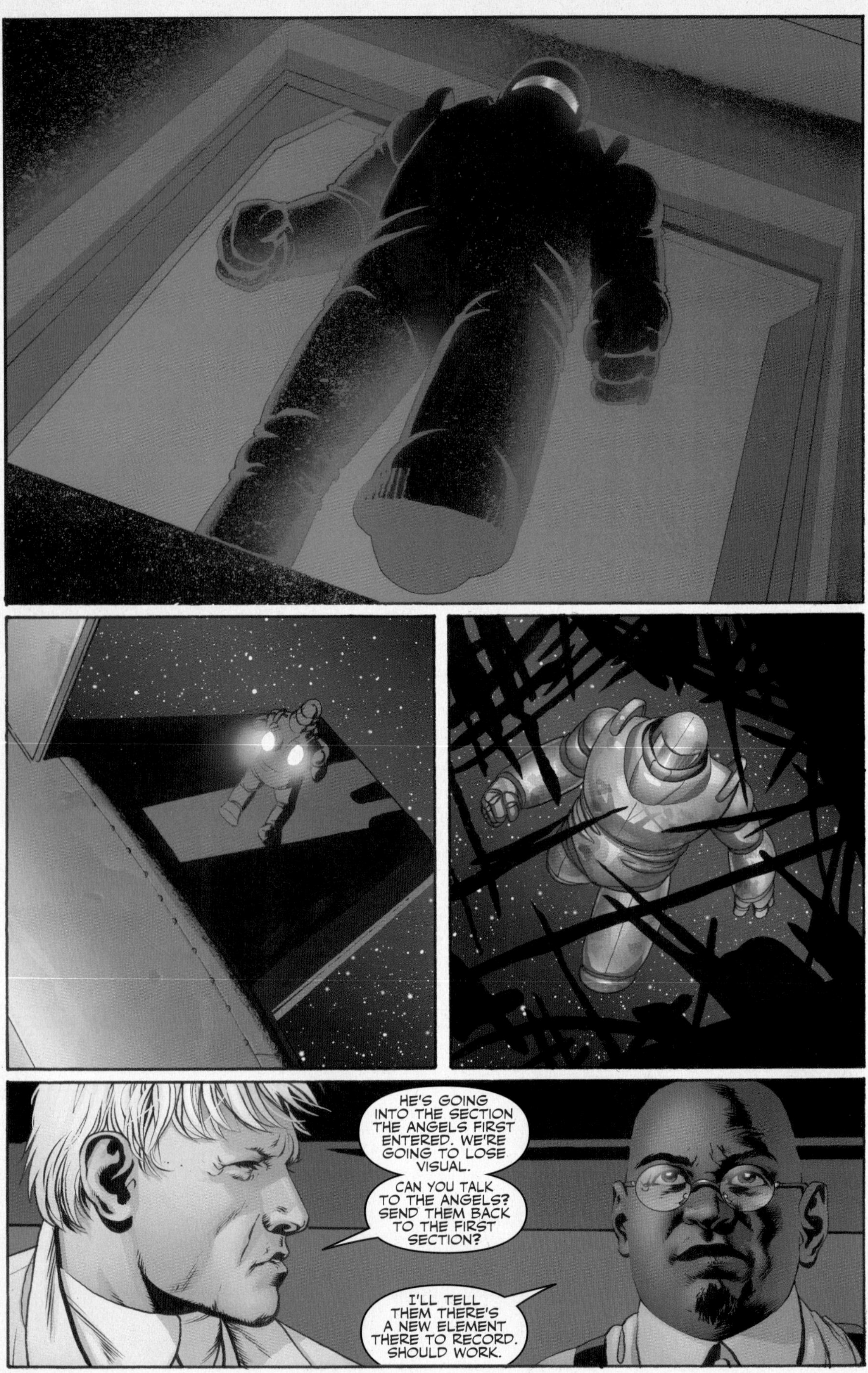
HE'S GOING INTO THE SECTION THE ANGELS FIRST ENTERED. WE'RE GOING TO LOSE VISUAL.
CAN YOU TALK TO THE ANGELS? SEND THEM BACK TO THE FIRST SECTION?
I'LL TELL THEM THERE'S A NEW ELEMENT THERE TO RECORD. SHOULD WORK.

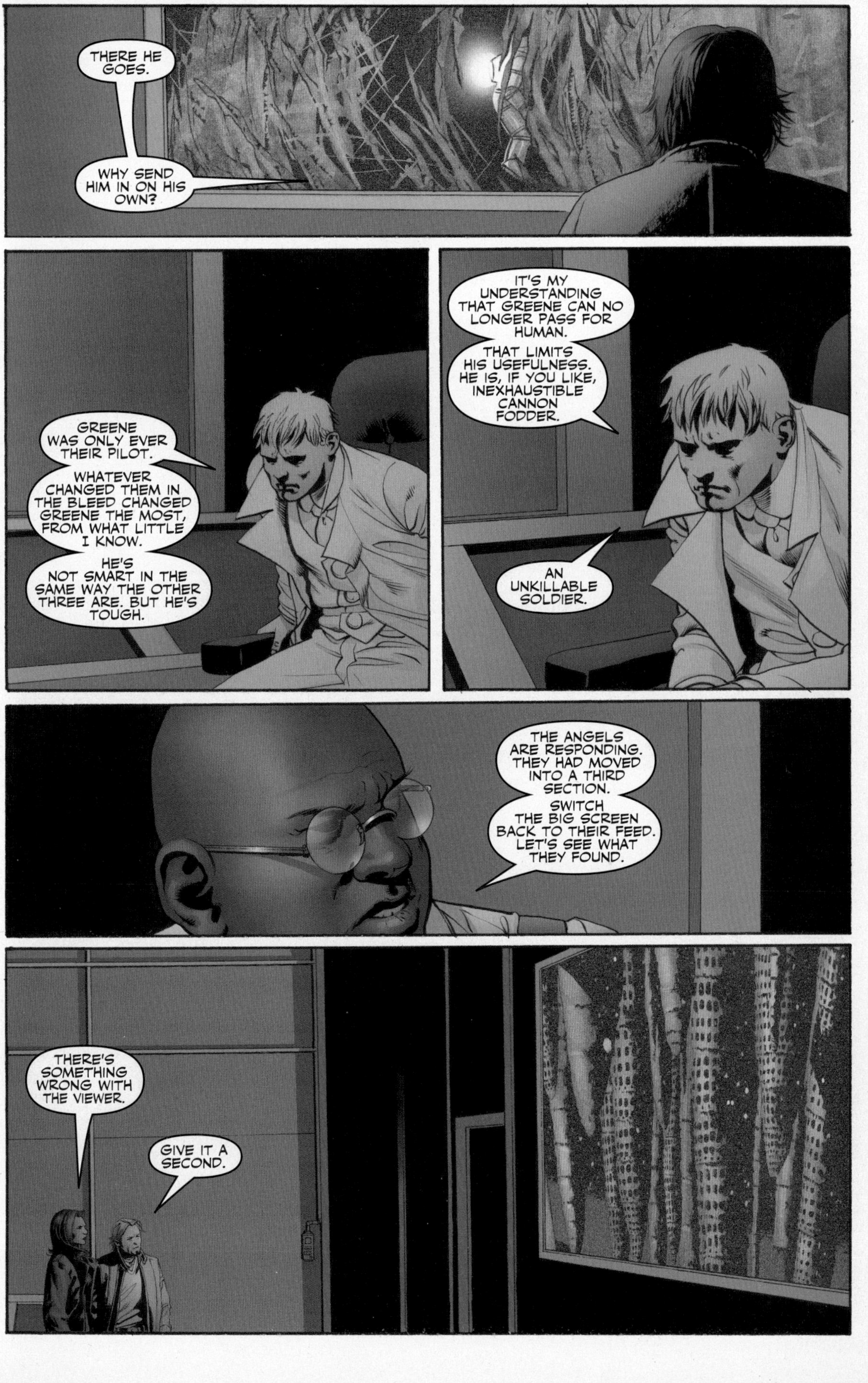
THERE HE GOES.
WHY SEND HIM IN ON HIS OWN?
GREENE WAS ONLY EVER THEIR PILOT.
WHATEVER CHANGED THEM IN THE BLEED CHANGED GREENE THE MOST, FROM WHAT LITTLE I KNOW.
HE'S NOT SMART IN THE SAME WAY THE OTHER THREE ARE. BUT HE'S TOUGH.
IT'S MY UNDERSTANDING THAT GREENE CAN NO LONGER PASS FOR HUMAN.
THAT LIMITS HIS USEFULNESS. HE IS, IF YOU LIKE, INEXHAUSTIBLE CANNON FODDER.
AN UNKILLABLE SOLDIER.
THE ANGELS ARE RESPONDING. THEY HAD MOVED INTO A THIRD SECTION.
SWITCH THE BIG SCREEN BACK TO THEIR FEED. LET'S SEE WHAT THEY FOUND.
THERE'S SOMETHING WRONG WITH THE VIEWER.
GIVE IT A SECOND.

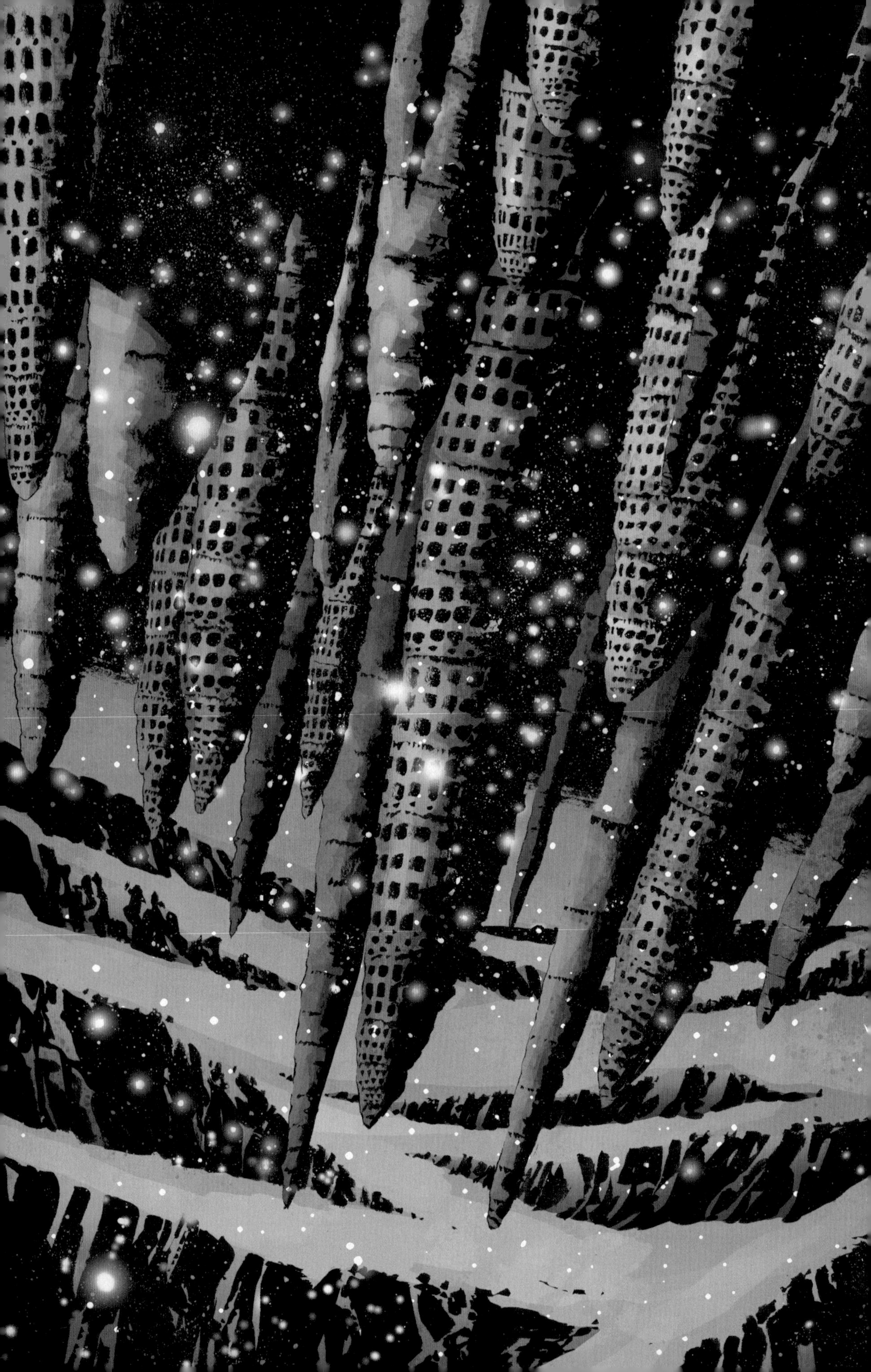

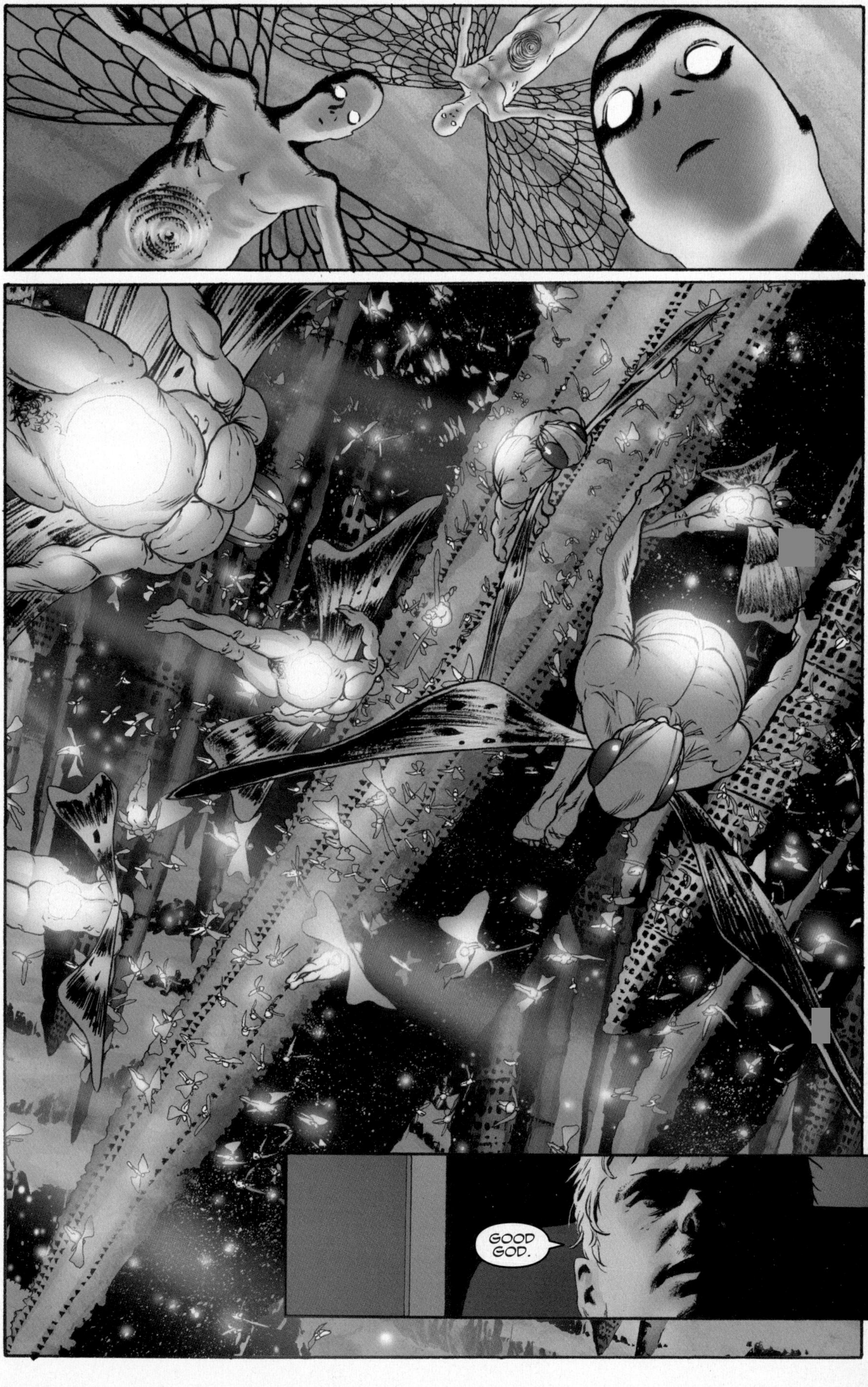
GOOD GOD.

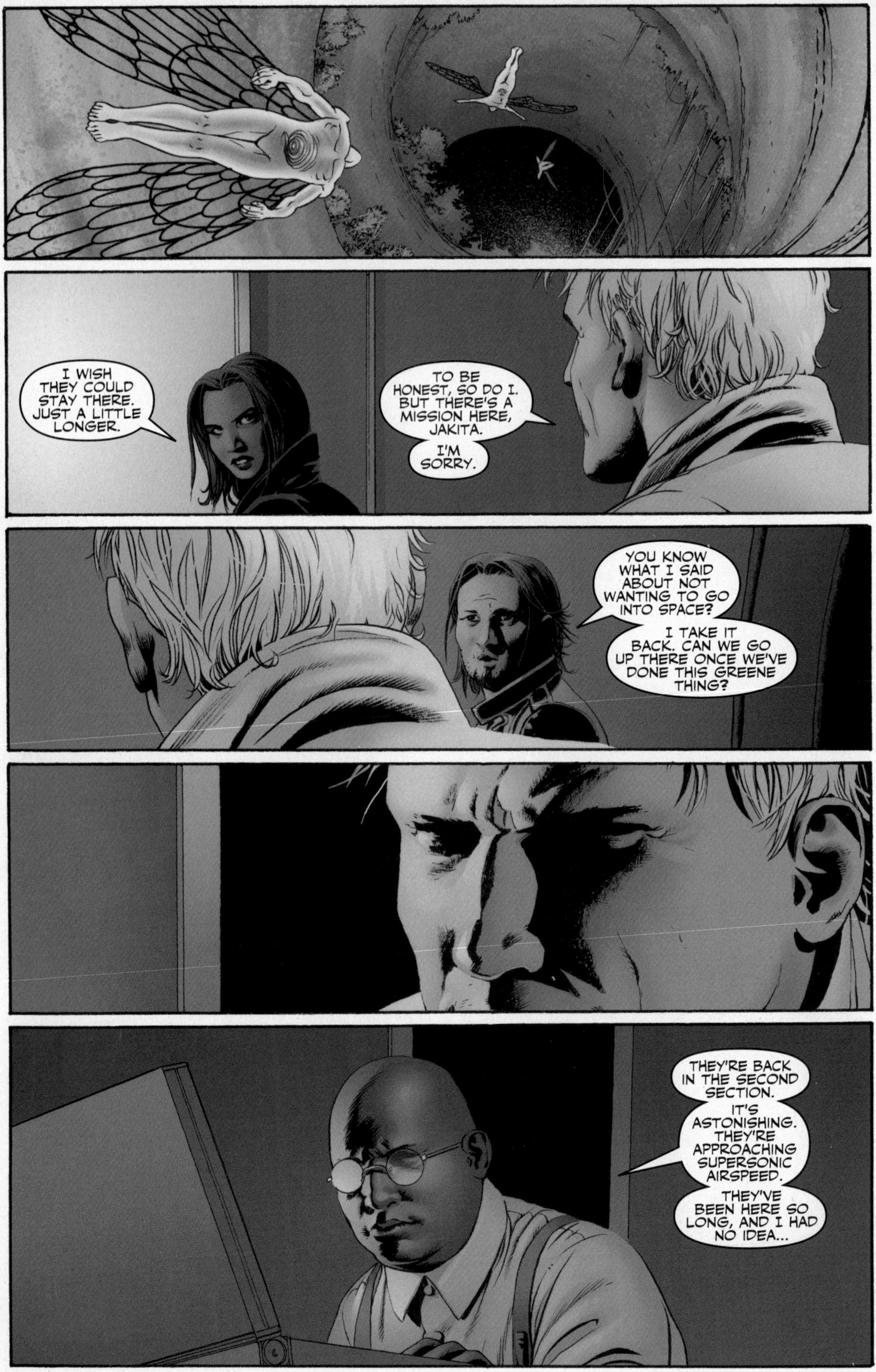
I WISH THEY COULD STAY THERE. JUST A LITTLE LONGER.
TO BE HONEST, SO DO I. BUT THERE'S A MISSION HERE, JAKITA.
I'M SORRY.
YOU KNOW WHAT I SAID ABOUT NOT WANTING TO GO INTO SPACE?
I TAKE IT BACK. CAN WE GO UP THERE ONCE WE'VE DONE THIS GREENE THING?
THEY'RE BACK IN THE SECOND SECTION.
IT'S ASTONISHING. THEY'RE APPROACHING SUPERSONIC AIRSPEED.
THEY'VE BEEN HERE SO LONG, AND I HAD NO IDEA...

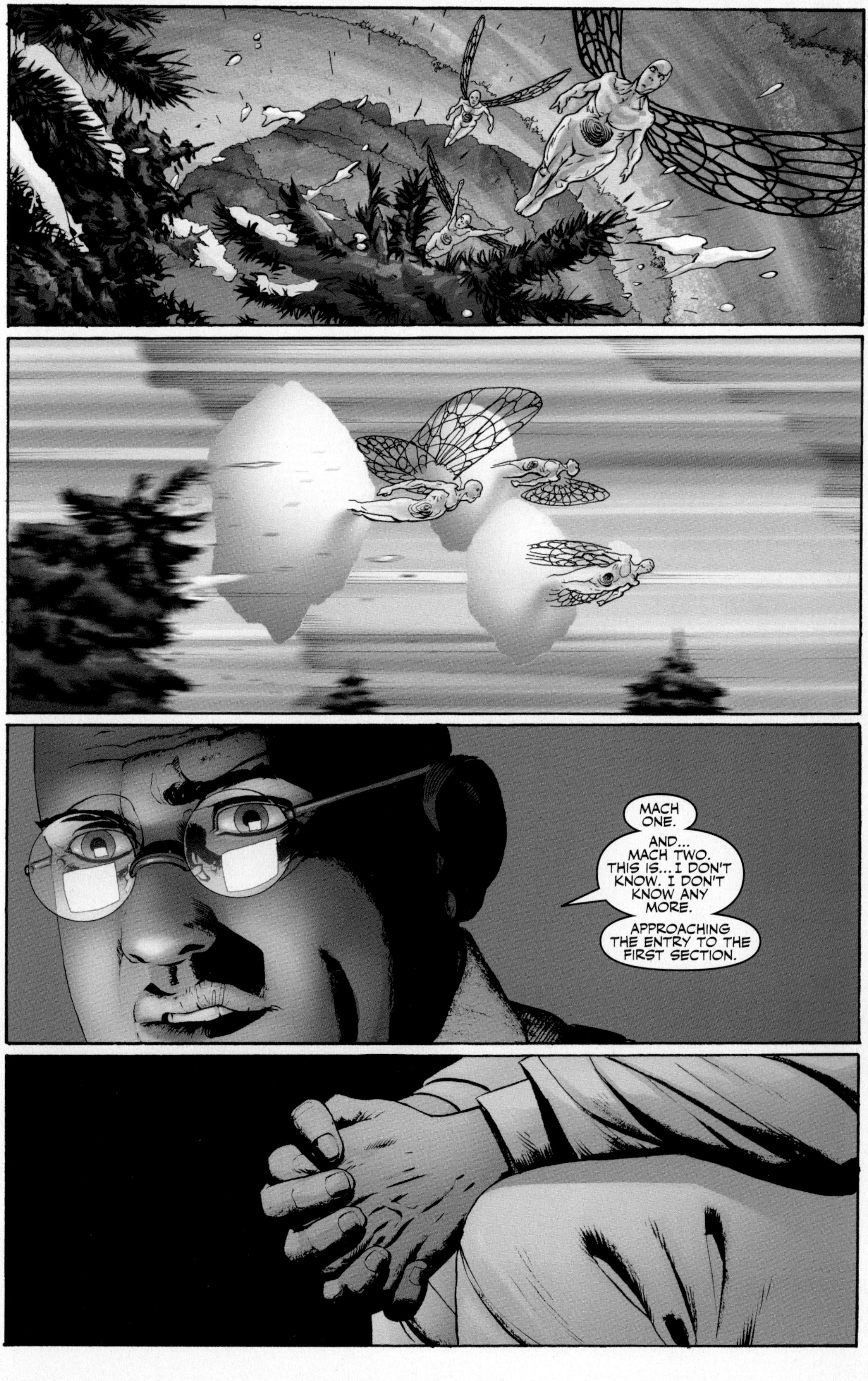
MACH ONE.
AND... MACH TWO. THIS IS... I DON'T KNOW. I DON'T KNOW ANY MORE.
APPROACHING THE ENTRY TO THE FIRST SECTION.

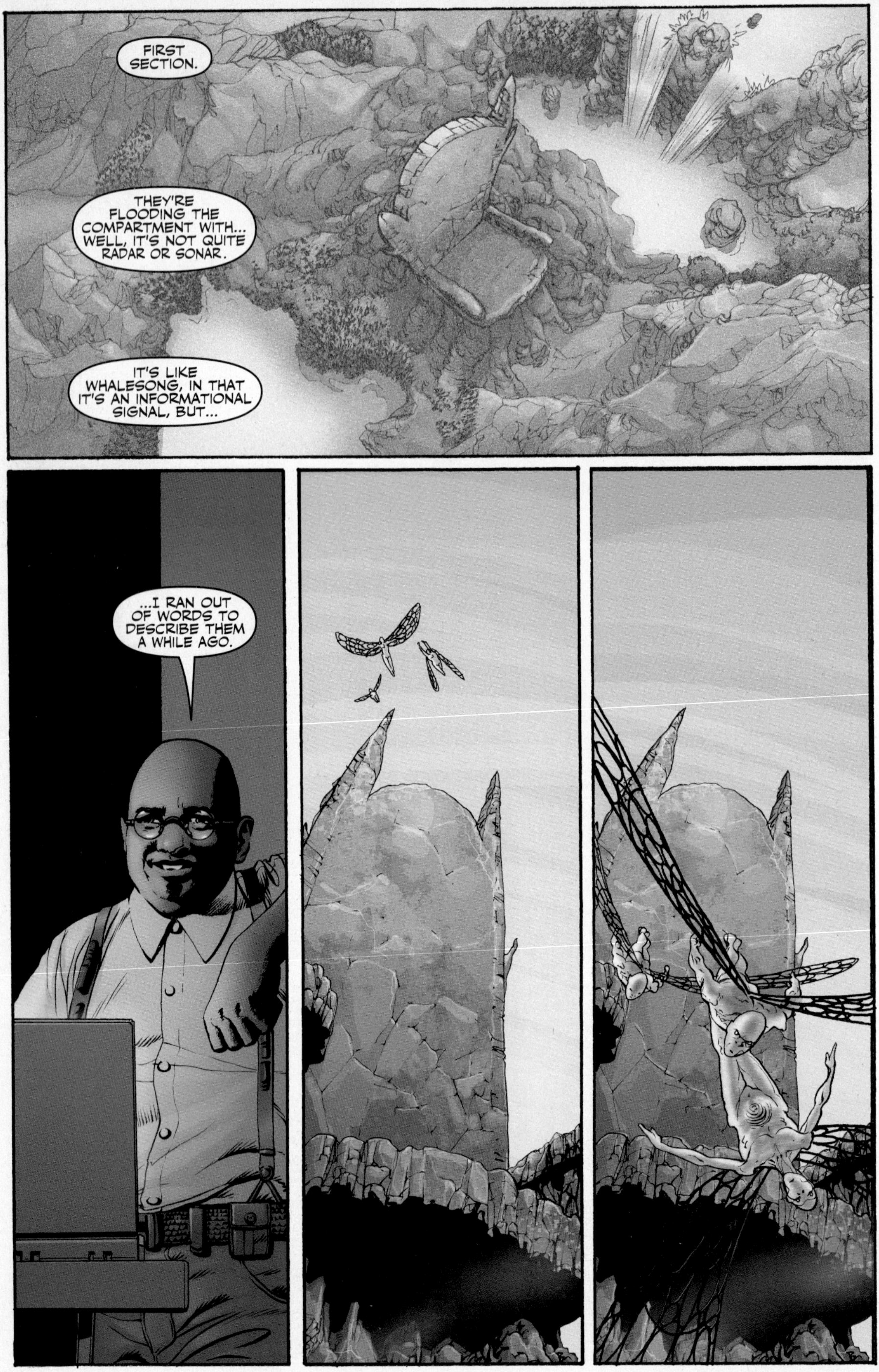
FIRST SECTION.
THEY'RE FLOODING THE COMPARTMENT WITH... WELL, IT'S NOT QUITE RADAR OR SONAR.
IT'S LIKE WHALESONG, IN THAT IT'S AN INFORMATIONAL SIGNAL, BUT...
...I RAN OUT OF WORDS TO DESCRIBE THEM A WHILE AGO.

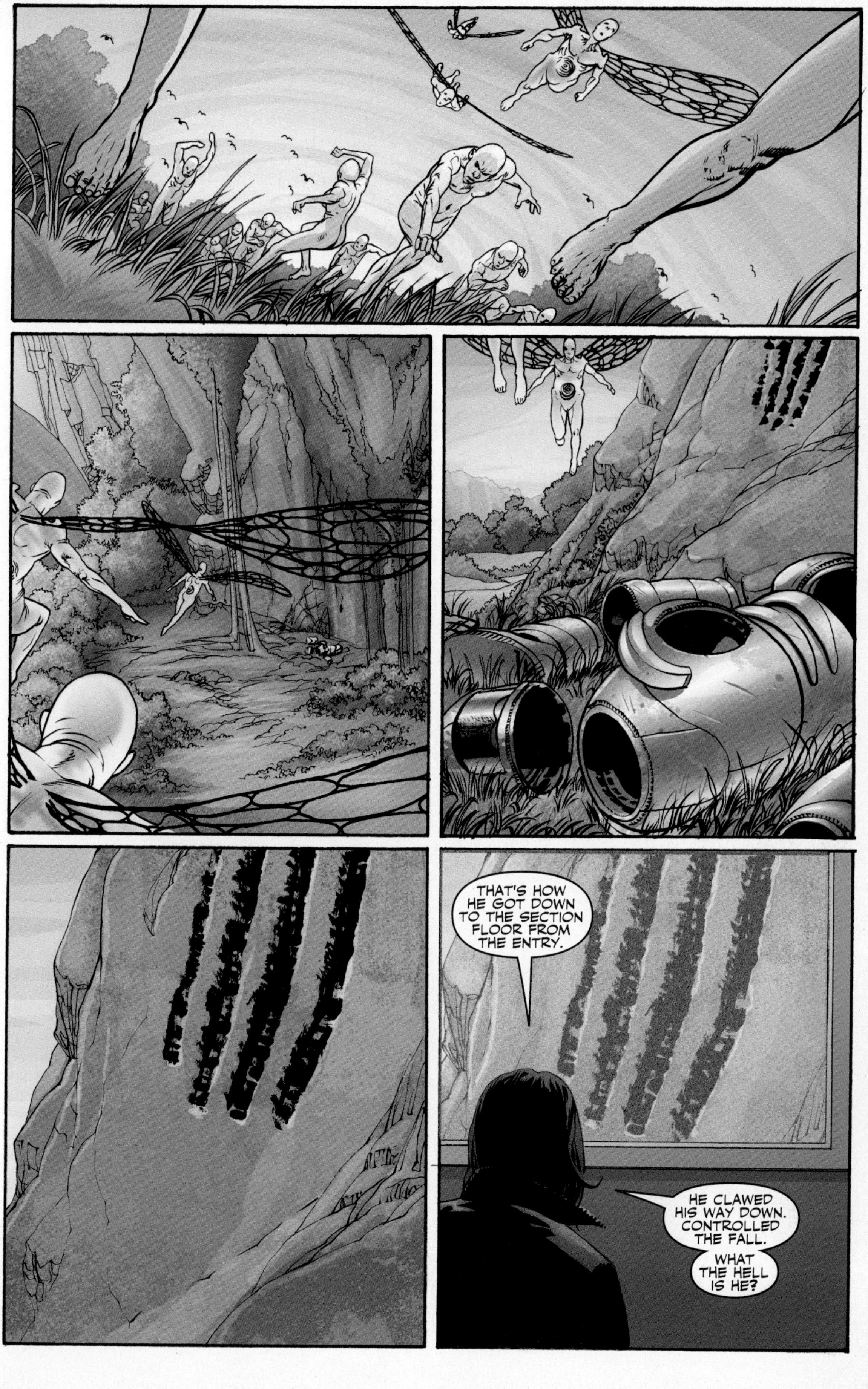
THAT'S HOW HE GOT DOWN TO THE SECTION FLOOR FROM THE ENTRY.
HE CLAWED HIS WAY DOWN. CONTROLLED THE FALL.
WHAT THE HELL IS HE?

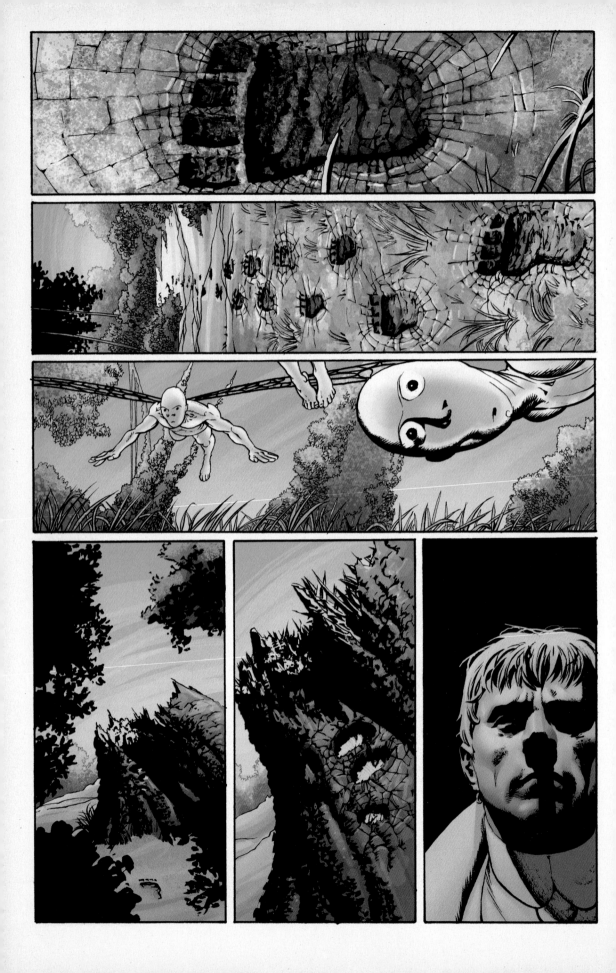

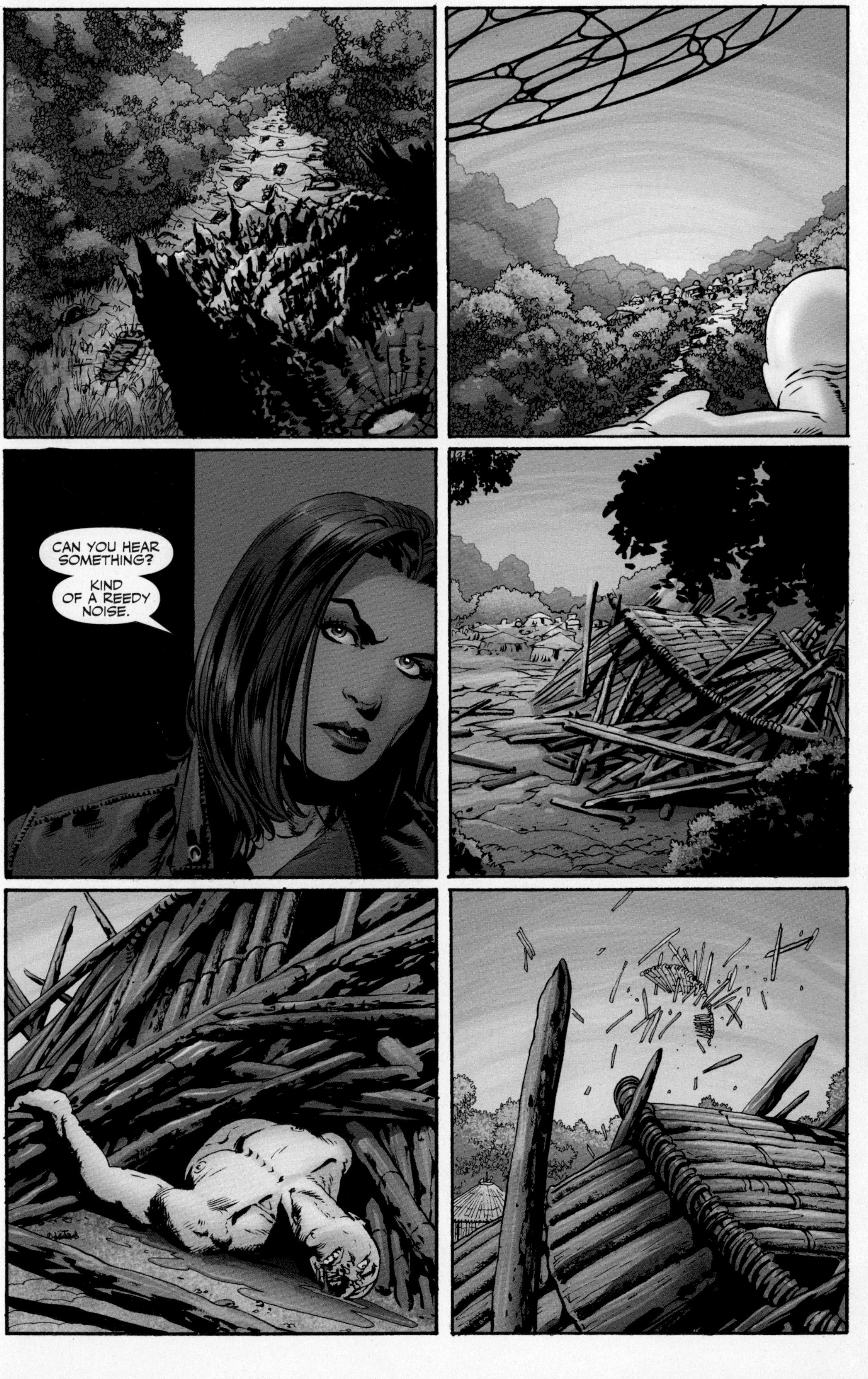
CAN YOU HEAR SOMETHING?
KIND OF A REEDY NOISE.

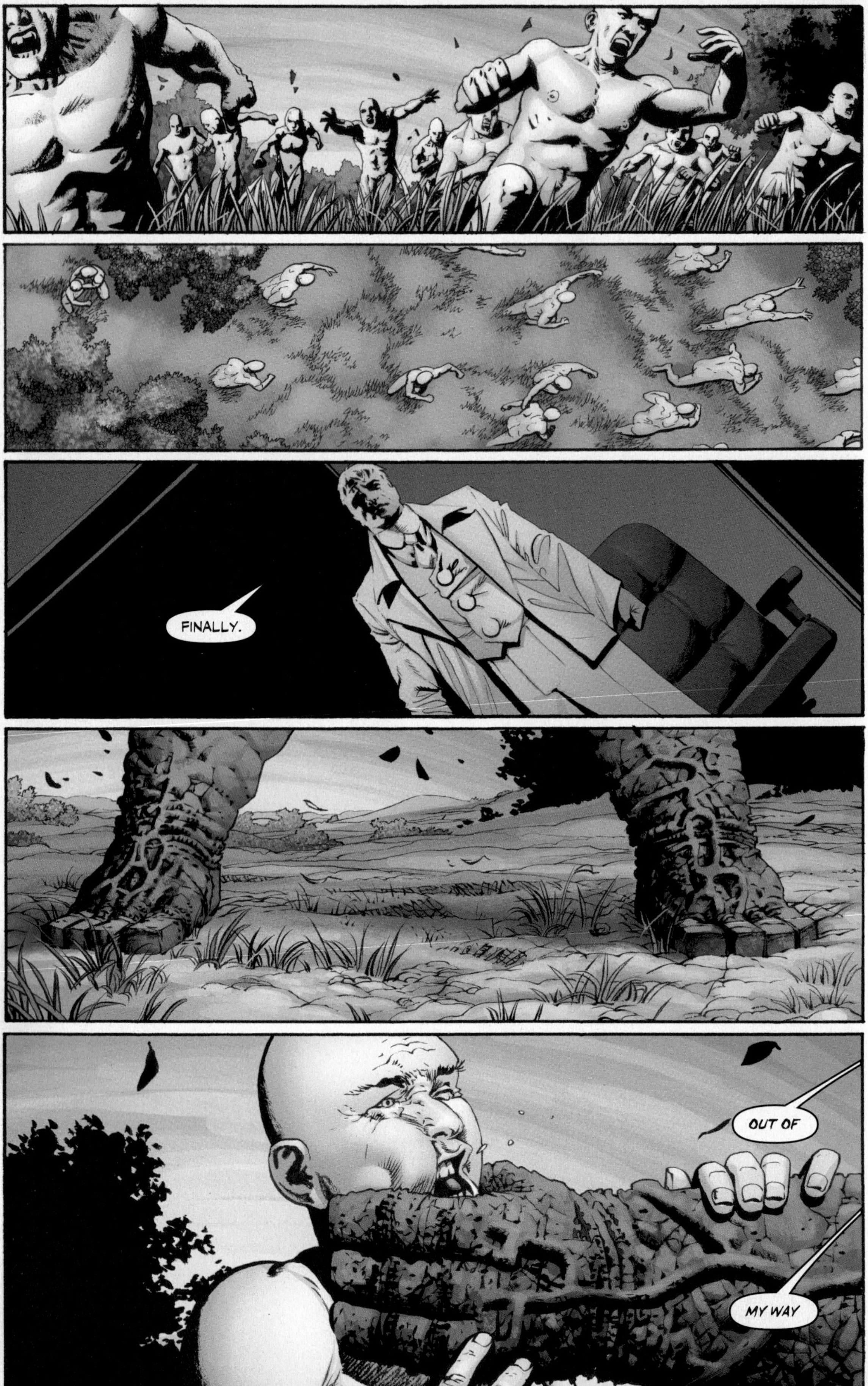
FINALLY.
OUT OF
MY WAY

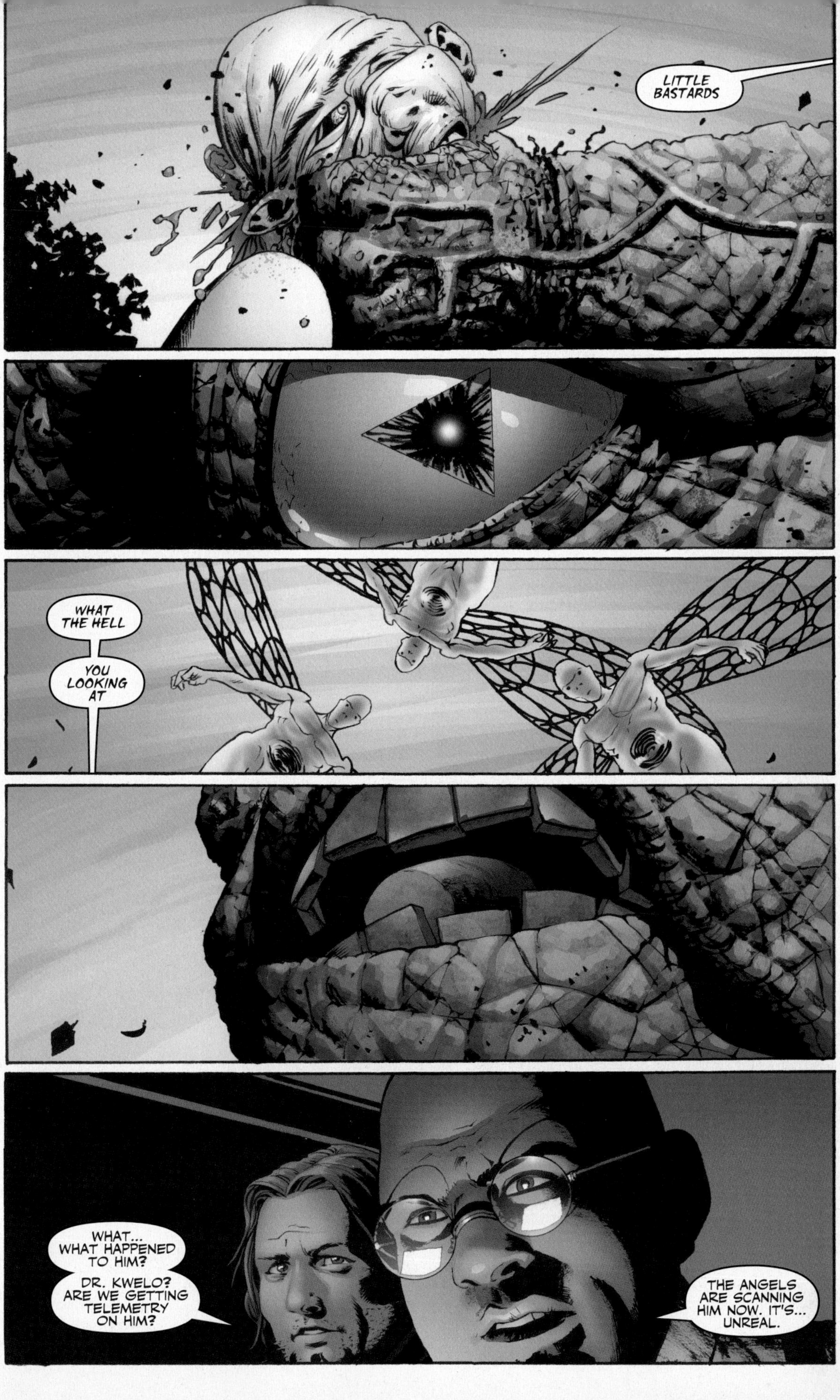
LITTLE BASTARDS
WHAT THE HELL
YOU LOOKING AT
WHAT... WHAT HAPPENED TO HIM?
DR. KWELO? ARE WE GETTING TELEMETRY ON HIM?
THE ANGELS ARE SCANNING HIM NOW. IT'S... UNREAL.

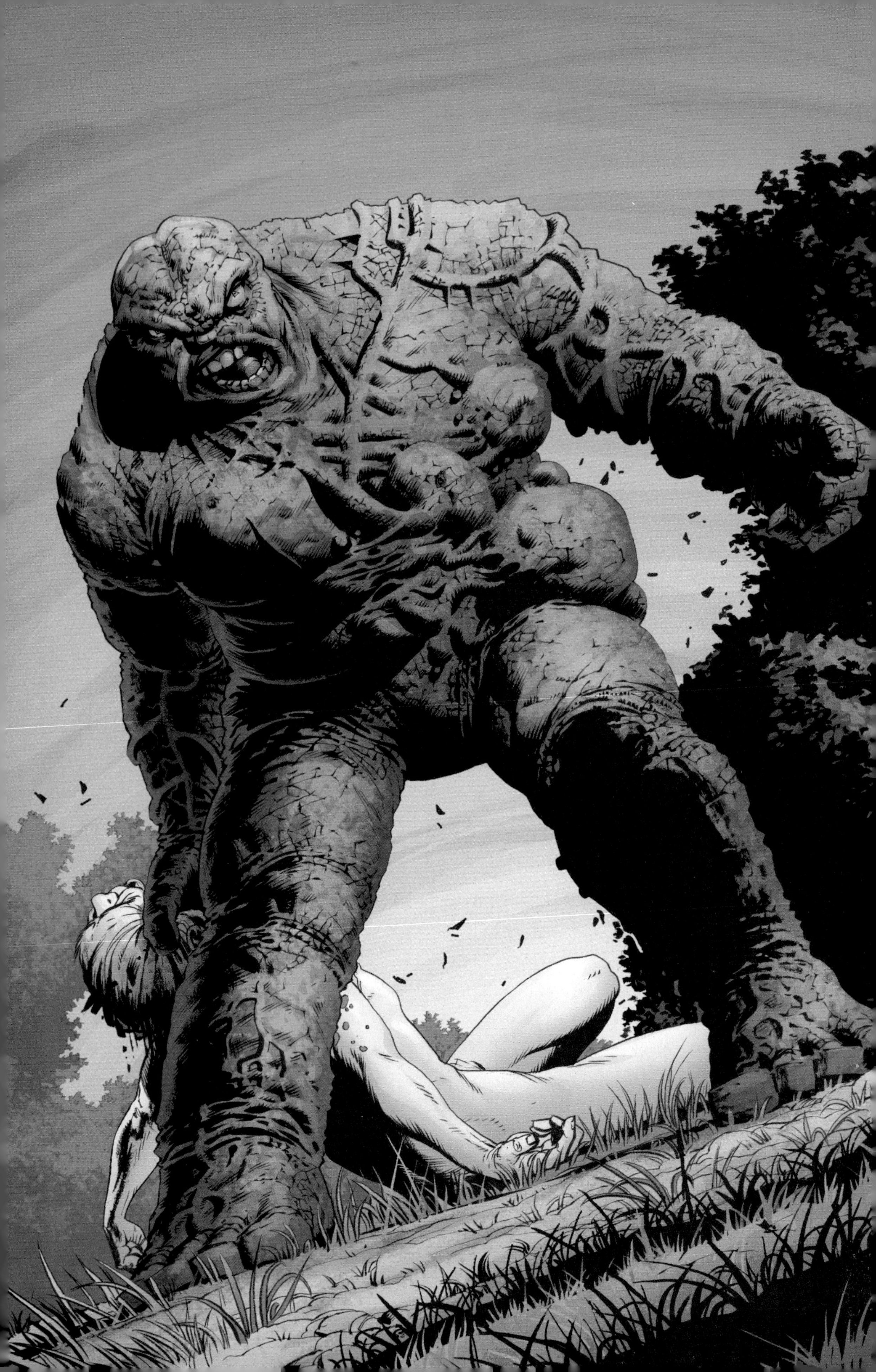

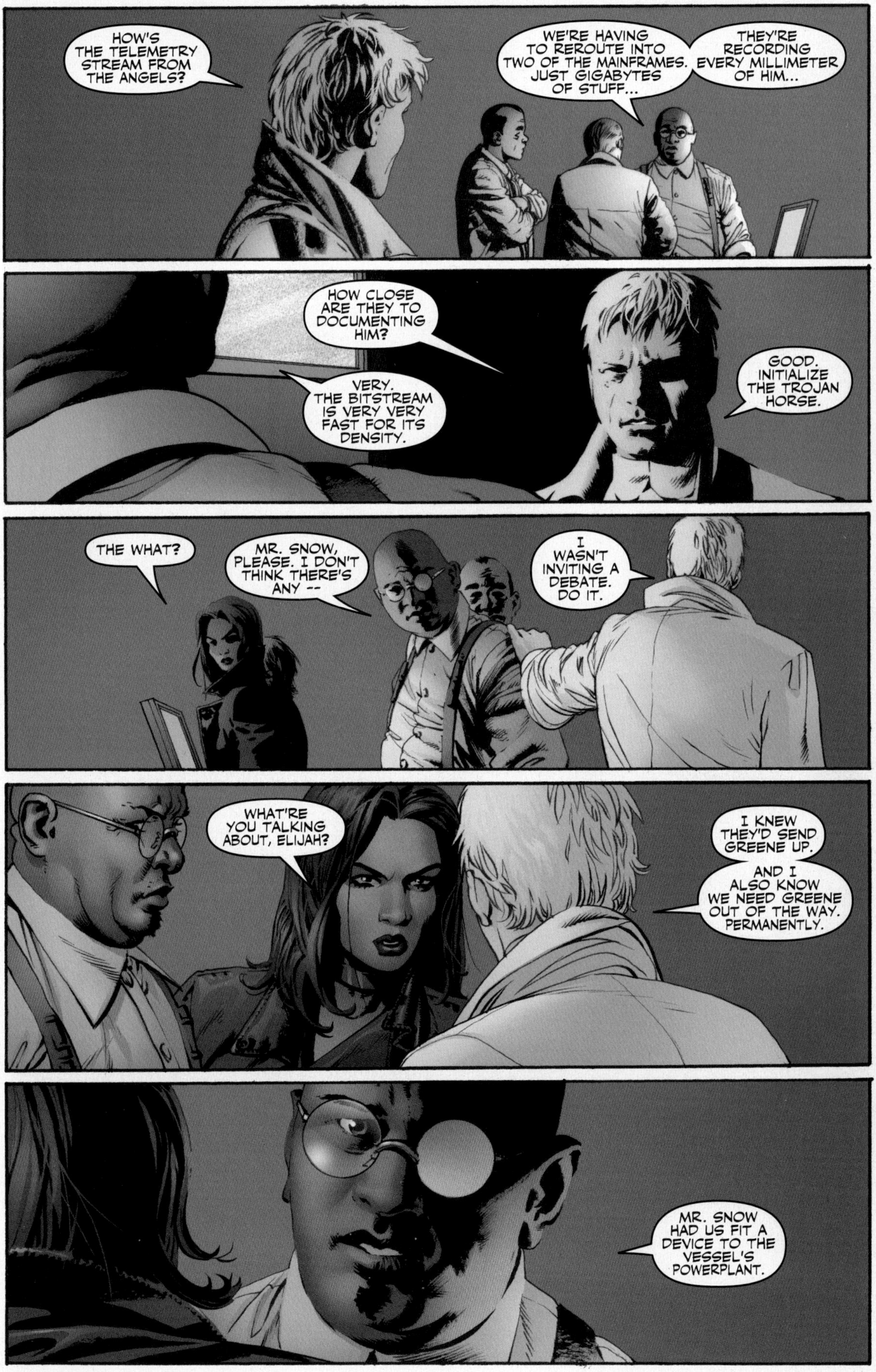
HOW'S THE TELEMETRY STREAM FROM THE ANGELS?
WE'RE HAVING TO REROUTE INTO TWO OF THE MAINFRAMES. JUST GIGABYTES OF STUFF...
THEY'RE RECORDING EVERY MILLIMETER OF HIM...
HOW CLOSE ARE THEY TO DOCUMENTING HIM?
VERY. THE BITSTREAM IS VERY VERY FAST FOR ITS DENSITY.
GOOD. INITIALIZE THE TROJAN HORSE.
THE WHAT?
MR. SNOW, PLEASE. I DON'T THINK THERE'S ANY --
I WASN'T INVITING A DEBATE. DO IT.
WHAT'RE YOU TALKING ABOUT, ELIJAH?
I KNEW THEY'D SEND GREENE UP.
AND I ALSO KNOW WE NEED GREENE OUT OF THE WAY. PERMANENTLY.
MR. SNOW HAD US FIT A DEVICE TO THE VESSEL'S POWERPLANT.

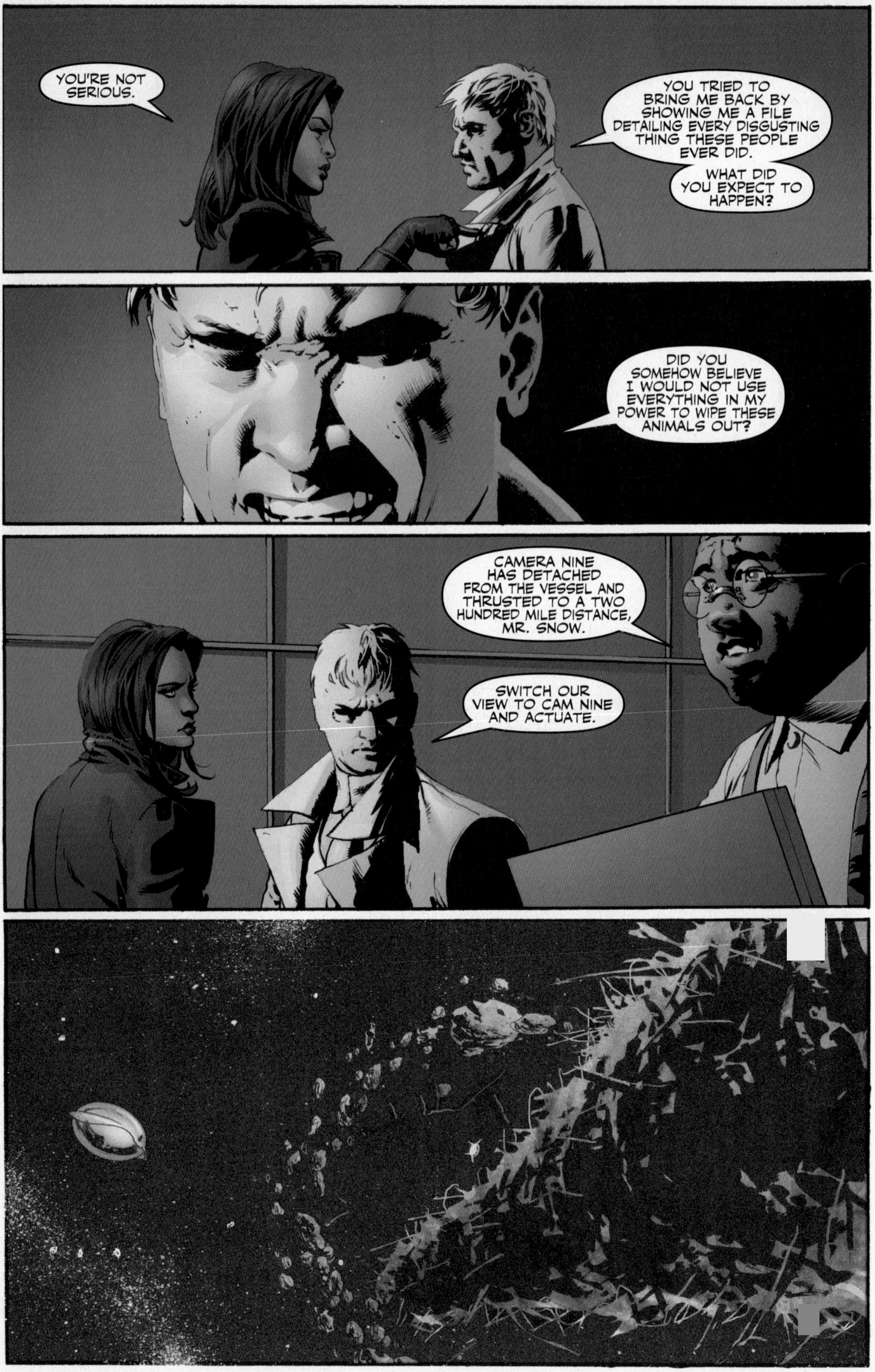
YOU'RE NOT SERIOUS.
YOU TRIED TO BRING ME BACK BY SHOWING ME A FILE DETAILING EVERY DISGUSTING THING THESE PEOPLE EVER DID.
WHAT DID YOU EXPECT TO HAPPEN?
DID YOU SOMEHOW BELIEVE I WOULD NOT USE EVERYTHING IN MY POWER TO WIPE THESE ANIMALS OUT?
CAMERA NINE HAS DETACHED FROM THE VESSEL AND THRUSTED TO A TWO HUNDRED MILE DISTANCE, MR. SNOW.
SWITCH OUR VIEW TO CAM NINE AND ACTUATE.

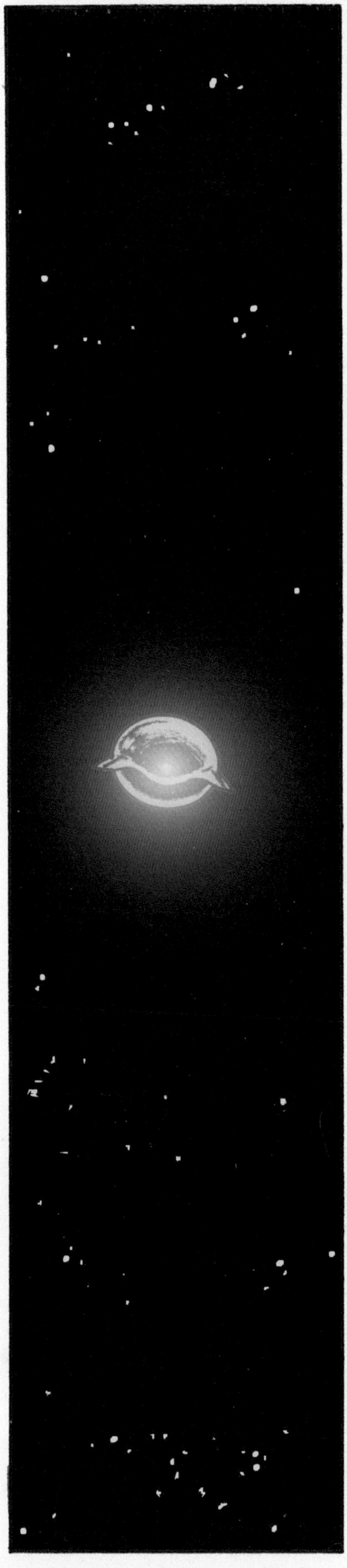
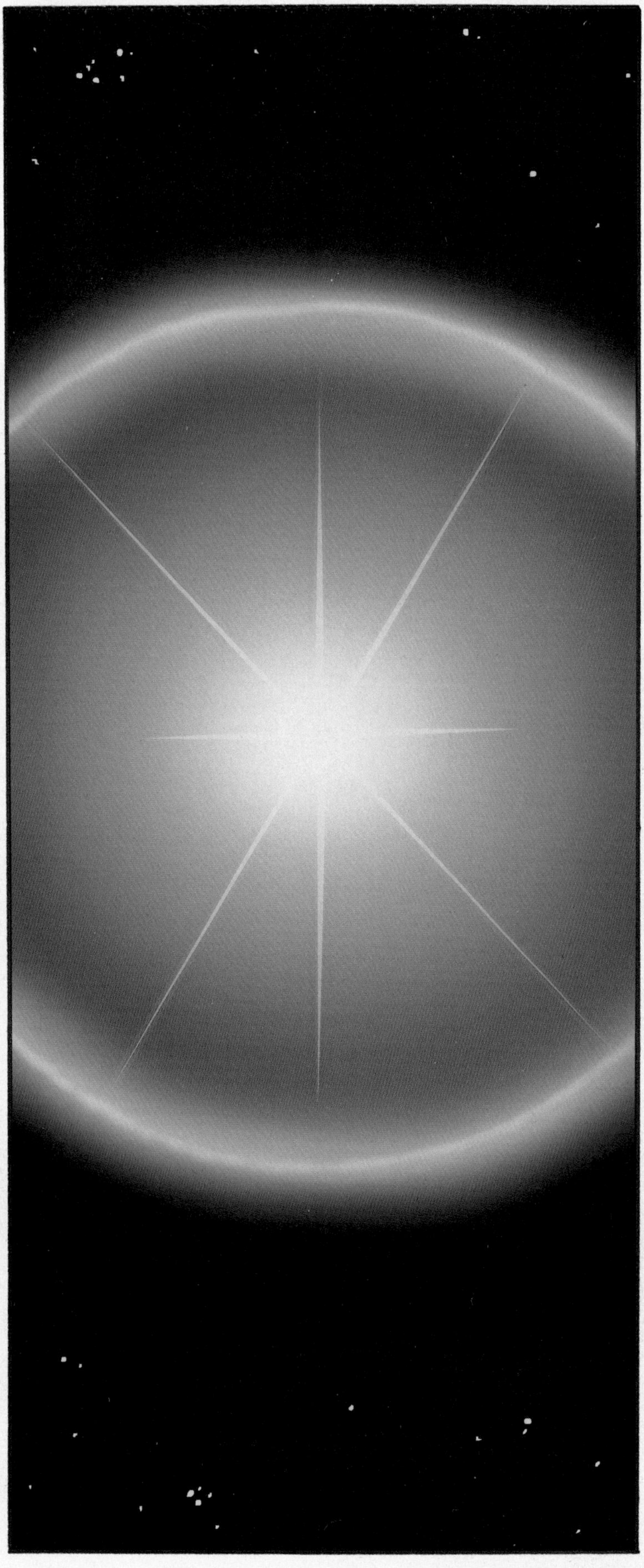

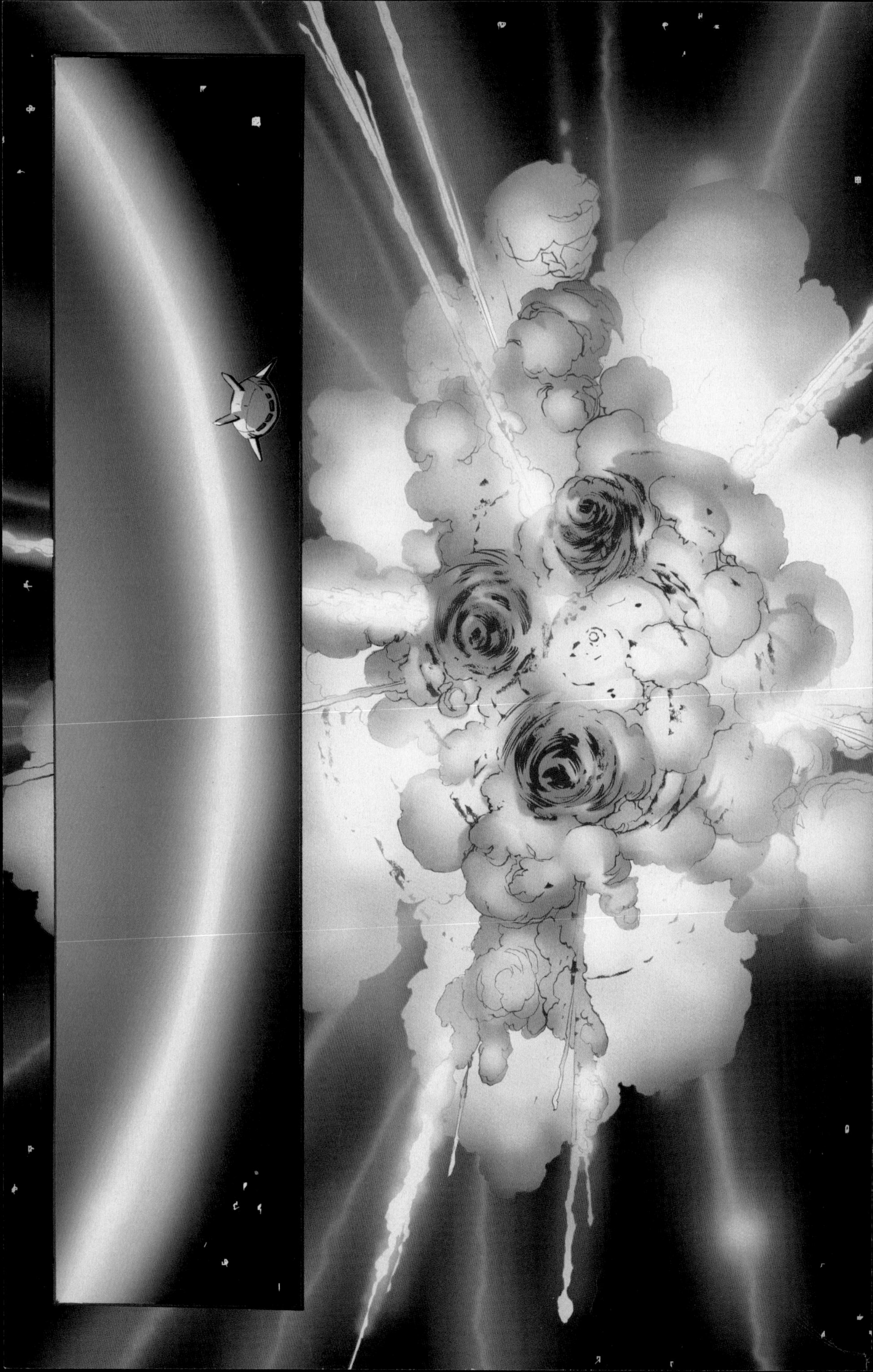

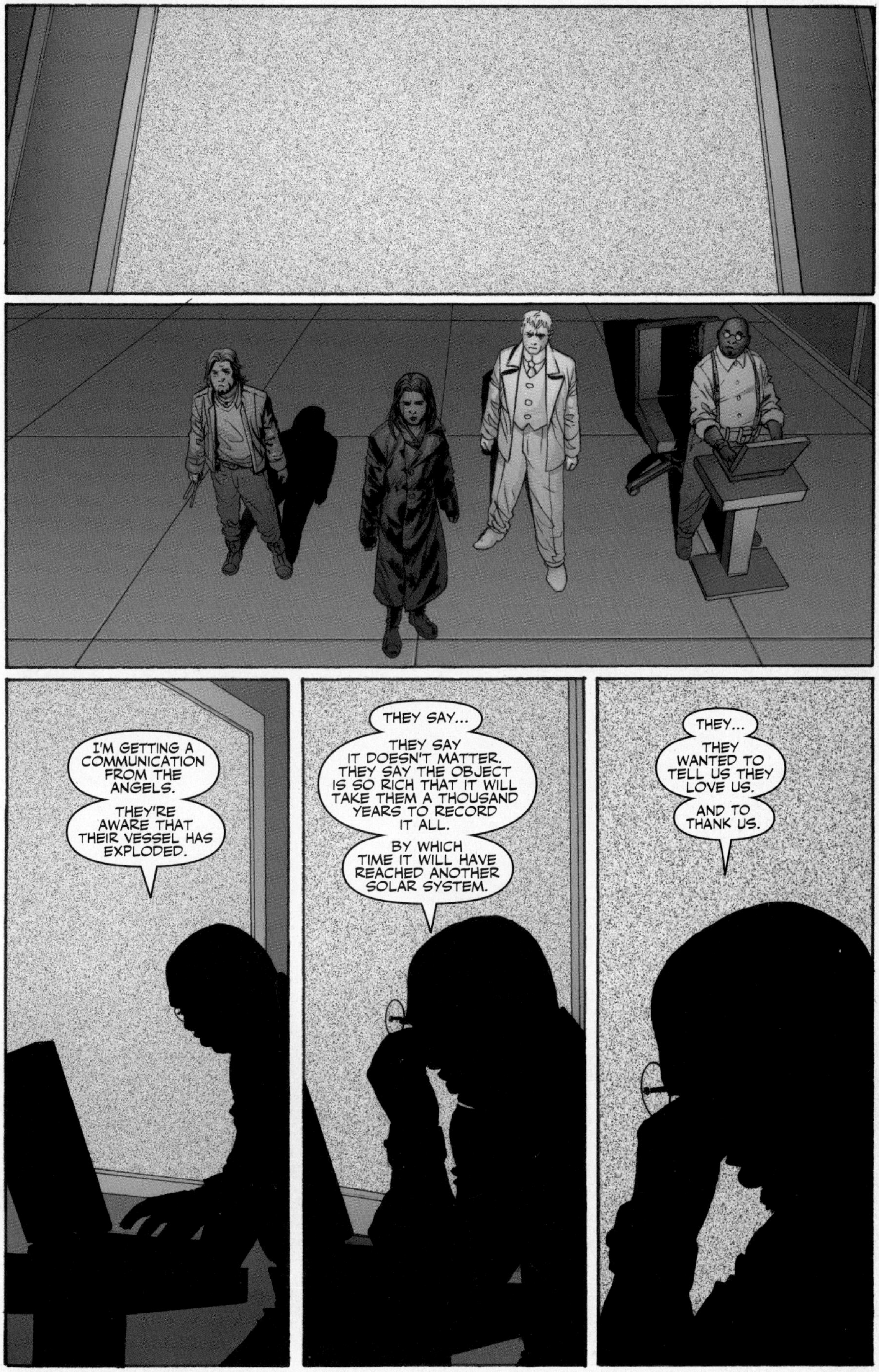
I'M GETTING A COMMUNICATION FROM THE ANGELS.
THEY'RE AWARE THAT THEIR VESSEL HAS EXPLODED.
THEY SAY...
THEY SAY IT DOESN'T MATTER. THEY SAY THE OBJECT IS SO RICH THAT IT WILL TAKE THEM A THOUSAND YEARS TO RECORD IT ALL.
BY WHICH TIME IT WILL HAVE REACHED ANOTHER SOLAR SYSTEM.
THEY...
THEY WANTED TO TELL US THEY LOVE US.
AND TO THANK US.

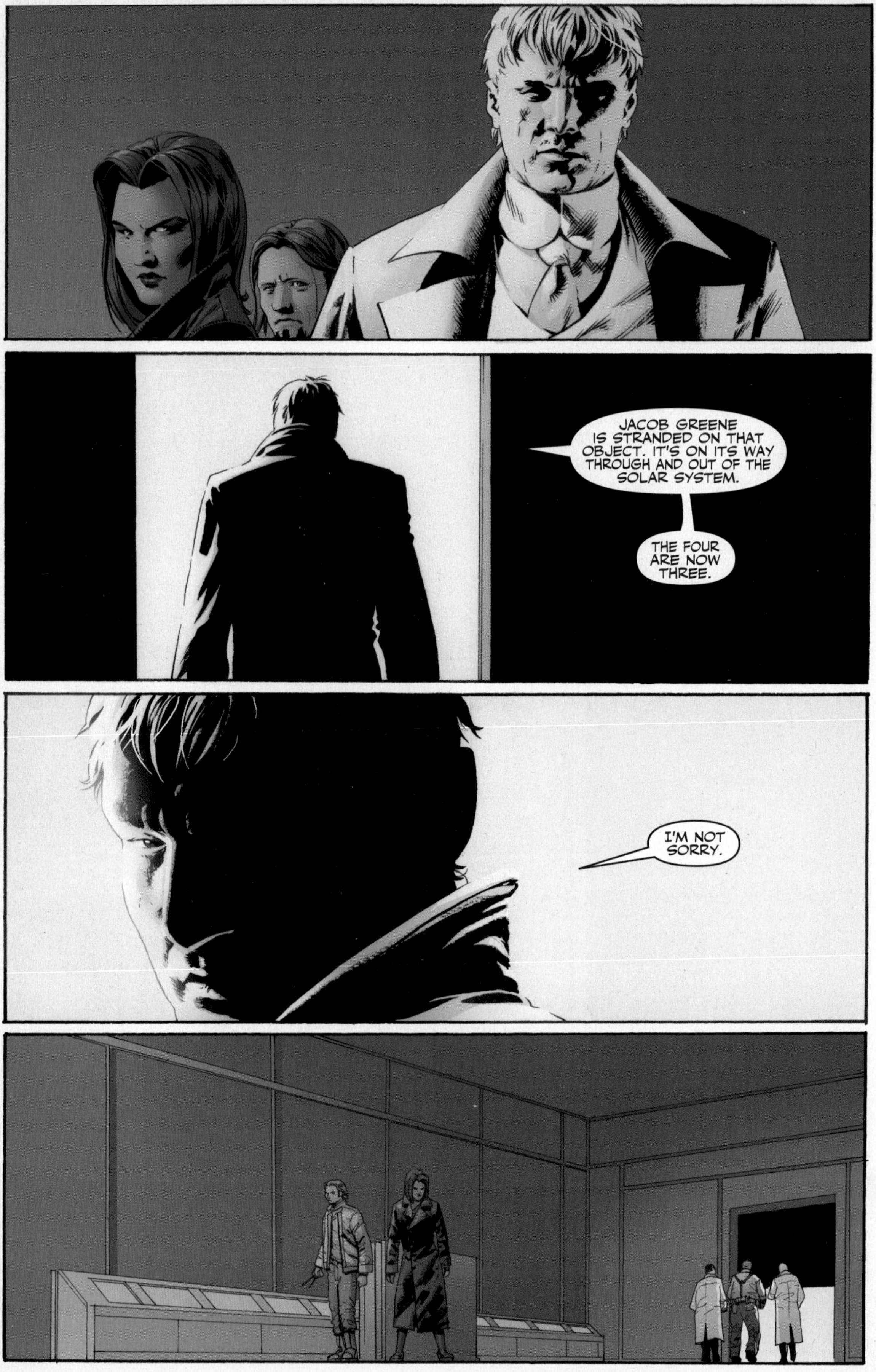
JACOB GREENE IS STRANDED ON THAT OBJECT. IT'S ON ITS WAY THROUGH AND OUT OF THE SOLAR SYSTEM.
THE FOUR ARE NOW THREE.
I'M NOT SORRY.

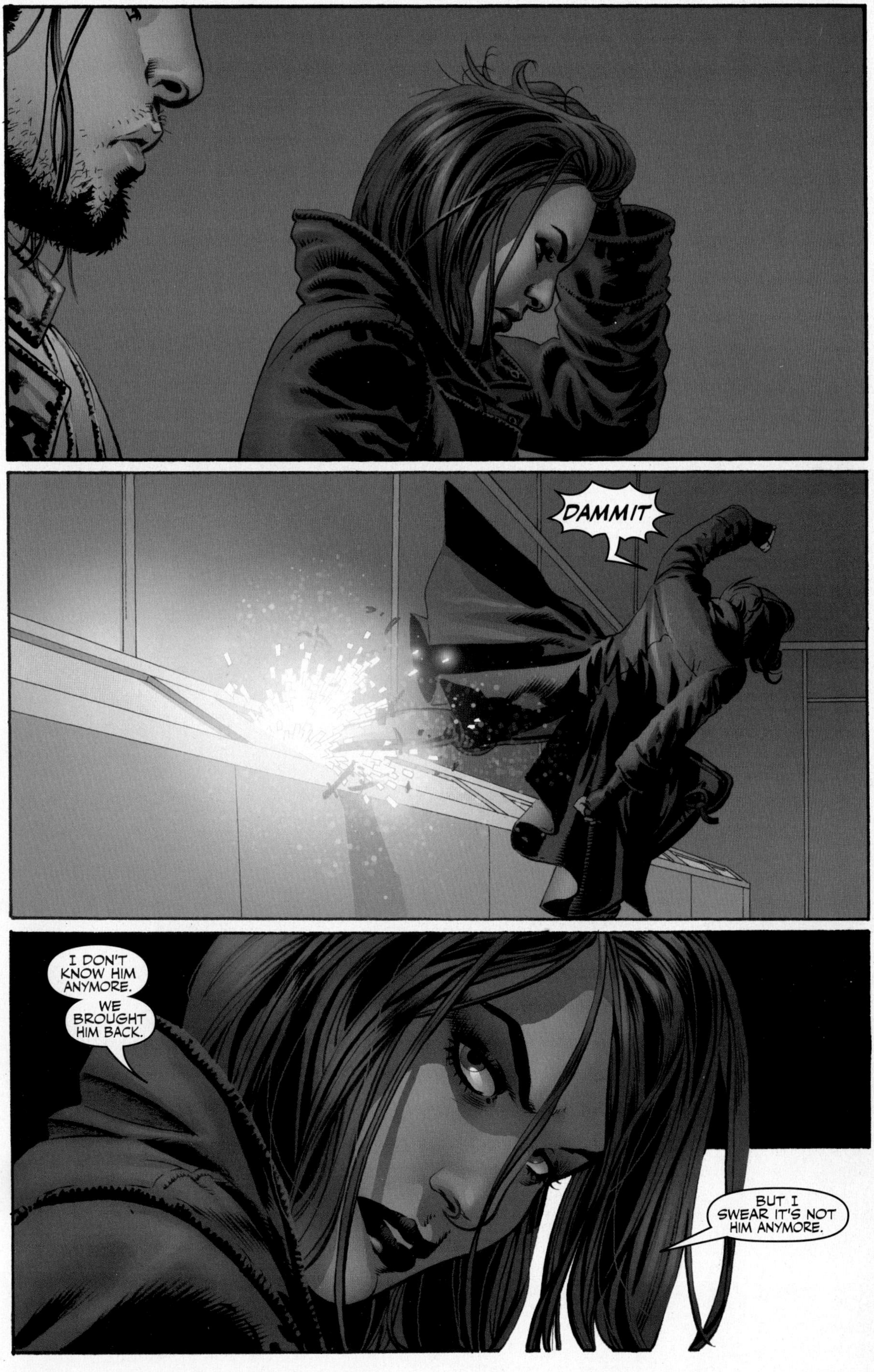
DAMMIT
I DON'T KNOW HIM ANYMORE.
WE BROUGHT HIM BACK.
BUT I SWEAR IT'S NOT HIM ANYMORE.

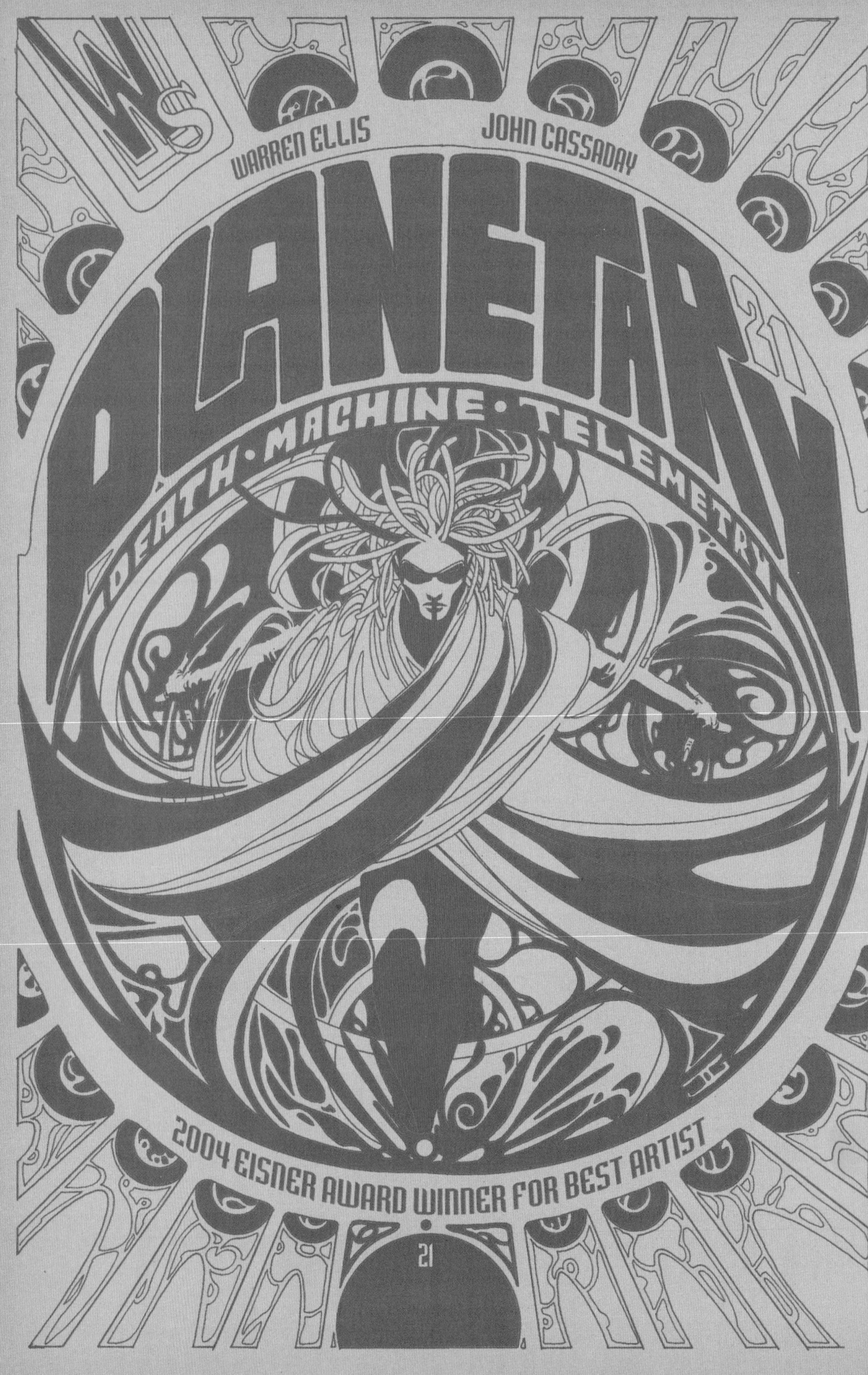
WS
WARREN ELLIS
JOHN CASSADAY
PLANETARY
21
DEATH • MACHINE • TELEMETRY
2004 EISNER AWARD WINNER FOR BEST ARTIST
21

DEATH MACHINE TELEMETRY

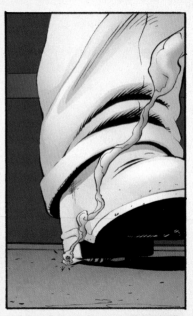

WRITTEN BY
WARREN ELLIS

LETTERING BY
RICHARD
STARKINGS

ASSISTANT EDITOR
KRISTY
QUINN

ART BY
JOHN CASSADAY

COLORING BY
LAURA
MARTIN

EDITOR
SCOTT
DUNBIER

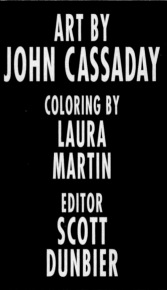

HELLO, MELANCTHA.

I'M HERE FOR MY CONSULTATION.

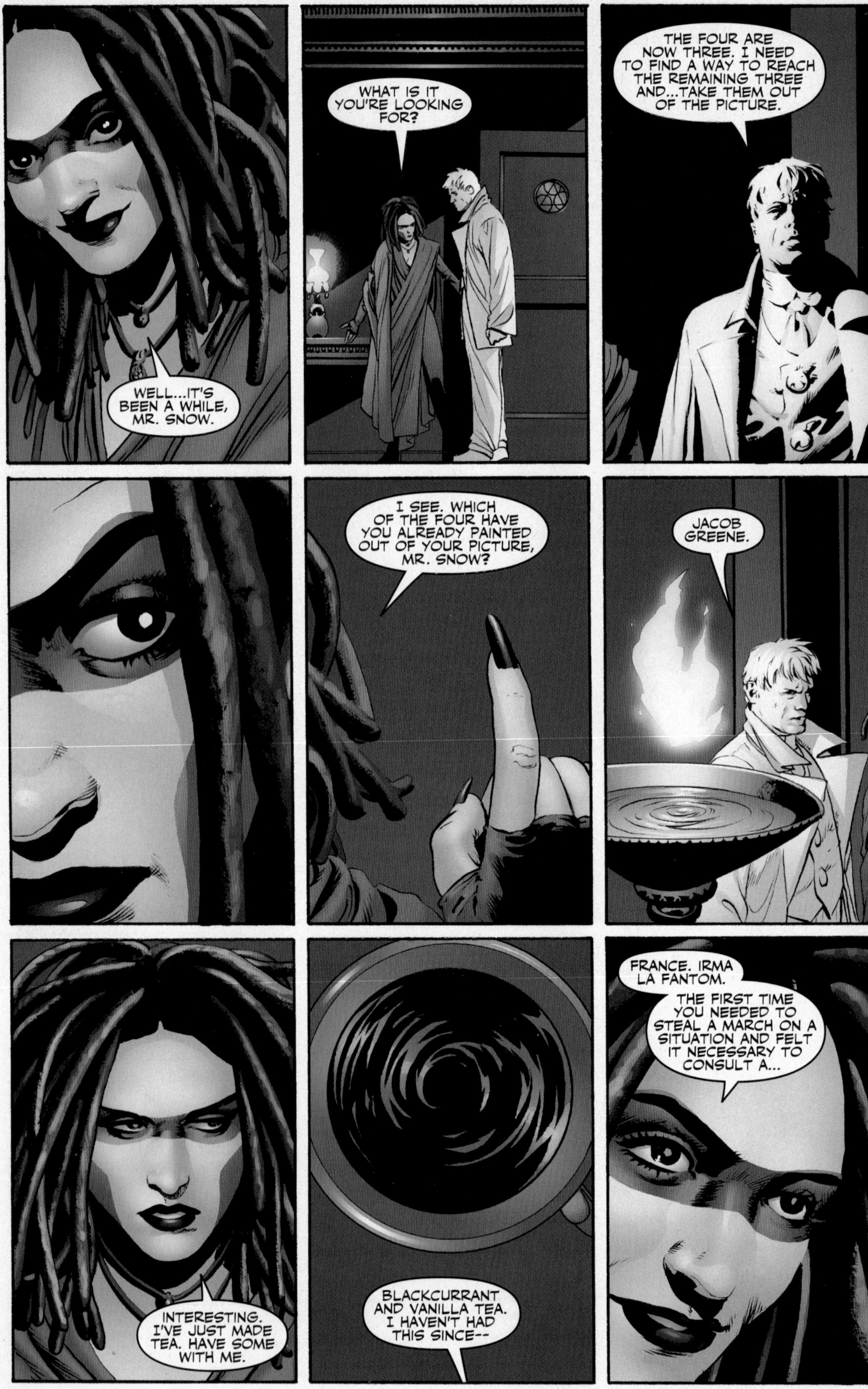
WELL...IT'S BEEN A WHILE, MR. SNOW.
WHAT IS IT YOU'RE LOOKING FOR?
THE FOUR ARE NOW THREE. I NEED TO FIND A WAY TO REACH THE REMAINING THREE AND...TAKE THEM OUT OF THE PICTURE.
I SEE. WHICH OF THE FOUR HAVE YOU ALREADY PAINTED OUT OF YOUR PICTURE, MR. SNOW?
JACOB GREENE.
INTERESTING. I'VE JUST MADE TEA. HAVE SOME WITH ME.
BLACKCURRANT AND VANILLA TEA. I HAVEN'T HAD THIS SINCE--
FRANCE. IRMA LA FANTOM.
THE FIRST TIME YOU NEEDED TO STEAL A MARCH ON A SITUATION AND FELT IT NECESSARY TO CONSULT A...

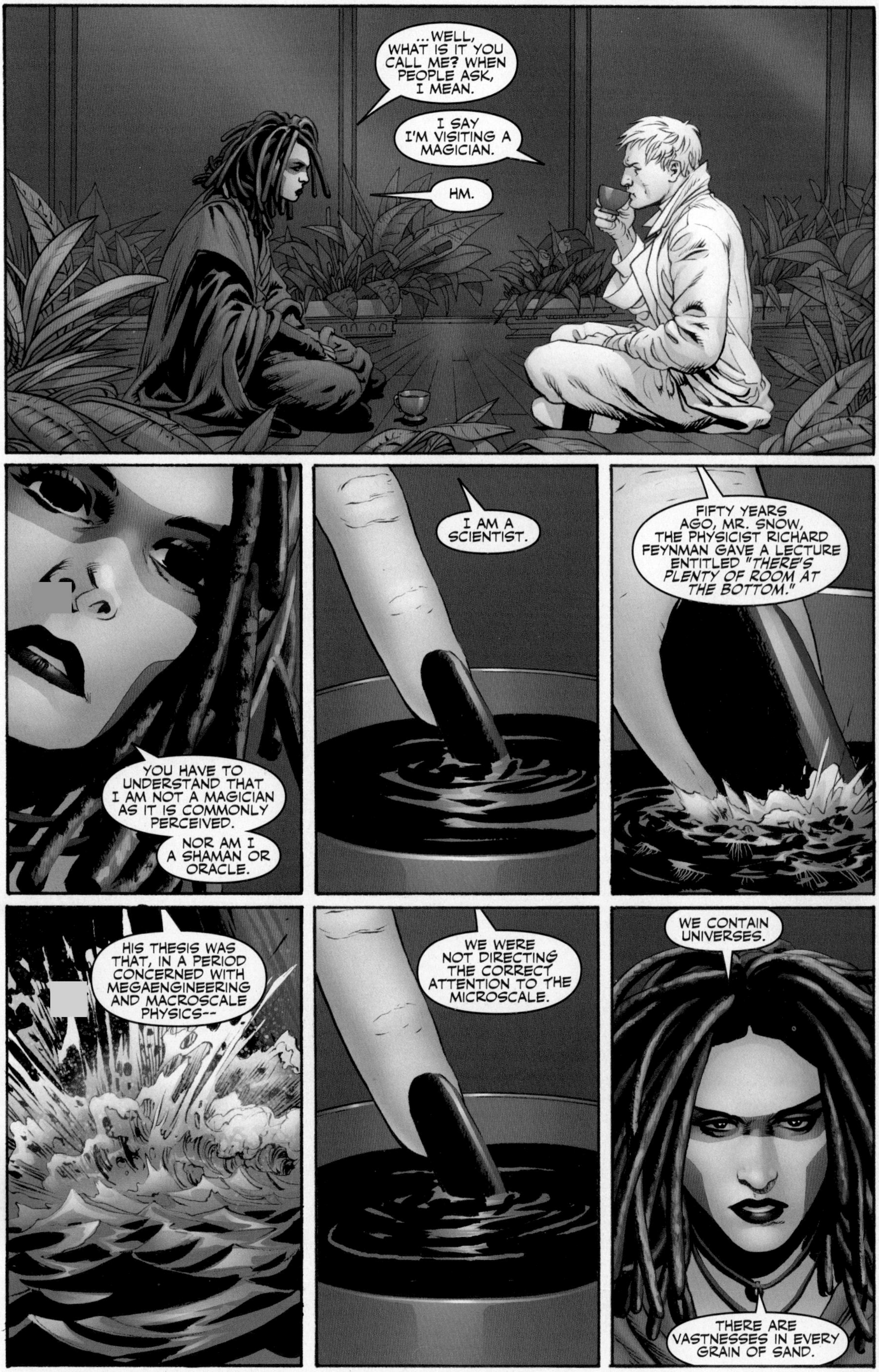
...WELL, WHAT IS IT YOU CALL ME? WHEN PEOPLE ASK, I MEAN.
I SAY I'M VISITING A MAGICIAN.
HM.
YOU HAVE TO UNDERSTAND THAT I AM NOT A MAGICIAN AS IT IS COMMONLY PERCEIVED.
NOR AM I A SHAMAN OR ORACLE.
I AM A SCIENTIST.
FIFTY YEARS AGO, MR. SNOW, THE PHYSICIST RICHARD FEYNMAN GAVE A LECTURE ENTITLED "THERE'S PLENTY OF ROOM AT THE BOTTOM."
HIS THESIS WAS THAT, IN A PERIOD CONCERNED WITH MEGAENGINEERING AND MACROSCALE PHYSICS--
WE WERE NOT DIRECTING THE CORRECT ATTENTION TO THE MICROSCALE.
WE CONTAIN UNIVERSES.
THERE ARE VASTNESSES IN EVERY GRAIN OF SAND.

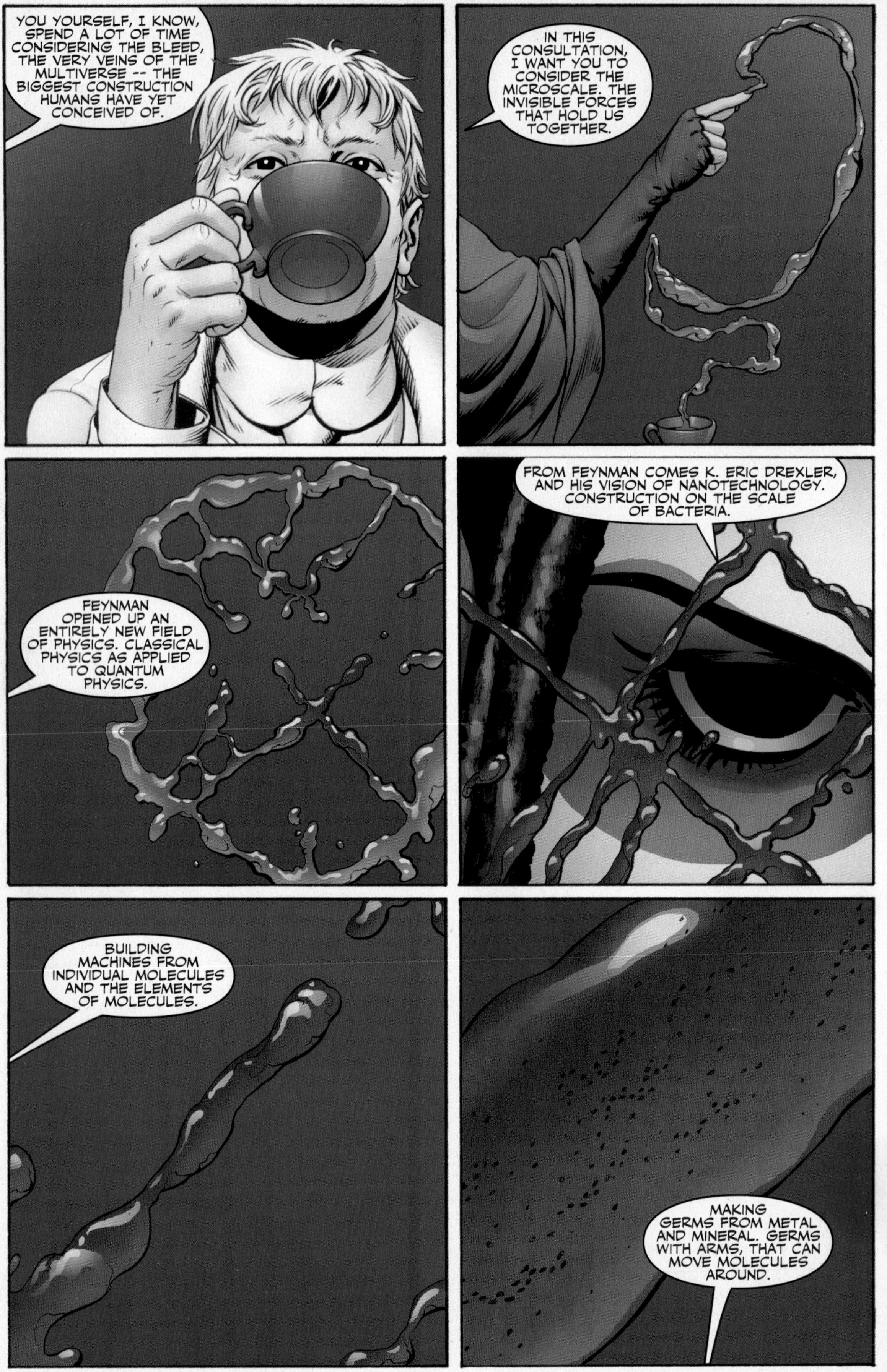
YOU YOURSELF, I KNOW, SPEND A LOT OF TIME CONSIDERING THE BLEED, THE VERY VEINS OF THE MULTIVERSE -- THE BIGGEST CONSTRUCTION HUMANS HAVE YET CONCEIVED OF.
IN THIS CONSULTATION, I WANT YOU TO CONSIDER THE MICROSCALE. THE INVISIBLE FORCES THAT HOLD US TOGETHER.
FEYNMAN OPENED UP AN ENTIRELY NEW FIELD OF PHYSICS. CLASSICAL PHYSICS AS APPLIED TO QUANTUM PHYSICS.
FROM FEYNMAN COMES K. ERIC DREXLER, AND HIS VISION OF NANOTECHNOLOGY. CONSTRUCTION ON THE SCALE OF BACTERIA.
BUILDING MACHINES FROM INDIVIDUAL MOLECULES AND THE ELEMENTS OF MOLECULES.
MAKING GERMS FROM METAL AND MINERAL. GERMS WITH ARMS, THAT CAN MOVE MOLECULES AROUND.

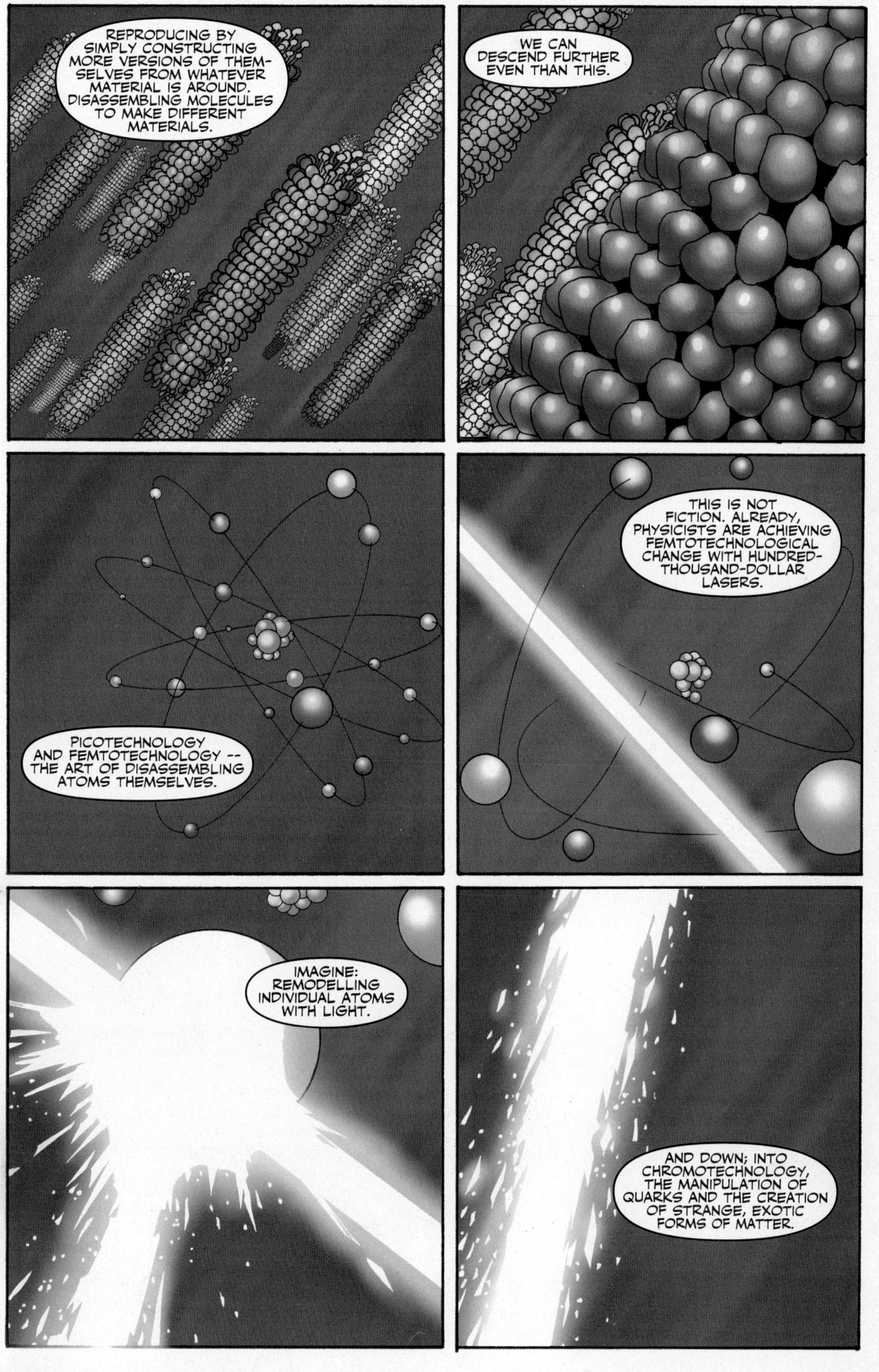
REPRODUCING BY SIMPLY CONSTRUCTING MORE VERSIONS OF THEMSELVES FROM WHATEVER MATERIAL IS AROUND. DISASSEMBLING MOLECULES TO MAKE DIFFERENT MATERIALS.
WE CAN DESCEND FURTHER EVEN THAN THIS.
PICOTECHNOLOGY AND FEMTOTECHNOLOGY -- THE ART OF DISASSEMBLING ATOMS THEMSELVES.
THIS IS NOT FICTION. ALREADY, PHYSICISTS ARE ACHIEVING FEMTOTECHNOLOGICAL CHANGE WITH HUNDRED-THOUSAND-DOLLAR LASERS.
IMAGINE: REMODELLING INDIVIDUAL ATOMS WITH LIGHT.
AND DOWN; INTO CHROMOTECHNOLOGY, THE MANIPULATION OF QUARKS AND THE CREATION OF STRANGE, EXOTIC FORMS OF MATTER.

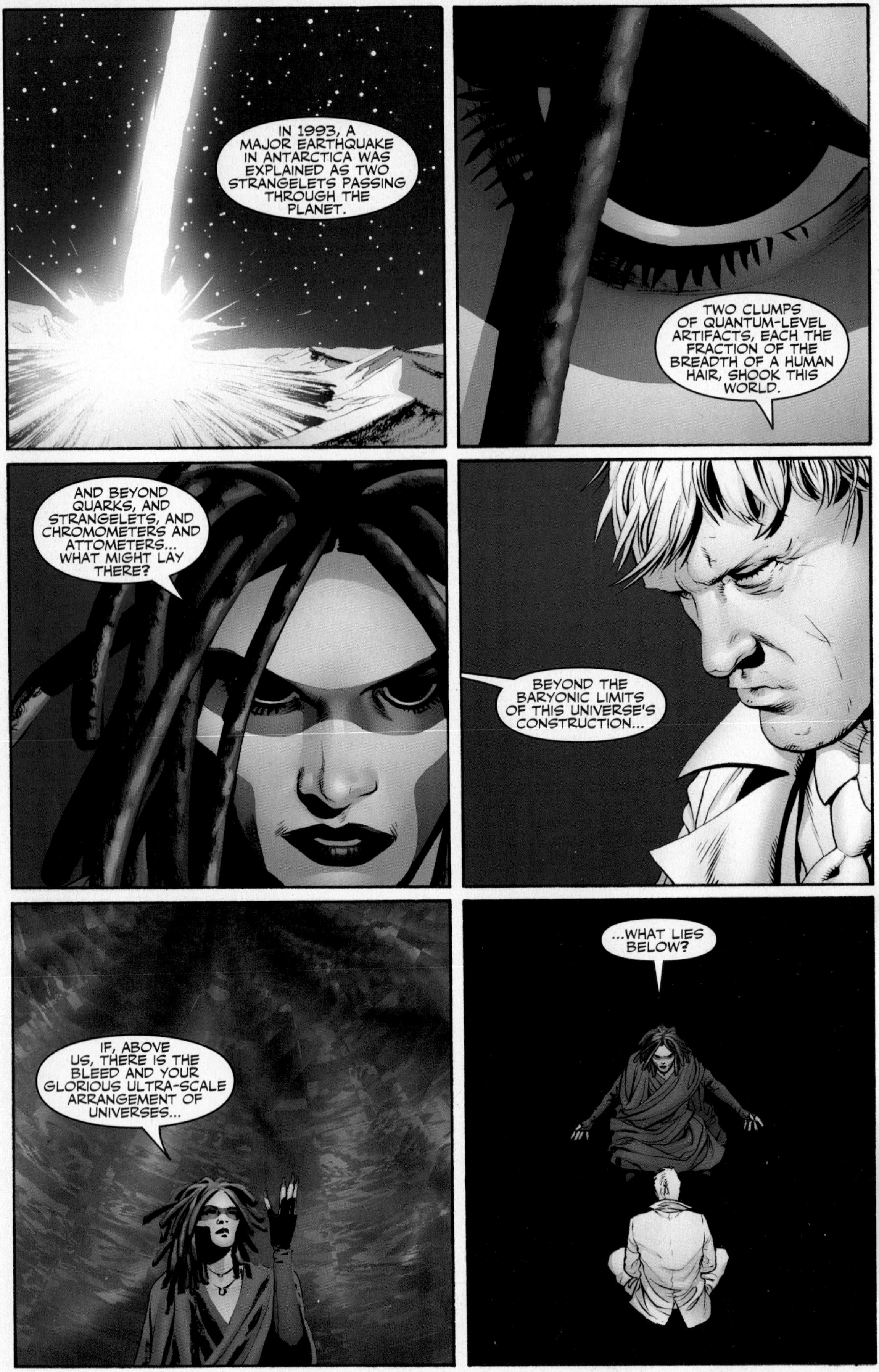
IN 1993, A MAJOR EARTHQUAKE IN ANTARCTICA WAS EXPLAINED AS TWO STRANGELETS PASSING THROUGH THE PLANET.
TWO CLUMPS OF QUANTUM-LEVEL ARTIFACTS, EACH THE FRACTION OF THE BREADTH OF A HUMAN HAIR, SHOOK THIS WORLD.
AND BEYOND QUARKS, AND STRANGELETS, AND CHROMOMETERS AND ATTOMETERS... WHAT MIGHT LAY THERE?
BEYOND THE BARYONIC LIMITS OF THIS UNIVERSE'S CONSTRUCTION...
IF, ABOVE US, THERE IS THE BLEED AND YOUR GLORIOUS ULTRA-SCALE ARRANGEMENT OF UNIVERSES...
...WHAT LIES BELOW?

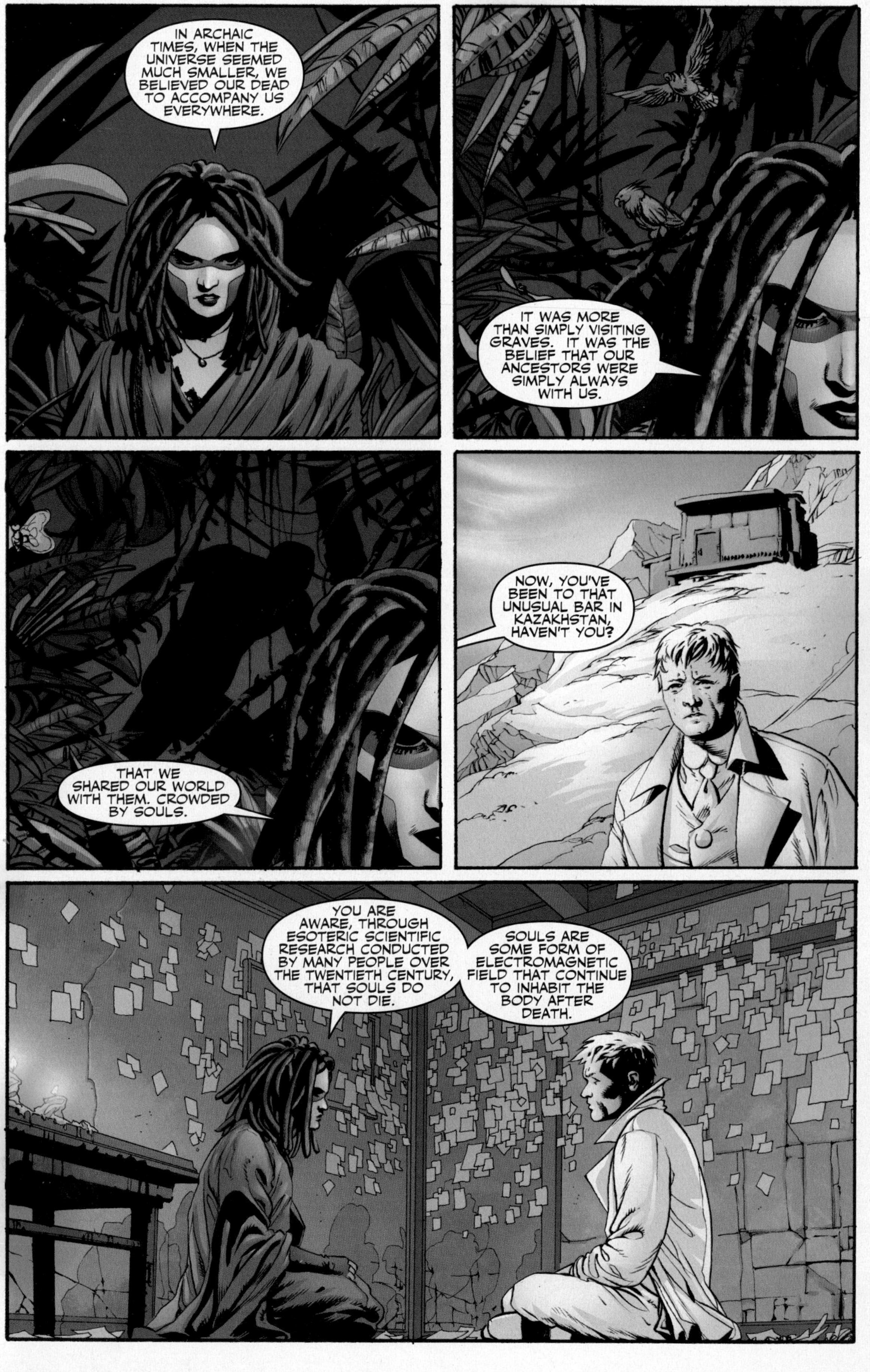
IN ARCHAIC TIMES, WHEN THE UNIVERSE SEEMED MUCH SMALLER, WE BELIEVED OUR DEAD TO ACCOMPANY US EVERYWHERE.
IT WAS MORE THAN SIMPLY VISITING GRAVES. IT WAS THE BELIEF THAT OUR ANCESTORS WERE SIMPLY ALWAYS WITH US.
THAT WE SHARED OUR WORLD WITH THEM. CROWDED BY SOULS.
NOW, YOU'VE BEEN TO THAT UNUSUAL BAR IN KAZAKHSTAN, HAVEN'T YOU?
YOU ARE AWARE, THROUGH ESOTERIC SCIENTIFIC RESEARCH CONDUCTED BY MANY PEOPLE OVER THE TWENTIETH CENTURY, THAT SOULS DO NOT DIE.
SOULS ARE SOME FORM OF ELECTROMAGNETIC FIELD THAT CONTINUE TO INHABIT THE BODY AFTER DEATH.

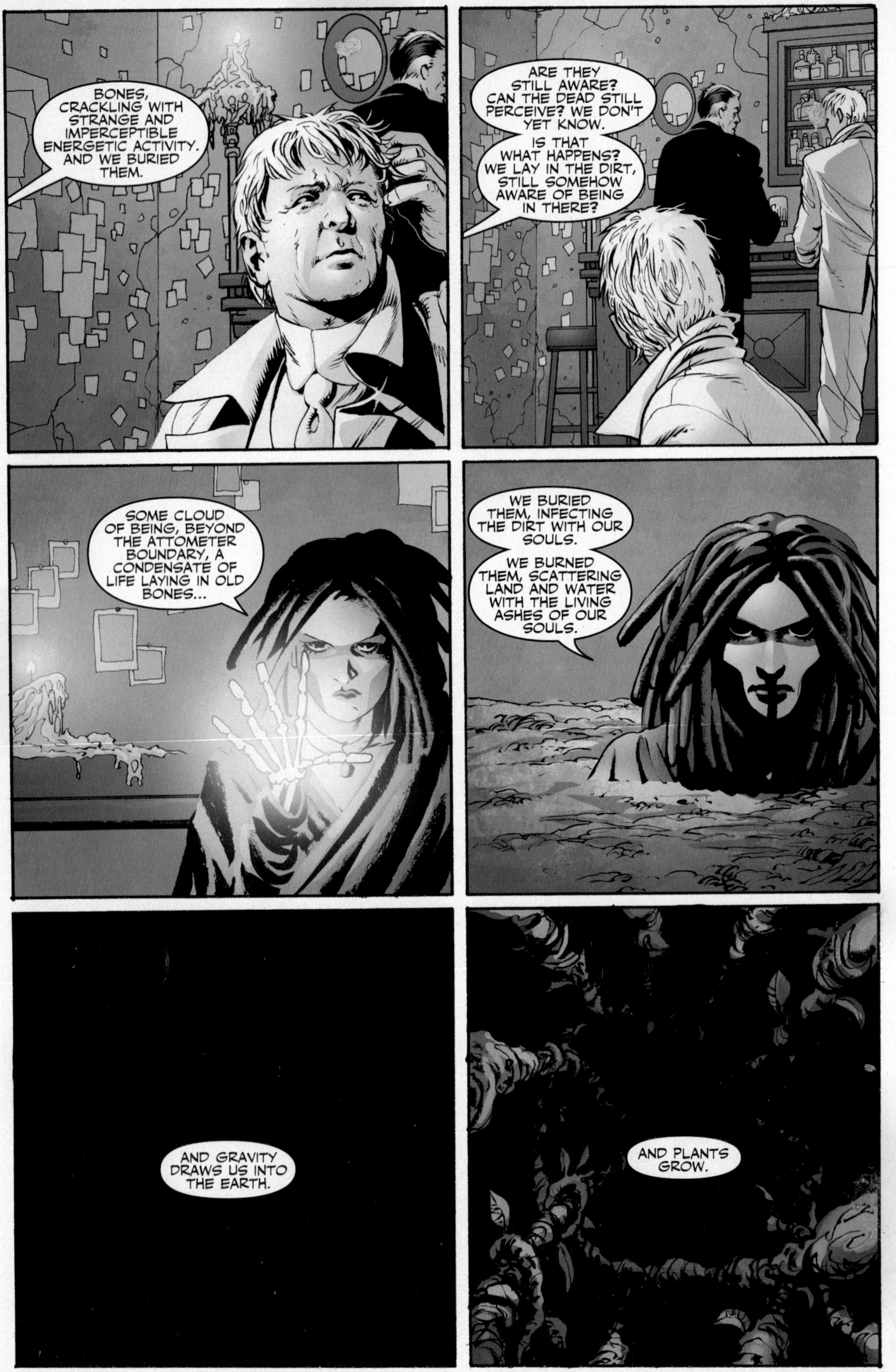
BONES, CRACKLING WITH STRANGE AND IMPERCEPTIBLE ENERGETIC ACTIVITY. AND WE BURIED THEM.
ARE THEY STILL AWARE? CAN THE DEAD STILL PERCEIVE? WE DON'T YET KNOW.
IS THAT WHAT HAPPENS? WE LAY IN THE DIRT, STILL SOMEHOW AWARE OF BEING IN THERE?
SOME CLOUD OF BEING, BEYOND THE ATTOMETER BOUNDARY, A CONDENSATE OF LIFE LAYING IN OLD BONES...
WE BURIED THEM, INFECTING THE DIRT WITH OUR SOULS.
WE BURNED THEM, SCATTERING LAND AND WATER WITH THE LIVING ASHES OF OUR SOULS.
AND GRAVITY DRAWS US INTO THE EARTH.
AND PLANTS GROW.

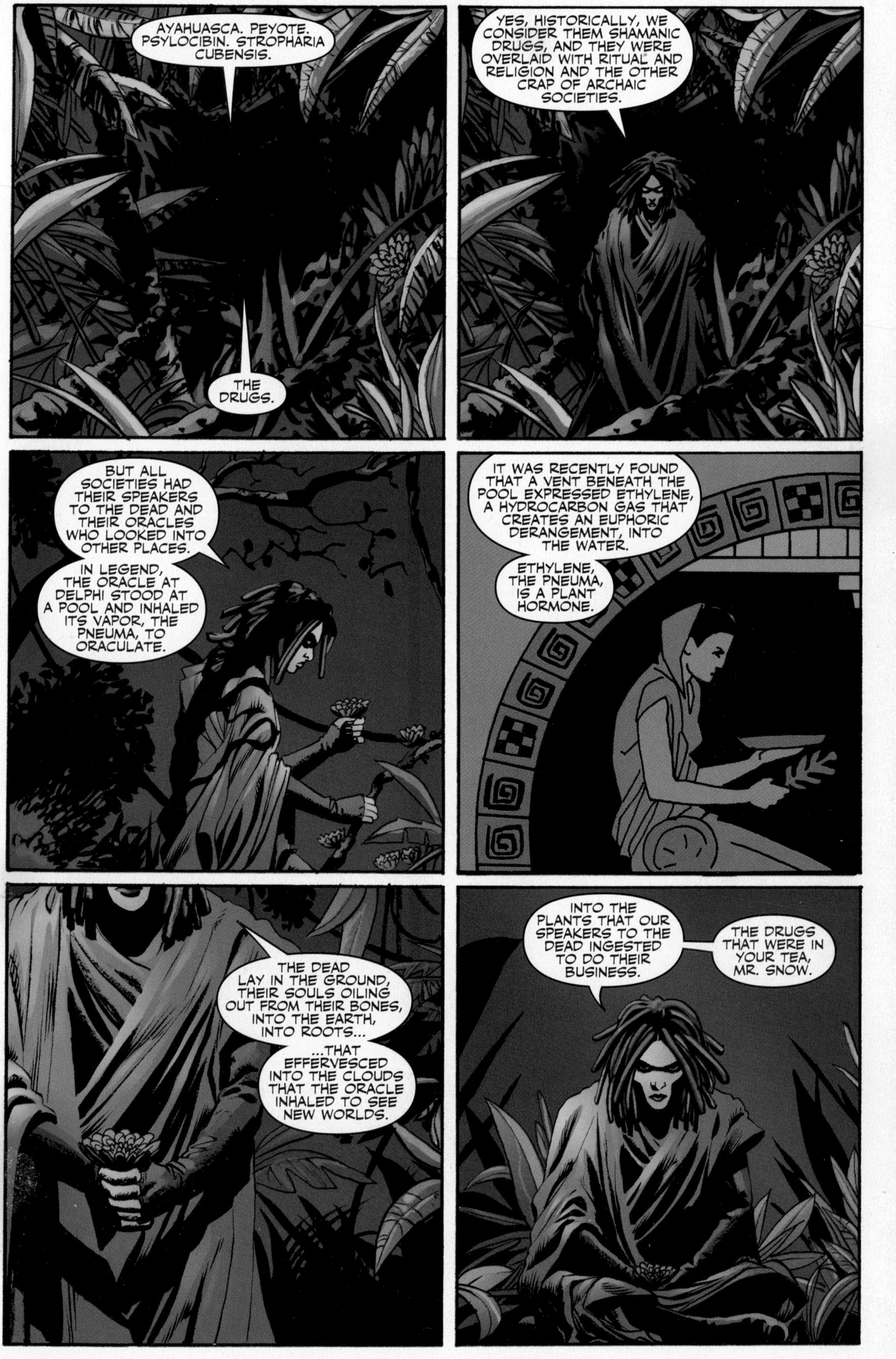
AYAHUASCA. PEYOTE. PSYLOCIBIN. STROPHARIA CUBENSIS.
THE DRUGS.
YES, HISTORICALLY, WE CONSIDER THEM SHAMANIC DRUGS, AND THEY WERE OVERLAID WITH RITUAL AND RELIGION AND THE OTHER CRAP OF ARCHAIC SOCIETIES.
BUT ALL SOCIETIES HAD THEIR SPEAKERS TO THE DEAD AND THEIR ORACLES WHO LOOKED INTO OTHER PLACES.
IN LEGEND, THE ORACLE AT DELPHI STOOD AT A POOL AND INHALED ITS VAPOR, THE PNEUMA, TO ORACULATE.
IT WAS RECENTLY FOUND THAT A VENT BENEATH THE POOL EXPRESSED ETHYLENE, A HYDROCARBON GAS THAT CREATES AN EUPHORIC DERANGEMENT, INTO THE WATER.
ETHYLENE, THE PNEUMA, IS A PLANT HORMONE.
THE DEAD LAY IN THE GROUND, THEIR SOULS OILING OUT FROM THEIR BONES, INTO THE EARTH, INTO ROOTS...
...THAT EFFERVESCED INTO THE CLOUDS THAT THE ORACLE INHALED TO SEE NEW WORLDS.
INTO THE PLANTS THAT OUR SPEAKERS TO THE DEAD INGESTED TO DO THEIR BUSINESS.
THE DRUGS THAT WERE IN YOUR TEA, MR. SNOW.

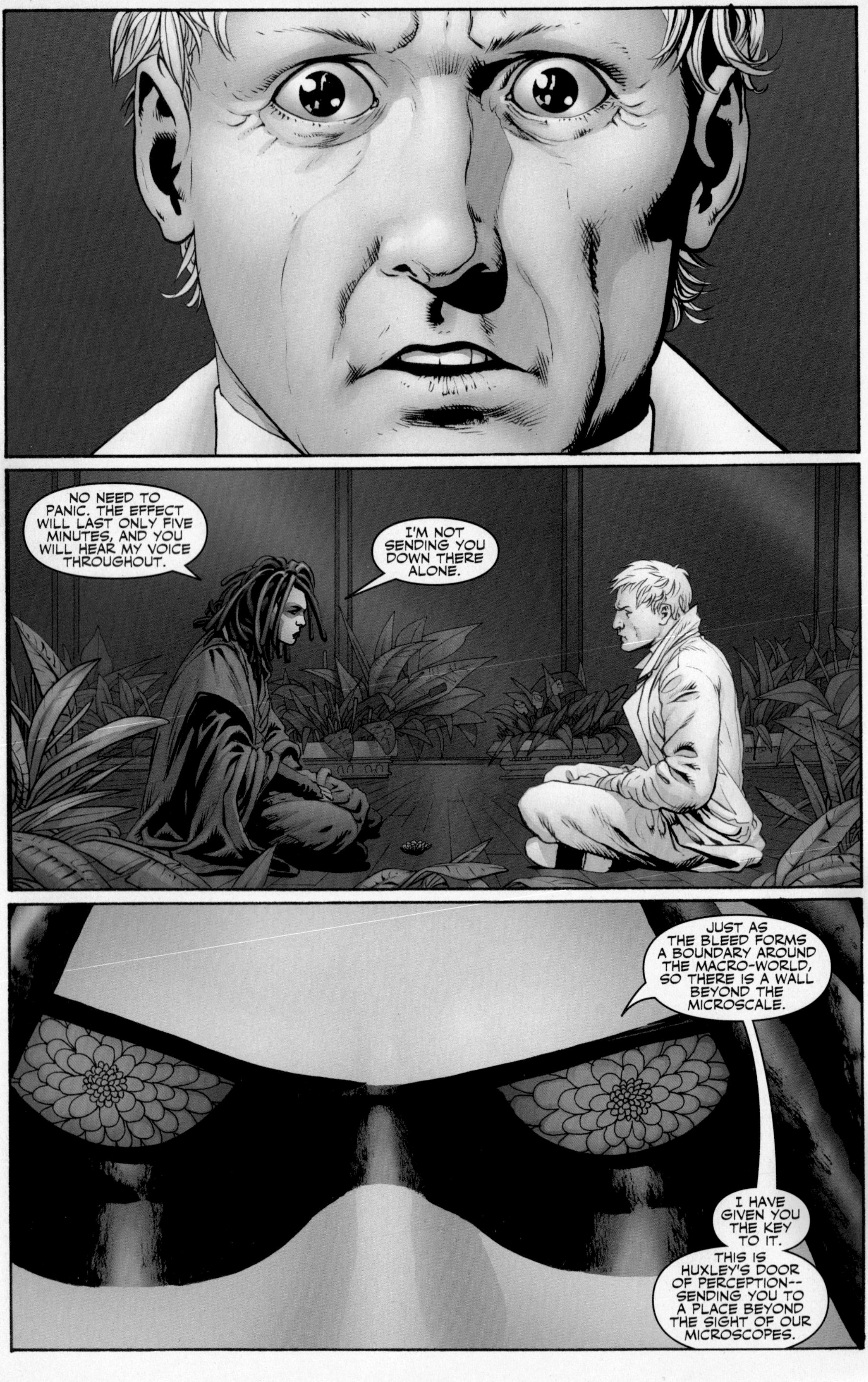
NO NEED TO PANIC. THE EFFECT WILL LAST ONLY FIVE MINUTES, AND YOU WILL HEAR MY VOICE THROUGHOUT.
I'M NOT SENDING YOU DOWN THERE ALONE.
JUST AS THE BLEED FORMS A BOUNDARY AROUND THE MACRO-WORLD, SO THERE IS A WALL BEYOND THE MICROSCALE.
I HAVE GIVEN YOU THE KEY TO IT.
THIS IS HUXLEY'S DOOR OF PERCEPTION-- SENDING YOU TO A PLACE BEYOND THE SIGHT OF OUR MICROSCOPES.

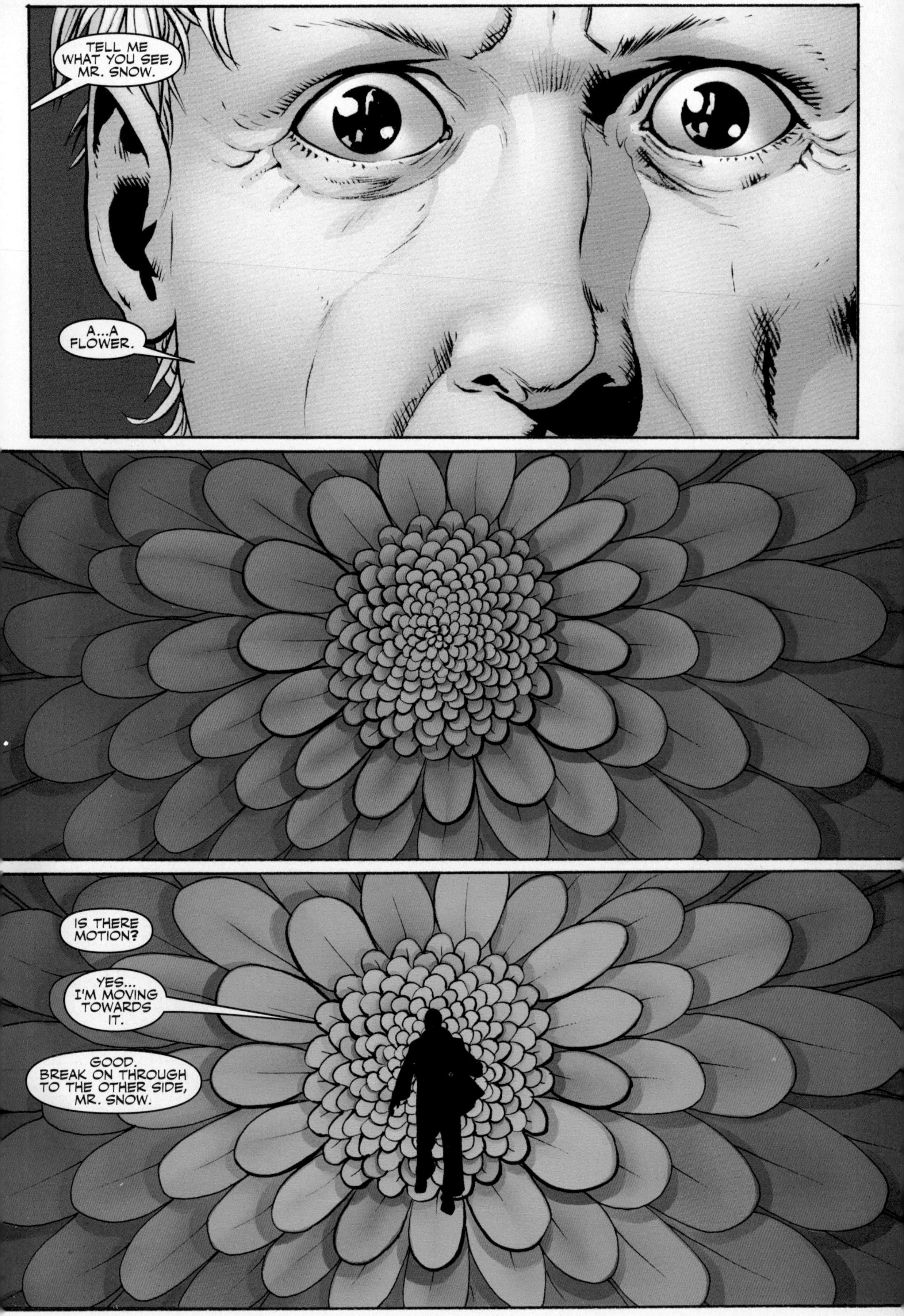
TELL ME WHAT YOU SEE, MR. SNOW.
A...A FLOWER.
IS THERE MOTION?
YES... I'M MOVING TOWARDS IT.
GOOD. BREAK ON THROUGH TO THE OTHER SIDE, MR. SNOW.

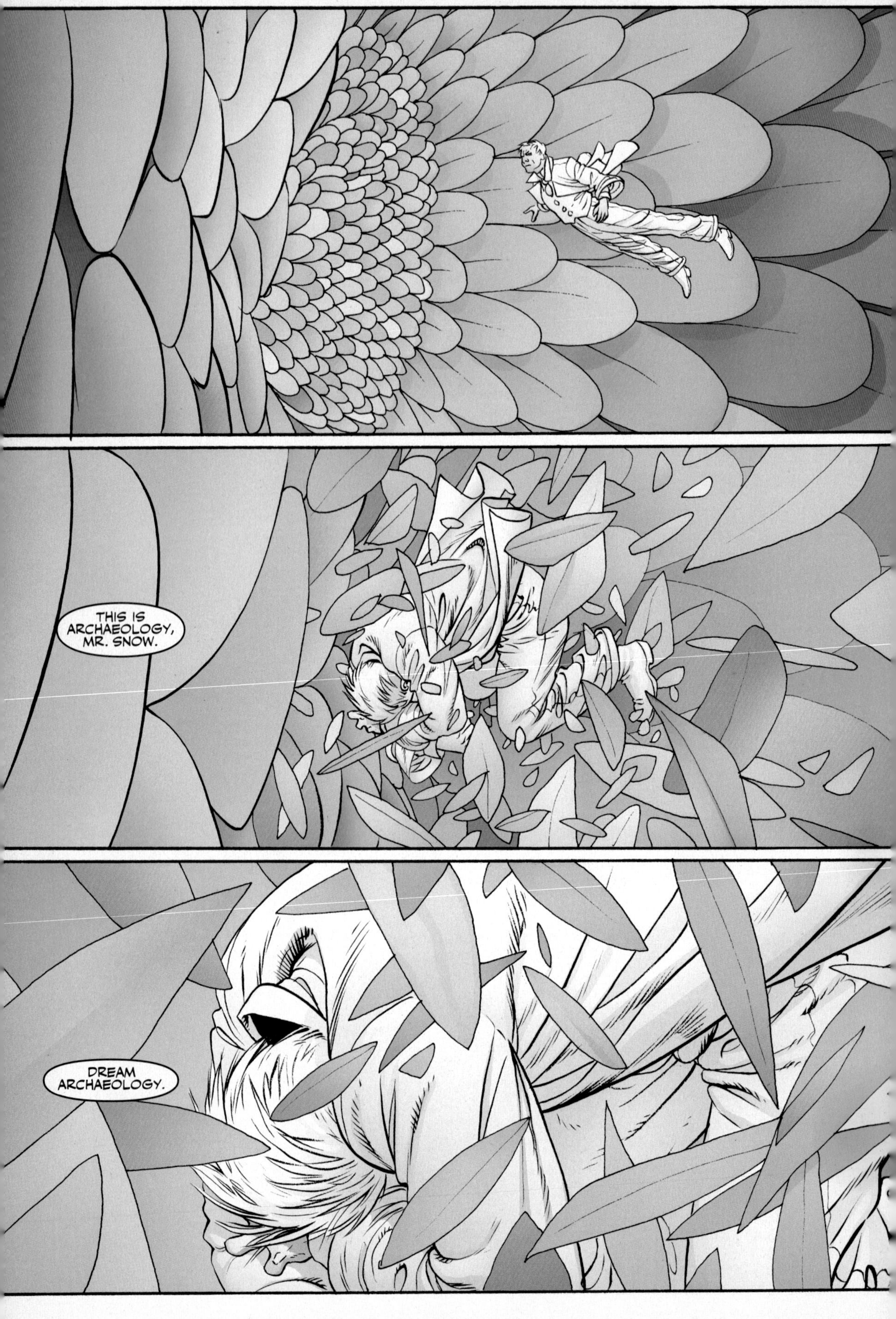
THIS IS ARCHAEOLOGY, MR. SNOW.
DREAM ARCHAEOLOGY.

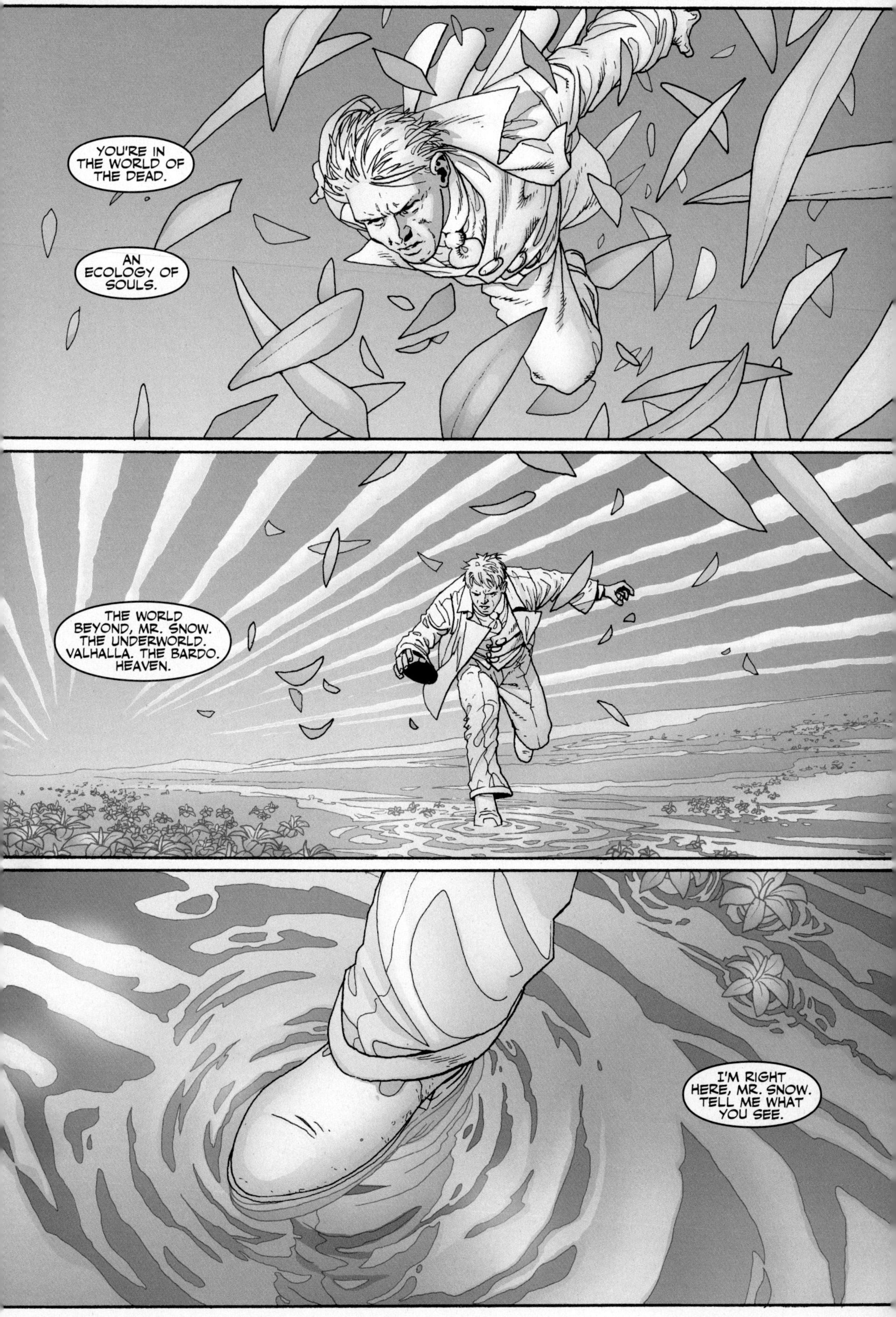
YOU'RE IN THE WORLD OF THE DEAD.
AN ECOLOGY OF SOULS.
THE WORLD BEYOND, MR. SNOW. THE UNDERWORLD. VALHALLA. THE BARDO. HEAVEN.
I'M RIGHT HERE, MR. SNOW. TELL ME WHAT YOU SEE.

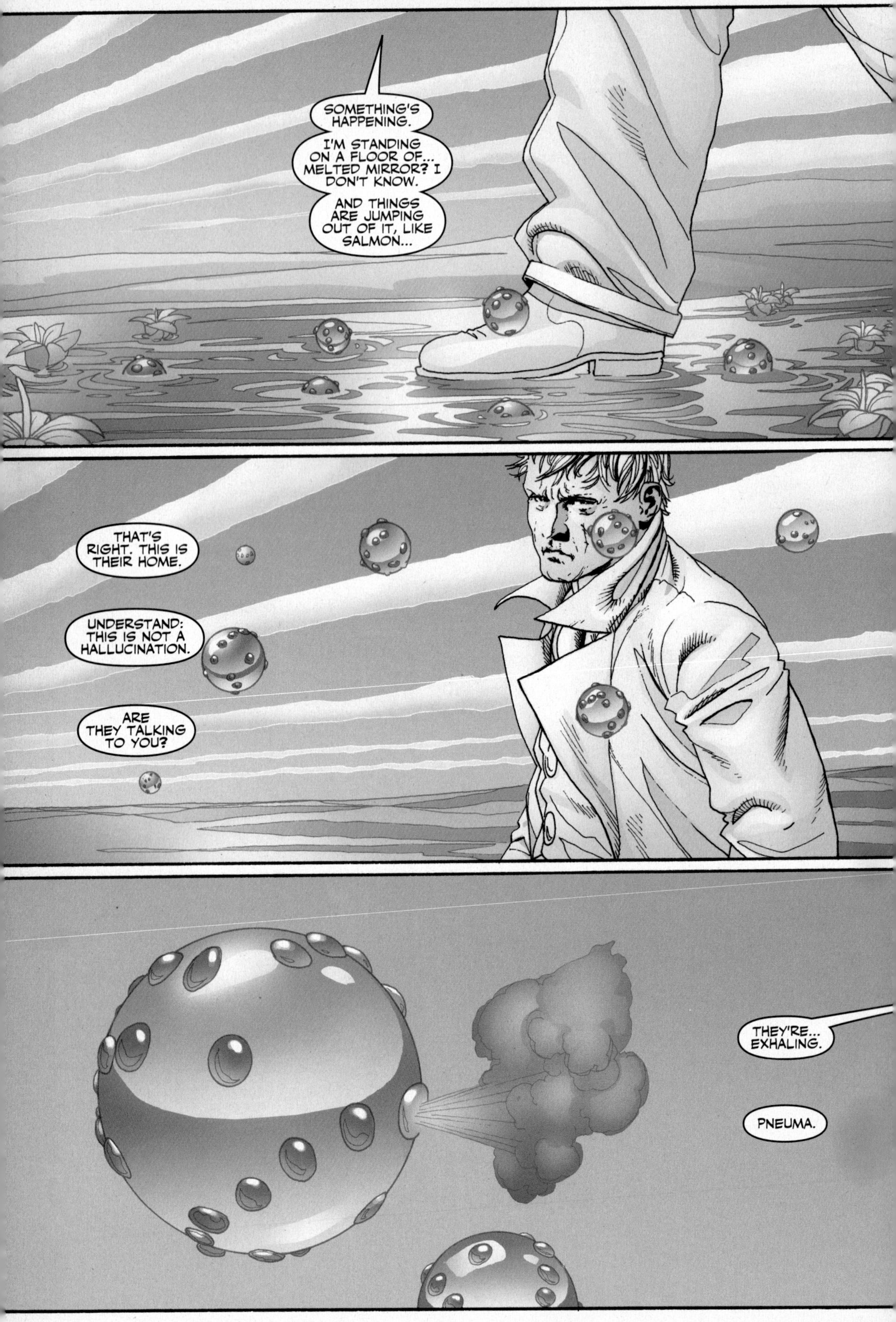
SOMETHING'S HAPPENING.
I'M STANDING ON A FLOOR OF... MELTED MIRROR? I DON'T KNOW.
AND THINGS ARE JUMPING OUT OF IT, LIKE SALMON...
THAT'S RIGHT. THIS IS THEIR HOME.
UNDERSTAND: THIS IS NOT A HALLUCINATION.
ARE THEY TALKING TO YOU?
THEY'RE... EXHALING.
PNEUMA.

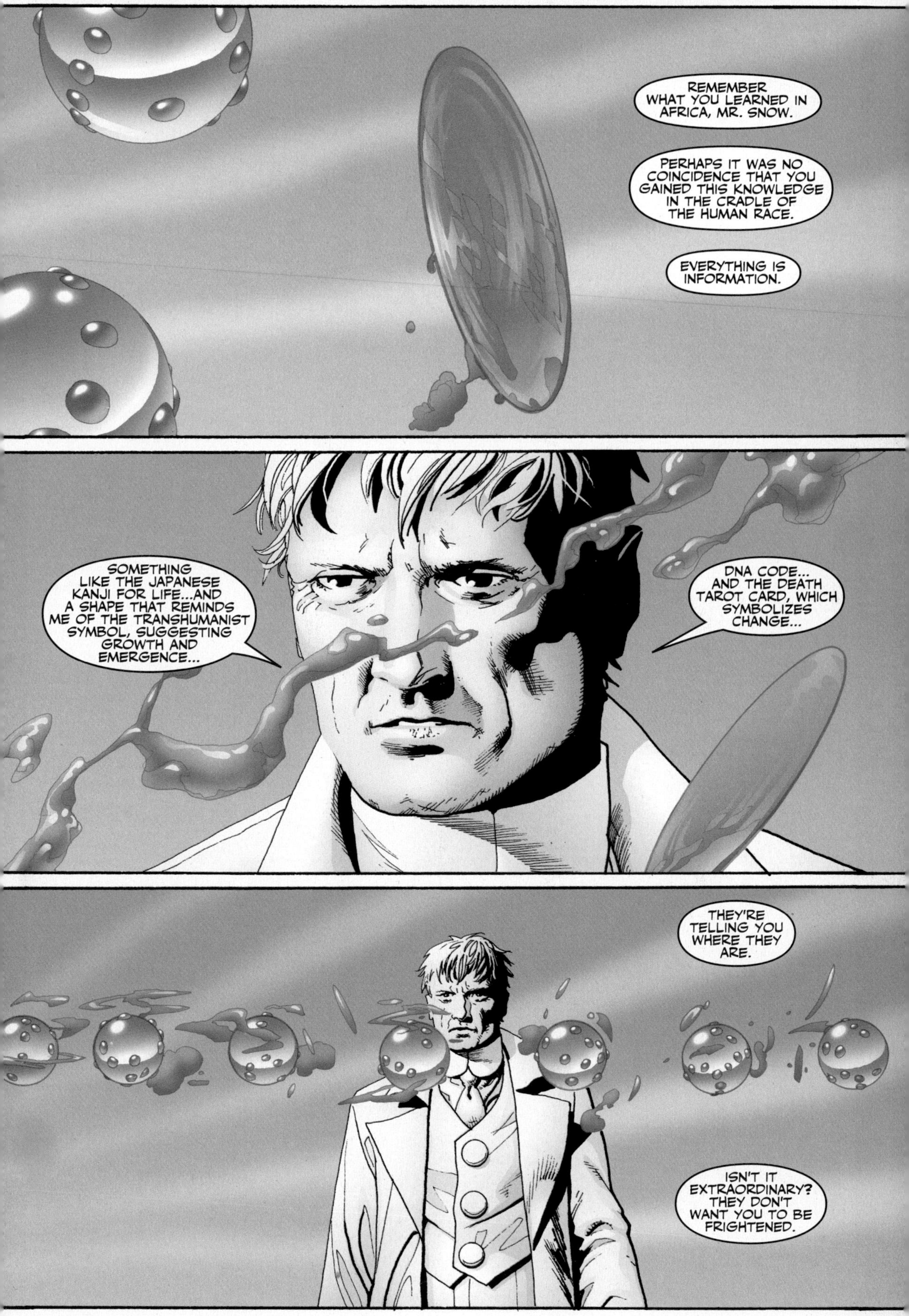
REMEMBER WHAT YOU LEARNED IN AFRICA, MR. SNOW.
PERHAPS IT WAS NO COINCIDENCE THAT YOU GAINED THIS KNOWLEDGE IN THE CRADLE OF THE HUMAN RACE.
EVERYTHING IS INFORMATION.
SOMETHING LIKE THE JAPANESE KANJI FOR LIFE...AND A SHAPE THAT REMINDS ME OF THE TRANSHUMANIST SYMBOL, SUGGESTING GROWTH AND EMERGENCE...
DNA CODE... AND THE DEATH TAROT CARD, WHICH SYMBOLIZES CHANGE...
THEY'RE TELLING YOU WHERE THEY ARE.
ISN'T IT EXTRAORDINARY? THEY DON'T WANT YOU TO BE FRIGHTENED.

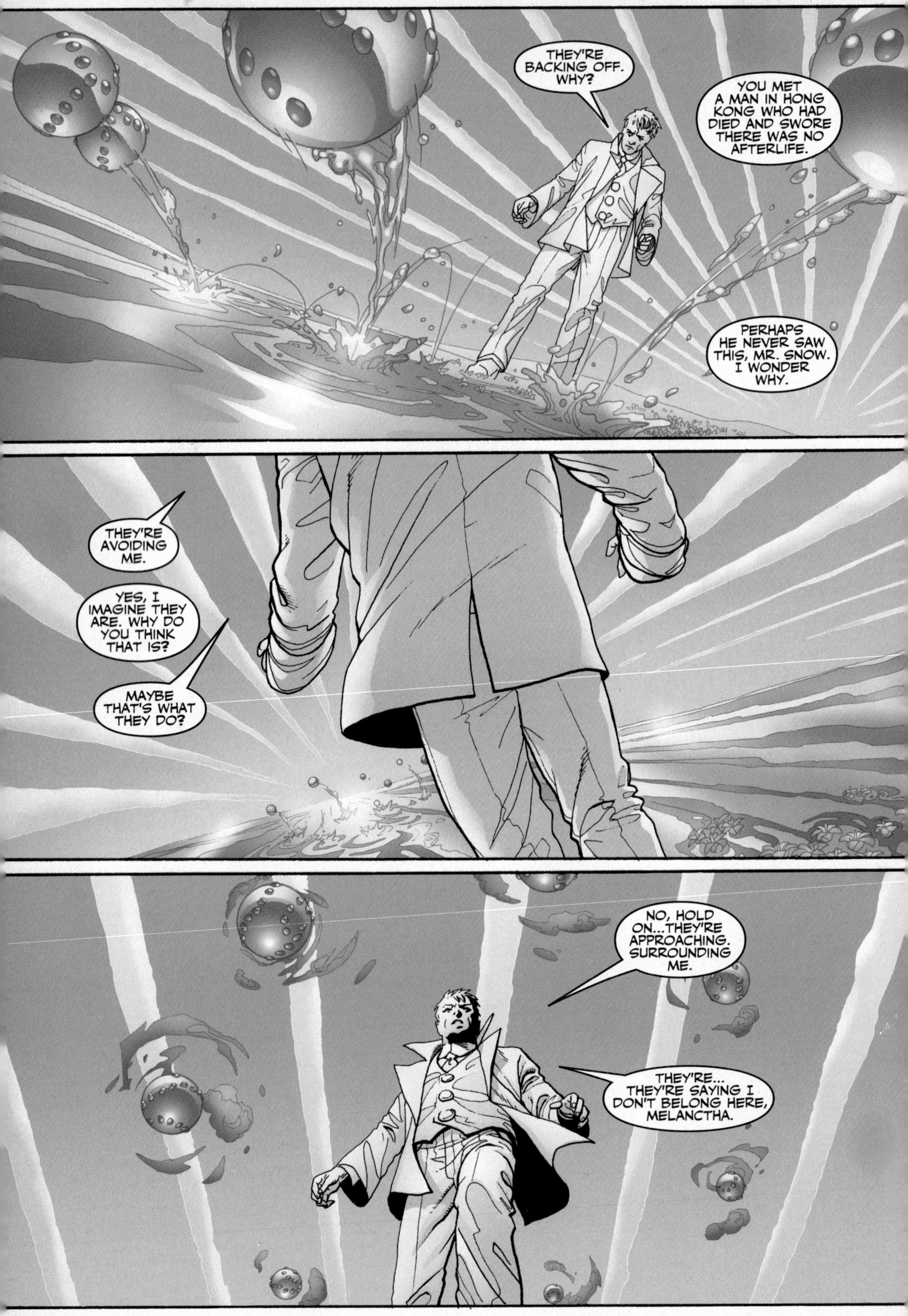
THEY'RE BACKING OFF. WHY?
YOU MET A MAN IN HONG KONG WHO HAD DIED AND SWORE THERE WAS NO AFTERLIFE.
PERHAPS HE NEVER SAW THIS, MR. SNOW. I WONDER WHY.
THEY'RE AVOIDING ME.
YES, I IMAGINE THEY ARE. WHY DO YOU THINK THAT IS?
MAYBE THAT'S WHAT THEY DO?
NO, HOLD ON...THEY'RE APPROACHING. SURROUNDING ME.
THEY'RE... THEY'RE SAYING I DON'T BELONG HERE, MELANCTHA.

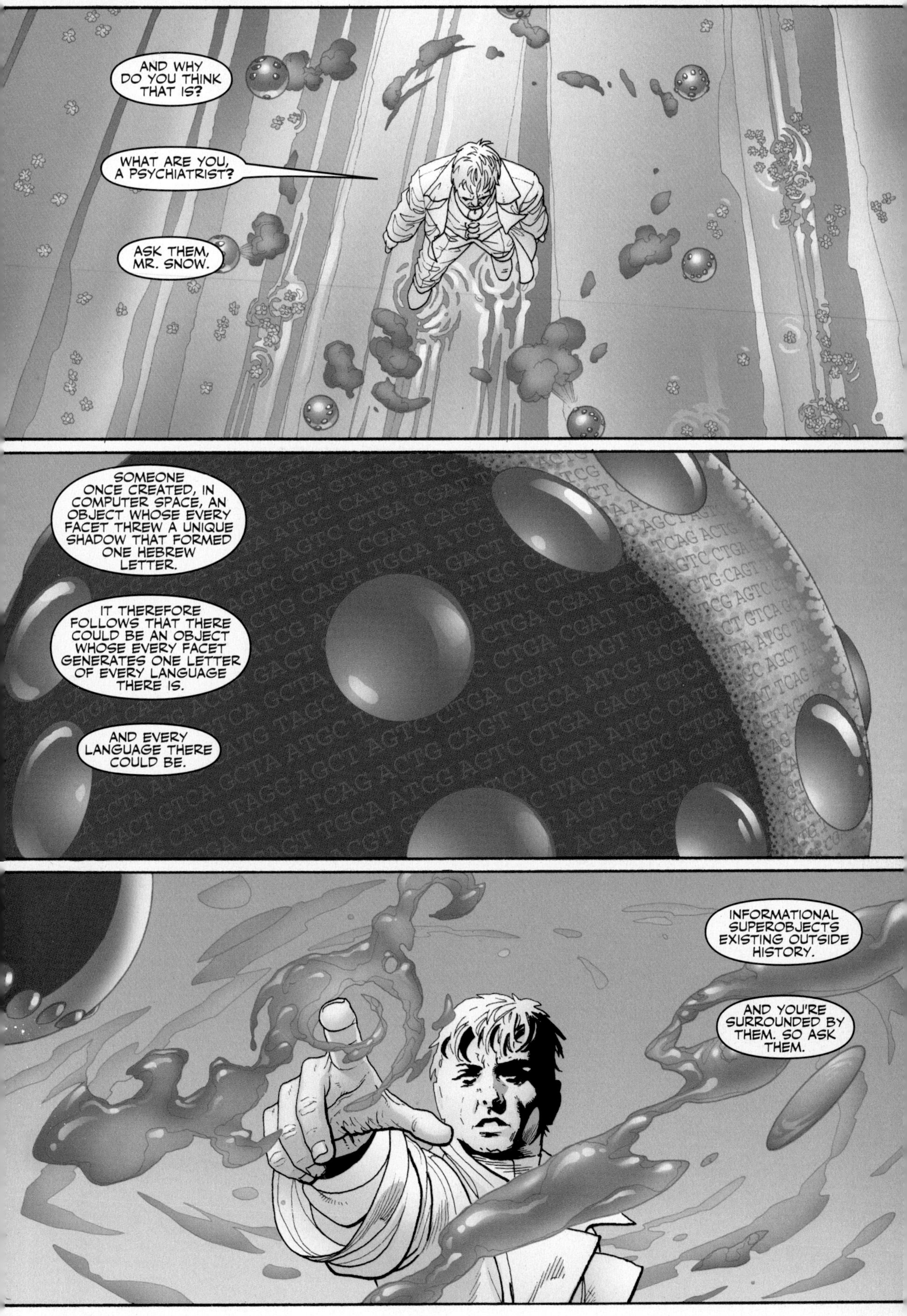
AND WHY DO YOU THINK THAT IS?
WHAT ARE YOU, A PSYCHIATRIST?
ASK THEM, MR. SNOW.
SOMEONE ONCE CREATED, IN COMPUTER SPACE, AN OBJECT WHOSE EVERY FACET THREW A UNIQUE SHADOW THAT FORMED ONE HEBREW LETTER.
IT THEREFORE FOLLOWS THAT THERE COULD BE AN OBJECT WHOSE EVERY FACET GENERATES ONE LETTER OF EVERY LANGUAGE THERE IS.
AND EVERY LANGUAGE THERE COULD BE.
INFORMATIONAL SUPEROBJECTS EXISTING OUTSIDE HISTORY.
AND YOU'RE SURROUNDED BY THEM. SO ASK THEM.

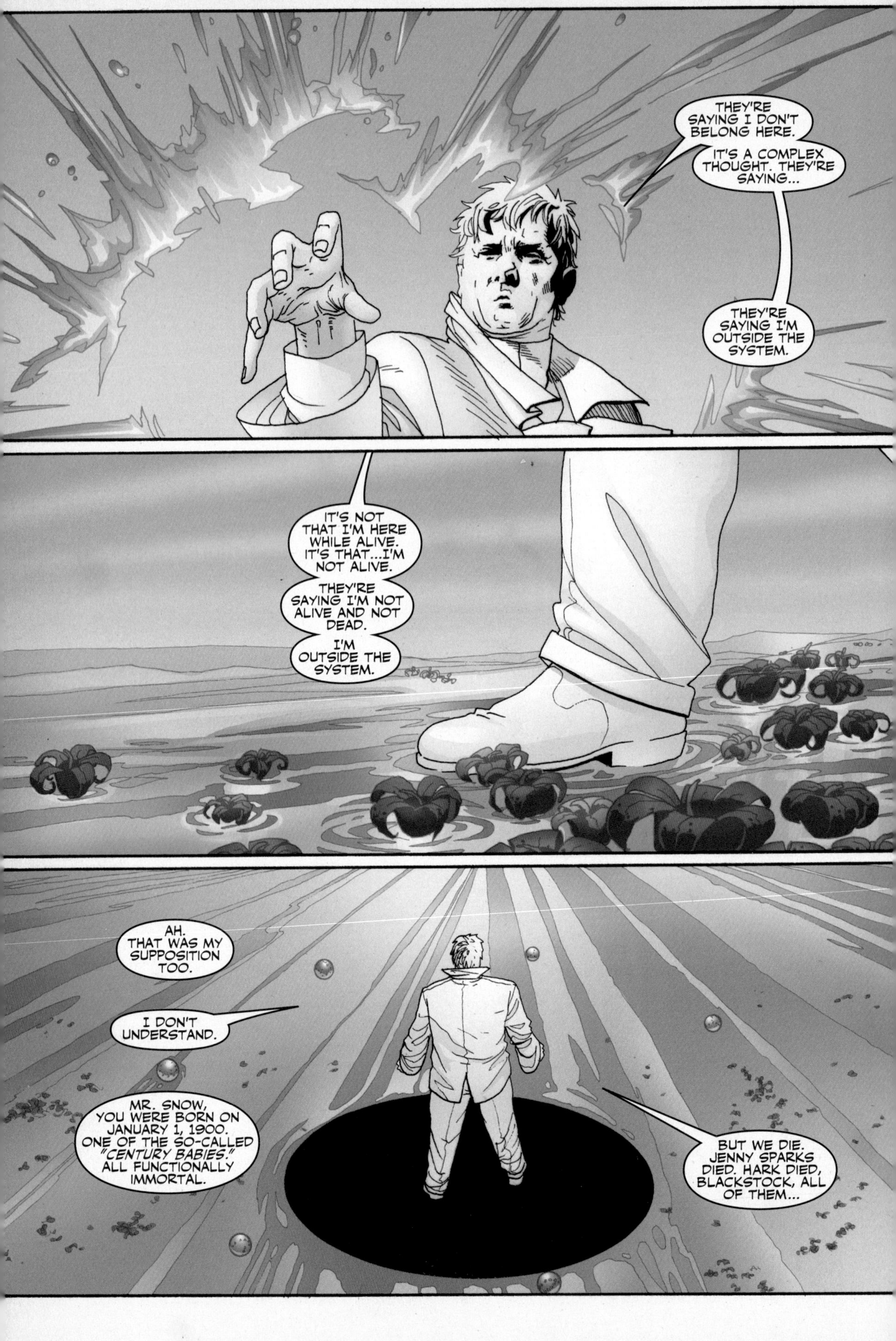
THEY'RE SAYING I DON'T BELONG HERE.
IT'S A COMPLEX THOUGHT. THEY'RE SAYING...
THEY'RE SAYING I'M OUTSIDE THE SYSTEM.
IT'S NOT THAT I'M HERE WHILE ALIVE. IT'S THAT...I'M NOT ALIVE.
THEY'RE SAYING I'M NOT ALIVE AND NOT DEAD.
I'M OUTSIDE THE SYSTEM.
AH. THAT WAS MY SUPPOSITION TOO.
I DON'T UNDERSTAND.
MR. SNOW, YOU WERE BORN ON JANUARY 1, 1900. ONE OF THE SO-CALLED "CENTURY BABIES." ALL FUNCTIONALLY IMMORTAL.
BUT WE DIE. JENNY SPARKS DIED. HARK DIED, BLACKSTOCK, ALL OF THEM...

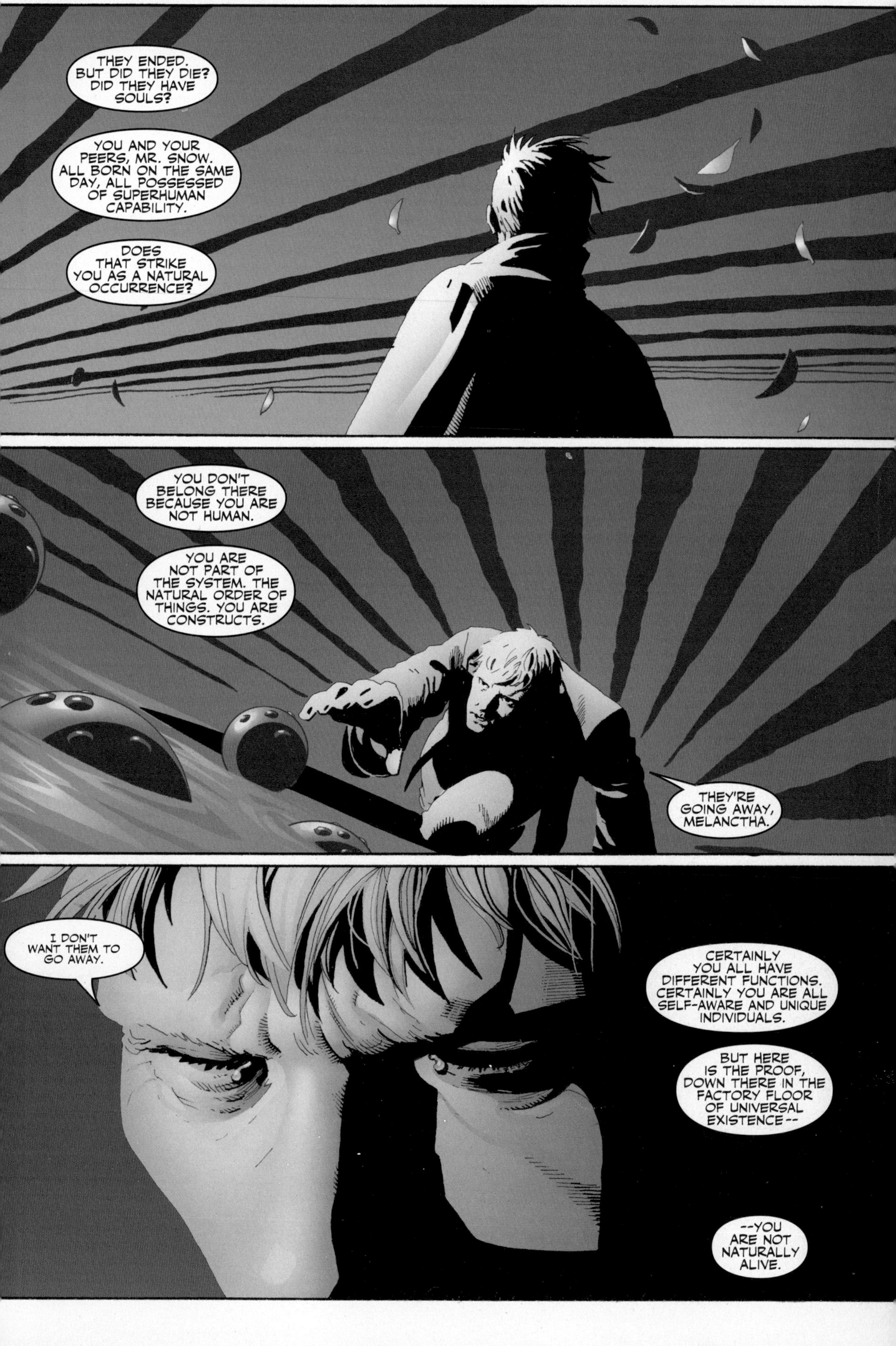
THEY ENDED. BUT DID THEY DIE? DID THEY HAVE SOULS?
YOU AND YOUR PEERS, MR. SNOW. ALL BORN ON THE SAME DAY, ALL POSSESSED OF SUPERHUMAN CAPABILITY.
DOES THAT STRIKE YOU AS A NATURAL OCCURRENCE?
YOU DON'T BELONG THERE BECAUSE YOU ARE NOT HUMAN.
YOU ARE NOT PART OF THE SYSTEM. THE NATURAL ORDER OF THINGS. YOU ARE CONSTRUCTS.
THEY'RE GOING AWAY, MELANCTHA.
I DON'T WANT THEM TO GO AWAY.
CERTAINLY YOU ALL HAVE DIFFERENT FUNCTIONS. CERTAINLY YOU ARE ALL SELF-AWARE AND UNIQUE INDIVIDUALS.
BUT HERE IS THE PROOF, DOWN THERE IN THE FACTORY FLOOR OF UNIVERSAL EXISTENCE--
--YOU ARE NOT NATURALLY ALIVE.

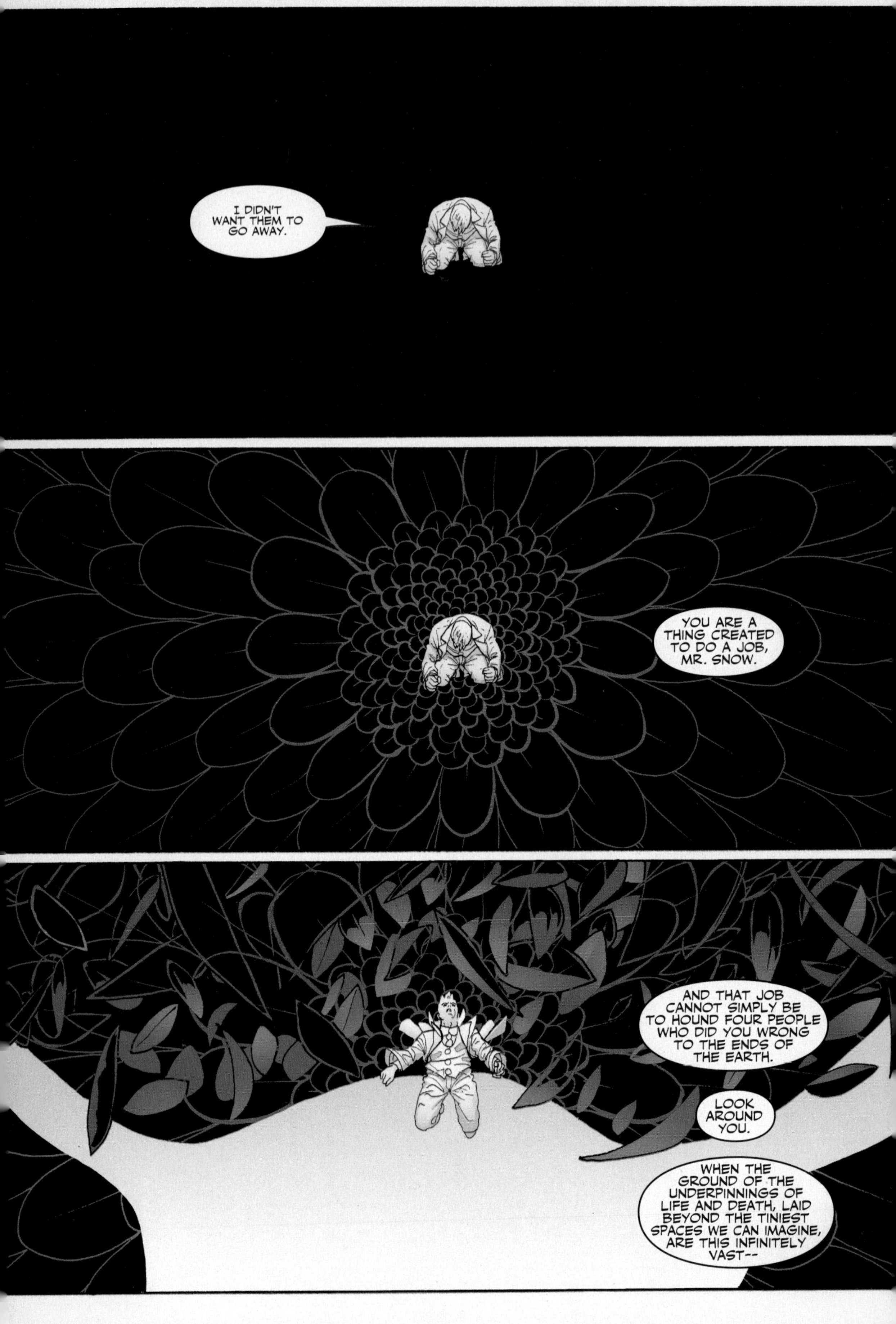
I DIDN'T WANT THEM TO GO AWAY.
YOU ARE A THING CREATED TO DO A JOB, MR. SNOW.
AND THAT JOB CANNOT SIMPLY BE TO HOUND FOUR PEOPLE WHO DID YOU WRONG TO THE ENDS OF THE EARTH.
LOOK AROUND YOU.
WHEN THE GROUND OF THE UNDERPINNINGS OF LIFE AND DEATH, LAID BEYOND THE TINIEST SPACES WE CAN IMAGINE, ARE THIS INFINITELY VAST--

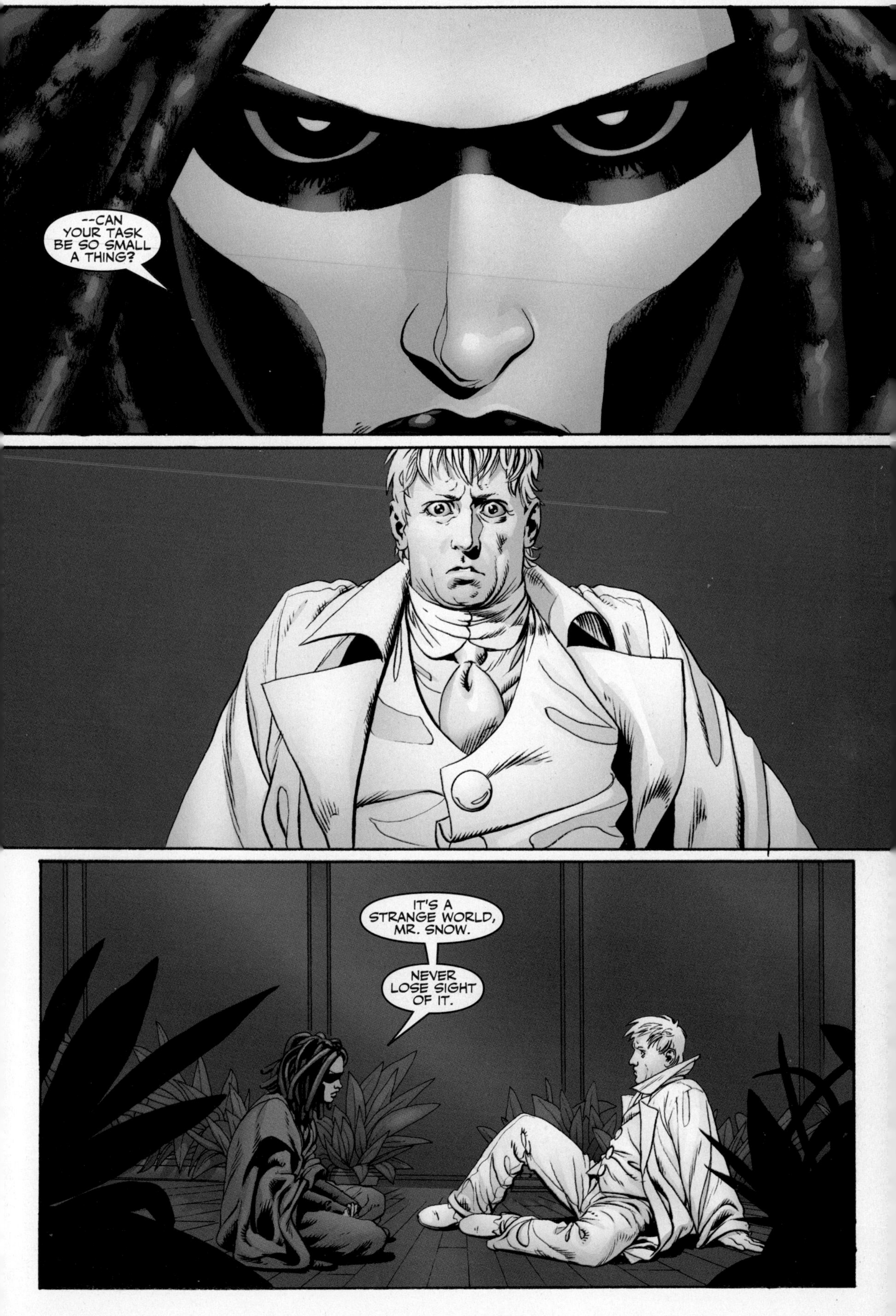
--CAN YOUR TASK BE SO SMALL A THING?
IT'S A STRANGE WORLD, MR. SNOW.
NEVER LOSE SIGHT OF IT.

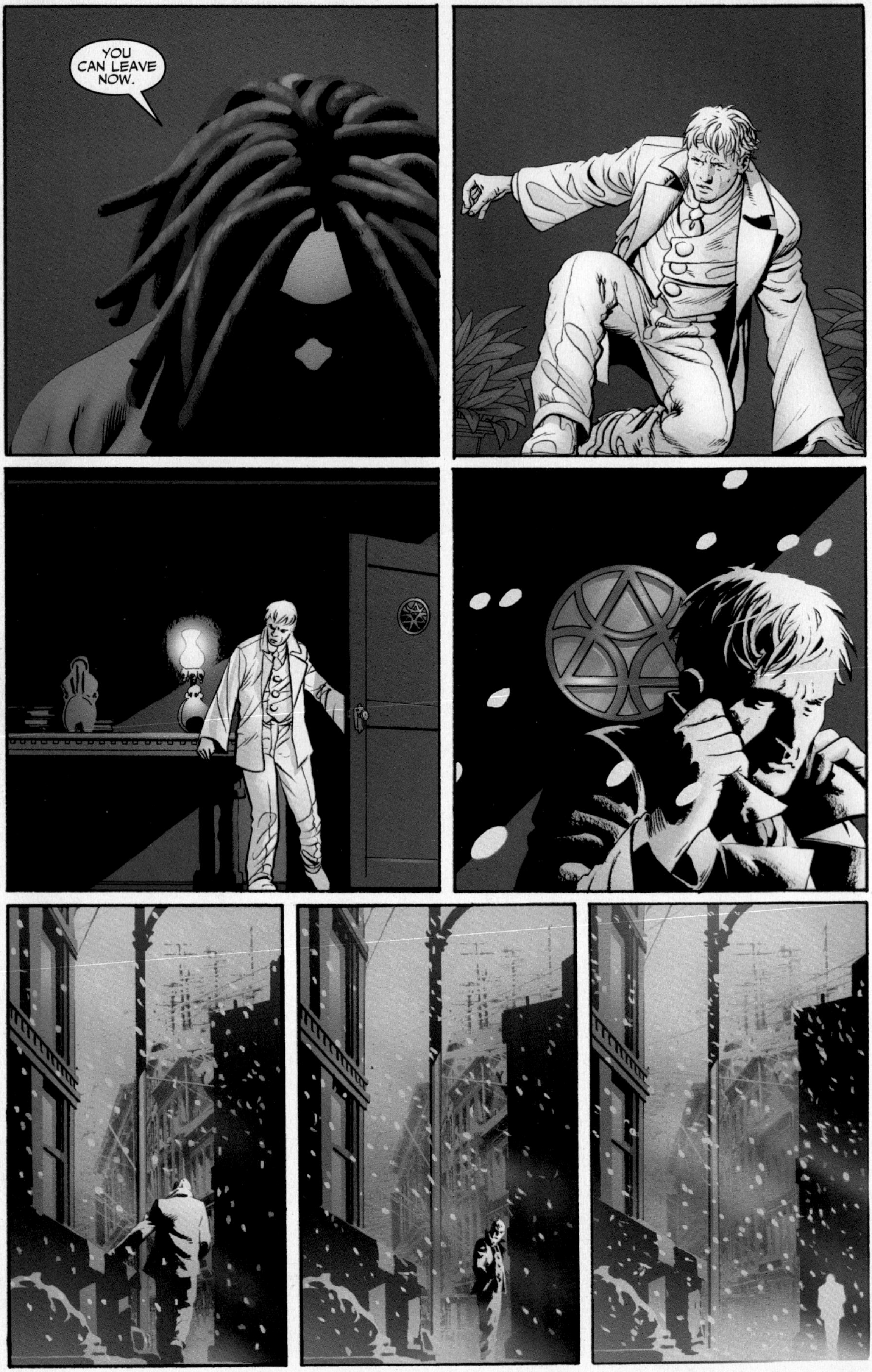
YOU CAN LEAVE NOW.

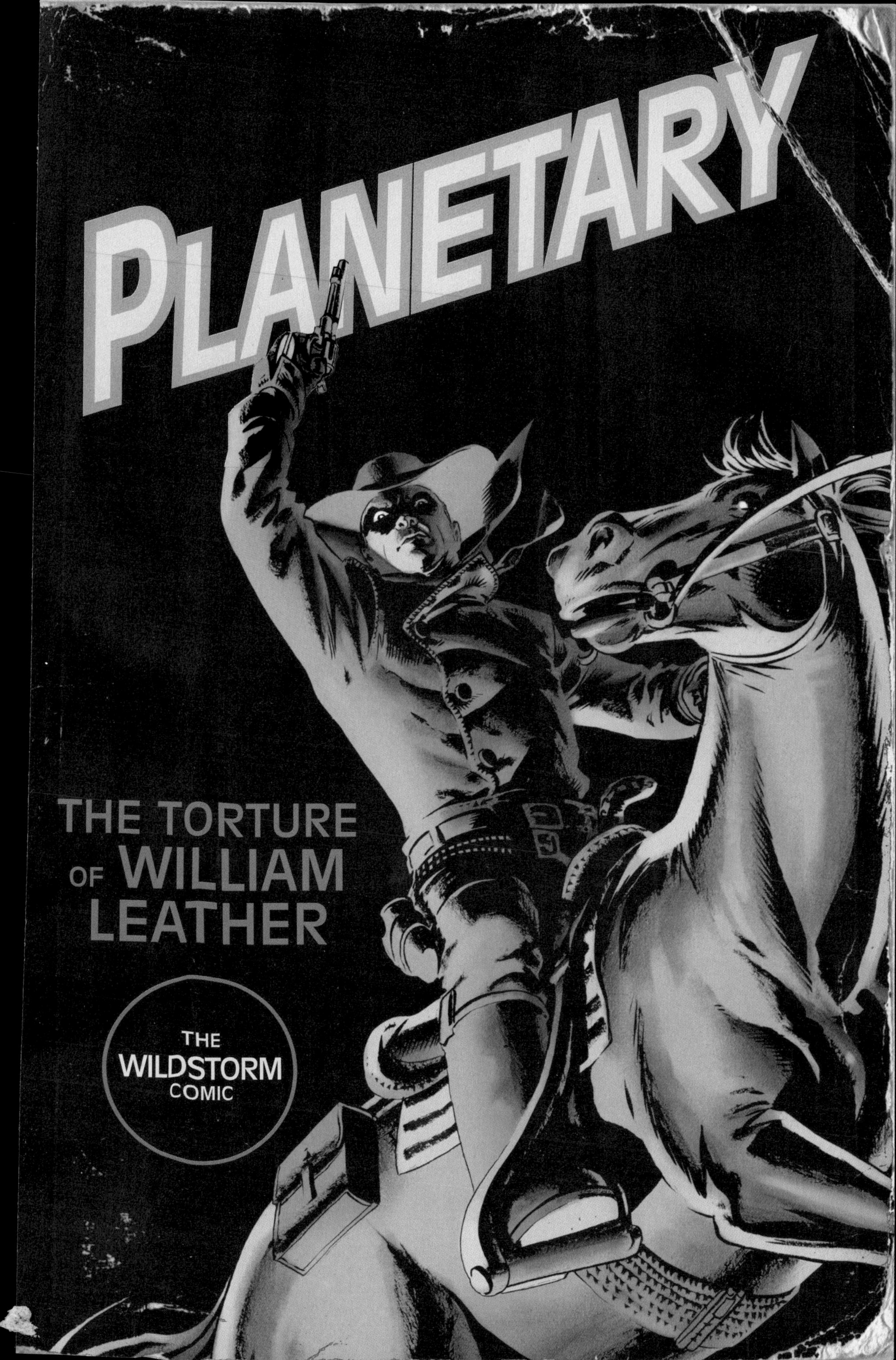
PLANETARY
THE TORTURE OF WILLIAM LEATHER
THE WILDSTORM COMIC

WARREN
ELLIS
JOHN
CASSADAY
LAURA
MARTIN
RICHARD
STARKINGS
SCOTT
DUNBIER

THE TORTURE OF WILLIAM LEATHER

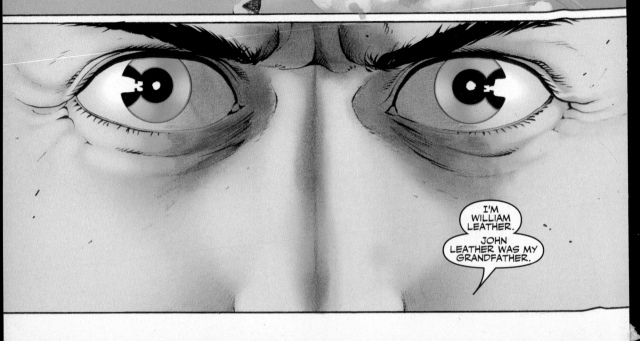

I'M WILLIAM LEATHER.

JOHN LEATHER WAS MY GRANDFATHER.

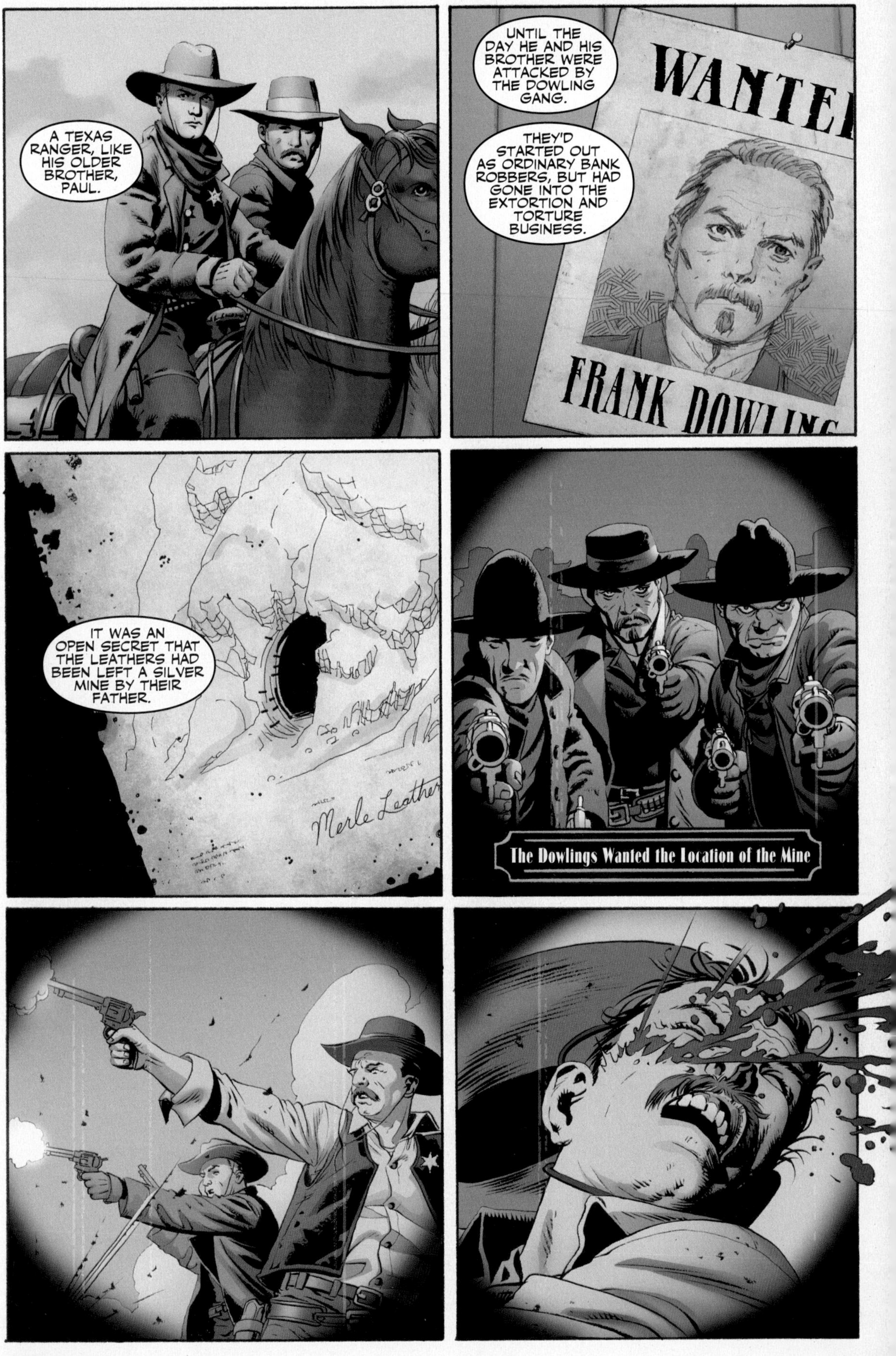
A TEXAS RANGER, LIKE HIS OLDER BROTHER, PAUL.
UNTIL THE DAY HE AND HIS BROTHER WERE ATTACKED BY THE DOWLING GANG.
THEY'D STARTED OUT AS ORDINARY BANK ROBBERS, BUT HAD GONE INTO THE EXTORTION AND TORTURE BUSINESS.
WANTE
FRANK DOWLING
IT WAS AN OPEN SECRET THAT THE LEATHERS HAD BEEN LEFT A SILVER MINE BY THEIR FATHER.
Merle Leather
The Dowlings Wanted the Location of the Mine

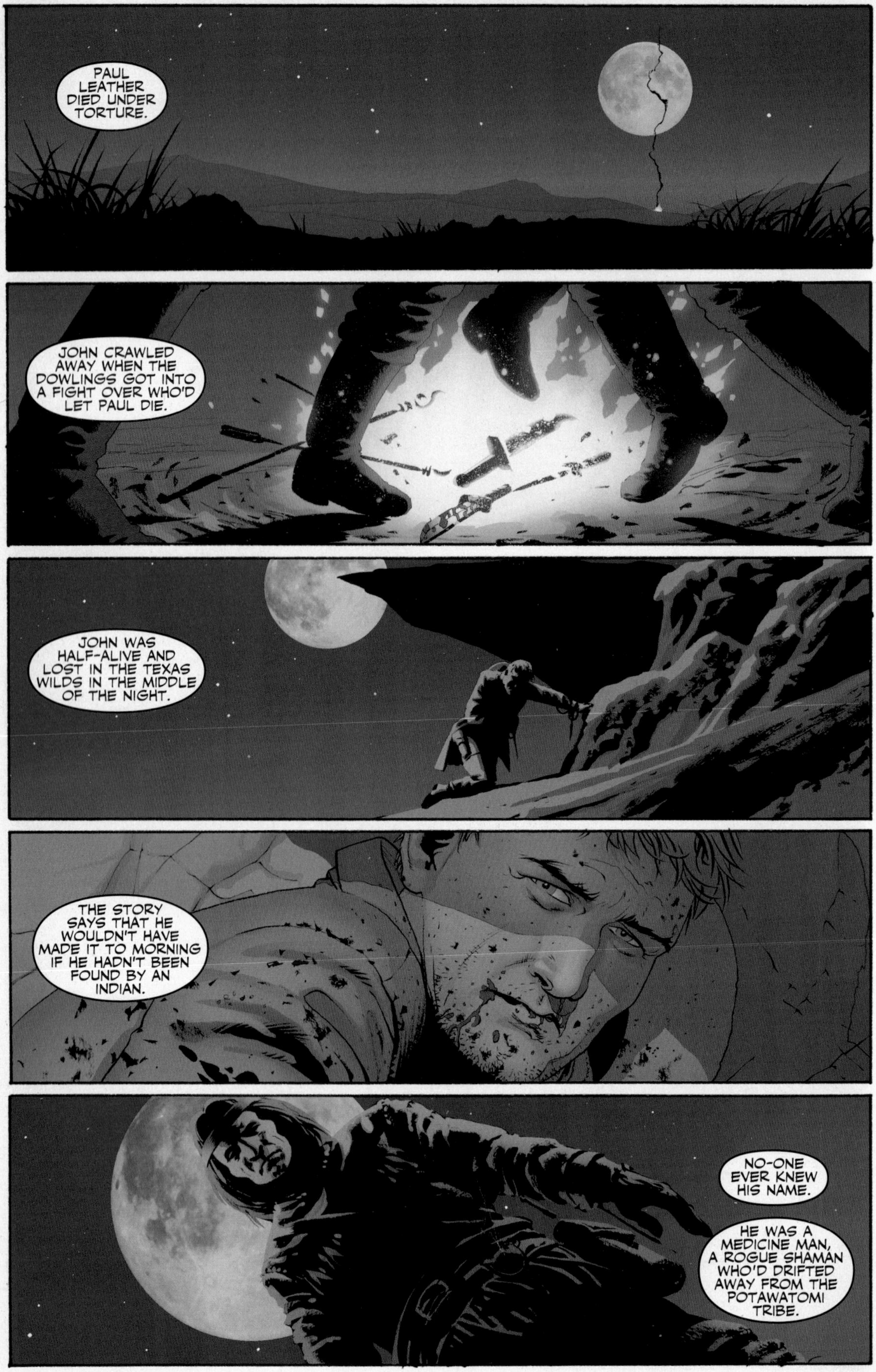
PAUL LEATHER DIED UNDER TORTURE.
JOHN CRAWLED AWAY WHEN THE DOWLINGS GOT INTO A FIGHT OVER WHO'D LET PAUL DIE.
JOHN WAS HALF-ALIVE AND LOST IN THE TEXAS WILDS IN THE MIDDLE OF THE NIGHT.
THE STORY SAYS THAT HE WOULDN'T HAVE MADE IT TO MORNING IF HE HADN'T BEEN FOUND BY AN INDIAN.
NO-ONE EVER KNEW HIS NAME.
HE WAS A MEDICINE MAN, A ROGUE SHAMAN WHO'D DRIFTED AWAY FROM THE POTAWATOMI TRIBE.

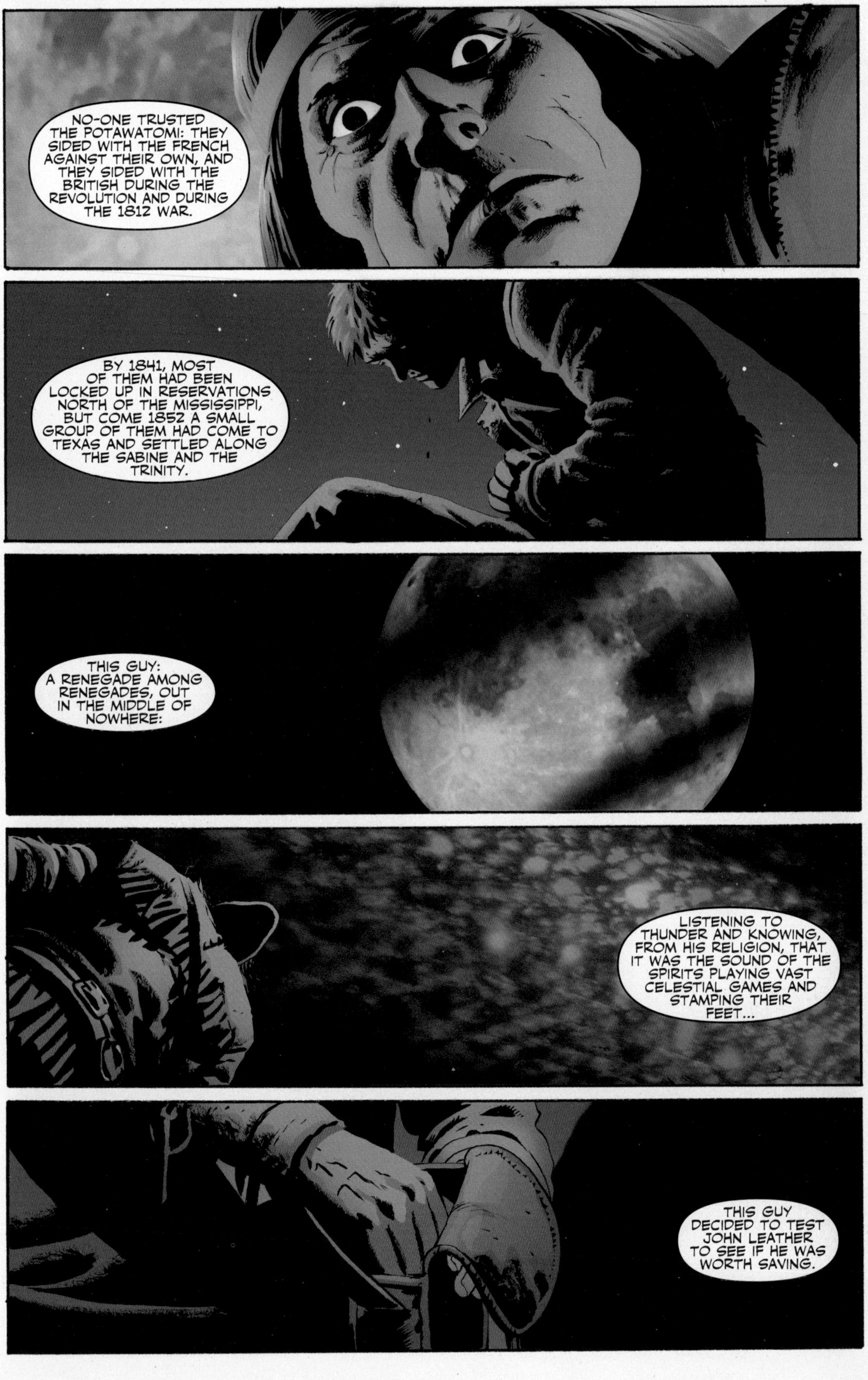
NO-ONE TRUSTED THE POTAWATOMI: THEY SIDED WITH THE FRENCH AGAINST THEIR OWN, AND THEY SIDED WITH THE BRITISH DURING THE REVOLUTION AND DURING THE 1812 WAR.
BY 1841, MOST OF THEM HAD BEEN LOCKED UP IN RESERVATIONS NORTH OF THE MISSISSIPPI, BUT COME 1852 A SMALL GROUP OF THEM HAD COME TO TEXAS AND SETTLED ALONG THE SABINE AND THE TRINITY.
THIS GUY: A RENEGADE AMONG RENEGADES, OUT IN THE MIDDLE OF NOWHERE:
LISTENING TO THUNDER AND KNOWING, FROM HIS RELIGION, THAT IT WAS THE SOUND OF THE SPIRITS PLAYING VAST CELESTIAL GAMES AND STAMPING THEIR FEET...
THIS GUY DECIDED TO TEST JOHN LEATHER TO SEE IF HE WAS WORTH SAVING.

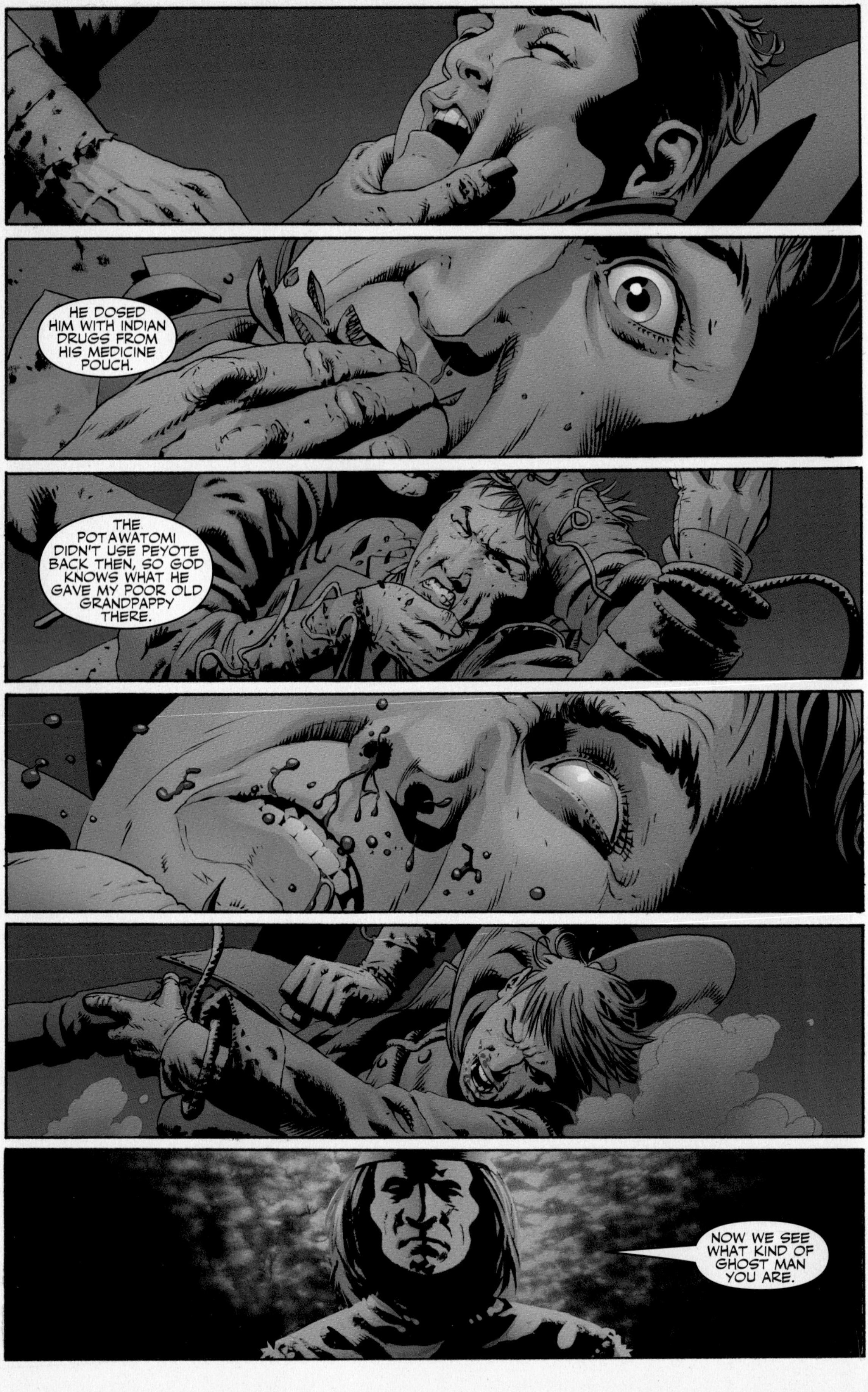
HE DOSED HIM WITH INDIAN DRUGS FROM HIS MEDICINE POUCH.
THE POTAWATOMI DIDN'T USE PEYOTE BACK THEN, SO GOD KNOWS WHAT HE GAVE MY POOR OLD GRANDPAPPY THERE.
NOW WE SEE WHAT KIND OF GHOST MAN YOU ARE.

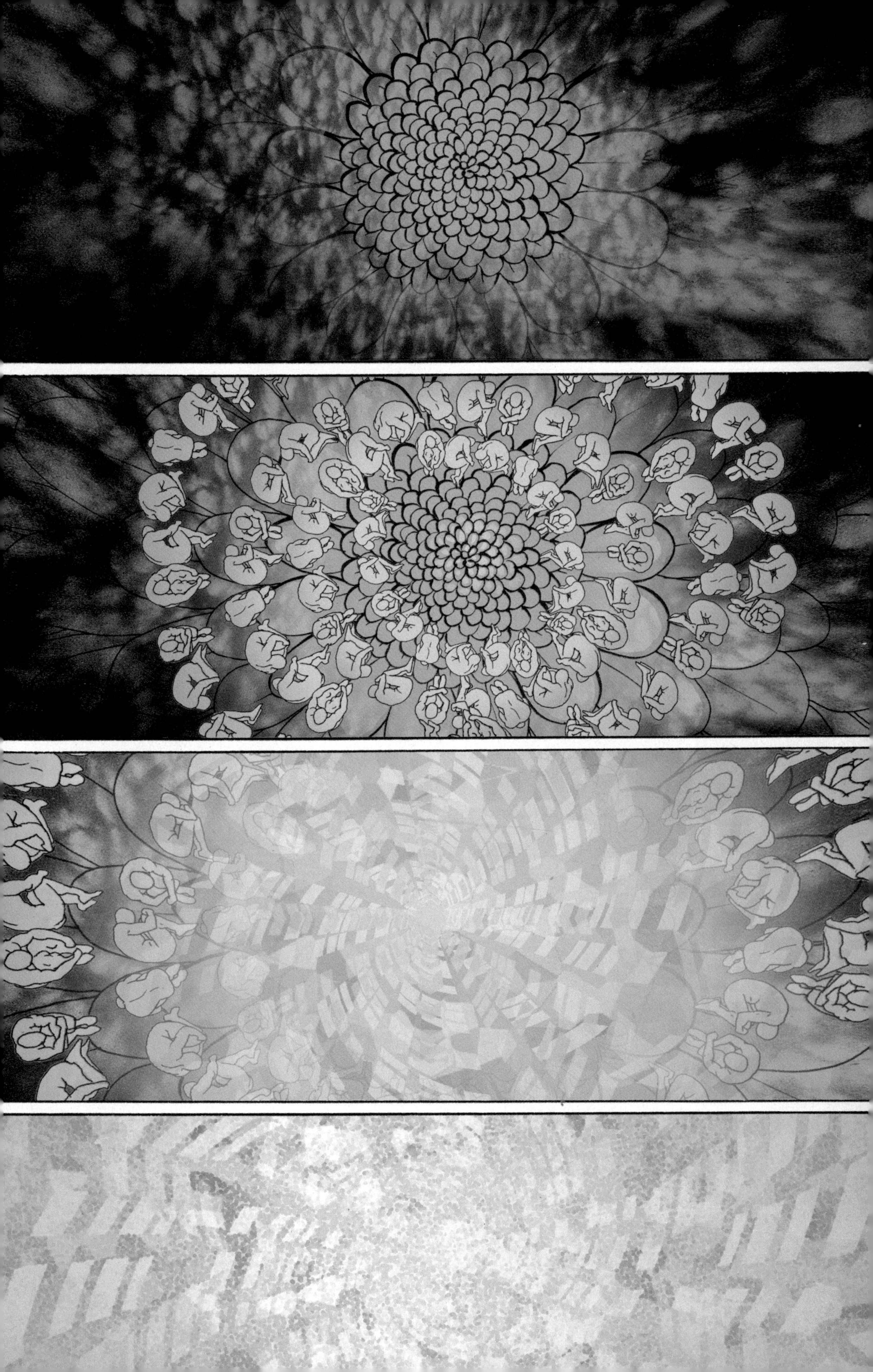

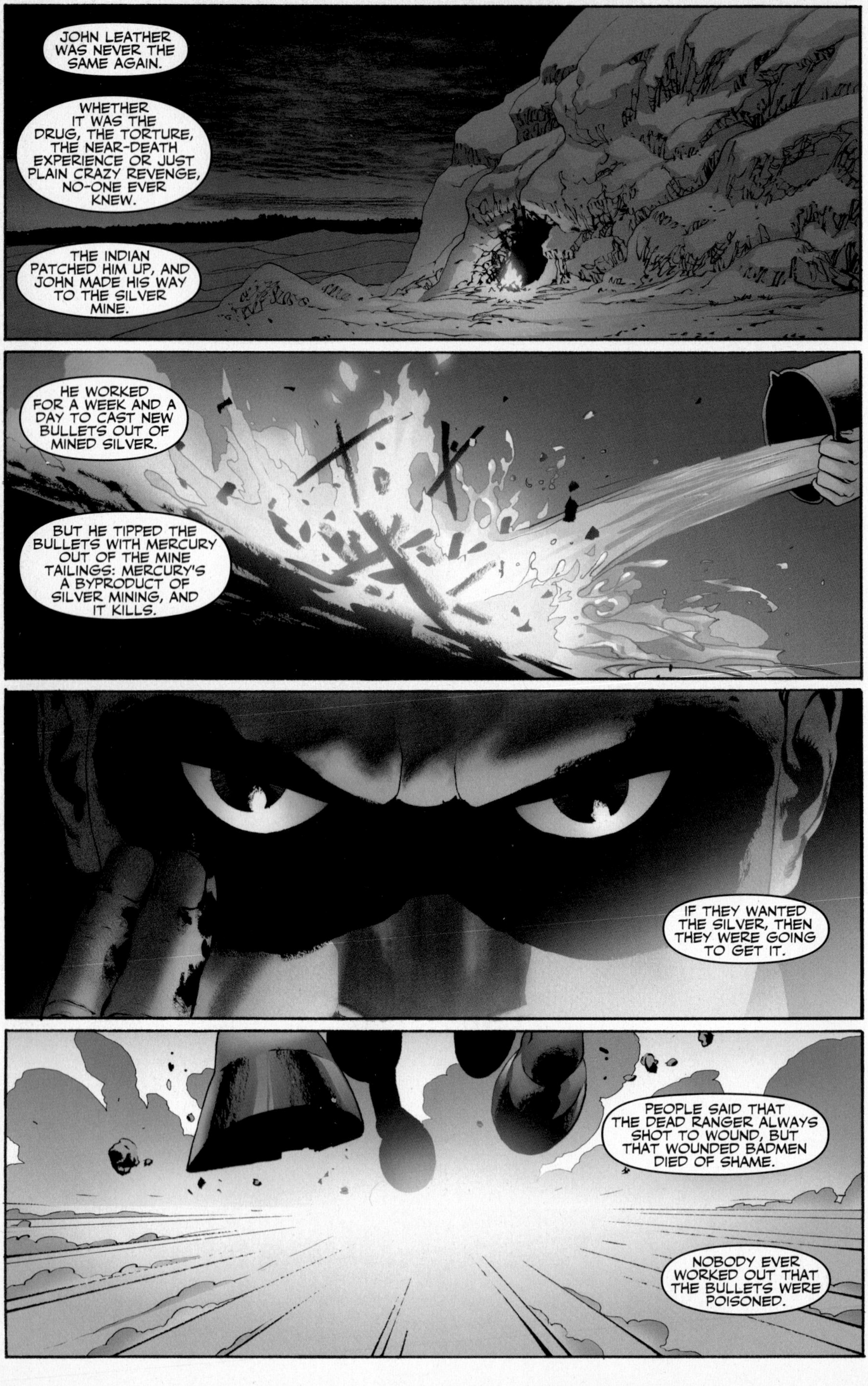
JOHN LEATHER WAS NEVER THE SAME AGAIN.
WHETHER IT WAS THE DRUG, THE TORTURE, THE NEAR-DEATH EXPERIENCE OR JUST PLAIN CRAZY REVENGE, NO-ONE EVER KNEW.
THE INDIAN PATCHED HIM UP, AND JOHN MADE HIS WAY TO THE SILVER MINE.
HE WORKED FOR A WEEK AND A DAY TO CAST NEW BULLETS OUT OF MINED SILVER.
BUT HE TIPPED THE BULLETS WITH MERCURY OUT OF THE MINE TAILINGS: MERCURY'S A BYPRODUCT OF SILVER MINING, AND IT KILLS.
IF THEY WANTED THE SILVER, THEN THEY WERE GOING TO GET IT.
PEOPLE SAID THAT THE DEAD RANGER ALWAYS SHOT TO WOUND, BUT THAT WOUNDED BADMEN DIED OF SHAME.
NOBODY EVER WORKED OUT THAT THE BULLETS WERE POISONED.

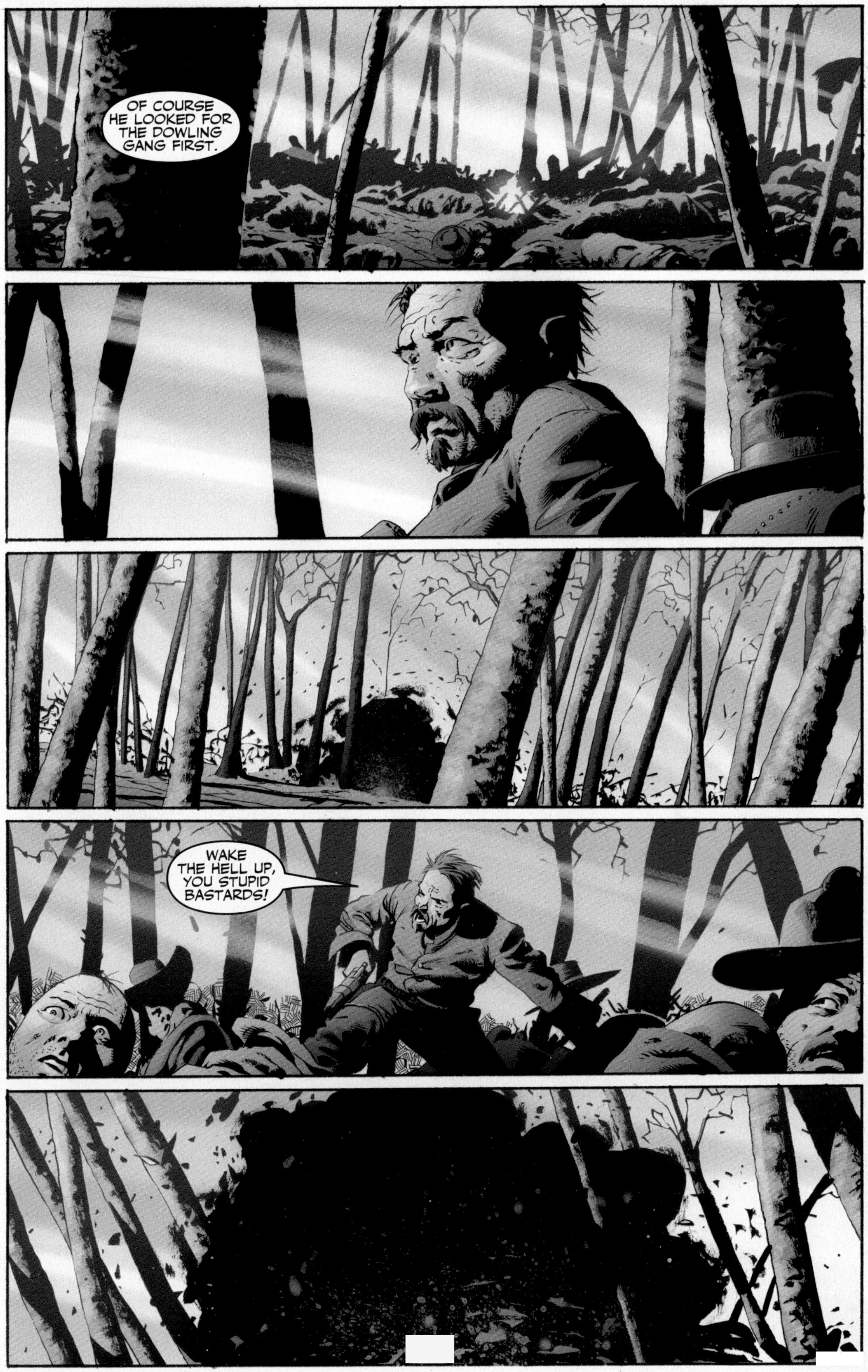
OF COURSE HE LOOKED FOR THE DOWLING GANG FIRST.
WAKE THE HELL UP, YOU STUPID BASTARDS!

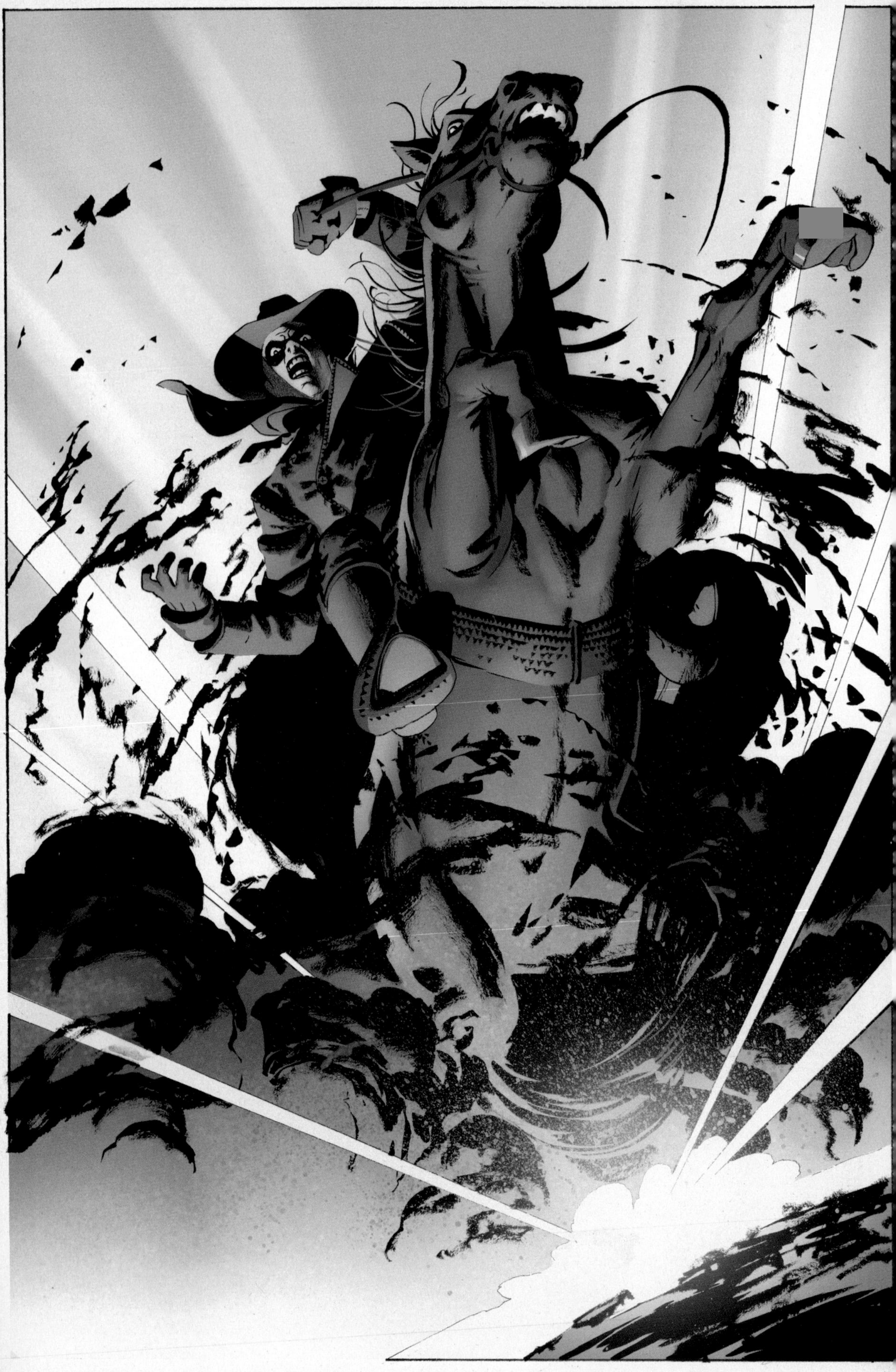

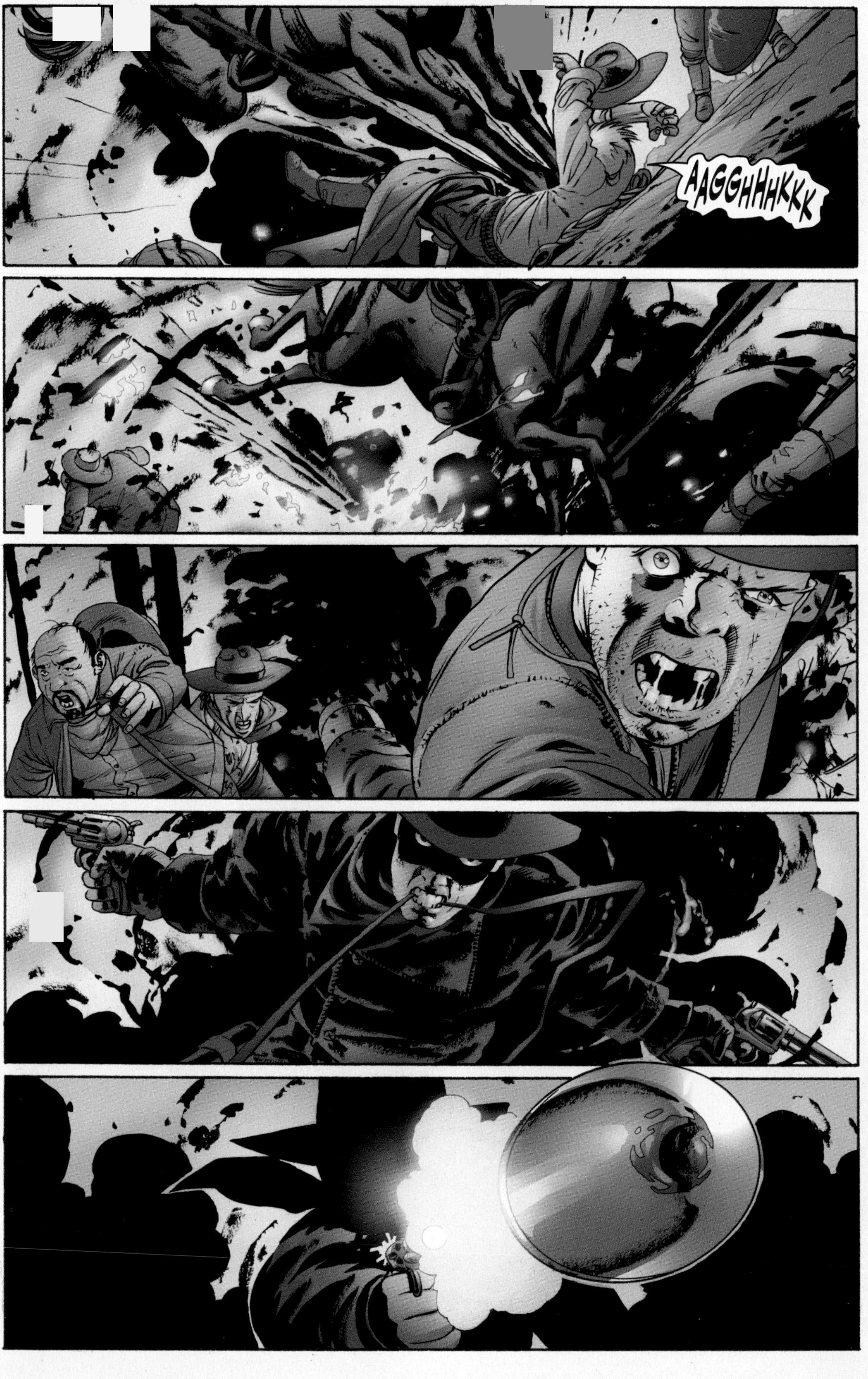
AAGGHHHKKK

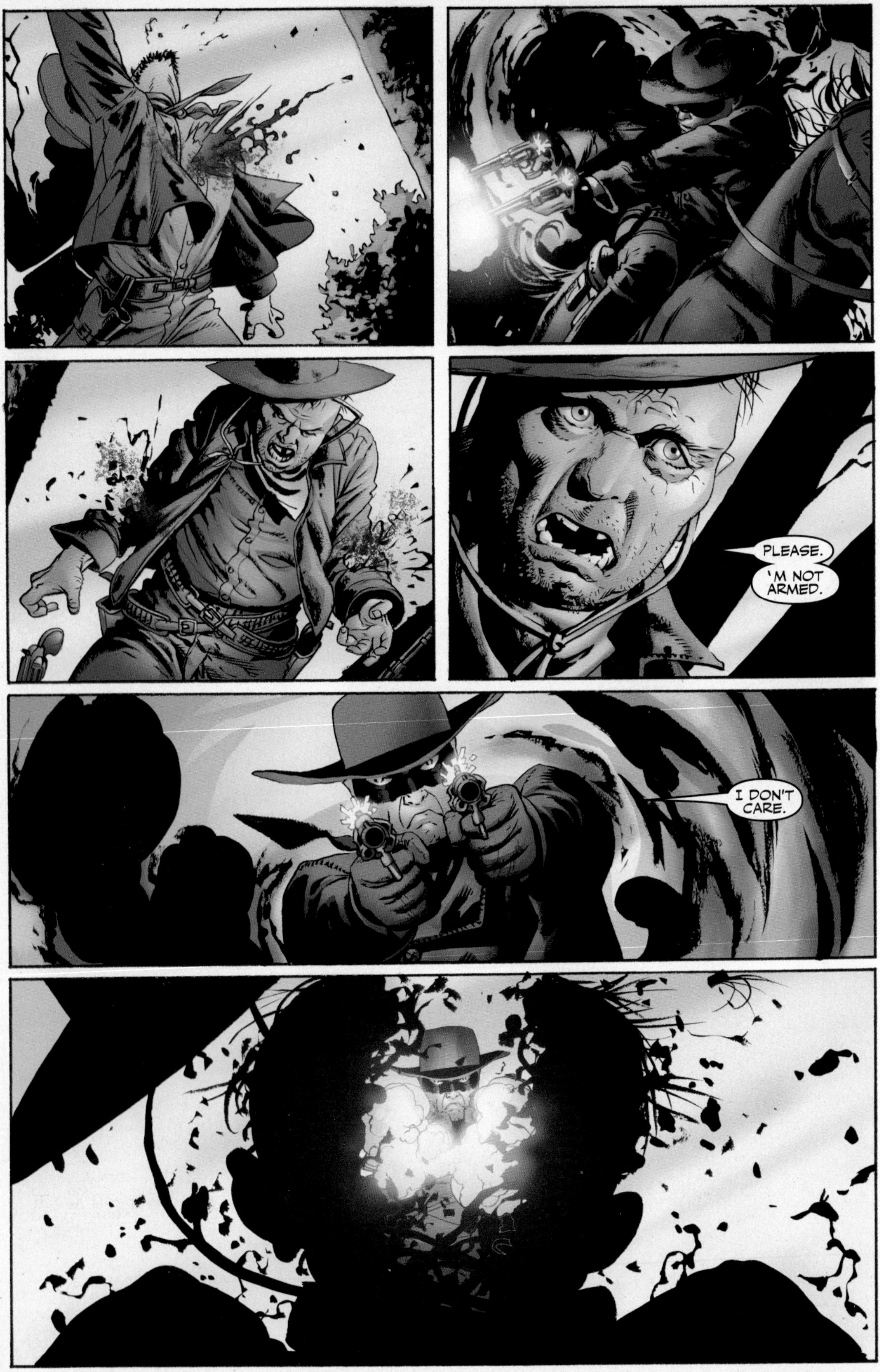
PLEASE.
'M NOT ARMED.
I DON'T CARE.

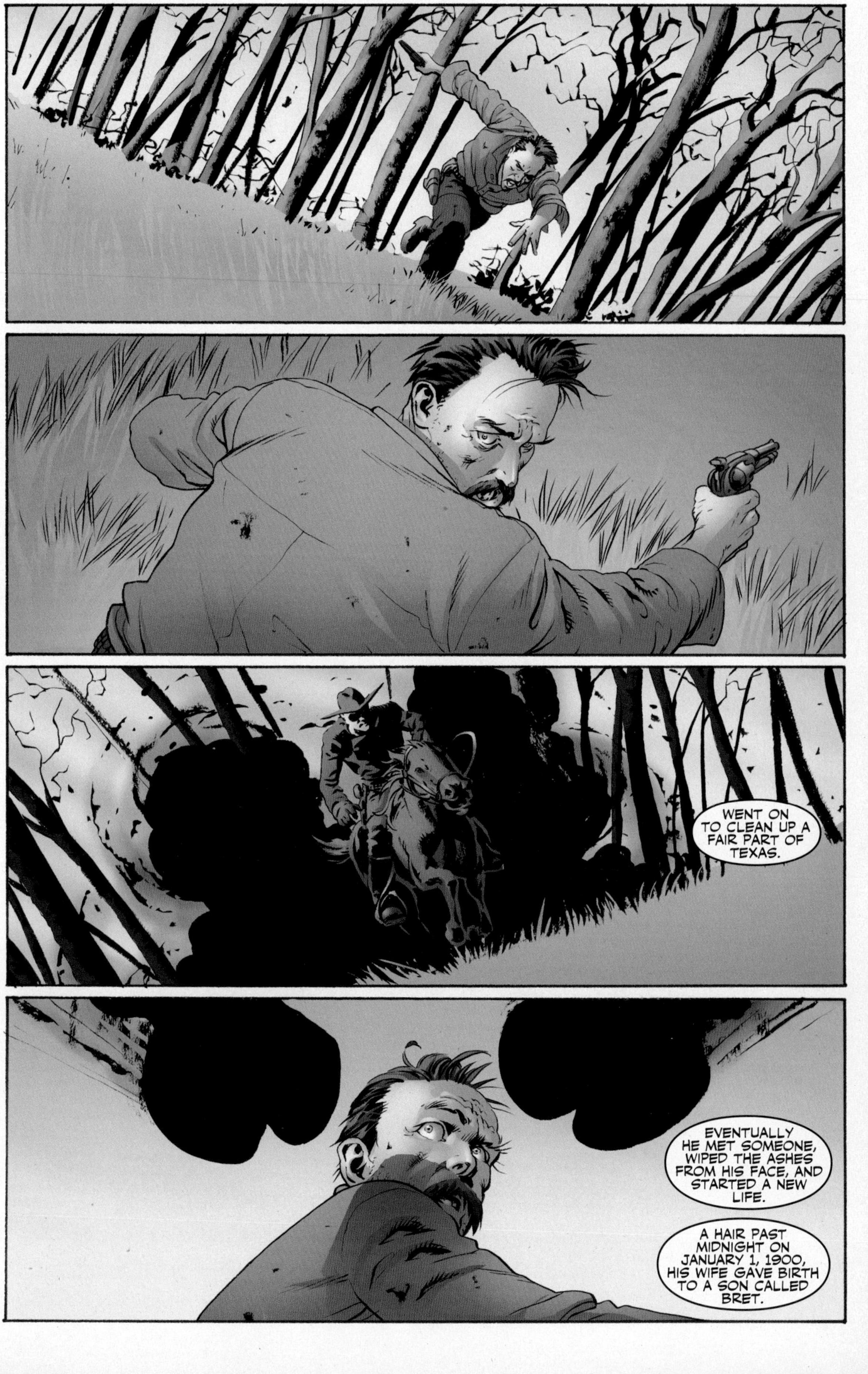
WENT ON TO CLEAN UP A FAIR PART OF TEXAS.
EVENTUALLY HE MET SOMEONE, WIPED THE ASHES FROM HIS FACE, AND STARTED A NEW LIFE.
A HAIR PAST MIDNIGHT ON JANUARY 1, 1900, HIS WIFE GAVE BIRTH TO A SON CALLED BRET.

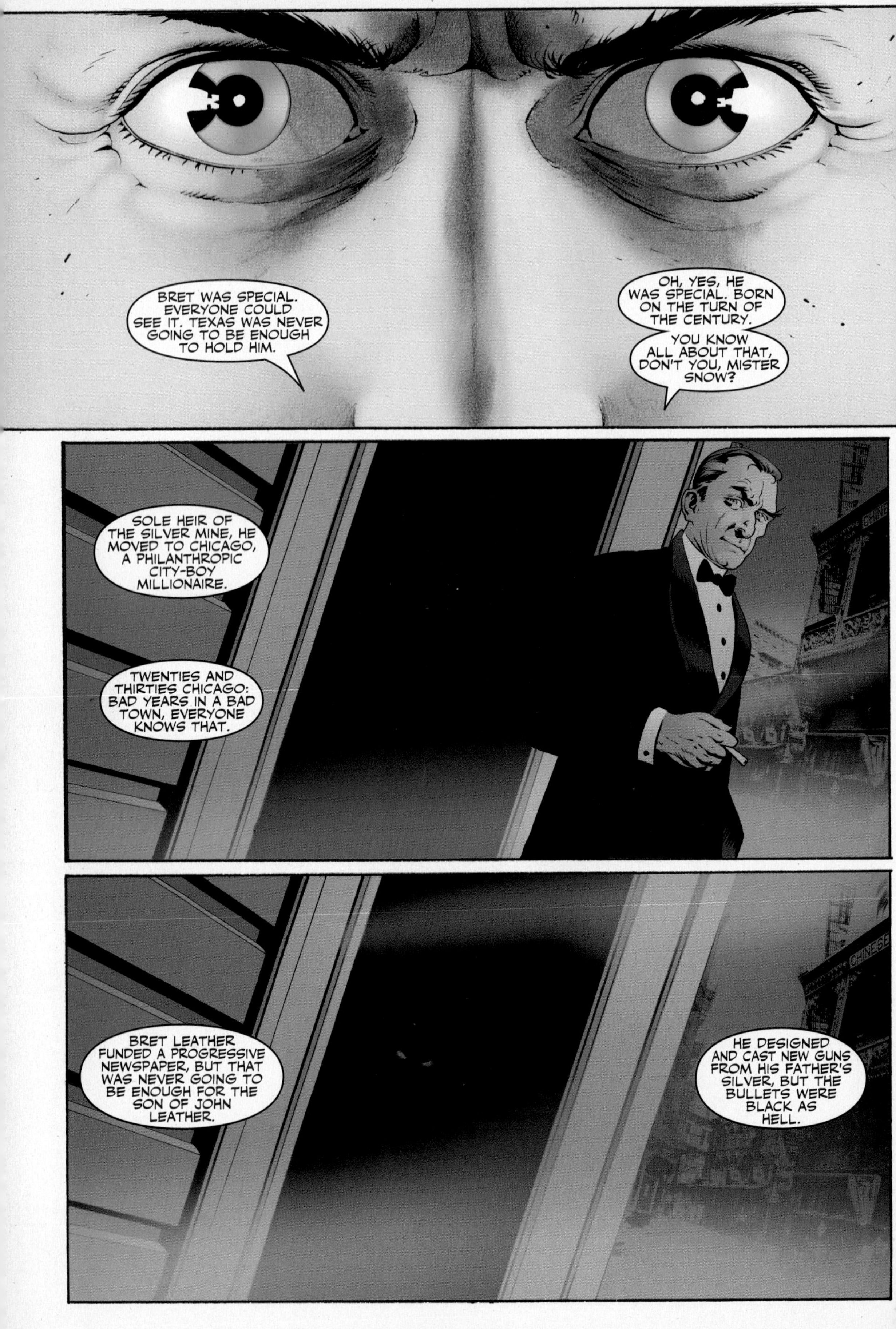
BRET WAS SPECIAL. EVERYONE COULD SEE IT. TEXAS WAS NEVER GOING TO BE ENOUGH TO HOLD HIM.
OH, YES, HE WAS SPECIAL. BORN ON THE TURN OF THE CENTURY.
YOU KNOW ALL ABOUT THAT, DON'T YOU, MISTER SNOW?
SOLE HEIR OF THE SILVER MINE, HE MOVED TO CHICAGO, A PHILANTHROPIC CITY-BOY MILLIONAIRE.
TWENTIES AND THIRTIES CHICAGO: BAD YEARS IN A BAD TOWN, EVERYONE KNOWS THAT.
BRET LEATHER FUNDED A PROGRESSIVE NEWSPAPER, BUT THAT WAS NEVER GOING TO BE ENOUGH FOR THE SON OF JOHN LEATHER.
HE DESIGNED AND CAST NEW GUNS FROM HIS FATHER'S SILVER, BUT THE BULLETS WERE BLACK AS HELL.

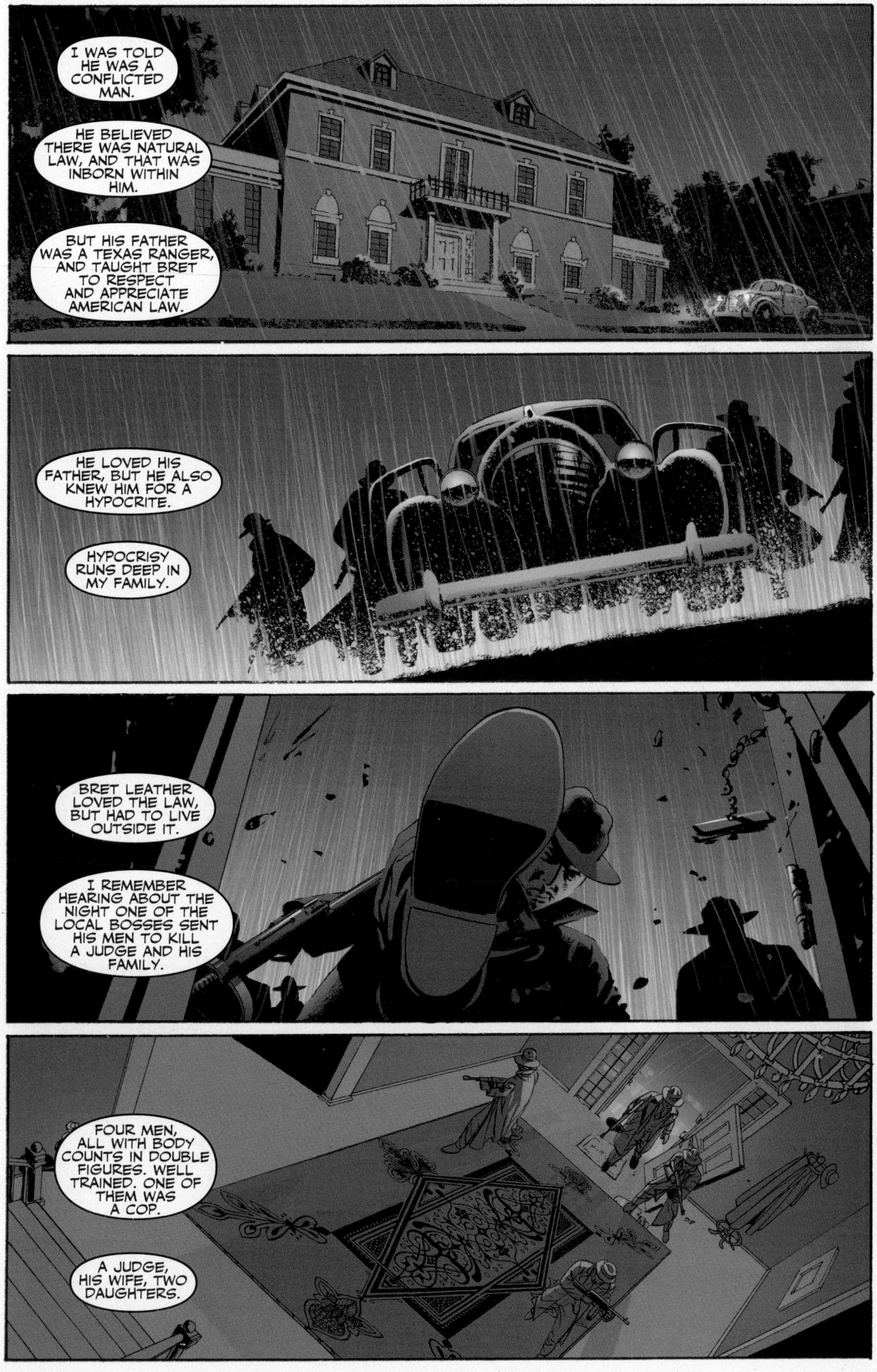
I WAS TOLD HE WAS A CONFLICTED MAN.
HE BELIEVED THERE WAS NATURAL LAW, AND THAT WAS INBORN WITHIN HIM.
BUT HIS FATHER WAS A TEXAS RANGER, AND TAUGHT BRET TO RESPECT AND APPRECIATE AMERICAN LAW.
HE LOVED HIS FATHER, BUT HE ALSO KNEW HIM FOR A HYPOCRITE.
HYPOCRISY RUNS DEEP IN MY FAMILY.
BRET LEATHER LOVED THE LAW, BUT HAD TO LIVE OUTSIDE IT.
I REMEMBER HEARING ABOUT THE NIGHT ONE OF THE LOCAL BOSSES SENT HIS MEN TO KILL A JUDGE AND HIS FAMILY.
FOUR MEN, ALL WITH BODY COUNTS IN DOUBLE FIGURES. WELL TRAINED. ONE OF THEM WAS A COP.
A JUDGE, HIS WIFE, TWO DAUGHTERS.

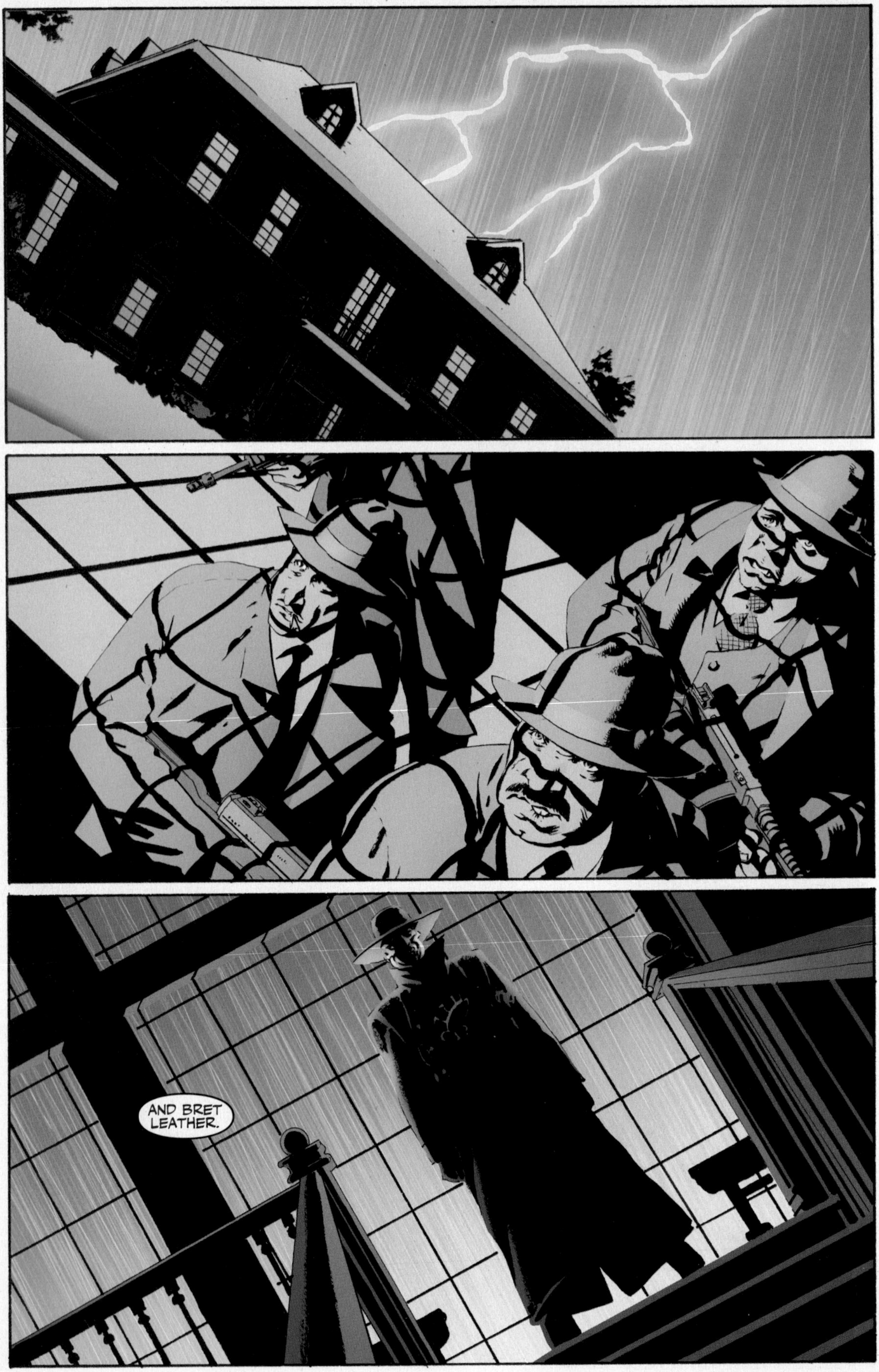
AND BRET LEATHER.

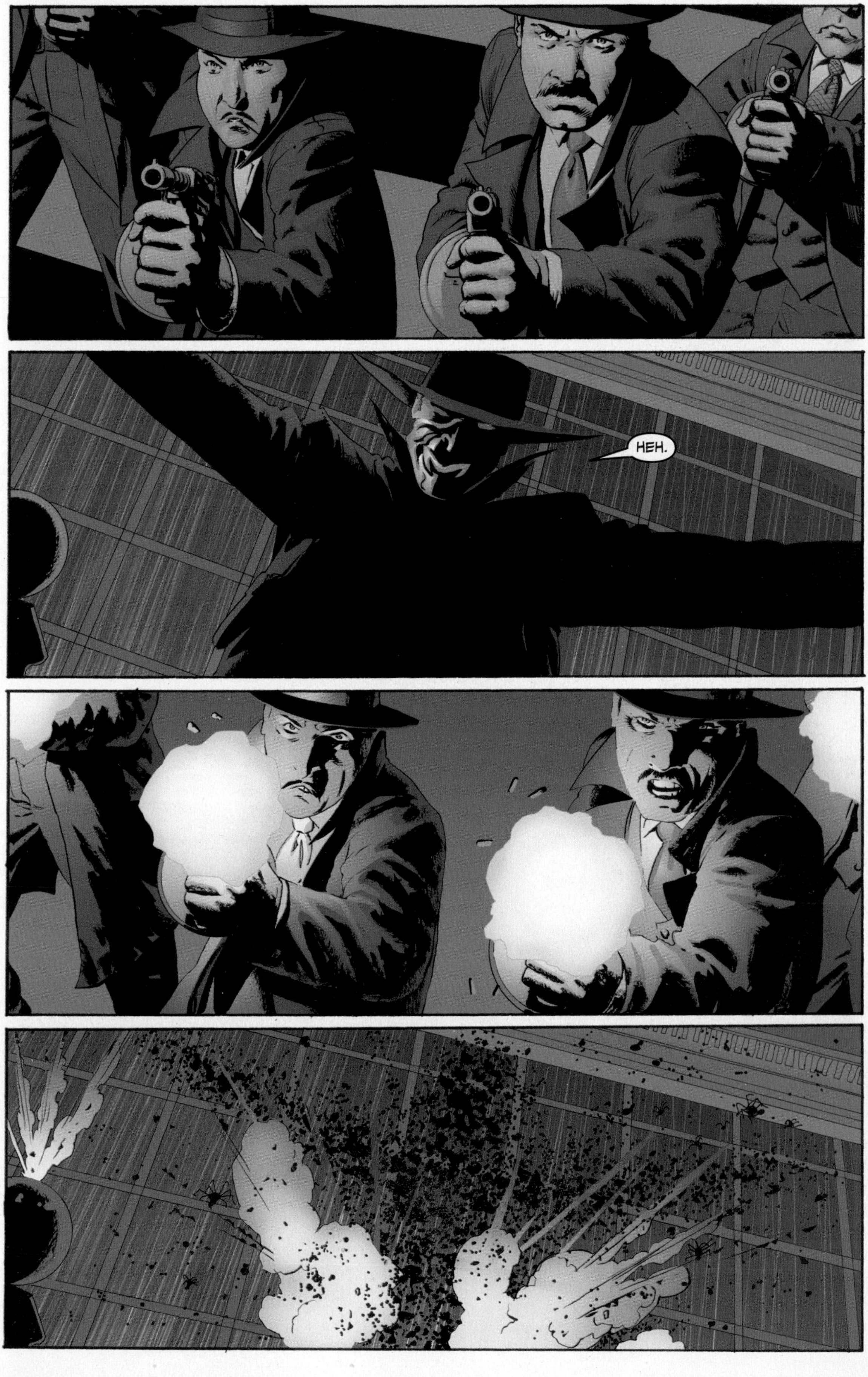
HEH.

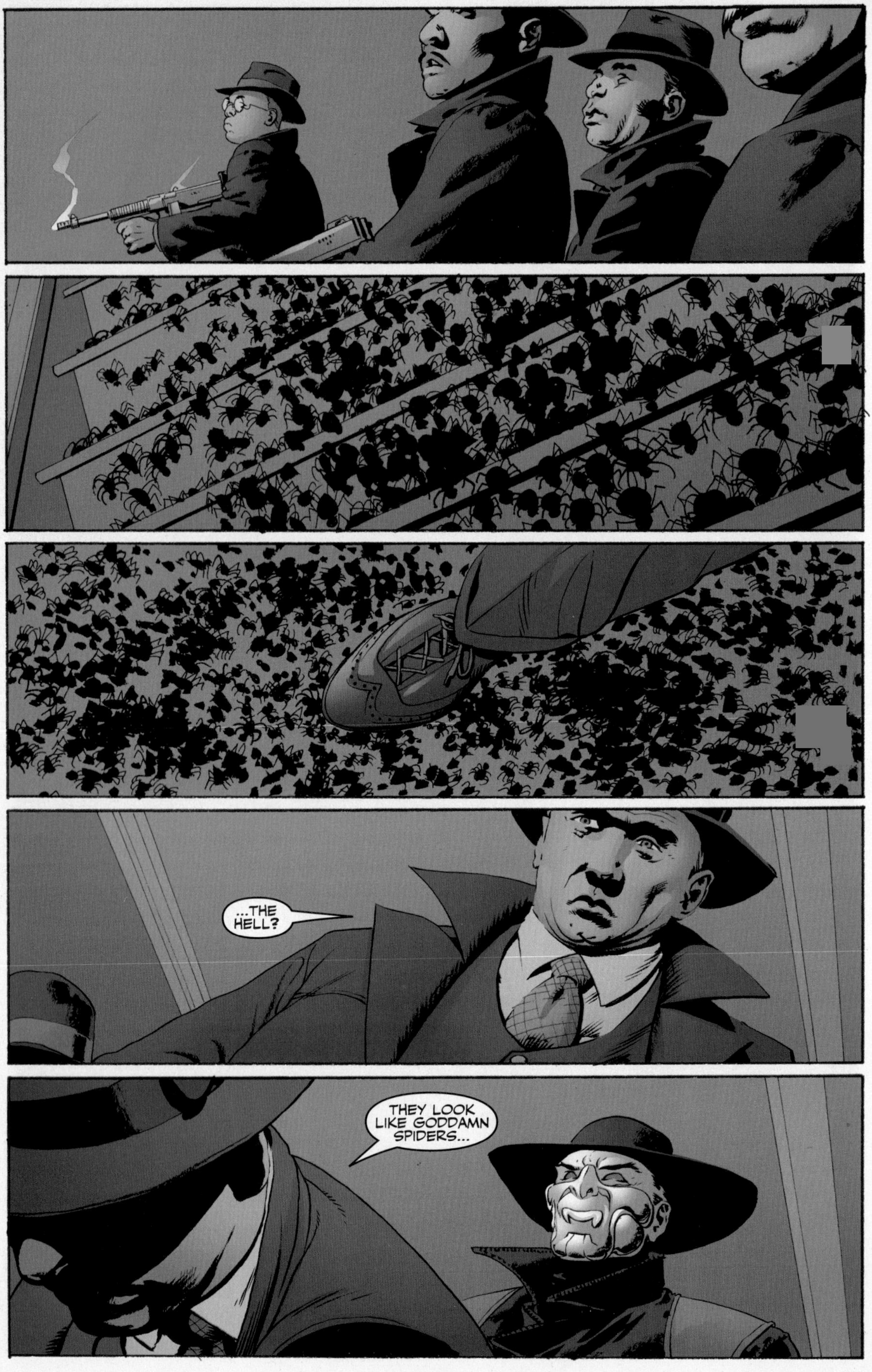
...THE HELL?
THEY LOOK LIKE GODDAMN SPIDERS...

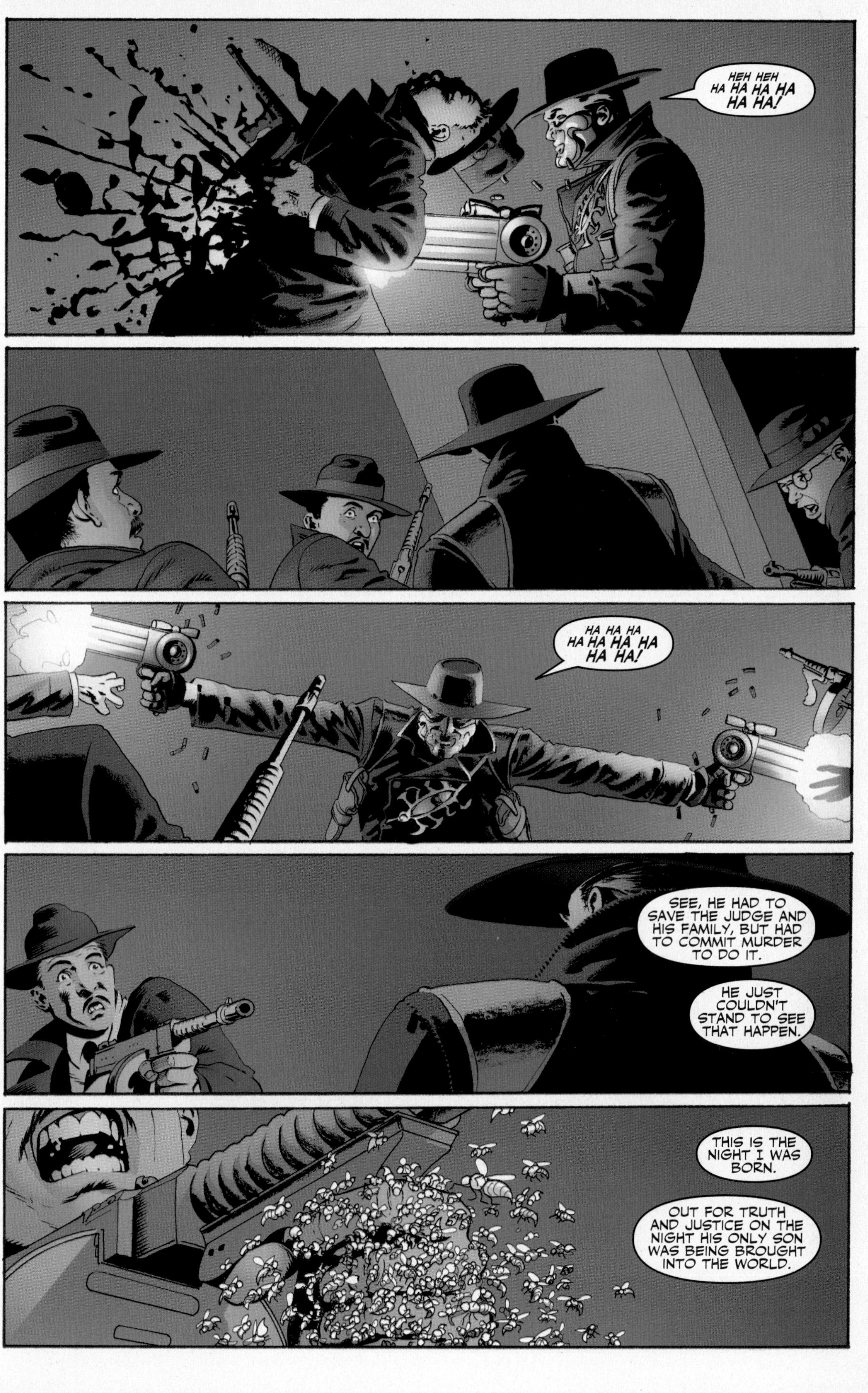
HEH HEH HA HA HA HA HA HA HA!
HA HA HA HA HA HA HA HA HA!
SEE, HE HAD TO SAVE THE JUDGE AND HIS FAMILY, BUT HAD TO COMMIT MURDER TO DO IT.
HE JUST COULDN'T STAND TO SEE THAT HAPPEN.
THIS IS THE NIGHT I WAS BORN.
OUT FOR TRUTH AND JUSTICE ON THE NIGHT HIS ONLY SON WAS BEING BROUGHT INTO THE WORLD.

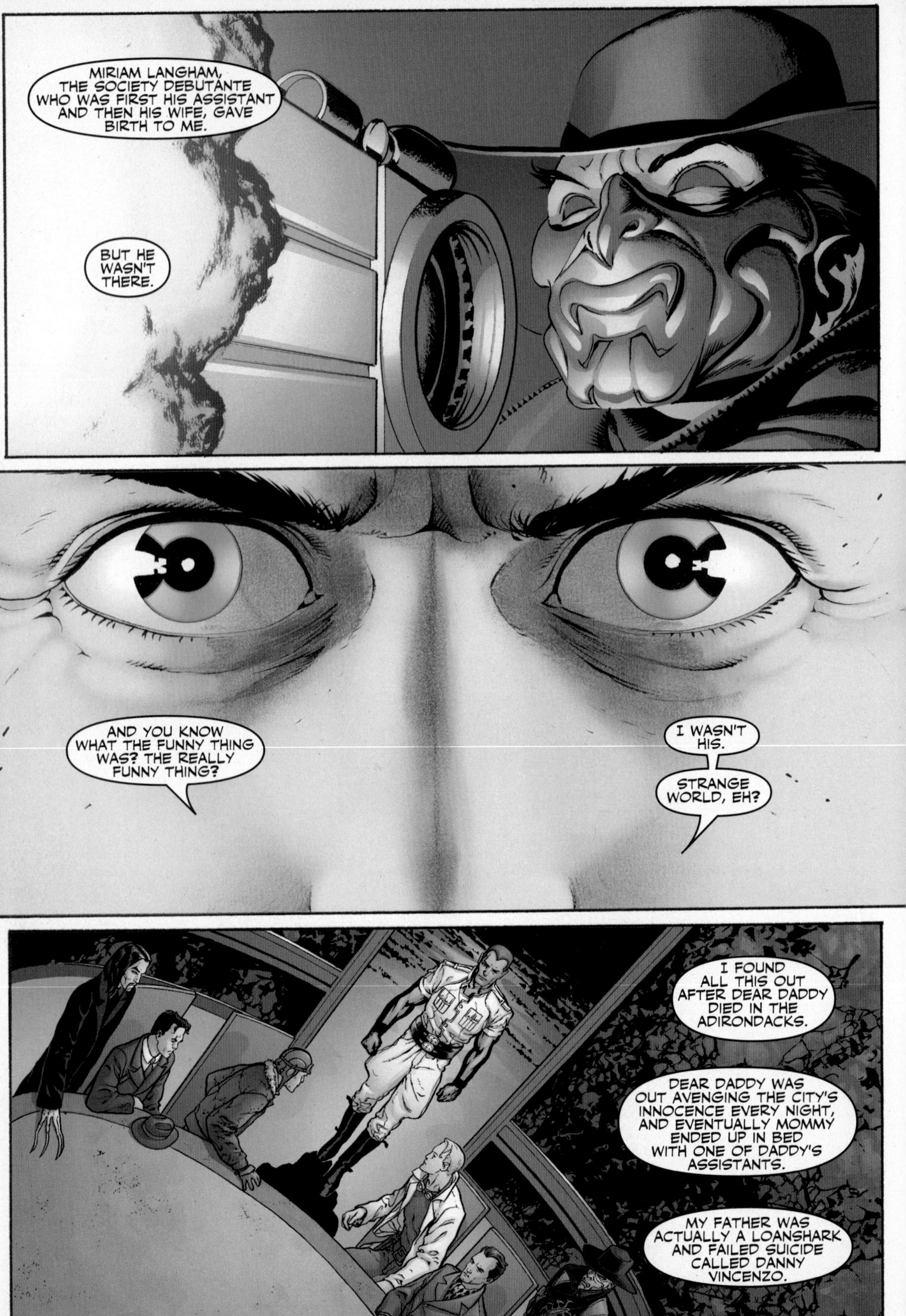
MIRIAM LANGHAM, THE SOCIETY DEBUTANTE WHO WAS FIRST HIS ASSISTANT AND THEN HIS WIFE, GAVE BIRTH TO ME.
BUT HE WASN'T THERE.
AND YOU KNOW WHAT THE FUNNY THING WAS? THE REALLY FUNNY THING?
I WASN'T HIS.
STRANGE WORLD, EH?
I FOUND ALL THIS OUT AFTER DEAR DADDY DIED IN THE ADIRONDACKS.
DEAR DADDY WAS OUT AVENGING THE CITY'S INNOCENCE EVERY NIGHT, AND EVENTUALLY MOMMY ENDED UP IN BED WITH ONE OF DADDY'S ASSISTANTS.
MY FATHER WAS ACTUALLY A LOANSHARK AND FAILED SUICIDE CALLED DANNY VINCENZO.

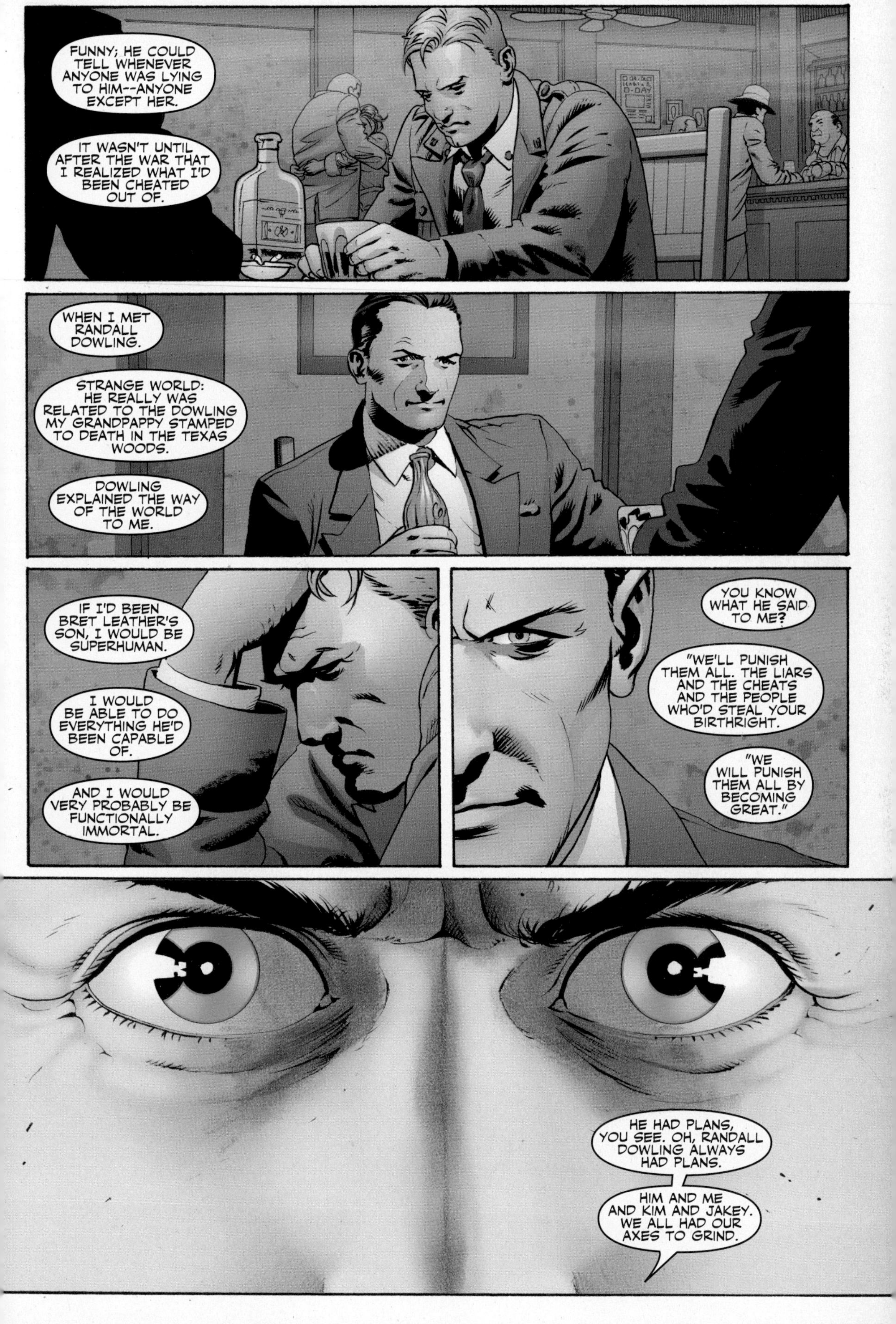
FUNNY; HE COULD TELL WHENEVER ANYONE WAS LYING TO HIM--ANYONE EXCEPT HER.
IT WASN'T UNTIL AFTER THE WAR THAT I REALIZED WHAT I'D BEEN CHEATED OUT OF.
WHEN I MET RANDALL DOWLING.
STRANGE WORLD: HE REALLY WAS RELATED TO THE DOWLING MY GRANDPAPPY STAMPED TO DEATH IN THE TEXAS WOODS.
DOWLING EXPLAINED THE WAY OF THE WORLD TO ME.
IF I'D BEEN BRET LEATHER'S SON, I WOULD BE SUPERHUMAN.
I WOULD BE ABLE TO DO EVERYTHING HE'D BEEN CAPABLE OF.
AND I WOULD VERY PROBABLY BE FUNCTIONALLY IMMORTAL.
YOU KNOW WHAT HE SAID TO ME?
"WE'LL PUNISH THEM ALL. THE LIARS AND THE CHEATS AND THE PEOPLE WHO'D STEAL YOUR BIRTHRIGHT.
"WE WILL PUNISH THEM ALL BY BECOMING GREAT."
HE HAD PLANS, YOU SEE. OH, RANDALL DOWLING ALWAYS HAD PLANS.
HIM AND ME AND KIM AND JAKEY. WE ALL HAD OUR AXES TO GRIND.

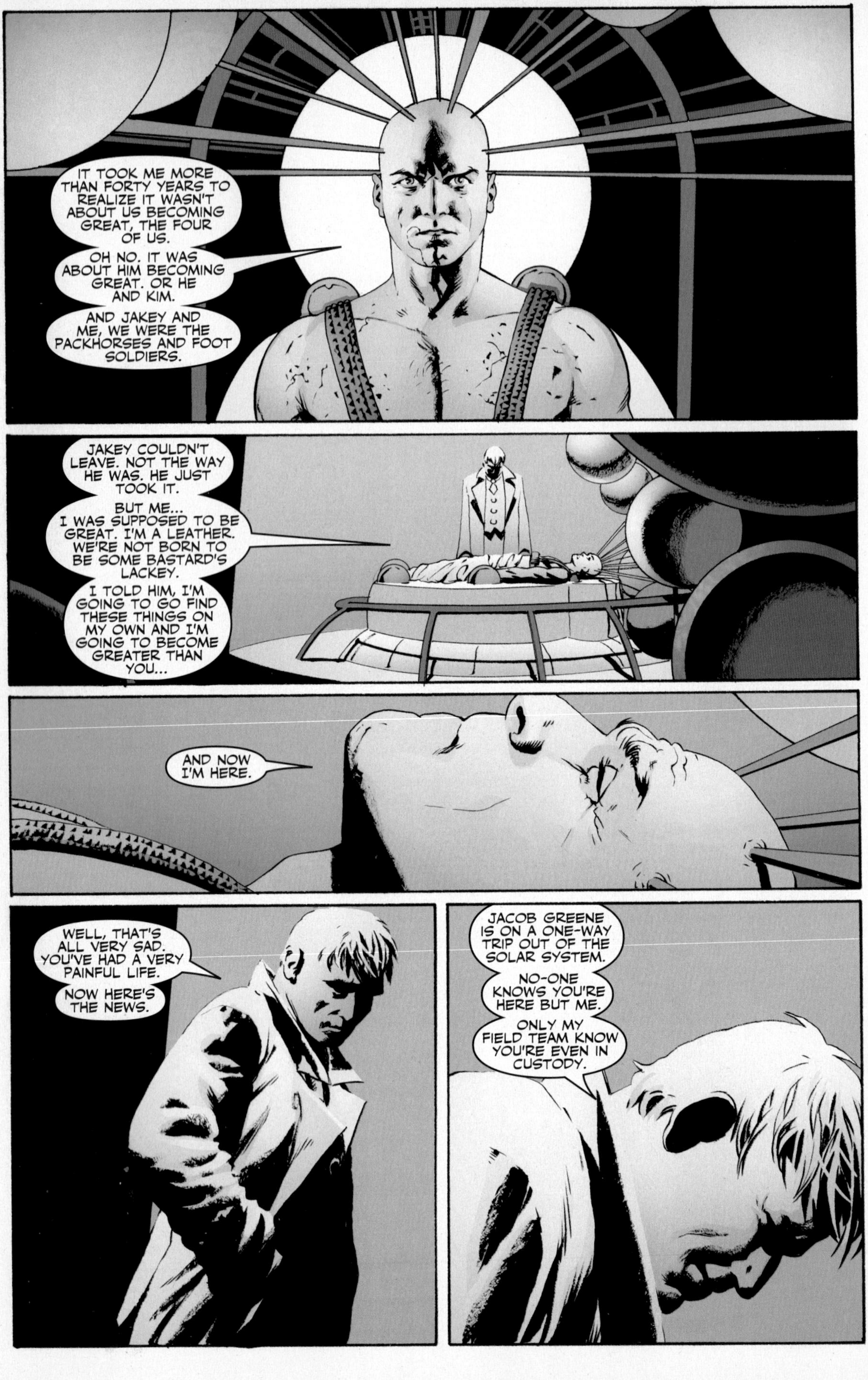
IT TOOK ME MORE THAN FORTY YEARS TO REALIZE IT WASN'T ABOUT US BECOMING GREAT, THE FOUR OF US.
OH NO. IT WAS ABOUT HIM BECOMING GREAT. OR HE AND KIM.
AND JAKEY AND ME, WE WERE THE PACKHORSES AND FOOT SOLDIERS.
JAKEY COULDN'T LEAVE. NOT THE WAY HE WAS. HE JUST TOOK IT.
BUT ME... I WAS SUPPOSED TO BE GREAT. I'M A LEATHER. WE'RE NOT BORN TO BE SOME BASTARD'S LACKEY.
I TOLD HIM, I'M GOING TO GO FIND THESE THINGS ON MY OWN AND I'M GOING TO BECOME GREATER THAN YOU...
AND NOW I'M HERE.
WELL, THAT'S ALL VERY SAD. YOU'VE HAD A VERY PAINFUL LIFE.
NOW HERE'S THE NEWS.
JACOB GREENE IS ON A ONE-WAY TRIP OUT OF THE SOLAR SYSTEM.
NO-ONE KNOWS YOU'RE HERE BUT ME.
ONLY MY FIELD TEAM KNOW YOU'RE EVEN IN CUSTODY.

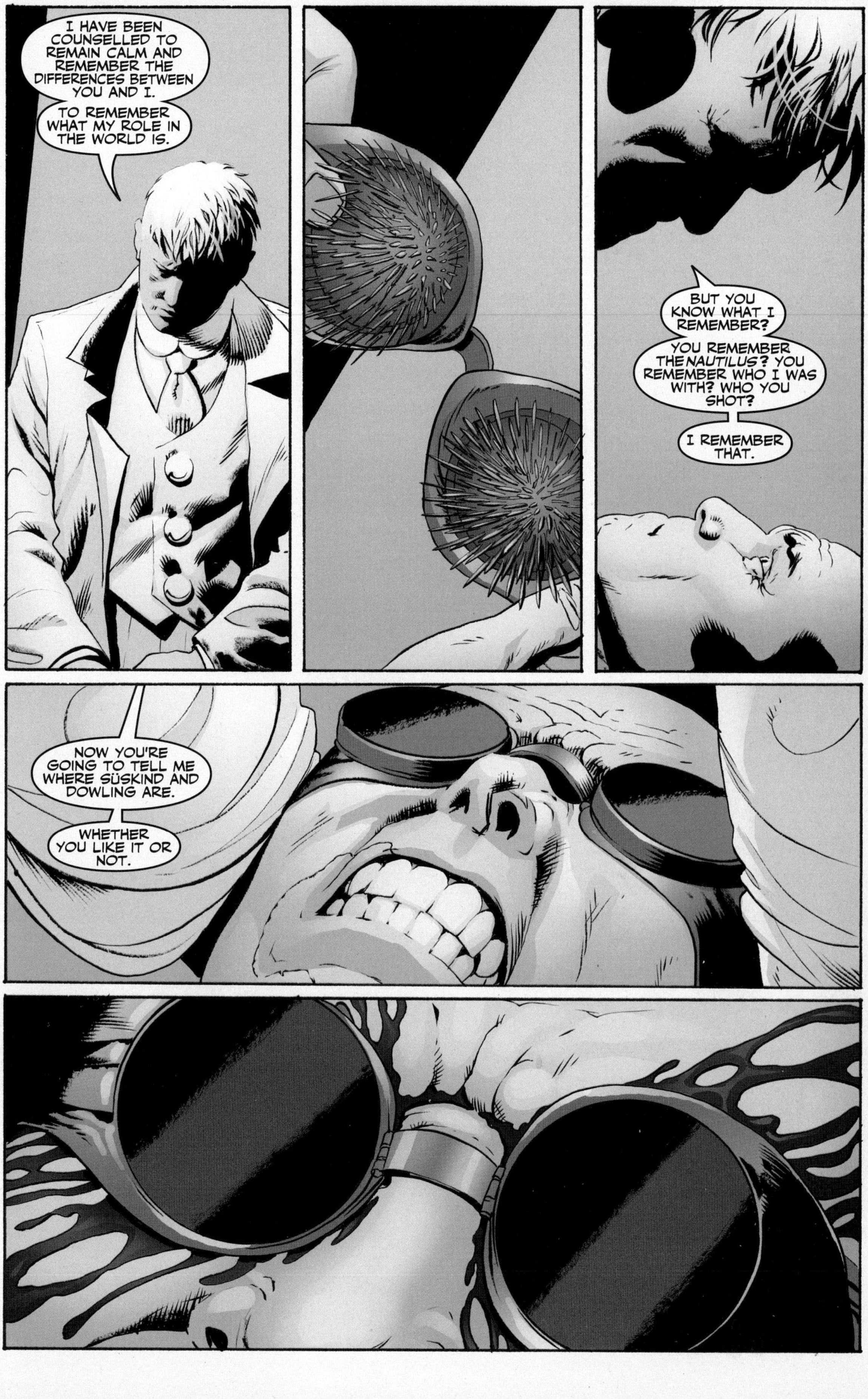
I HAVE BEEN COUNSELLED TO REMAIN CALM AND REMEMBER THE DIFFERENCES BETWEEN YOU AND I.
TO REMEMBER WHAT MY ROLE IN THE WORLD IS.
BUT YOU KNOW WHAT I REMEMBER?
YOU REMEMBER THE *NAUTILUS*? YOU REMEMBER WHO I WAS WITH? WHO YOU SHOT?
I REMEMBER THAT.
NOW YOU'RE GOING TO TELL ME WHERE SÜSKIND AND DOWLING ARE.
WHETHER YOU LIKE IT OR NOT.

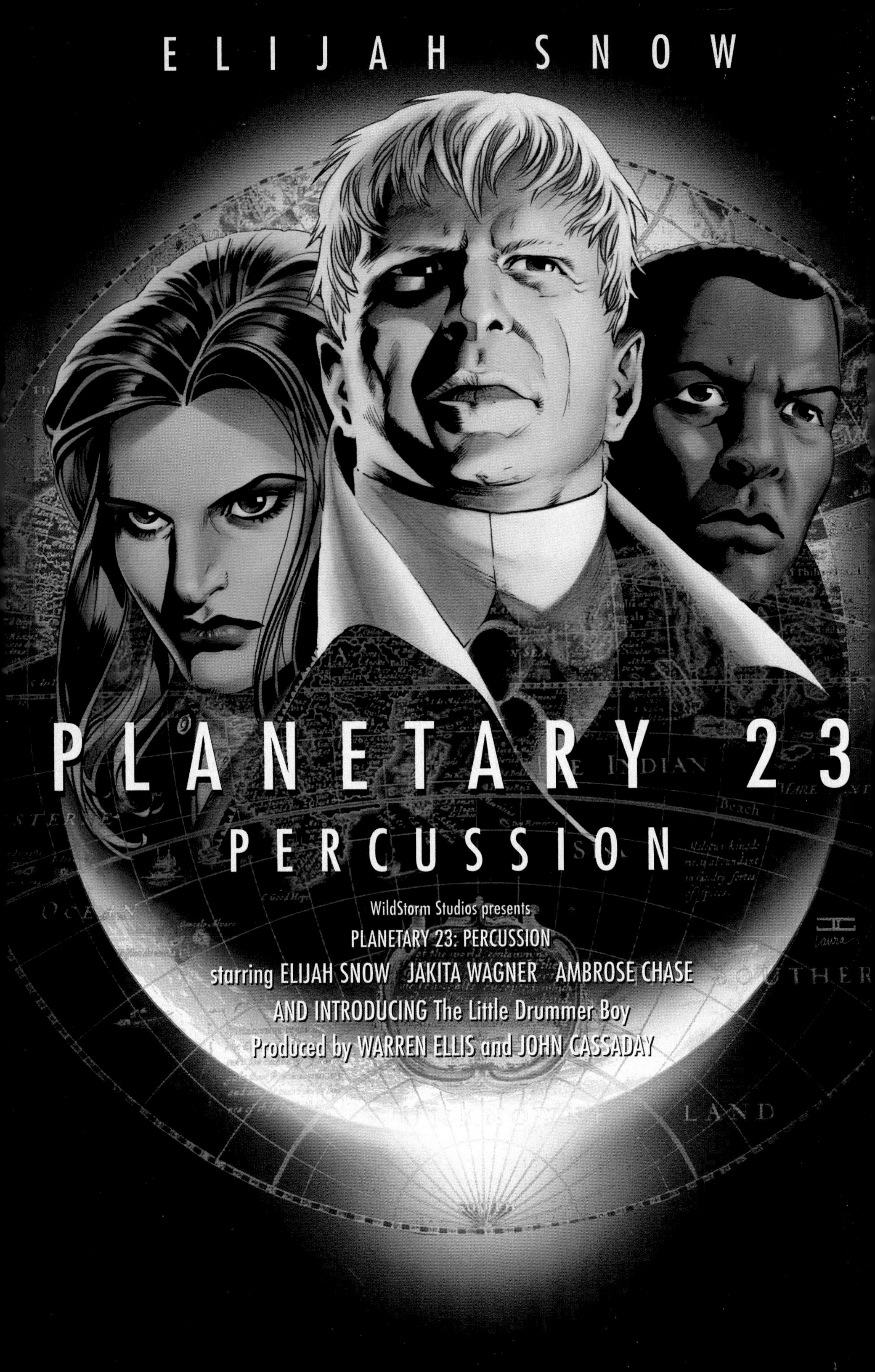
ELIJAH SNOW
PLANETARY 23
PERCUSSION
WildStorm Studios presents
PLANETARY 23: PERCUSSION
starring ELIJAH SNOW JAKITA WAGNER AMBROSE CHASE
AND INTRODUCING The Little Drummer Boy
Produced by WARREN ELLIS and JOHN CASSADAY

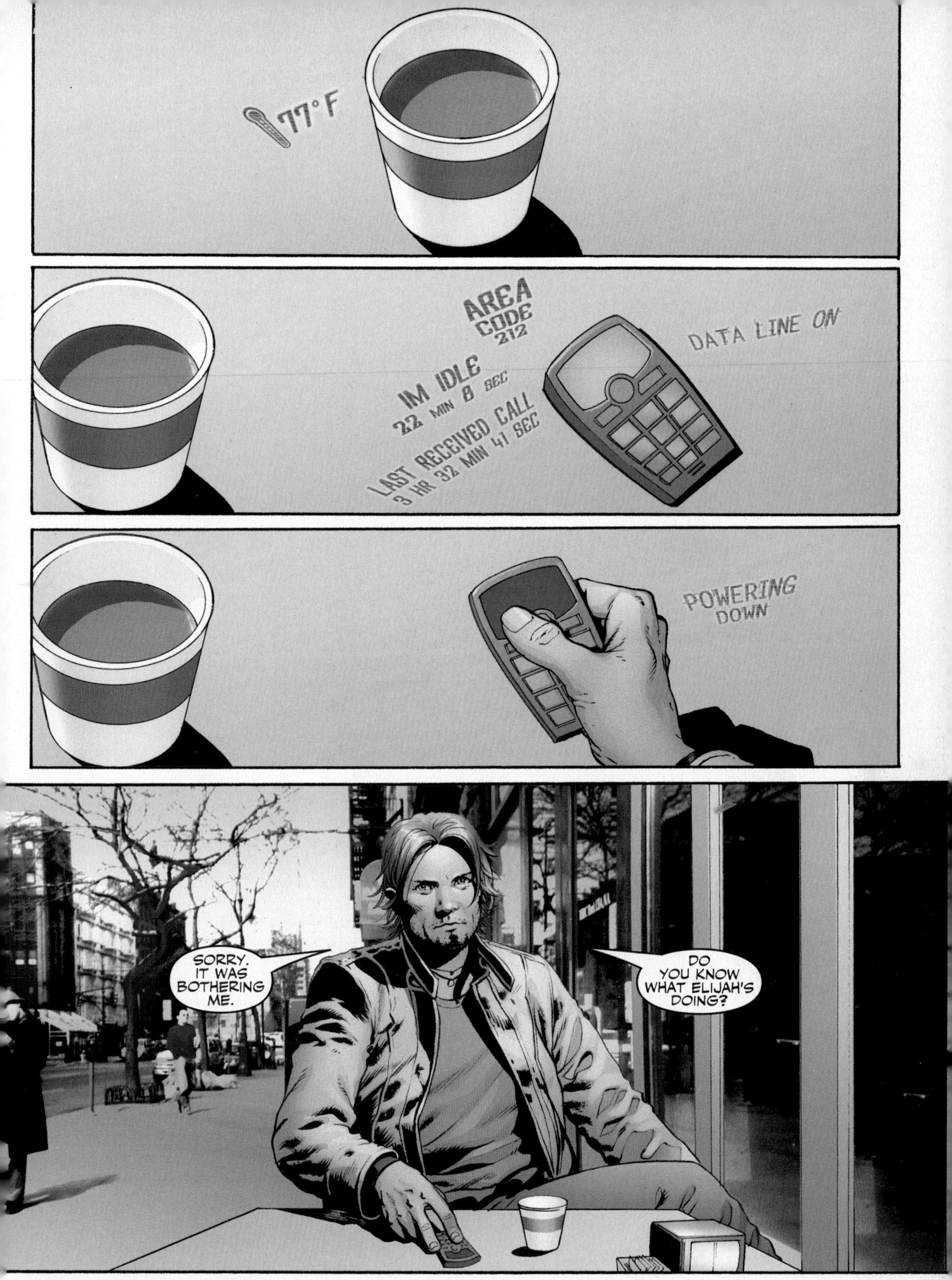
77° F
AREA CODE 212
IM IDLE 22 MIN 8 SEC
LAST RECEIVED CALL 3 HR 32 MIN 41 SEC
DATA LINE ON
POWERING DOWN
SORRY. IT WAS BOTHERING ME.
DO YOU KNOW WHAT ELIJAH'S DOING?

PERCUSSION

WARREN ELLIS JOHN CASSADAY

LAURA MARTIN RICHARD STARKINGS SCOTT DUNBIER

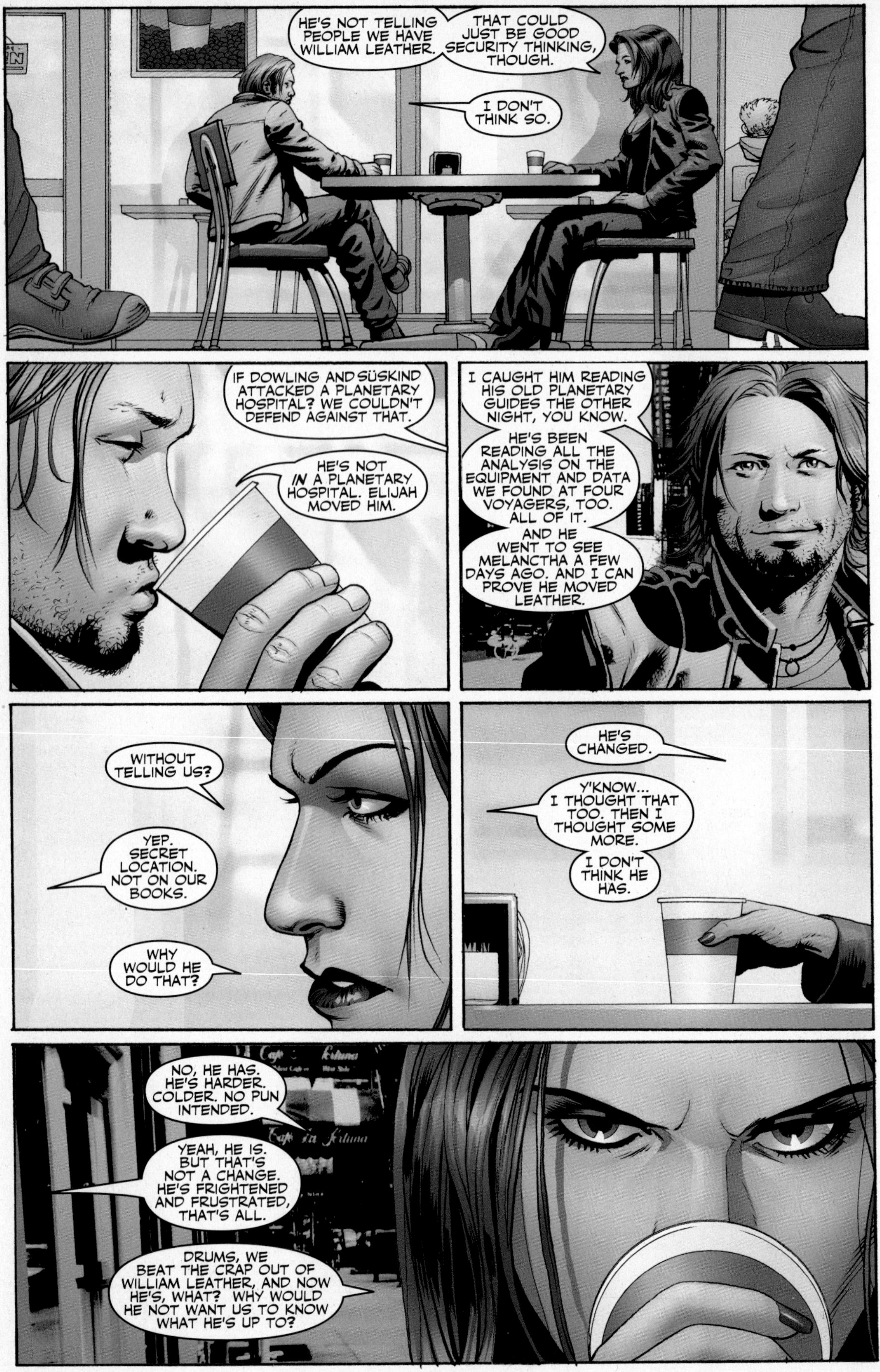

HE'S NOT TELLING PEOPLE WE HAVE WILLIAM LEATHER.
THAT COULD JUST BE GOOD SECURITY THINKING, THOUGH.
I DON'T THINK SO.
IF DOWLING AND SÜSKIND ATTACKED A PLANETARY HOSPITAL? WE COULDN'T DEFEND AGAINST THAT.
HE'S NOT *IN* A PLANETARY HOSPITAL. ELIJAH MOVED HIM.
I CAUGHT HIM READING HIS OLD PLANETARY GUIDES THE OTHER NIGHT, YOU KNOW.
HE'S BEEN READING ALL THE ANALYSIS ON THE EQUIPMENT AND DATA WE FOUND AT FOUR VOYAGERS, TOO. ALL OF IT.
AND HE WENT TO SEE MELANCTHA A FEW DAYS AGO. AND I CAN PROVE HE MOVED LEATHER.
WITHOUT TELLING US?
YEP. SECRET LOCATION. NOT ON OUR BOOKS.
WHY WOULD HE DO THAT?
HE'S CHANGED.
Y'KNOW... I THOUGHT THAT TOO. THEN I THOUGHT SOME MORE.
I DON'T THINK HE HAS.
NO, HE HAS. HE'S HARDER. COLDER. NO PUN INTENDED.
YEAH, HE IS. BUT THAT'S NOT A CHANGE. HE'S FRIGHTENED AND FRUSTRATED, THAT'S ALL.
DRUMS, WE BEAT THE CRAP OUT OF WILLIAM LEATHER, AND NOW HE'S, WHAT? WHY WOULD HE NOT WANT US TO KNOW WHAT HE'S UP TO?

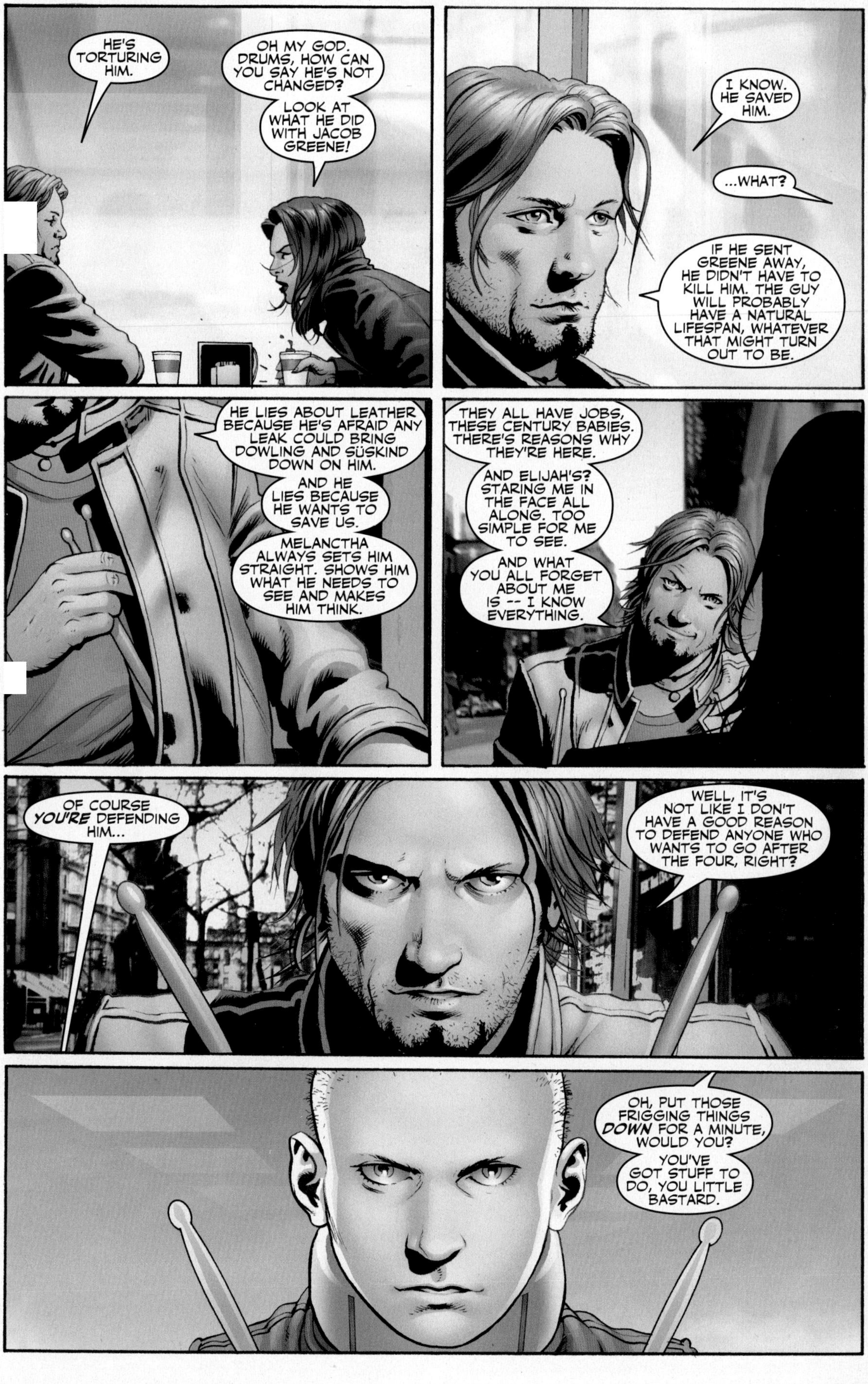
HE'S TORTURING HIM.
OH MY GOD. DRUMS, HOW CAN YOU SAY HE'S NOT CHANGED?
LOOK AT WHAT HE DID WITH JACOB GREENE!
I KNOW. HE SAVED HIM.
...WHAT?
IF HE SENT GREENE AWAY, HE DIDN'T HAVE TO KILL HIM. THE GUY WILL PROBABLY HAVE A NATURAL LIFESPAN, WHATEVER THAT MIGHT TURN OUT TO BE.
HE LIES ABOUT LEATHER BECAUSE HE'S AFRAID ANY LEAK COULD BRING DOWLING AND SÜSKIND DOWN ON HIM.
AND HE LIES BECAUSE HE WANTS TO SAVE US.
MELANCTHA ALWAYS SETS HIM STRAIGHT. SHOWS HIM WHAT HE NEEDS TO SEE AND MAKES HIM THINK.
THEY ALL HAVE JOBS, THESE CENTURY BABIES. THERE'S REASONS WHY THEY'RE HERE.
AND ELIJAH'S? STARING ME IN THE FACE ALL ALONG. TOO SIMPLE FOR ME TO SEE.
AND WHAT YOU ALL FORGET ABOUT ME IS -- I KNOW EVERYTHING.
OF COURSE YOU'RE DEFENDING HIM...
WELL, IT'S NOT LIKE I DON'T HAVE A GOOD REASON TO DEFEND ANYONE WHO WANTS TO GO AFTER THE FOUR, RIGHT?
OH, PUT THOSE FRIGGING THINGS DOWN FOR A MINUTE, WOULD YOU?
YOU'VE GOT STUFF TO DO, YOU LITTLE BASTARD.

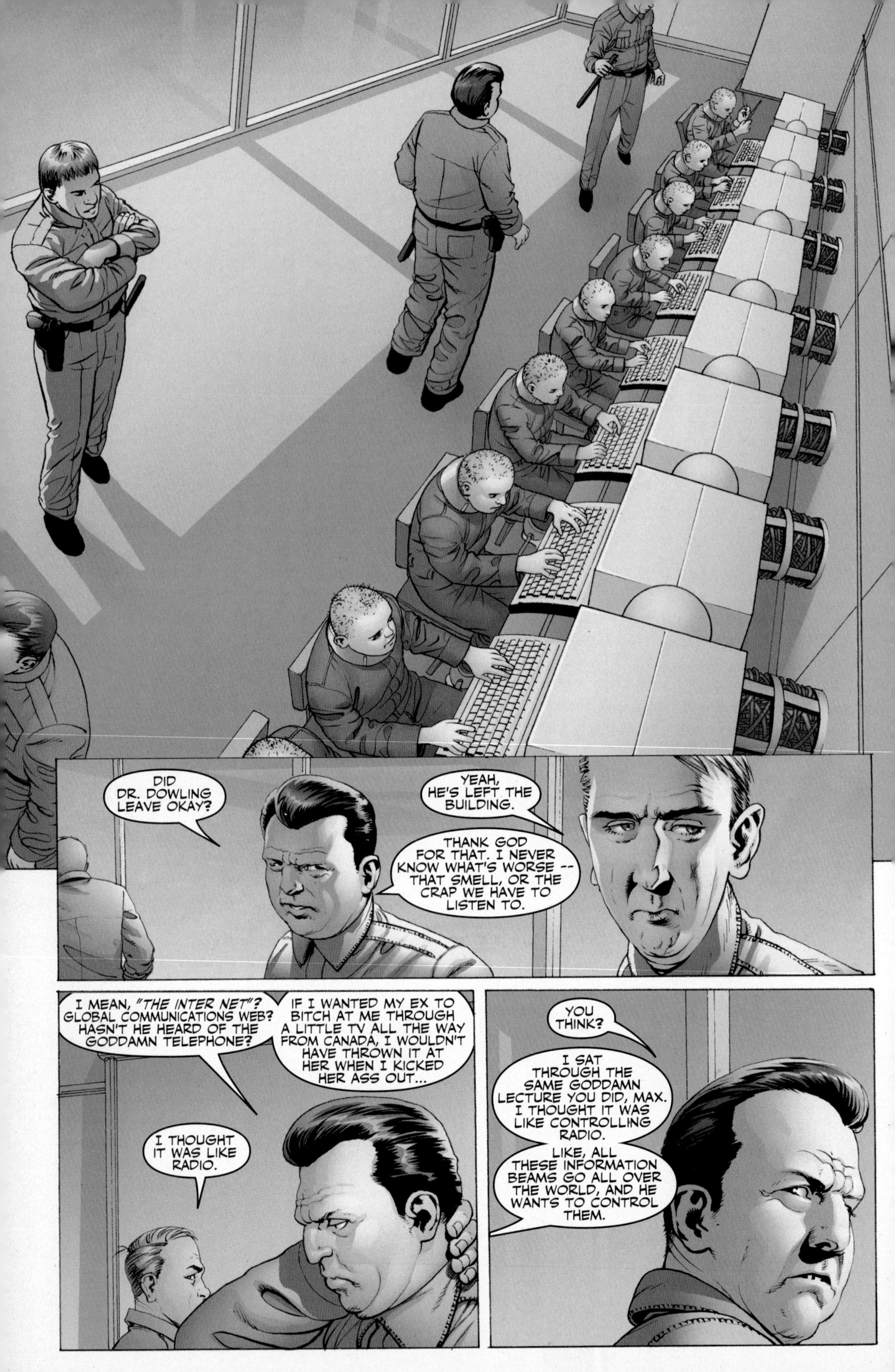
DID DR. DOWLING LEAVE OKAY?
YEAH, HE'S LEFT THE BUILDING.
THANK GOD FOR THAT. I NEVER KNOW WHAT'S WORSE -- THAT SMELL, OR THE CRAP WE HAVE TO LISTEN TO.
I MEAN, *"THE INTER NET"*? GLOBAL COMMUNICATIONS WEB? HASN'T HE HEARD OF THE GODDAMN TELEPHONE?
IF I WANTED MY EX TO BITCH AT ME THROUGH A LITTLE TV ALL THE WAY FROM CANADA, I WOULDN'T HAVE THROWN IT AT HER WHEN I KICKED HER ASS OUT...
I THOUGHT IT WAS LIKE RADIO.
YOU THINK?
I SAT THROUGH THE SAME GODDAMN LECTURE YOU DID, MAX. I THOUGHT IT WAS LIKE CONTROLLING RADIO.
LIKE, ALL THESE INFORMATION BEAMS GO ALL OVER THE WORLD, AND HE WANTS TO CONTROL THEM.

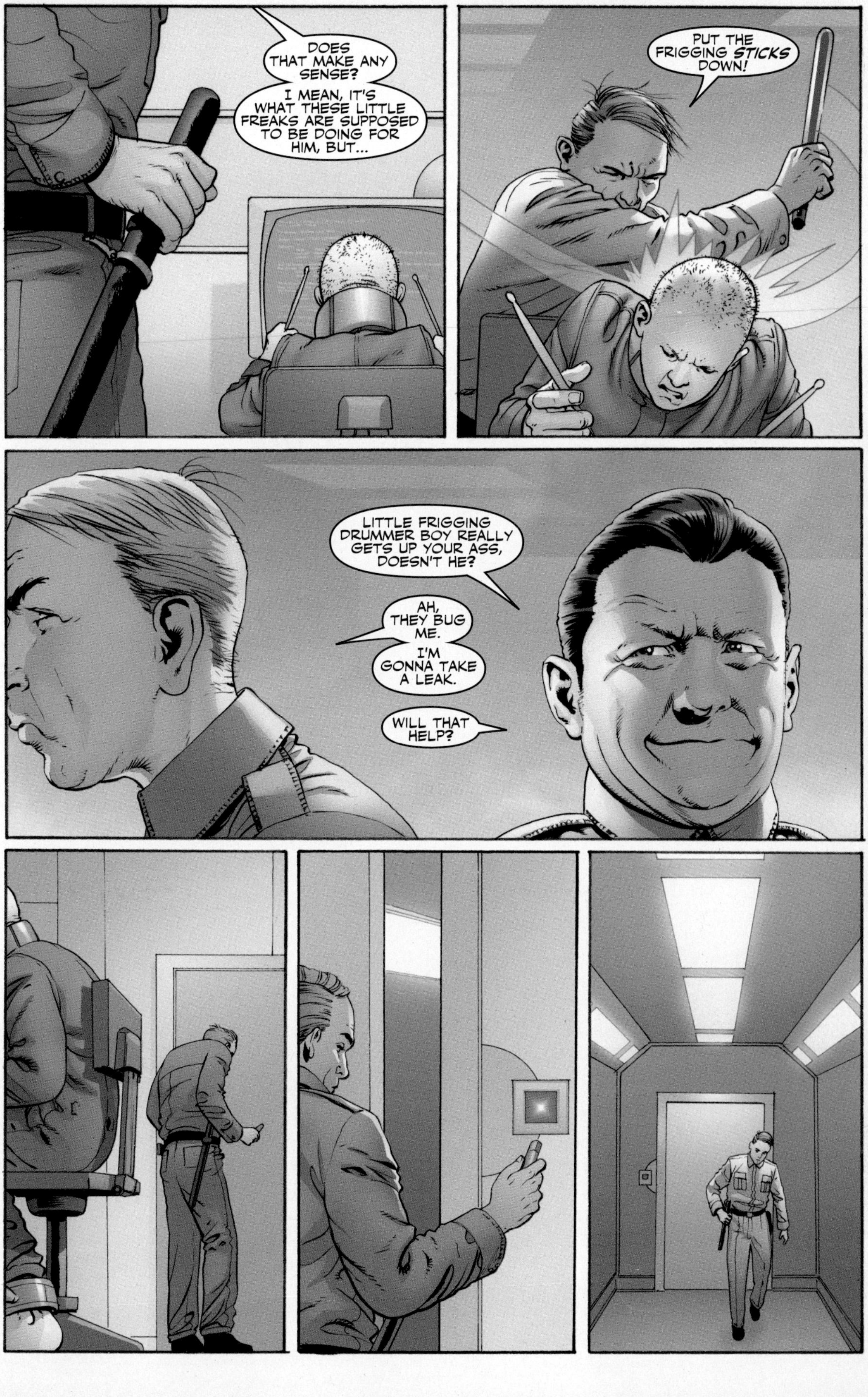
DOES THAT MAKE ANY SENSE?
I MEAN, IT'S WHAT THESE LITTLE FREAKS ARE SUPPOSED TO BE DOING FOR HIM, BUT...
PUT THE FRIGGING STICKS DOWN!
LITTLE FRIGGING DRUMMER BOY REALLY GETS UP YOUR ASS, DOESN'T HE?
AH, THEY BUG ME.
I'M GONNA TAKE A LEAK.
WILL THAT HELP?

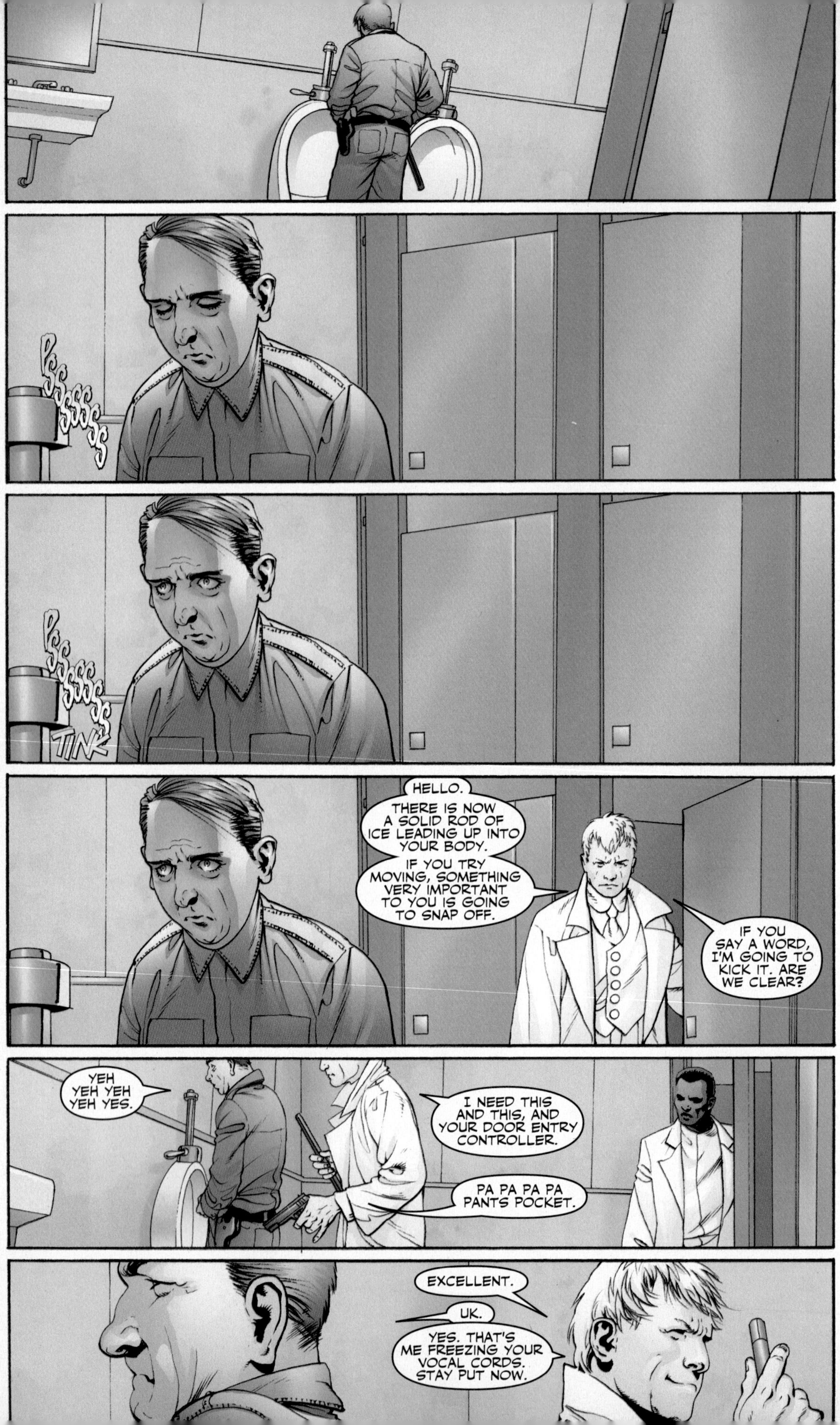
PSSSSSSSS
PSSSSSSSS
TINK
HELLO.
THERE IS NOW A SOLID ROD OF ICE LEADING UP INTO YOUR BODY.
IF YOU TRY MOVING, SOMETHING VERY IMPORTANT TO YOU IS GOING TO SNAP OFF.
IF YOU SAY A WORD, I'M GOING TO KICK IT. ARE WE CLEAR?
YEH YEH YEH YEH YES.
I NEED THIS AND THIS, AND YOUR DOOR ENTRY CONTROLLER.
PA PA PA PA PANTS POCKET.
EXCELLENT.
UK.
YES. THAT'S ME FREEZING YOUR VOCAL CORDS. STAY PUT NOW.

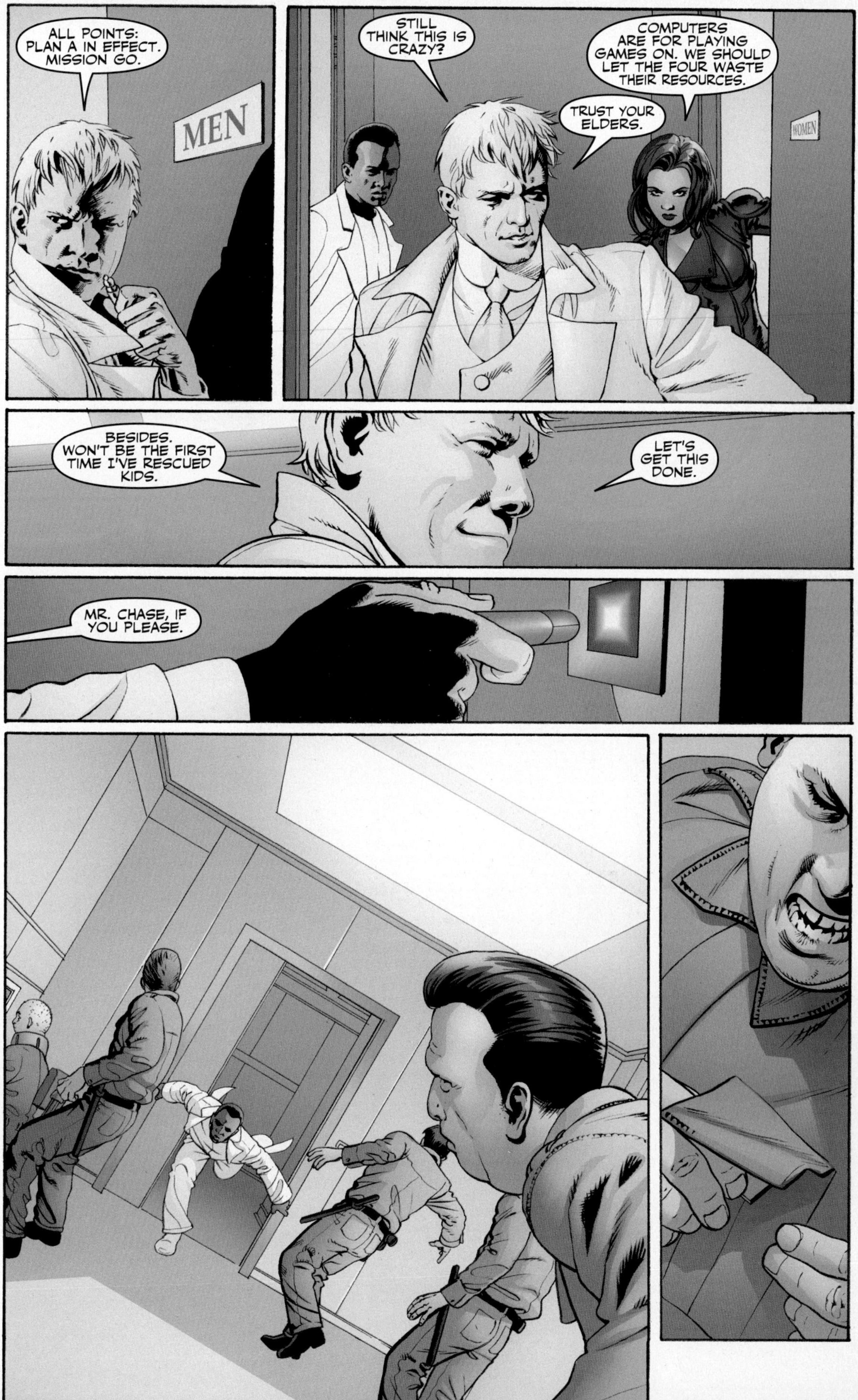
ALL POINTS: PLAN A IN EFFECT. MISSION GO.
MEN
STILL THINK THIS IS CRAZY?
COMPUTERS ARE FOR PLAYING GAMES ON. WE SHOULD LET THE FOUR WASTE THEIR RESOURCES.
TRUST YOUR ELDERS.
WOMEN
BESIDES. WON'T BE THE FIRST TIME I'VE RESCUED KIDS.
LET'S GET THIS DONE.
MR. CHASE, IF YOU PLEASE.

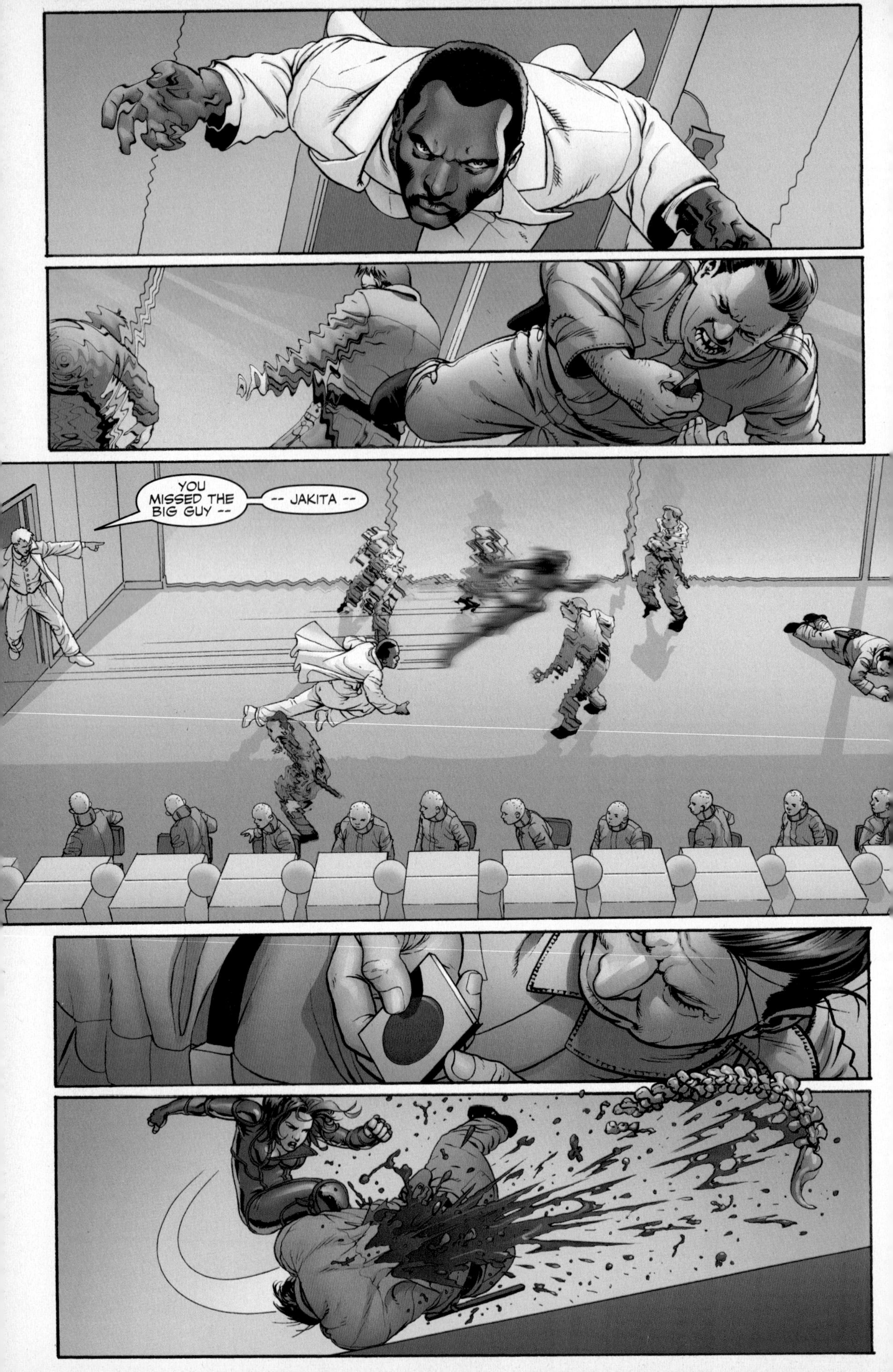
YOU MISSED THE BIG GUY --
-- JAKITA --

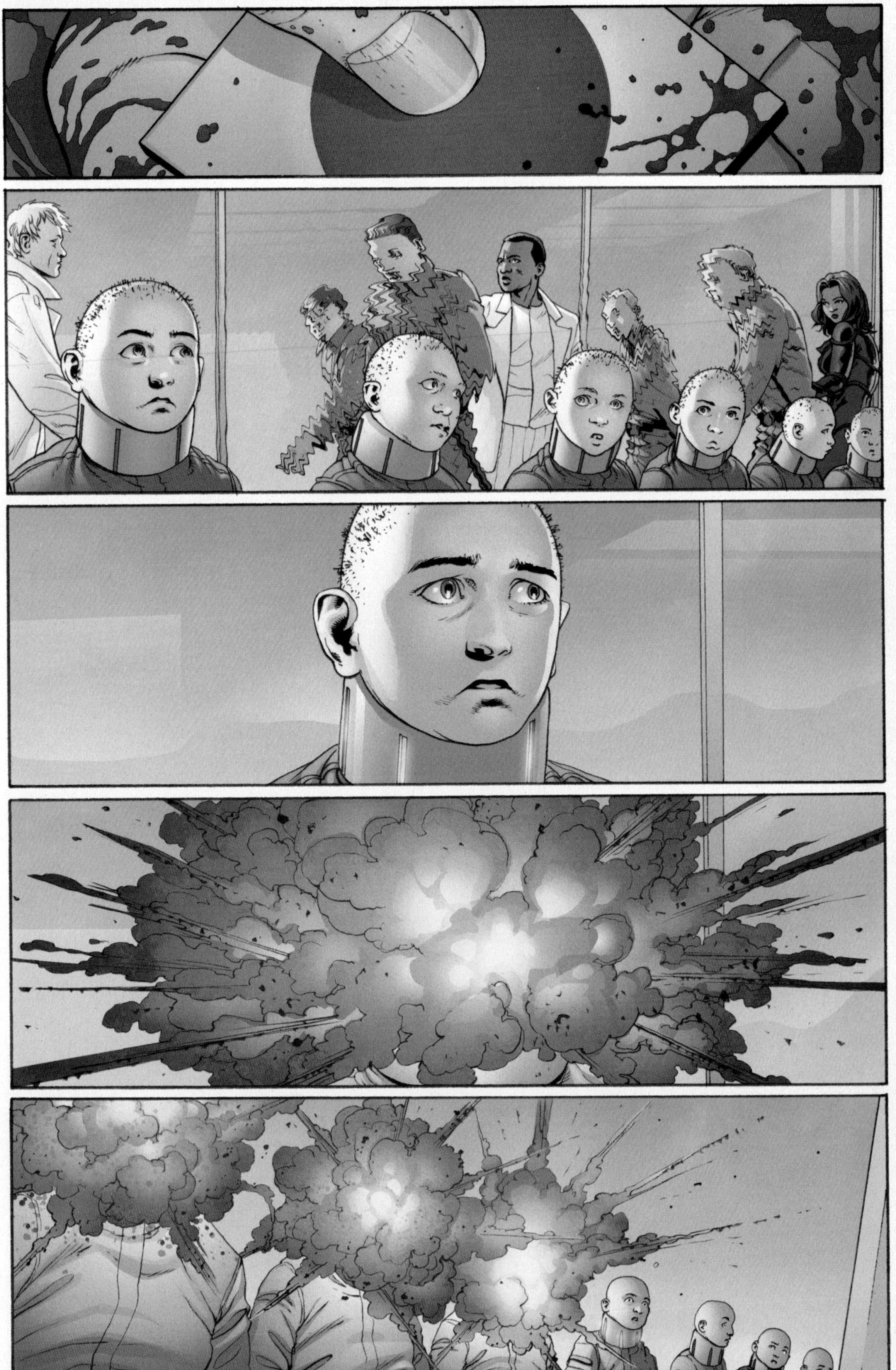

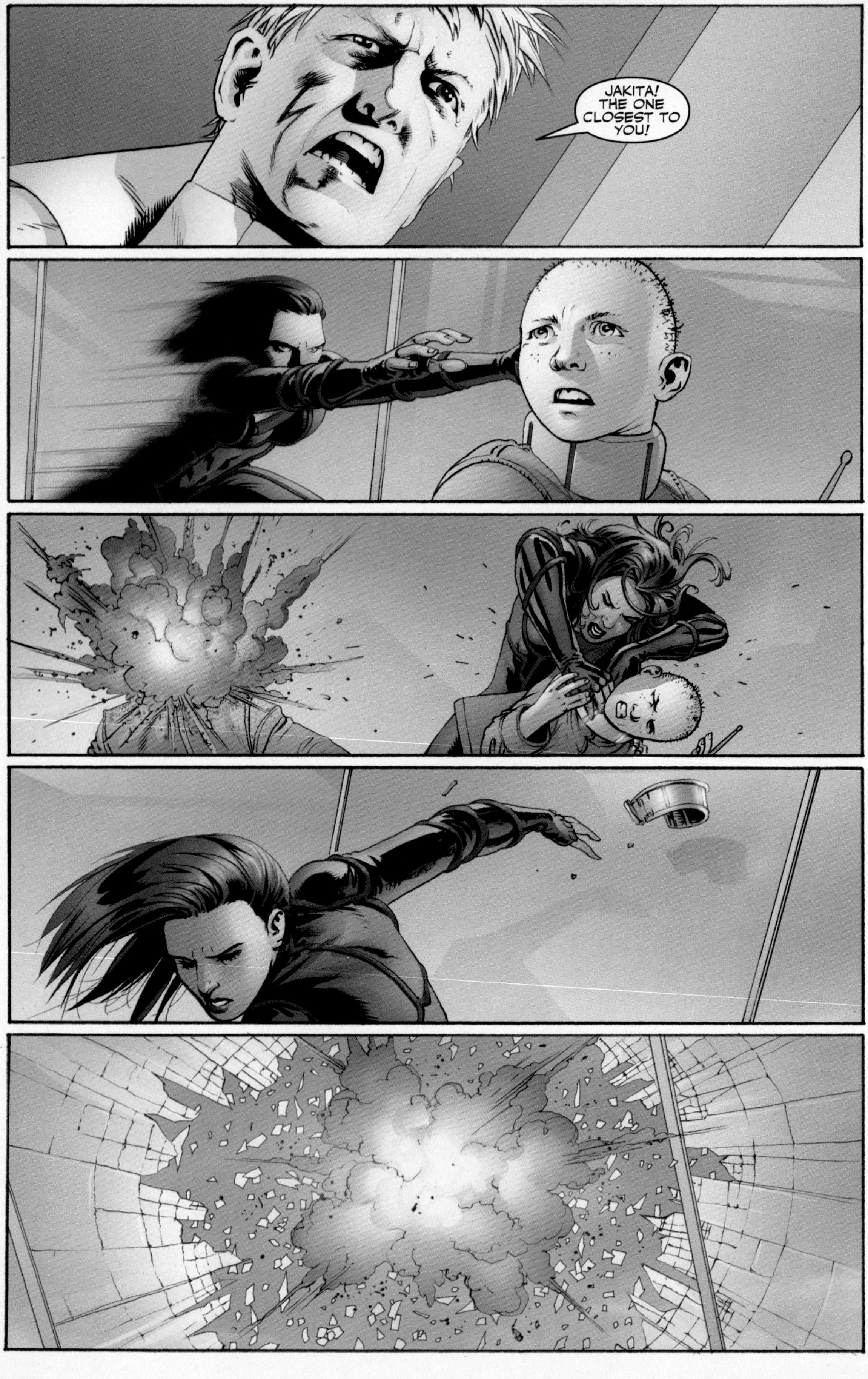
JAKITA! THE ONE CLOSEST TO YOU!

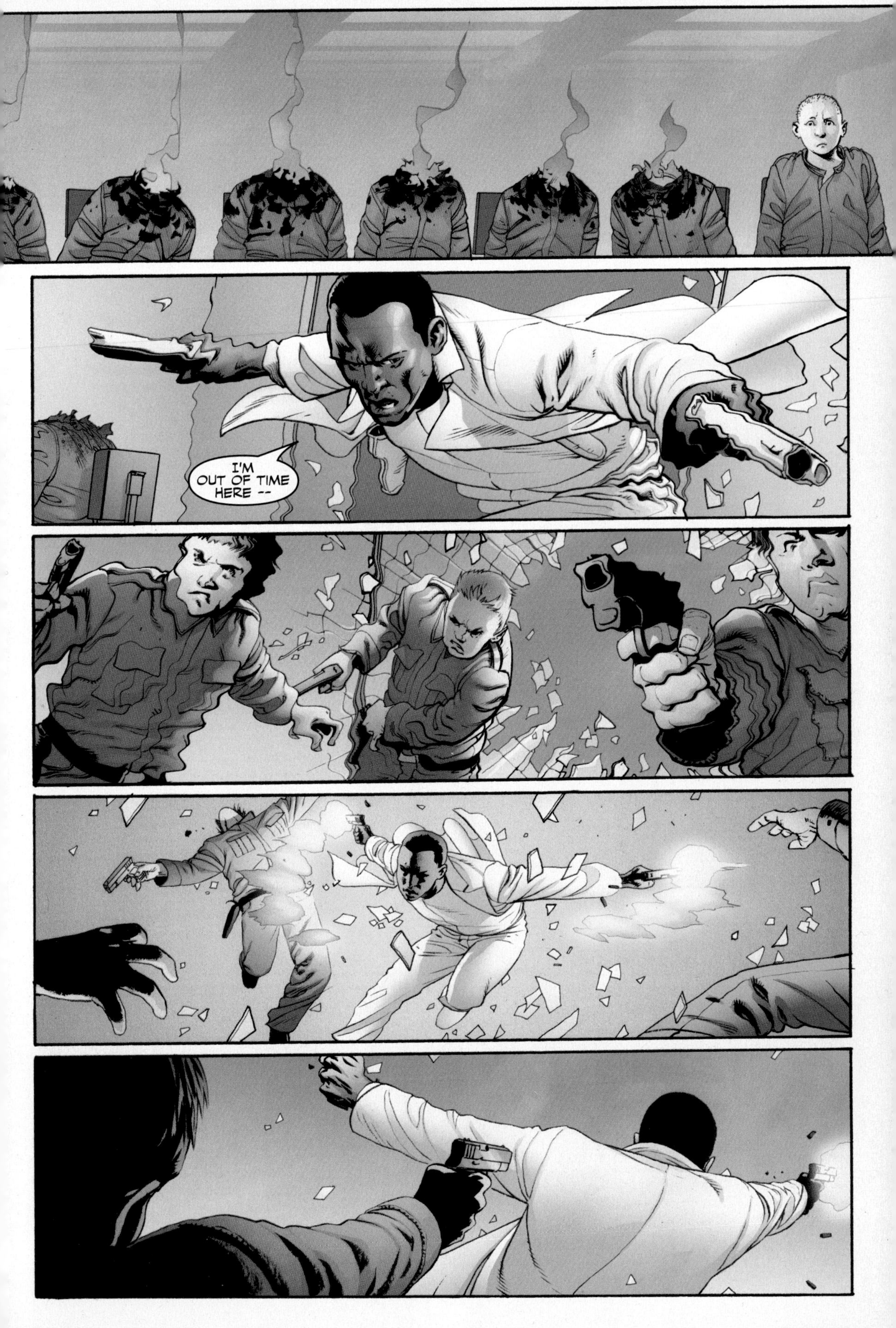
I'M OUT OF TIME HERE --

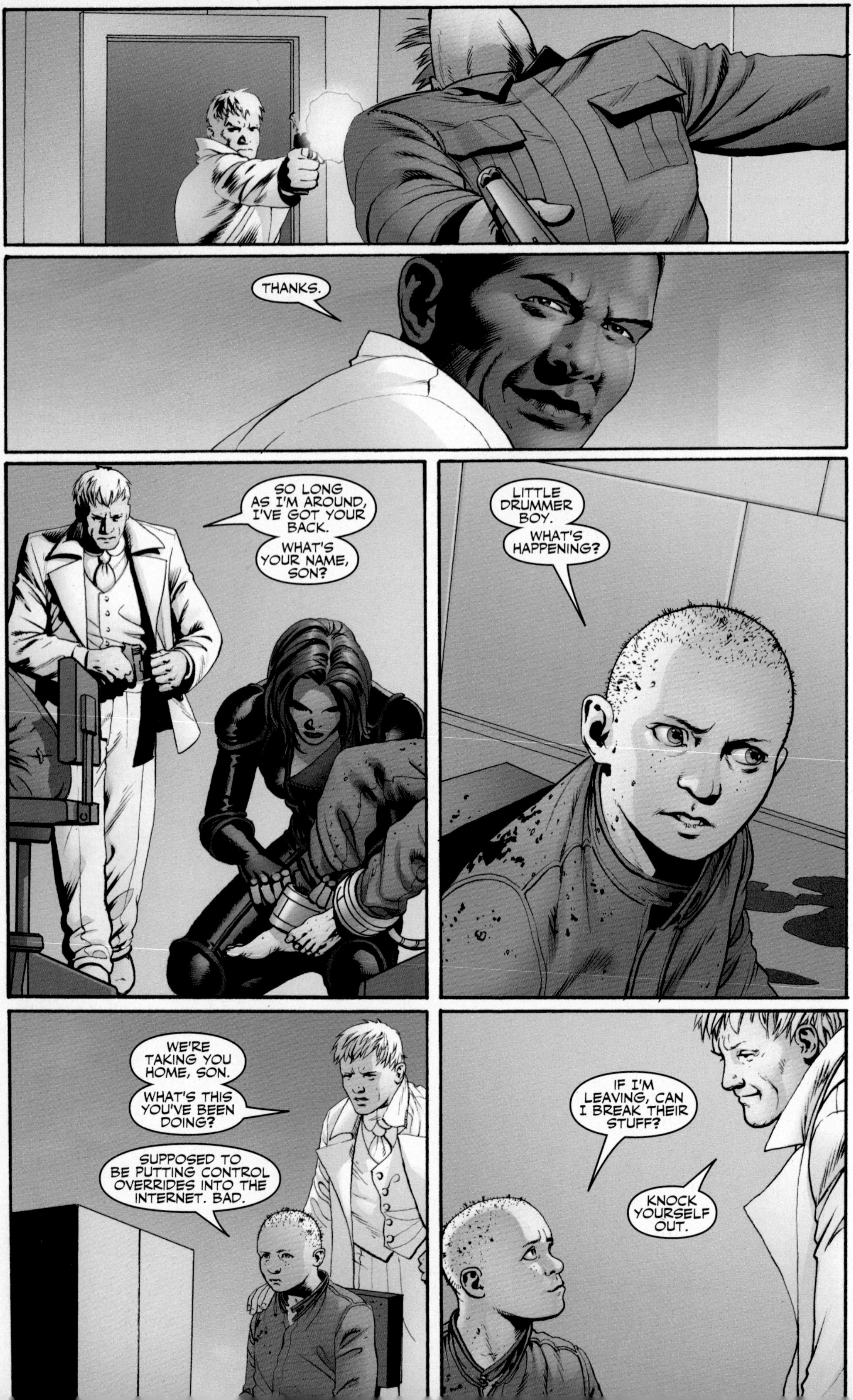
THANKS.
SO LONG AS I'M AROUND, I'VE GOT YOUR BACK.
WHAT'S YOUR NAME, SON?
LITTLE DRUMMER BOY.
WHAT'S HAPPENING?
WE'RE TAKING YOU HOME, SON.
WHAT'S THIS YOU'VE BEEN DOING?
SUPPOSED TO BE PUTTING CONTROL OVERRIDES INTO THE INTERNET. BAD.
IF I'M LEAVING, CAN I BREAK THEIR STUFF?
KNOCK YOURSELF OUT.

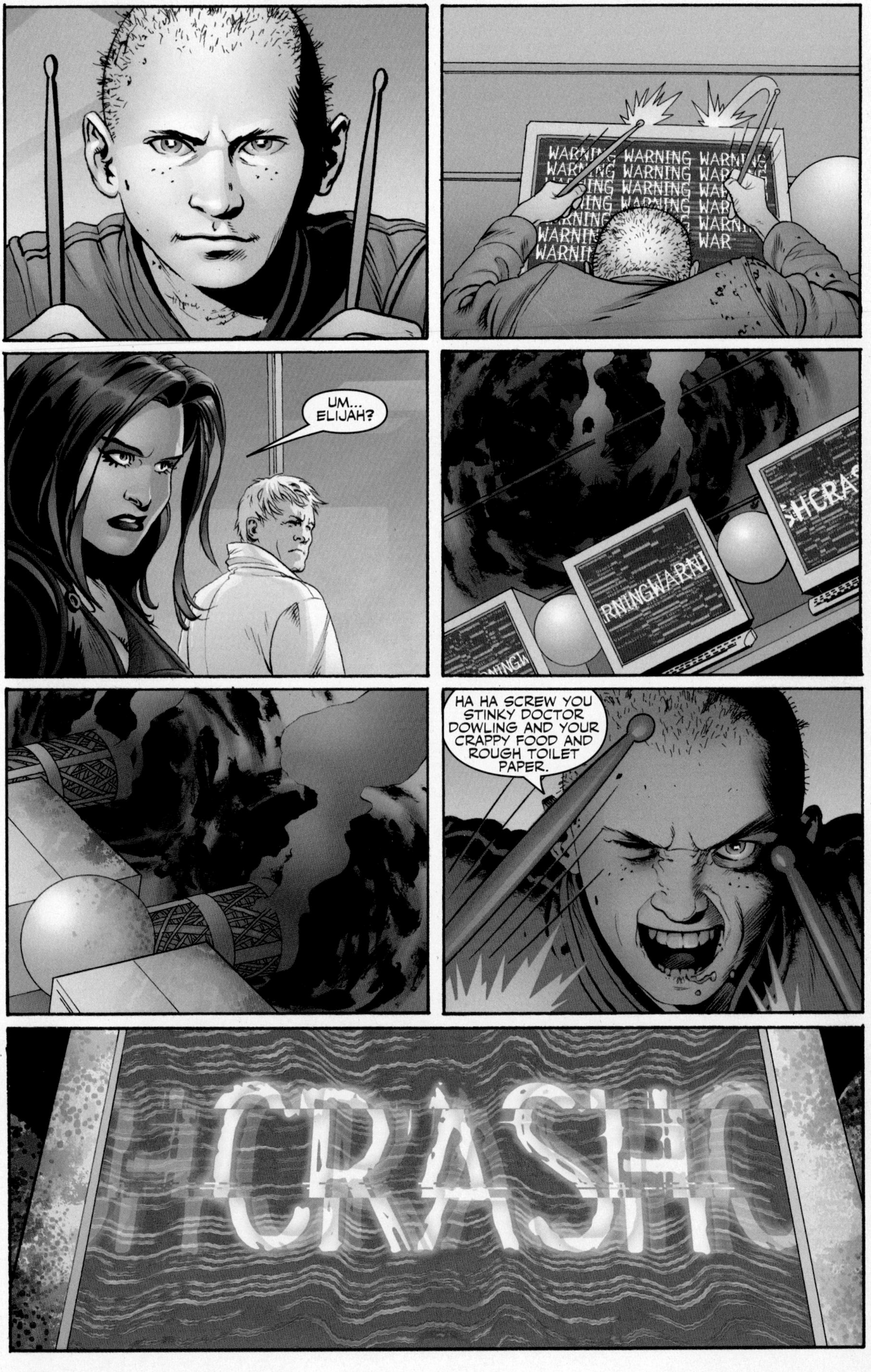
WARNING WARNING WARNING
UM... ELIJAH?
RNINGWARNI
HCRAS
HA HA SCREW YOU STINKY DOCTOR DOWLING AND YOUR CRAPPY FOOD AND ROUGH TOILET PAPER.
CRASH

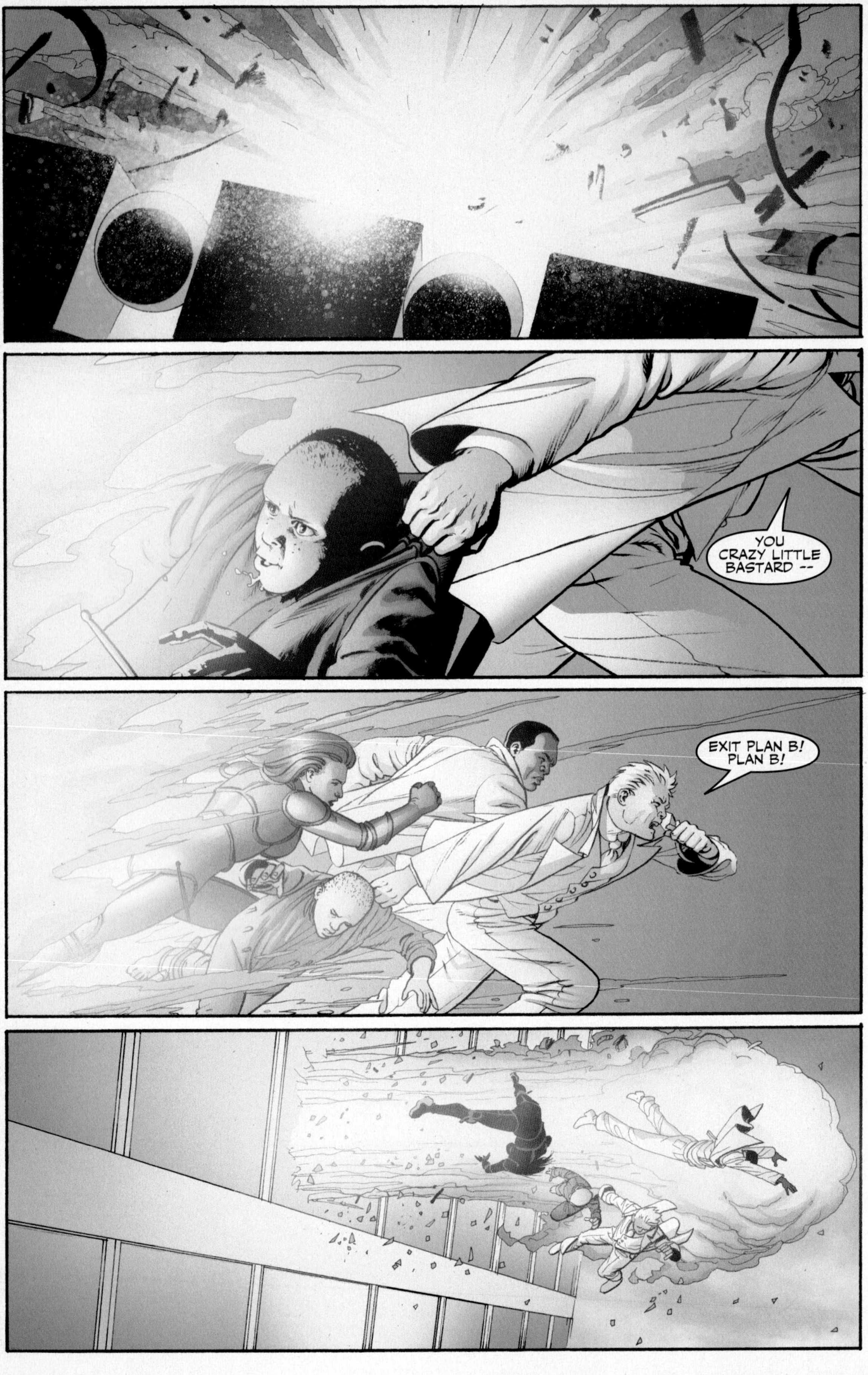
YOU CRAZY LITTLE BASTARD --
EXIT PLAN B! PLAN B!

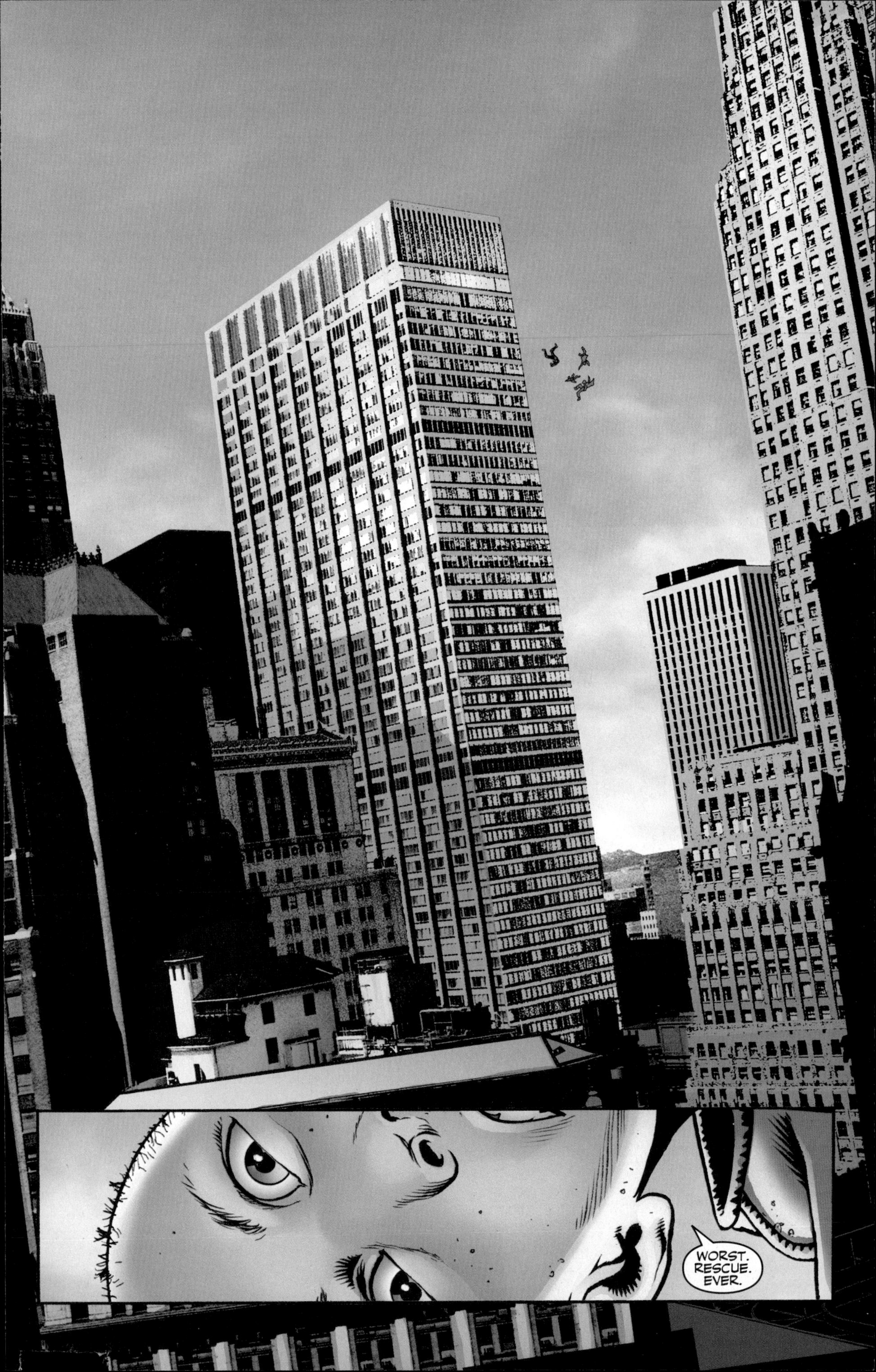
WORST. RESCUE. EVER.

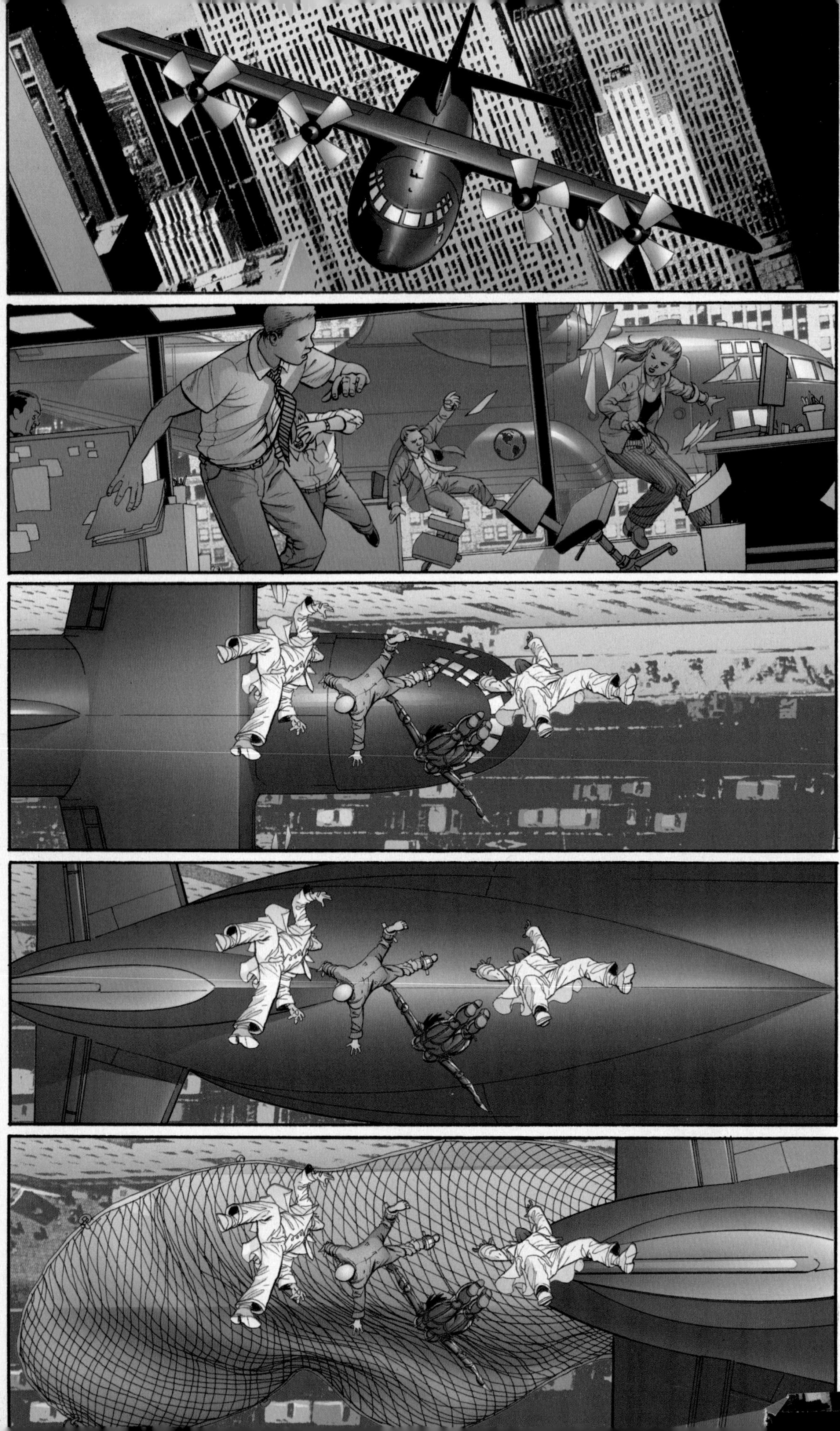

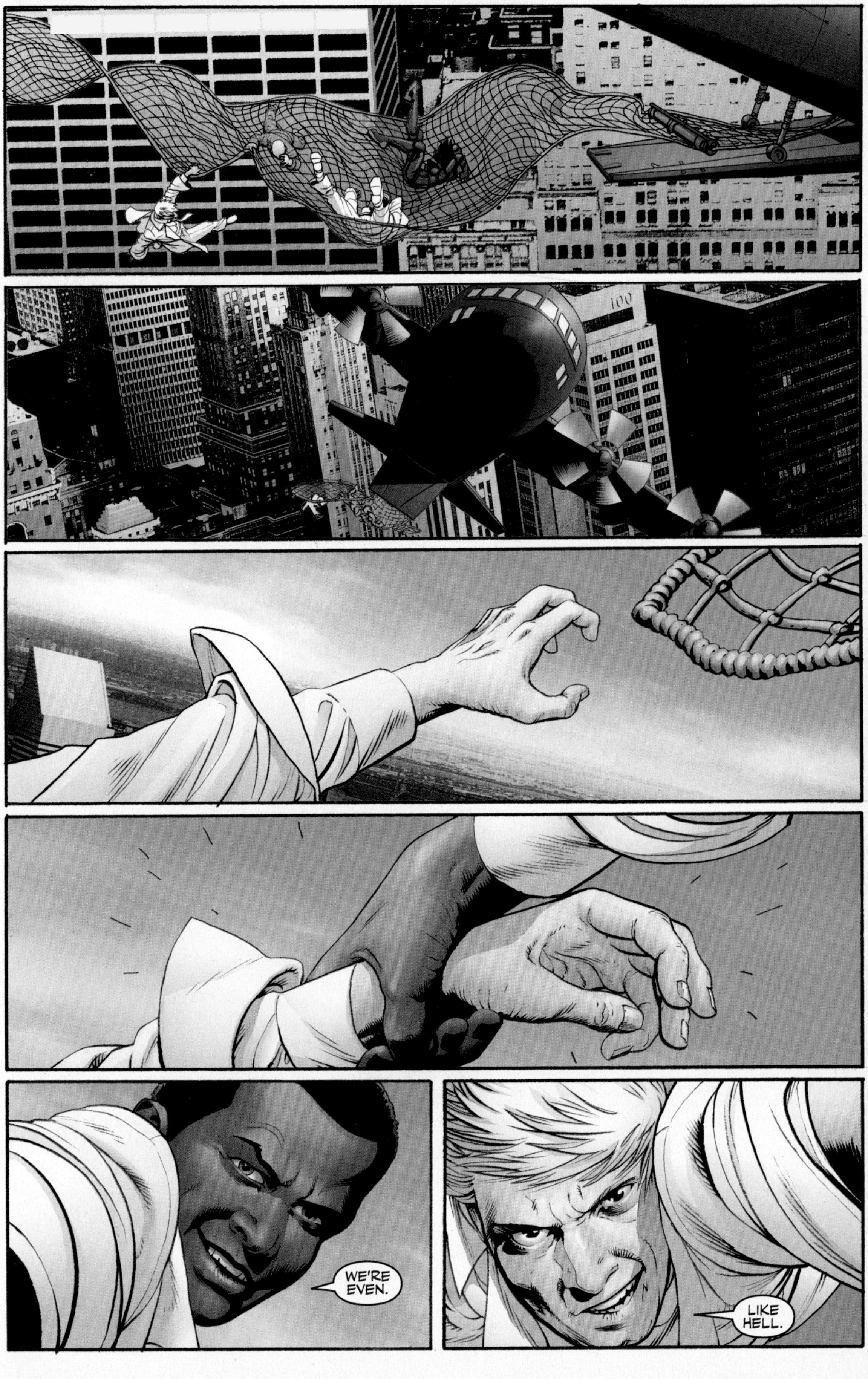
WE'RE EVEN.
LIKE HELL.

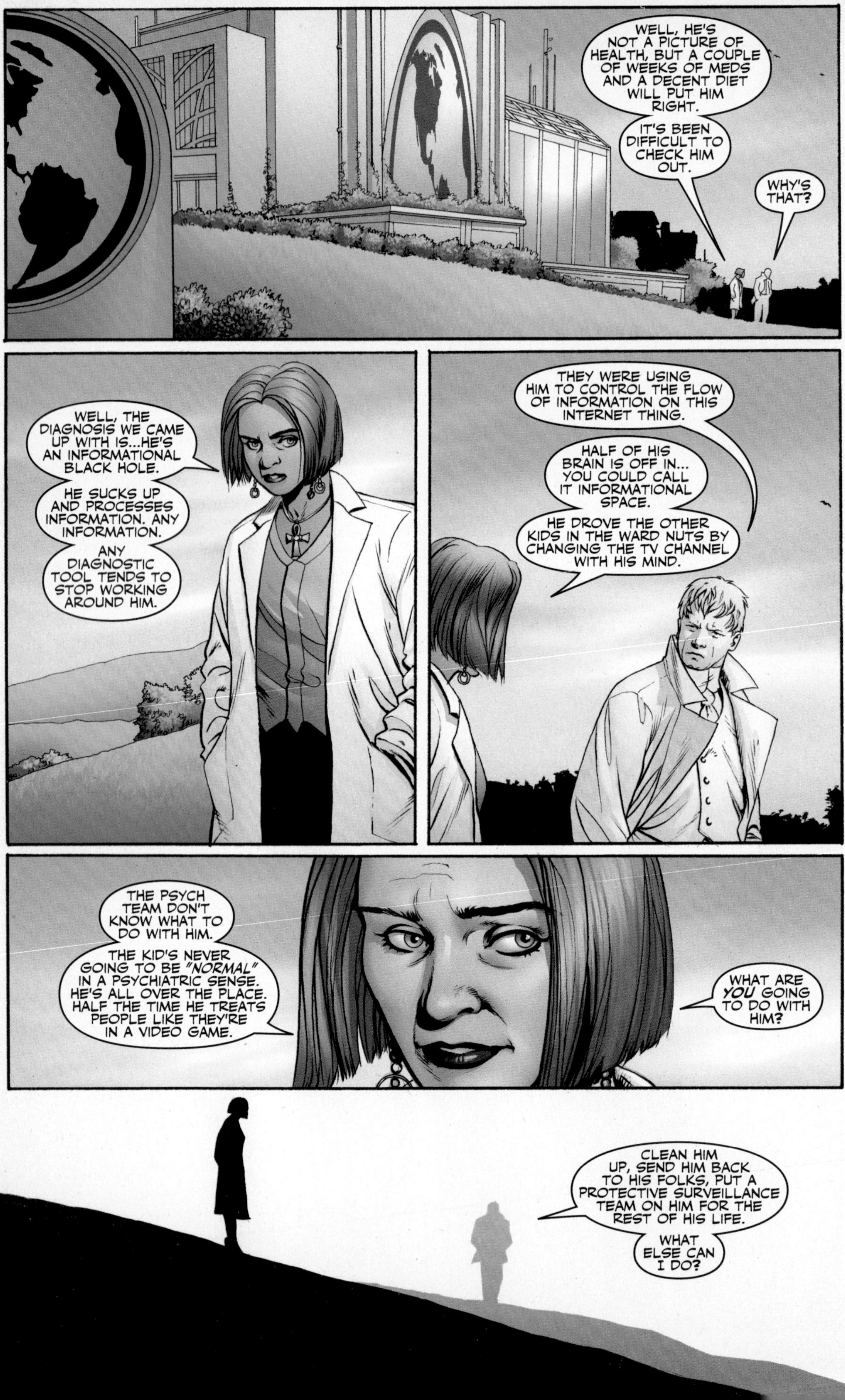
WELL, HE'S NOT A PICTURE OF HEALTH, BUT A COUPLE OF WEEKS OF MEDS AND A DECENT DIET WILL PUT HIM RIGHT.
IT'S BEEN DIFFICULT TO CHECK HIM OUT.
WHY'S THAT?
WELL, THE DIAGNOSIS WE CAME UP WITH IS...HE'S AN INFORMATIONAL BLACK HOLE.
HE SUCKS UP AND PROCESSES INFORMATION. ANY INFORMATION.
ANY DIAGNOSTIC TOOL TENDS TO STOP WORKING AROUND HIM.
THEY WERE USING HIM TO CONTROL THE FLOW OF INFORMATION ON THIS INTERNET THING.
HALF OF HIS BRAIN IS OFF IN... YOU COULD CALL IT INFORMATIONAL SPACE.
HE DROVE THE OTHER KIDS IN THE WARD NUTS BY CHANGING THE TV CHANNEL WITH HIS MIND.
THE PSYCH TEAM DON'T KNOW WHAT TO DO WITH HIM.
THE KID'S NEVER GOING TO BE "NORMAL" IN A PSYCHIATRIC SENSE. HE'S ALL OVER THE PLACE. HALF THE TIME HE TREATS PEOPLE LIKE THEY'RE IN A VIDEO GAME.
WHAT ARE YOU GOING TO DO WITH HIM?
CLEAN HIM UP, SEND HIM BACK TO HIS FOLKS, PUT A PROTECTIVE SURVEILLANCE TEAM ON HIM FOR THE REST OF HIS LIFE.
WHAT ELSE CAN I DO?

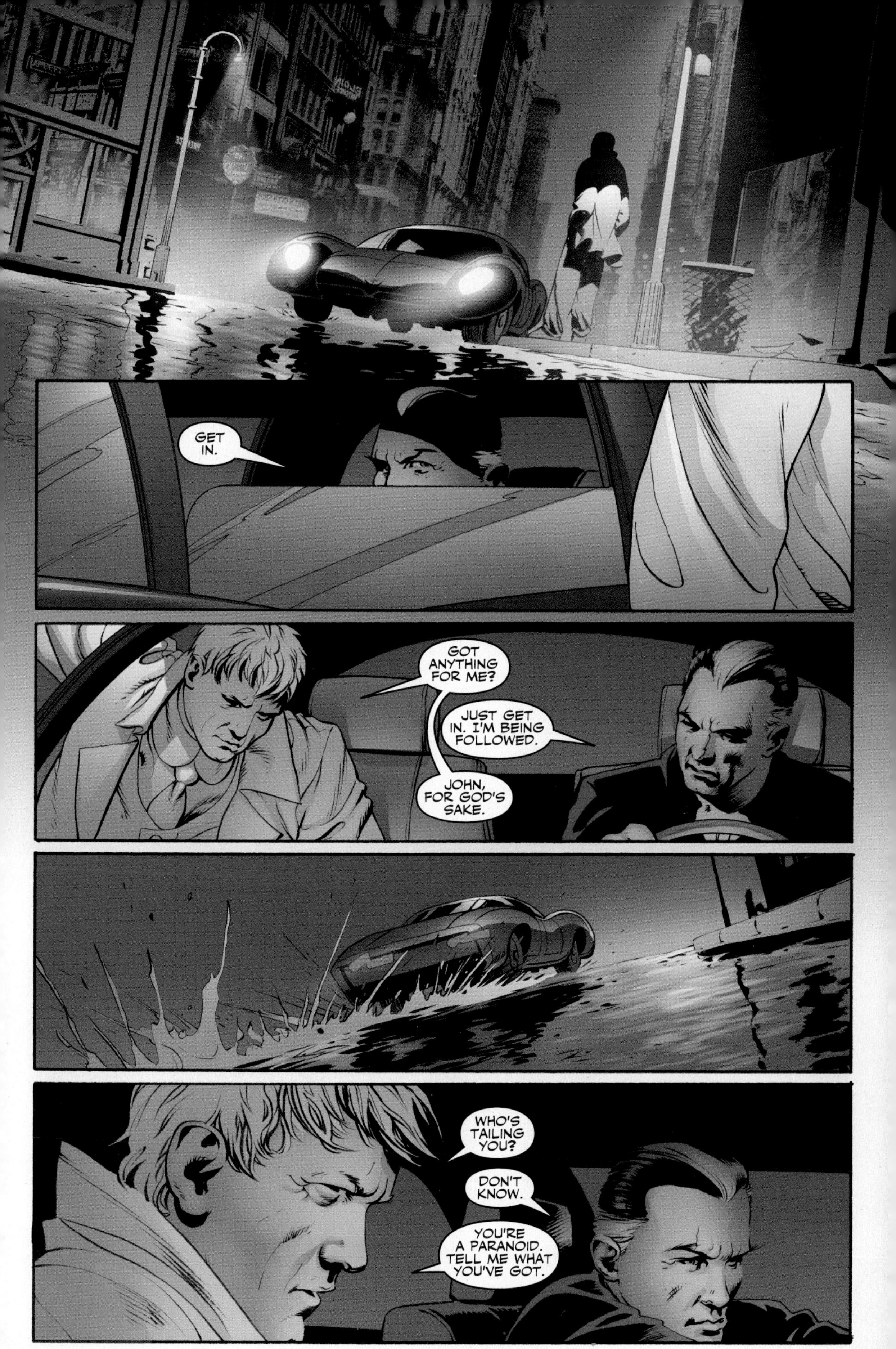
GET IN.
GOT ANYTHING FOR ME?
JUST GET IN. I'M BEING FOLLOWED.
JOHN, FOR GOD'S SAKE.
WHO'S TAILING YOU?
DON'T KNOW.
YOU'RE A PARANOID. TELL ME WHAT YOU'VE GOT.

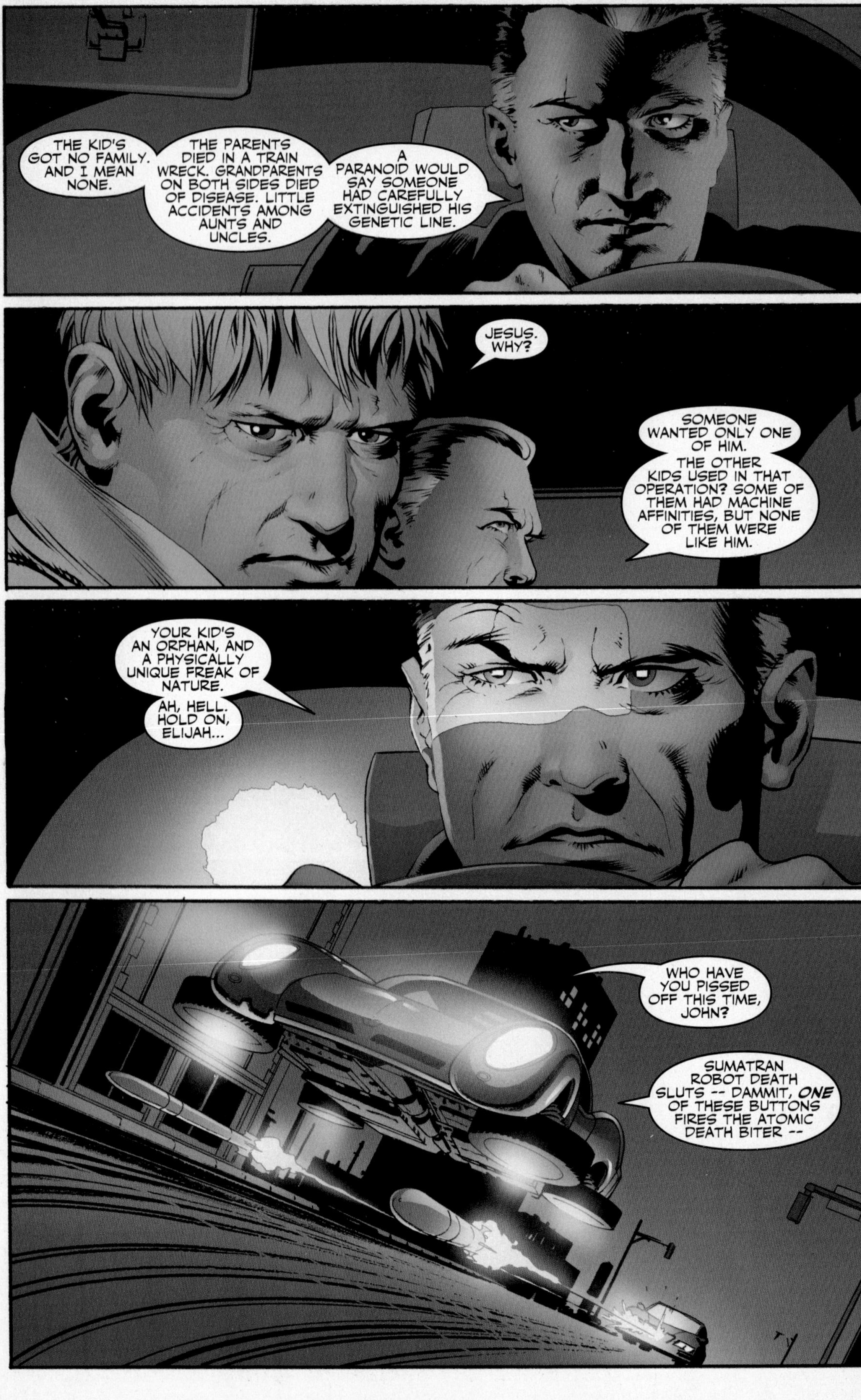
THE KID'S GOT NO FAMILY. AND I MEAN NONE.
THE PARENTS DIED IN A TRAIN WRECK. GRANDPARENTS ON BOTH SIDES DIED OF DISEASE. LITTLE ACCIDENTS AMONG AUNTS AND UNCLES.
A PARANOID WOULD SAY SOMEONE HAD CAREFULLY EXTINGUISHED HIS GENETIC LINE.
JESUS. WHY?
SOMEONE WANTED ONLY ONE OF HIM.
THE OTHER KIDS USED IN THAT OPERATION? SOME OF THEM HAD MACHINE AFFINITIES, BUT NONE OF THEM WERE LIKE HIM.
YOUR KID'S AN ORPHAN, AND A PHYSICALLY UNIQUE FREAK OF NATURE.
AH, HELL. HOLD ON, ELIJAH...
WHO HAVE YOU PISSED OFF THIS TIME, JOHN?
SUMATRAN ROBOT DEATH SLUTS -- DAMMIT, *ONE* OF THESE BUTTONS FIRES THE ATOMIC DEATH BITER --

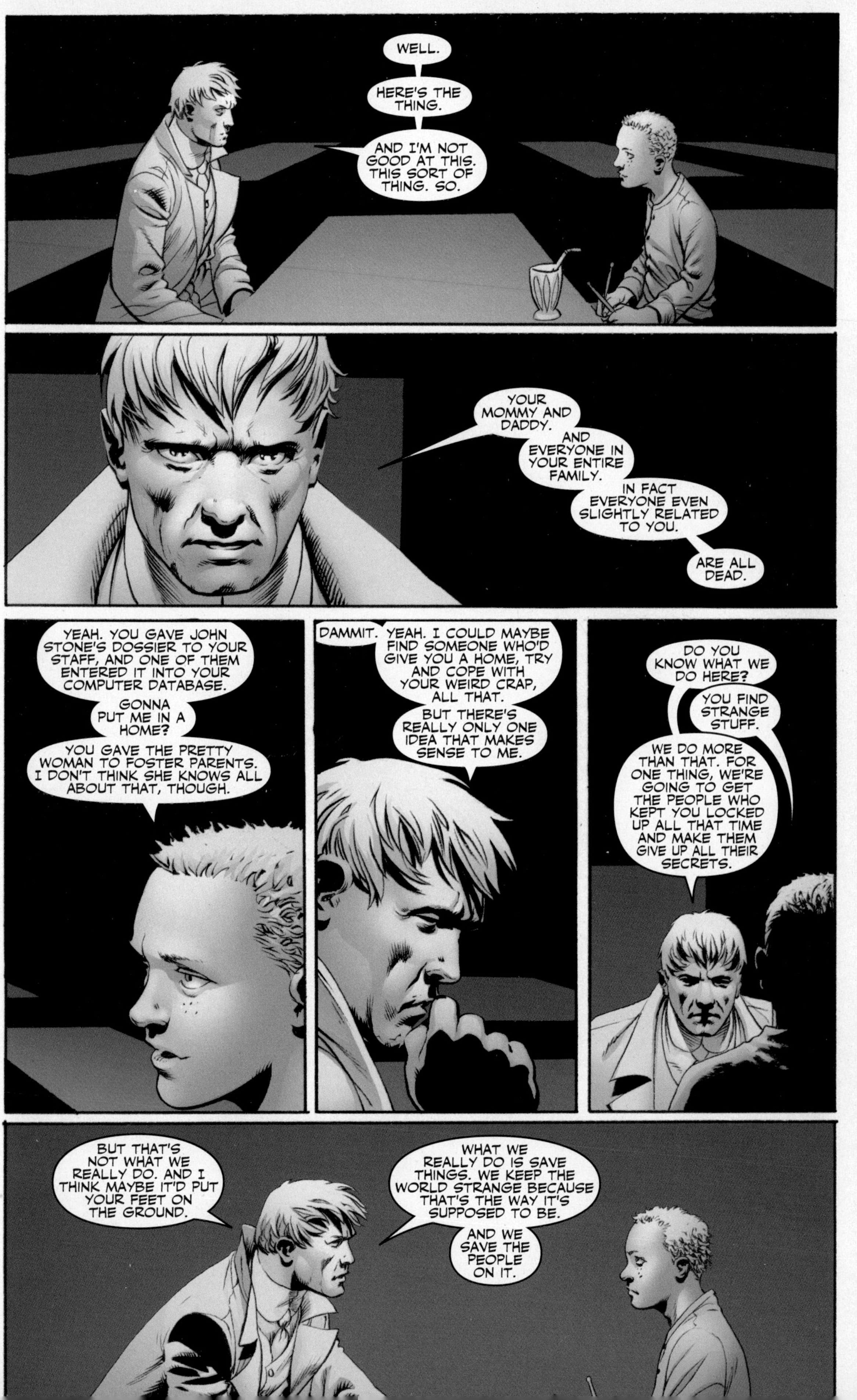
WELL.
HERE'S THE THING.
AND I'M NOT GOOD AT THIS. THIS SORT OF THING. SO.
YOUR MOMMY AND DADDY.
AND EVERYONE IN YOUR ENTIRE FAMILY.
IN FACT EVERYONE EVEN SLIGHTLY RELATED TO YOU.
ARE ALL DEAD.
YEAH. YOU GAVE JOHN STONE'S DOSSIER TO YOUR STAFF, AND ONE OF THEM ENTERED IT INTO YOUR COMPUTER DATABASE.
GONNA PUT ME IN A HOME?
YOU GAVE THE PRETTY WOMAN TO FOSTER PARENTS. I DON'T THINK SHE KNOWS ALL ABOUT THAT, THOUGH.
DAMMIT.
YEAH. I COULD MAYBE FIND SOMEONE WHO'D GIVE YOU A HOME, TRY AND COPE WITH YOUR WEIRD CRAP, ALL THAT.
BUT THERE'S REALLY ONLY ONE IDEA THAT MAKES SENSE TO ME.
DO YOU KNOW WHAT WE DO HERE?
YOU FIND STRANGE STUFF.
WE DO MORE THAN THAT. FOR ONE THING, WE'RE GOING TO GET THE PEOPLE WHO KEPT YOU LOCKED UP ALL THAT TIME AND MAKE THEM GIVE UP ALL THEIR SECRETS.
BUT THAT'S NOT WHAT WE REALLY DO. AND I THINK MAYBE IT'D PUT YOUR FEET ON THE GROUND.
WHAT WE REALLY DO IS SAVE THINGS. WE KEEP THE WORLD STRANGE BECAUSE THAT'S THE WAY IT'S SUPPOSED TO BE.
AND WE SAVE THE PEOPLE ON IT.

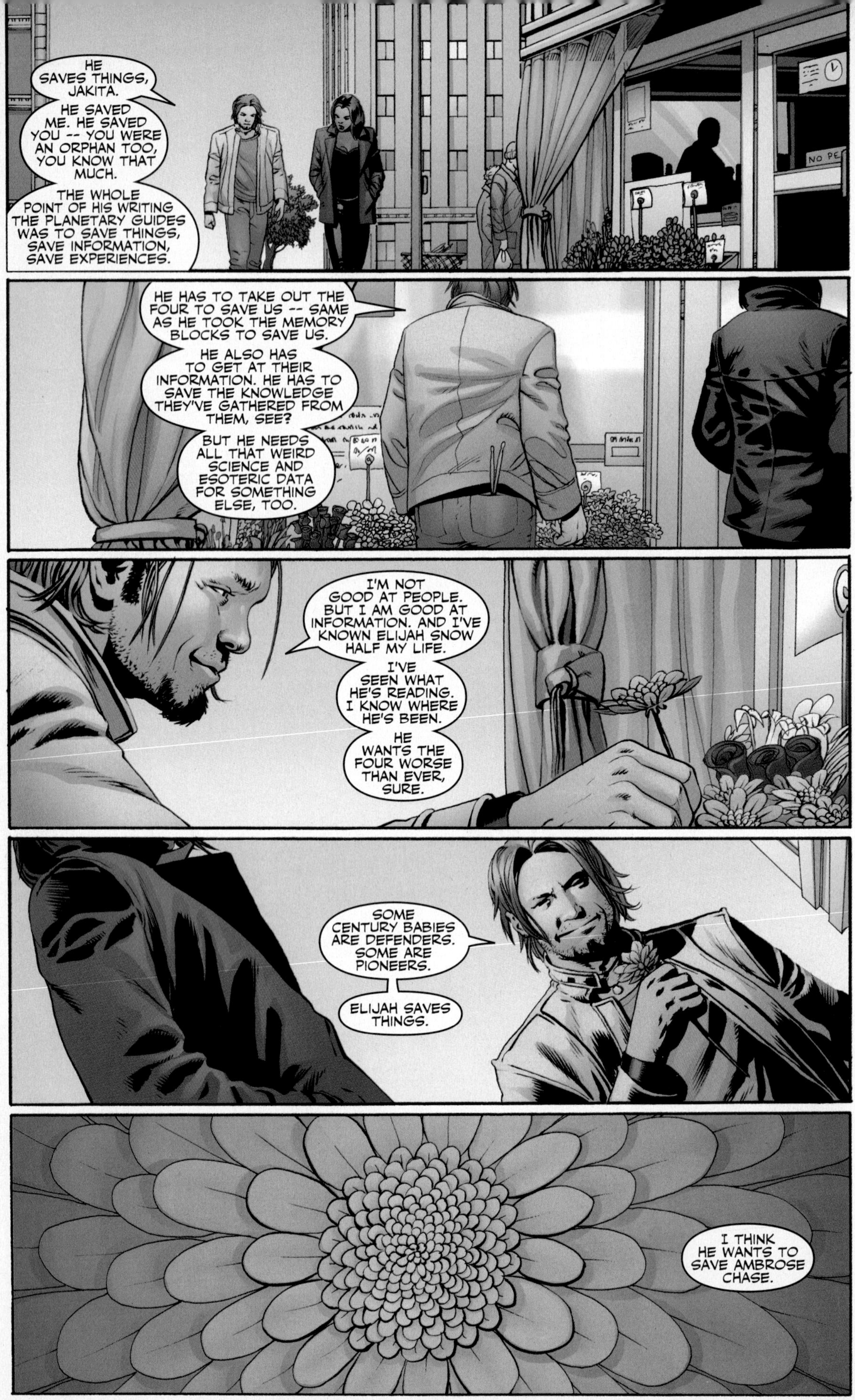
HE SAVES THINGS, JAKITA.
HE SAVED ME. HE SAVED YOU -- YOU WERE AN ORPHAN TOO, YOU KNOW THAT MUCH.
THE WHOLE POINT OF HIS WRITING THE PLANETARY GUIDES WAS TO SAVE THINGS, SAVE INFORMATION, SAVE EXPERIENCES.
HE HAS TO TAKE OUT THE FOUR TO SAVE US -- SAME AS HE TOOK THE MEMORY BLOCKS TO SAVE US.
HE ALSO HAS TO GET AT THEIR INFORMATION. HE HAS TO SAVE THE KNOWLEDGE THEY'VE GATHERED FROM THEM, SEE?
BUT HE NEEDS ALL THAT WEIRD SCIENCE AND ESOTERIC DATA FOR SOMETHING ELSE, TOO.
I'M NOT GOOD AT PEOPLE. BUT I AM GOOD AT INFORMATION. AND I'VE KNOWN ELIJAH SNOW HALF MY LIFE.
I'VE SEEN WHAT HE'S READING. I KNOW WHERE HE'S BEEN.
HE WANTS THE FOUR WORSE THAN EVER, SURE.
SOME CENTURY BABIES ARE DEFENDERS. SOME ARE PIONEERS.
ELIJAH SAVES THINGS.
I THINK HE WANTS TO SAVE AMBROSE CHASE.

PLANETARY

GUIDE
NUMBER 24

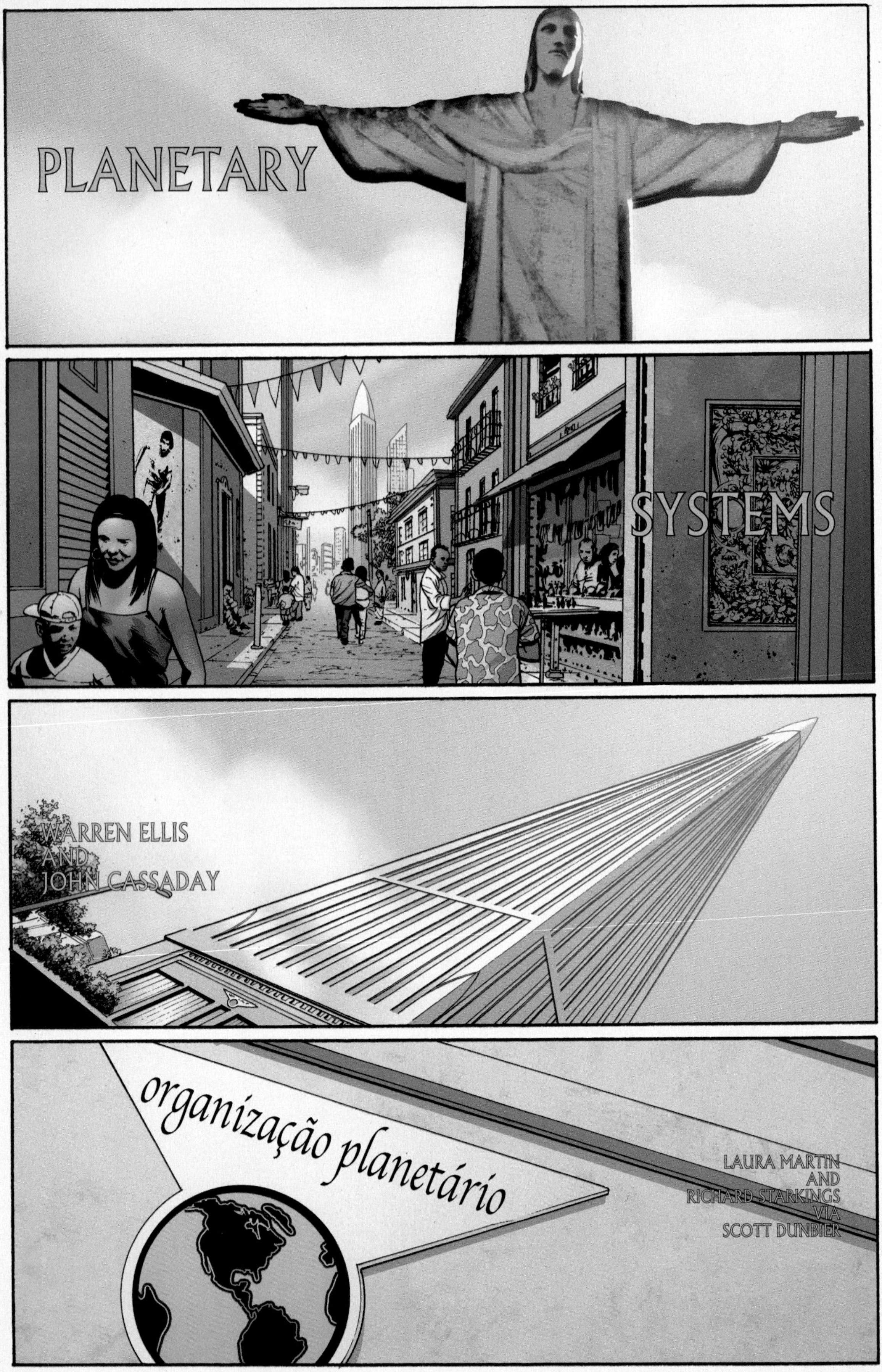
PLANETARY
SYSTEMS
WARREN ELLIS
AND
JOHN CASSADAY
organização planetário
LAURA MARTIN
AND
RICHARD STARKINGS
VIA
SCOTT DUNBIER

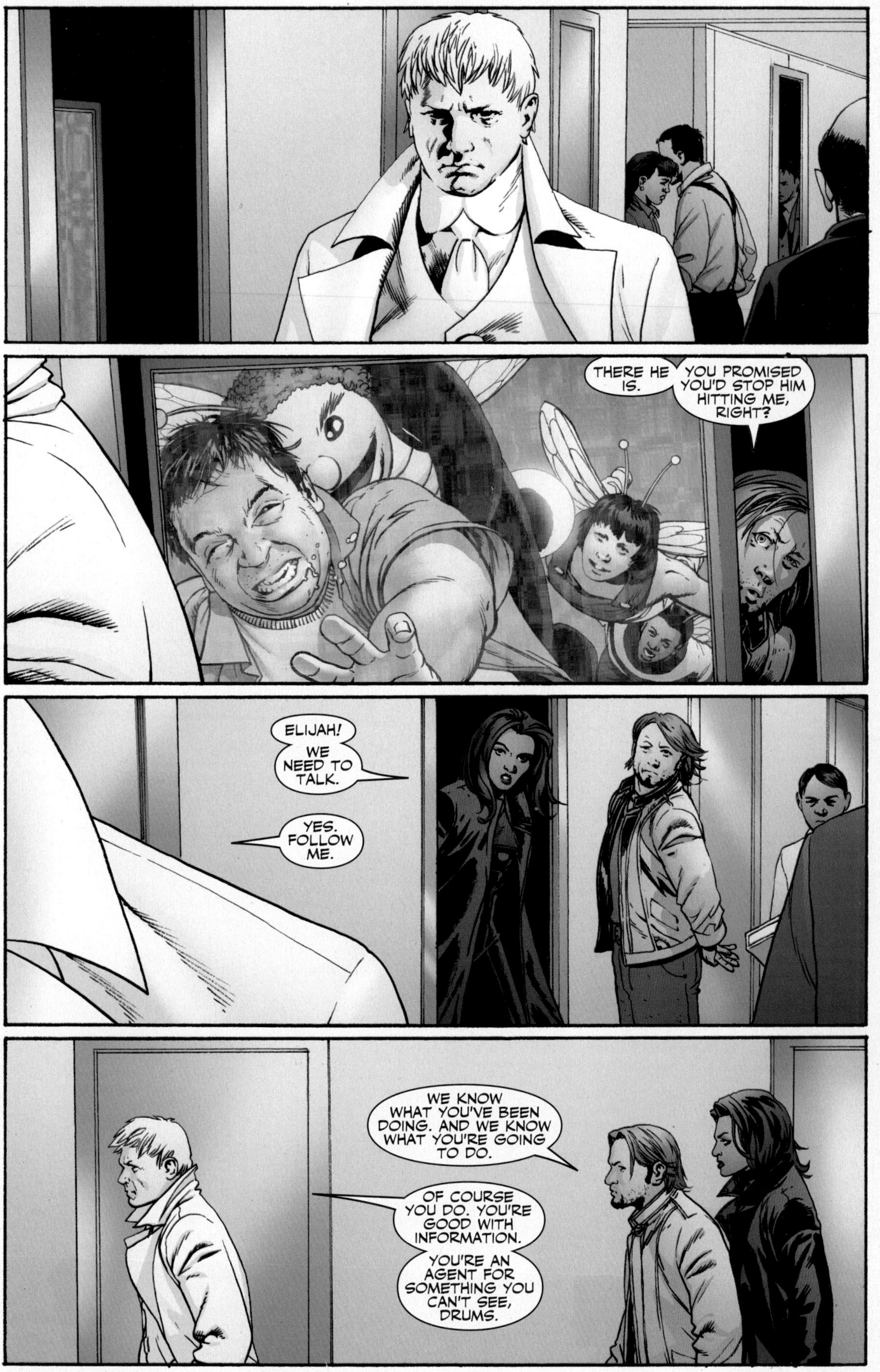
THERE HE IS.
YOU PROMISED YOU'D STOP HIM HITTING ME, RIGHT?
ELIJAH! WE NEED TO TALK.
YES. FOLLOW ME.
WE KNOW WHAT YOU'VE BEEN DOING. AND WE KNOW WHAT YOU'RE GOING TO DO.
OF COURSE YOU DO. YOU'RE GOOD WITH INFORMATION.
YOU'RE AN AGENT FOR SOMETHING YOU CAN'T SEE, DRUMS.

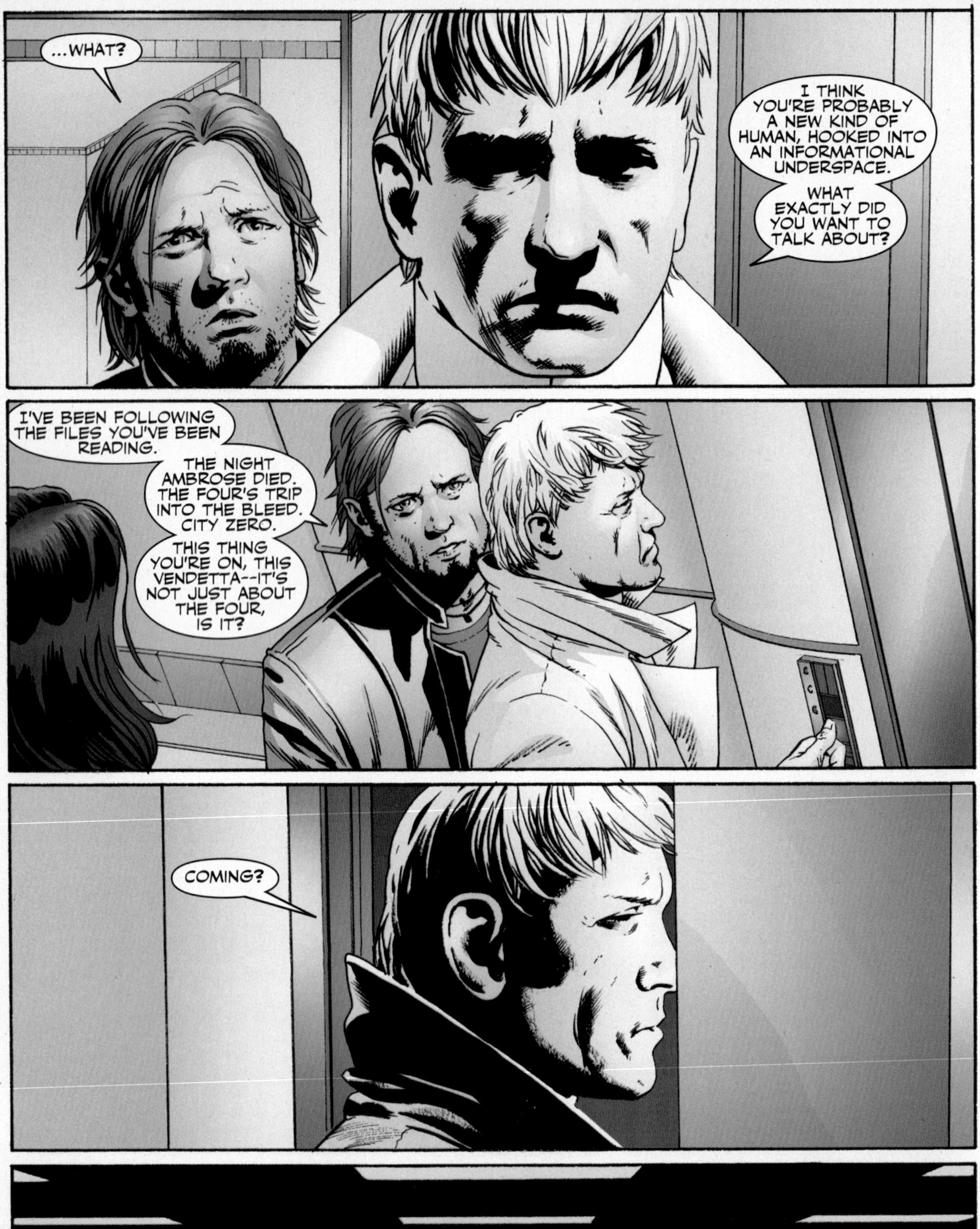
...WHAT?
I THINK YOU'RE PROBABLY A NEW KIND OF HUMAN, HOOKED INTO AN INFORMATIONAL UNDERSPACE.
WHAT EXACTLY DID YOU WANT TO TALK ABOUT?
I'VE BEEN FOLLOWING THE FILES YOU'VE BEEN READING.
THE NIGHT AMBROSE DIED. THE FOUR'S TRIP INTO THE BLEED. CITY ZERO.
THIS THING YOU'RE ON, THIS VENDETTA--IT'S NOT JUST ABOUT THE FOUR, IS IT?
COMING?
HAVE YOU BEEN DOWN TO THE TERMINAL LEVEL BEFORE? ABSOLUTE BASEMENT OF THE BUILDING.
ROCK BOTTOM.
WHAT HAVE YOU BEEN DOING WITH WILLIAM LEATHER?

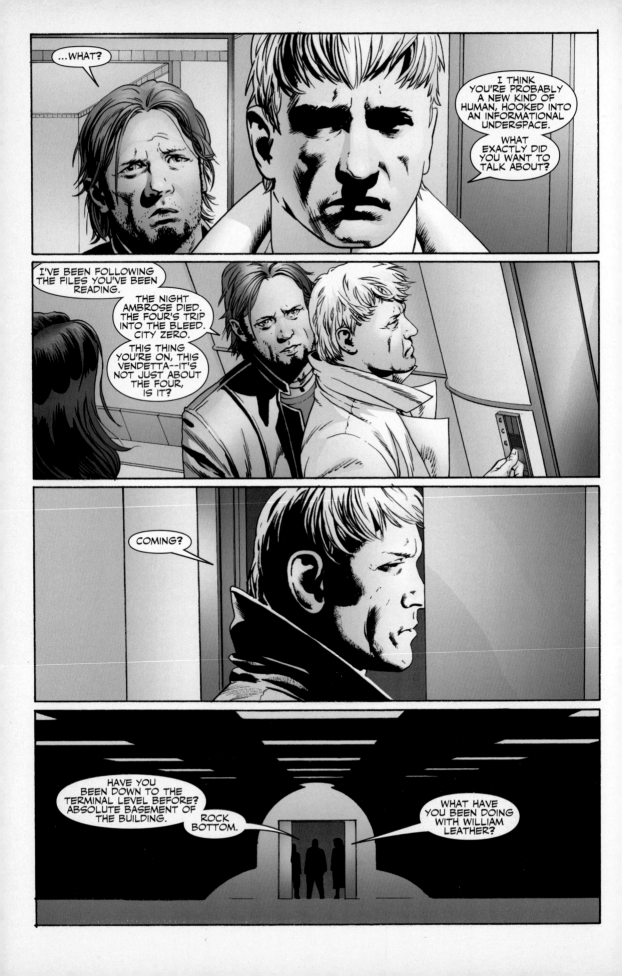

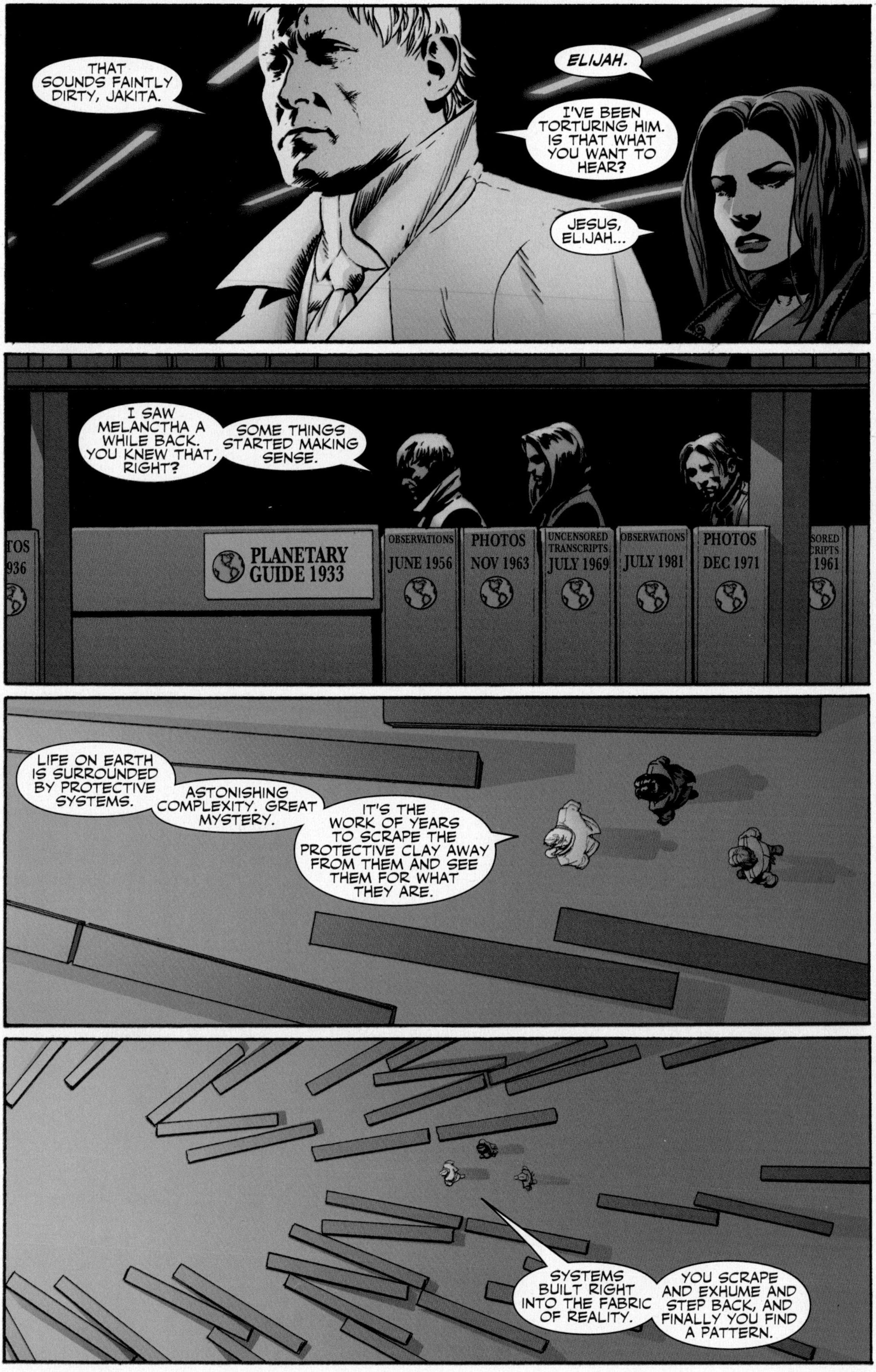
THAT SOUNDS FAINTLY DIRTY, JAKITA.
ELIJAH.
I'VE BEEN TORTURING HIM. IS THAT WHAT YOU WANT TO HEAR?
JESUS, ELIJAH...
I SAW MELANCTHA A WHILE BACK. YOU KNEW THAT, RIGHT?
SOME THINGS STARTED MAKING SENSE.
PLANETARY GUIDE 1933
OBSERVATIONS JUNE 1956
PHOTOS NOV 1963
UNCENSORED TRANSCRIPTS JULY 1969
OBSERVATIONS JULY 1981
PHOTOS DEC 1971
LIFE ON EARTH IS SURROUNDED BY PROTECTIVE SYSTEMS.
ASTONISHING COMPLEXITY. GREAT MYSTERY.
IT'S THE WORK OF YEARS TO SCRAPE THE PROTECTIVE CLAY AWAY FROM THEM AND SEE THEM FOR WHAT THEY ARE.
SYSTEMS BUILT RIGHT INTO THE FABRIC OF REALITY.
YOU SCRAPE AND EXHUME AND STEP BACK, AND FINALLY YOU FIND A PATTERN.

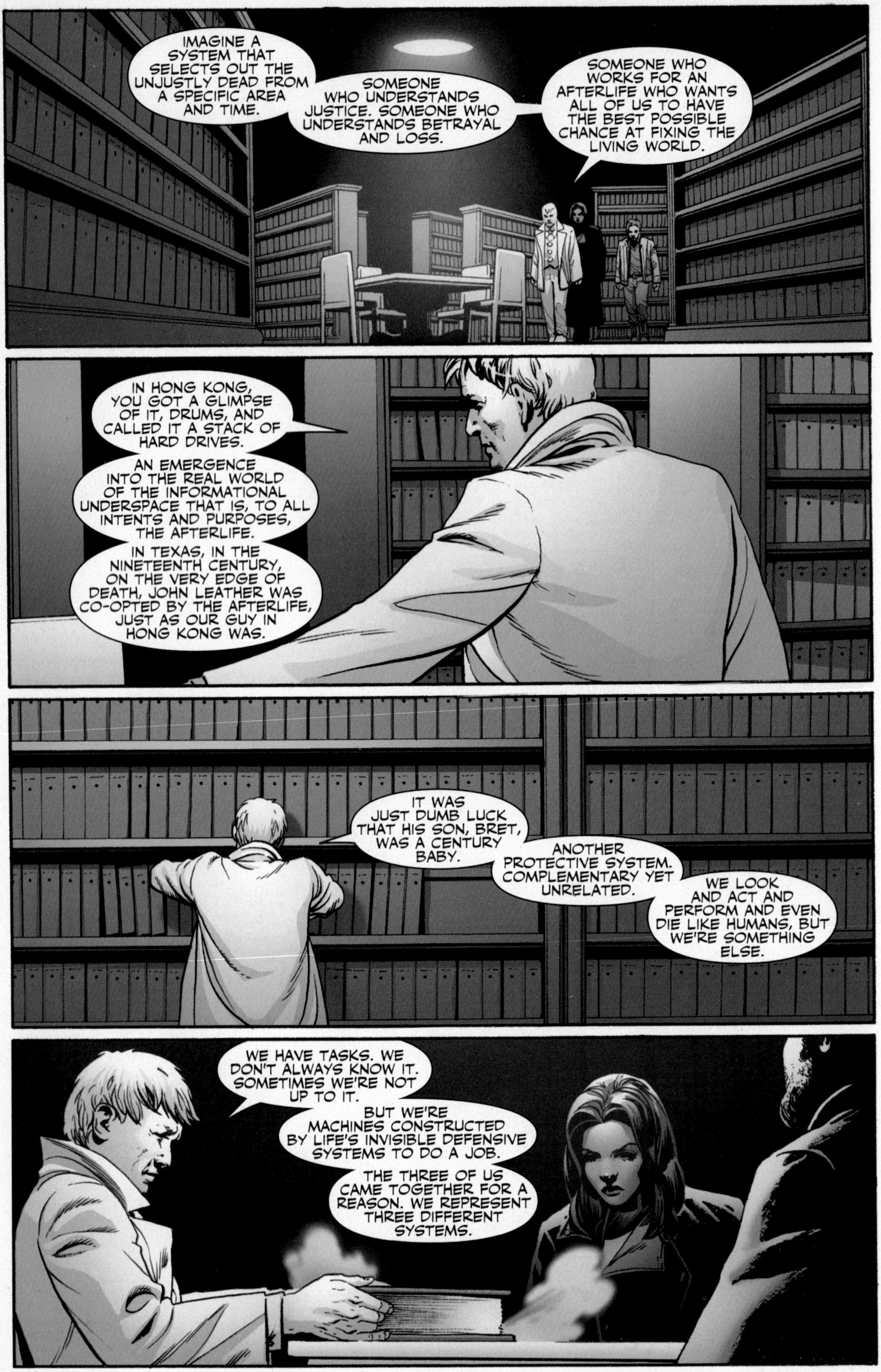
IMAGINE A SYSTEM THAT SELECTS OUT THE UNJUSTLY DEAD FROM A SPECIFIC AREA AND TIME.
SOMEONE WHO UNDERSTANDS JUSTICE. SOMEONE WHO UNDERSTANDS BETRAYAL AND LOSS.
SOMEONE WHO WORKS FOR AN AFTERLIFE WHO WANTS ALL OF US TO HAVE THE BEST POSSIBLE CHANCE AT FIXING THE LIVING WORLD.
IN HONG KONG, YOU GOT A GLIMPSE OF IT, DRUMS, AND CALLED IT A STACK OF HARD DRIVES.
AN EMERGENCE INTO THE REAL WORLD OF THE INFORMATIONAL UNDERSPACE THAT IS, TO ALL INTENTS AND PURPOSES, THE AFTERLIFE.
IN TEXAS, IN THE NINETEENTH CENTURY, ON THE VERY EDGE OF DEATH, JOHN LEATHER WAS CO-OPTED BY THE AFTERLIFE, JUST AS OUR GUY IN HONG KONG WAS.
IT WAS JUST DUMB LUCK THAT HIS SON, BRET, WAS A CENTURY BABY.
ANOTHER PROTECTIVE SYSTEM. COMPLEMENTARY YET UNRELATED.
WE LOOK AND ACT AND PERFORM AND EVEN DIE LIKE HUMANS, BUT WE'RE SOMETHING ELSE.
WE HAVE TASKS. WE DON'T ALWAYS KNOW IT. SOMETIMES WE'RE NOT UP TO IT.
BUT WE'RE MACHINES CONSTRUCTED BY LIFE'S INVISIBLE DEFENSIVE SYSTEMS TO DO A JOB.
THE THREE OF US CAME TOGETHER FOR A REASON. WE REPRESENT THREE DIFFERENT SYSTEMS.

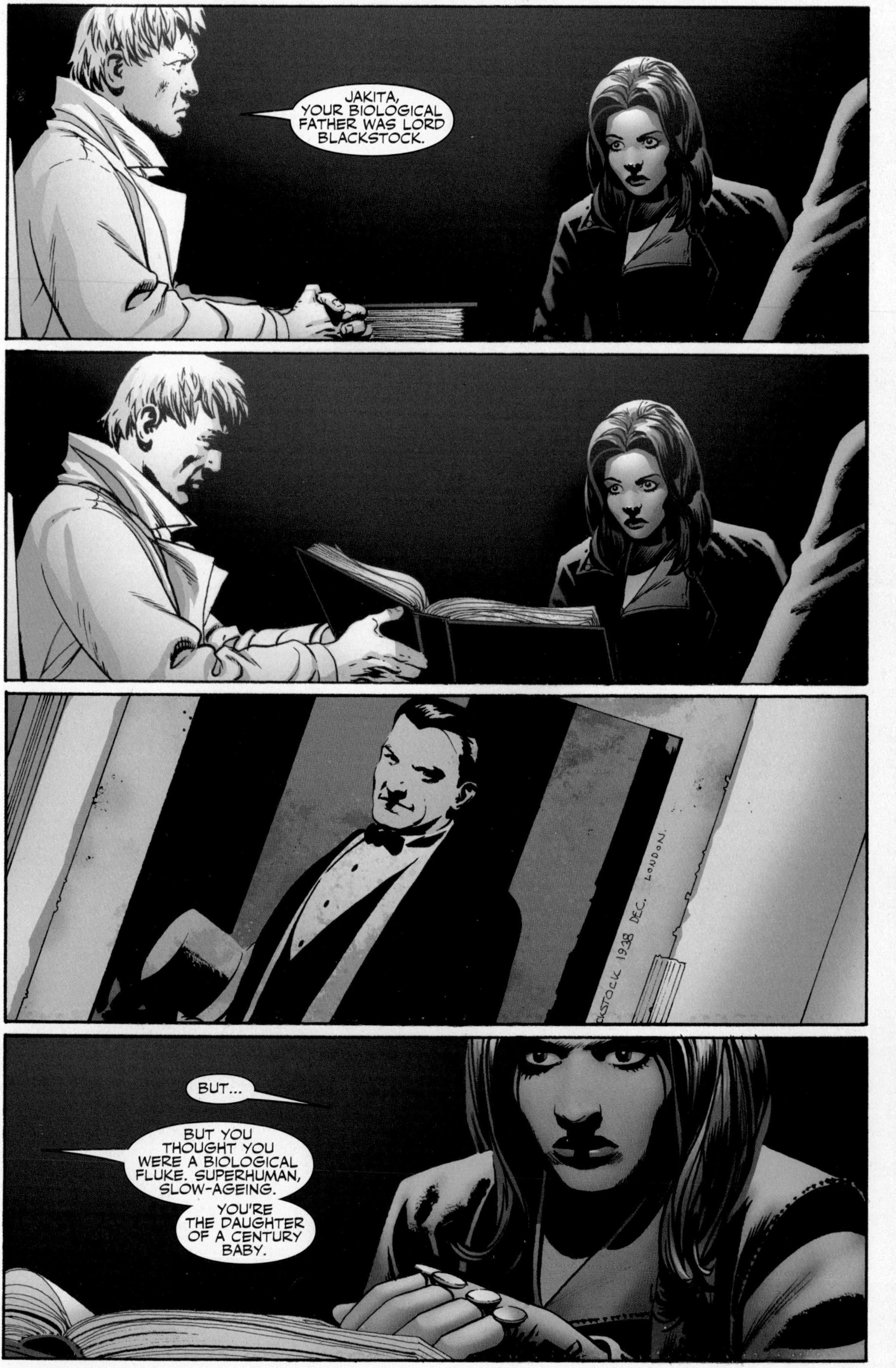
JAKITA, YOUR BIOLOGICAL FATHER WAS LORD BLACKSTOCK.
CKSTOCK. 1938 DEC. LONDON.
BUT...
BUT YOU THOUGHT YOU WERE A BIOLOGICAL FLUKE. SUPERHUMAN, SLOW-AGEING.
YOU'RE THE DAUGHTER OF A CENTURY BABY.

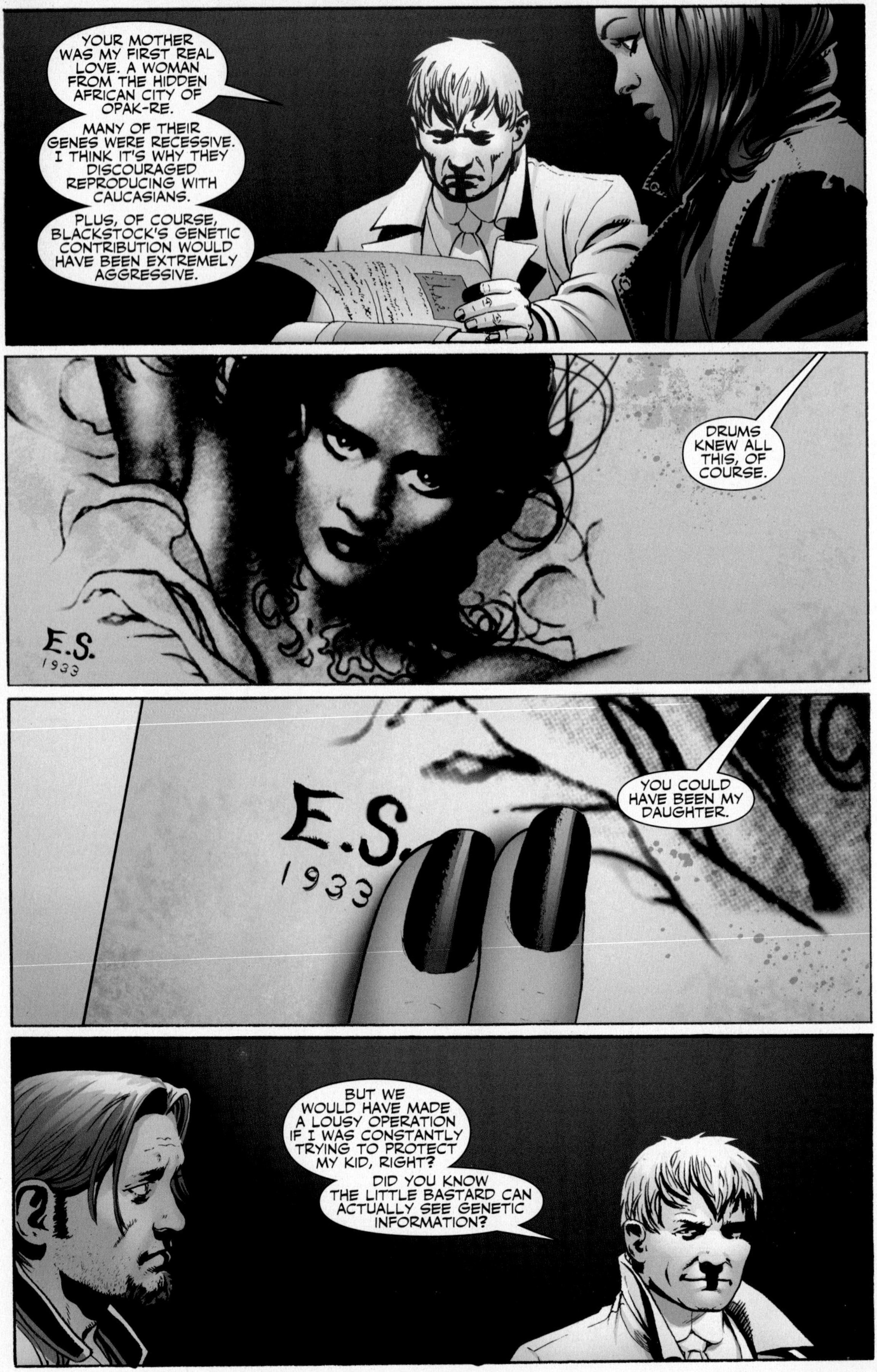
YOUR MOTHER WAS MY FIRST REAL LOVE. A WOMAN FROM THE HIDDEN AFRICAN CITY OF OPAK-RE.
MANY OF THEIR GENES WERE RECESSIVE. I THINK IT'S WHY THEY DISCOURAGED REPRODUCING WITH CAUCASIANS.
PLUS, OF COURSE, BLACKSTOCK'S GENETIC CONTRIBUTION WOULD HAVE BEEN EXTREMELY AGGRESSIVE.
DRUMS KNEW ALL THIS, OF COURSE.
E.S. 1933
YOU COULD HAVE BEEN MY DAUGHTER.
E.S. 1933
BUT WE WOULD HAVE MADE A LOUSY OPERATION IF I WAS CONSTANTLY TRYING TO PROTECT MY KID, RIGHT?
DID YOU KNOW THE LITTLE BASTARD CAN ACTUALLY SEE GENETIC INFORMATION?

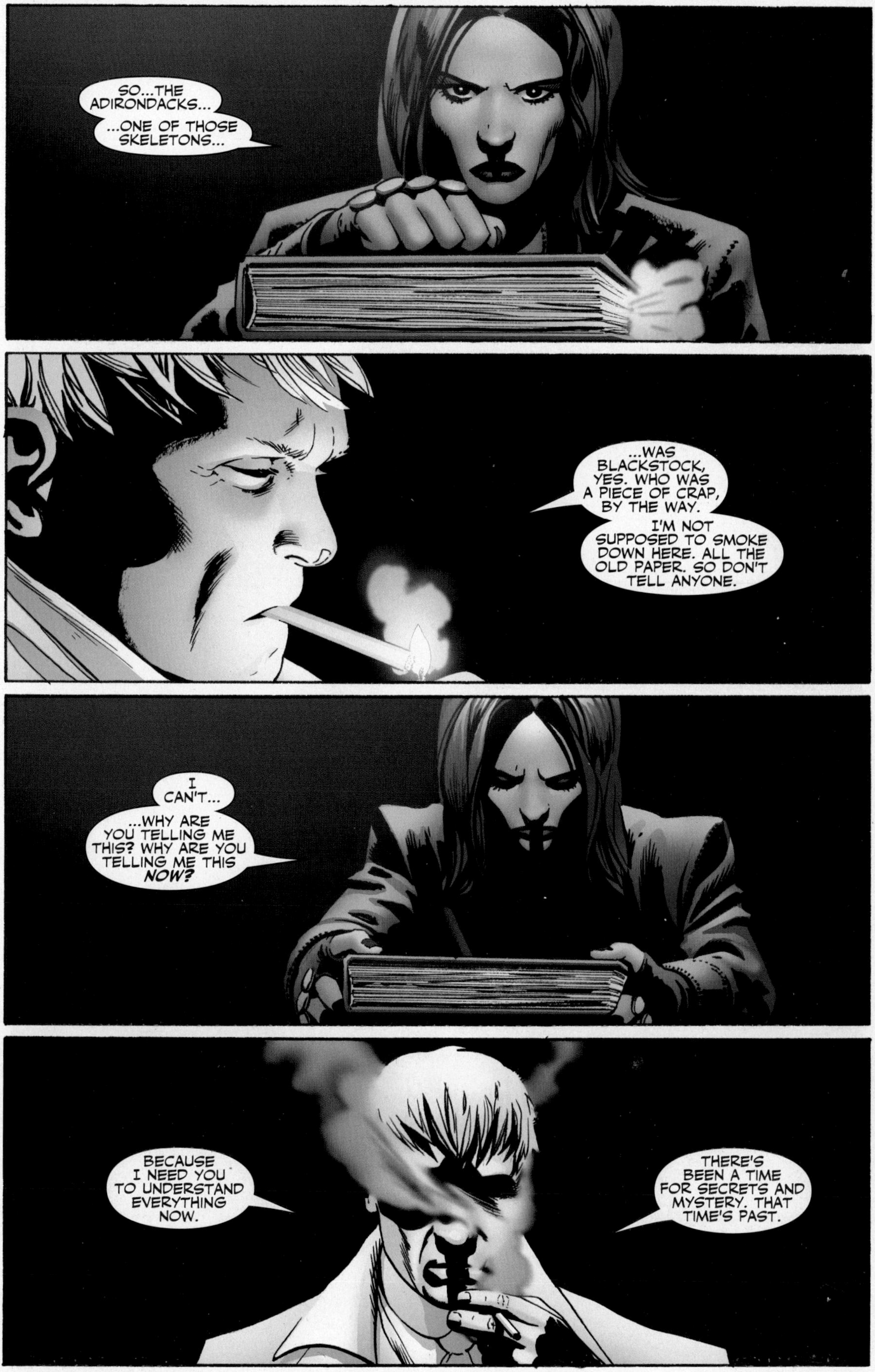
SO...THE ADIRONDACKS...
...ONE OF THOSE SKELETONS...
...WAS BLACKSTOCK, YES. WHO WAS A PIECE OF CRAP, BY THE WAY.
I'M NOT SUPPOSED TO SMOKE DOWN HERE. ALL THE OLD PAPER. SO DON'T TELL ANYONE.
I CAN'T...
...WHY ARE YOU TELLING ME THIS? WHY ARE YOU TELLING ME THIS NOW?
BECAUSE I NEED YOU TO UNDERSTAND EVERYTHING NOW.
THERE'S BEEN A TIME FOR SECRETS AND MYSTERY. THAT TIME'S PAST.

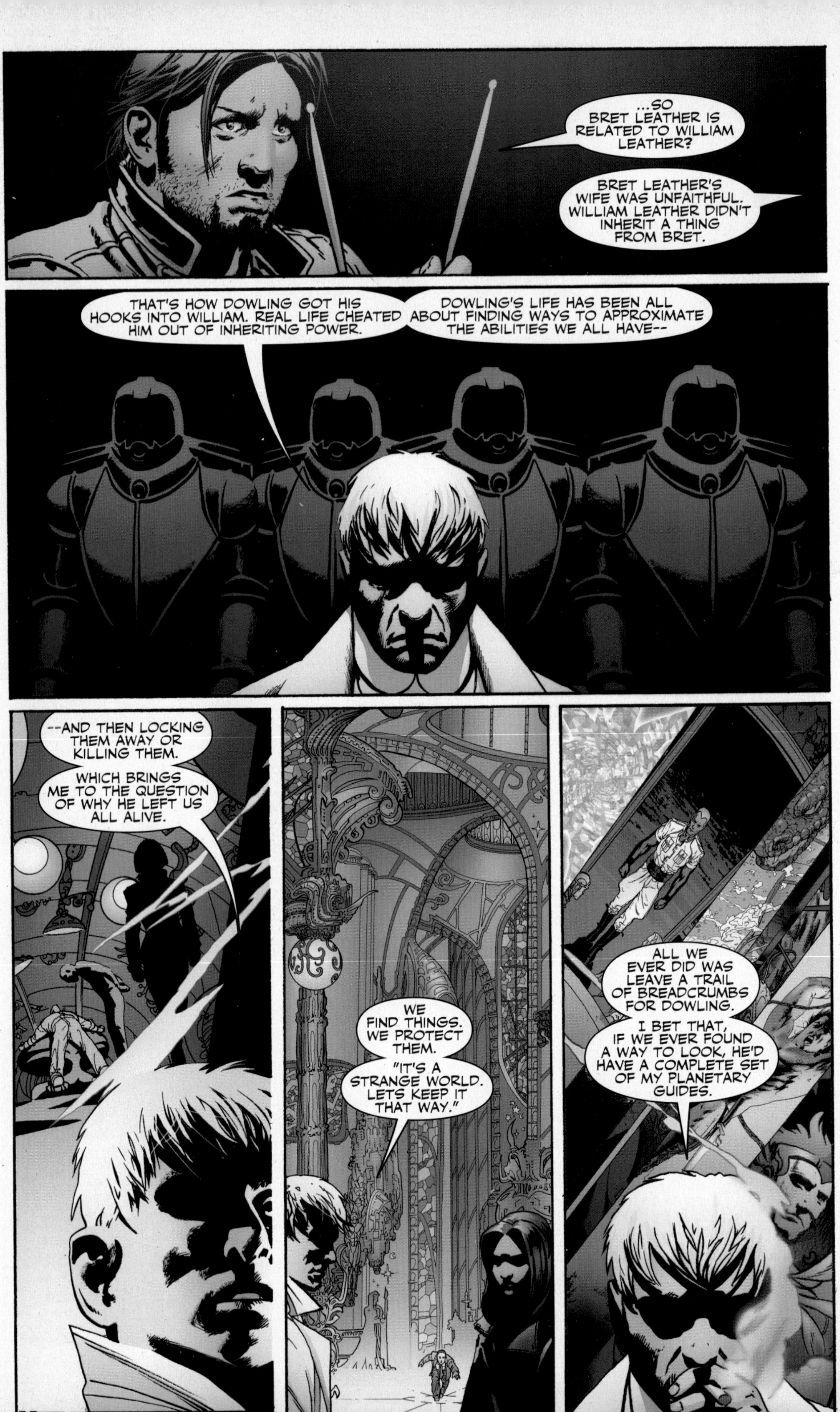
...SO BRET LEATHER IS RELATED TO WILLIAM LEATHER?
BRET LEATHER'S WIFE WAS UNFAITHFUL. WILLIAM LEATHER DIDN'T INHERIT A THING FROM BRET.
THAT'S HOW DOWLING GOT HIS HOOKS INTO WILLIAM. REAL LIFE CHEATED HIM OUT OF INHERITING POWER.
DOWLING'S LIFE HAS BEEN ALL ABOUT FINDING WAYS TO APPROXIMATE THE ABILITIES WE ALL HAVE--
--AND THEN LOCKING THEM AWAY OR KILLING THEM.
WHICH BRINGS ME TO THE QUESTION OF WHY HE LEFT US ALL ALIVE.
WE FIND THINGS. WE PROTECT THEM.
"IT'S A STRANGE WORLD. LETS KEEP IT THAT WAY."
ALL WE EVER DID WAS LEAVE A TRAIL OF BREADCRUMBS FOR DOWLING.
I BET THAT, IF WE EVER FOUND A WAY TO LOOK, HE'D HAVE A COMPLETE SET OF MY PLANETARY GUIDES.

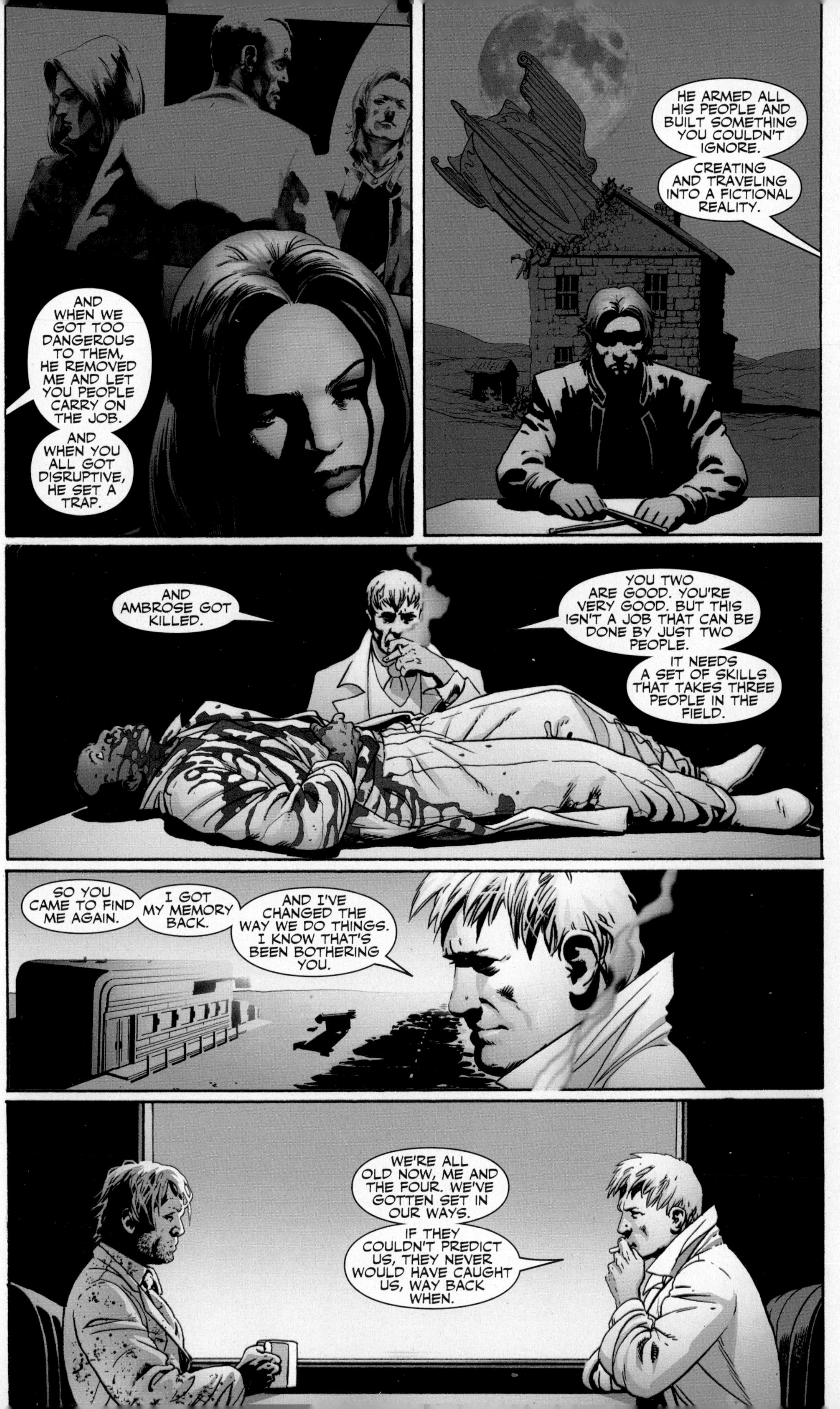
AND WHEN WE GOT TOO DANGEROUS TO THEM, HE REMOVED ME AND LET YOU PEOPLE CARRY ON THE JOB.
AND WHEN YOU ALL GOT DISRUPTIVE, HE SET A TRAP.
HE ARMED ALL HIS PEOPLE AND BUILT SOMETHING YOU COULDN'T IGNORE.
CREATING AND TRAVELING INTO A FICTIONAL REALITY.
AND AMBROSE GOT KILLED.
YOU TWO ARE GOOD. YOU'RE VERY GOOD. BUT THIS ISN'T A JOB THAT CAN BE DONE BY JUST TWO PEOPLE.
IT NEEDS A SET OF SKILLS THAT TAKES THREE PEOPLE IN THE FIELD.
SO YOU CAME TO FIND ME AGAIN.
I GOT MY MEMORY BACK.
AND I'VE CHANGED THE WAY WE DO THINGS. I KNOW THAT'S BEEN BOTHERING YOU.
WE'RE ALL OLD NOW, ME AND THE FOUR. WE'VE GOTTEN SET IN OUR WAYS.
IF THEY COULDN'T PREDICT US, THEY NEVER WOULD HAVE CAUGHT US, WAY BACK WHEN.

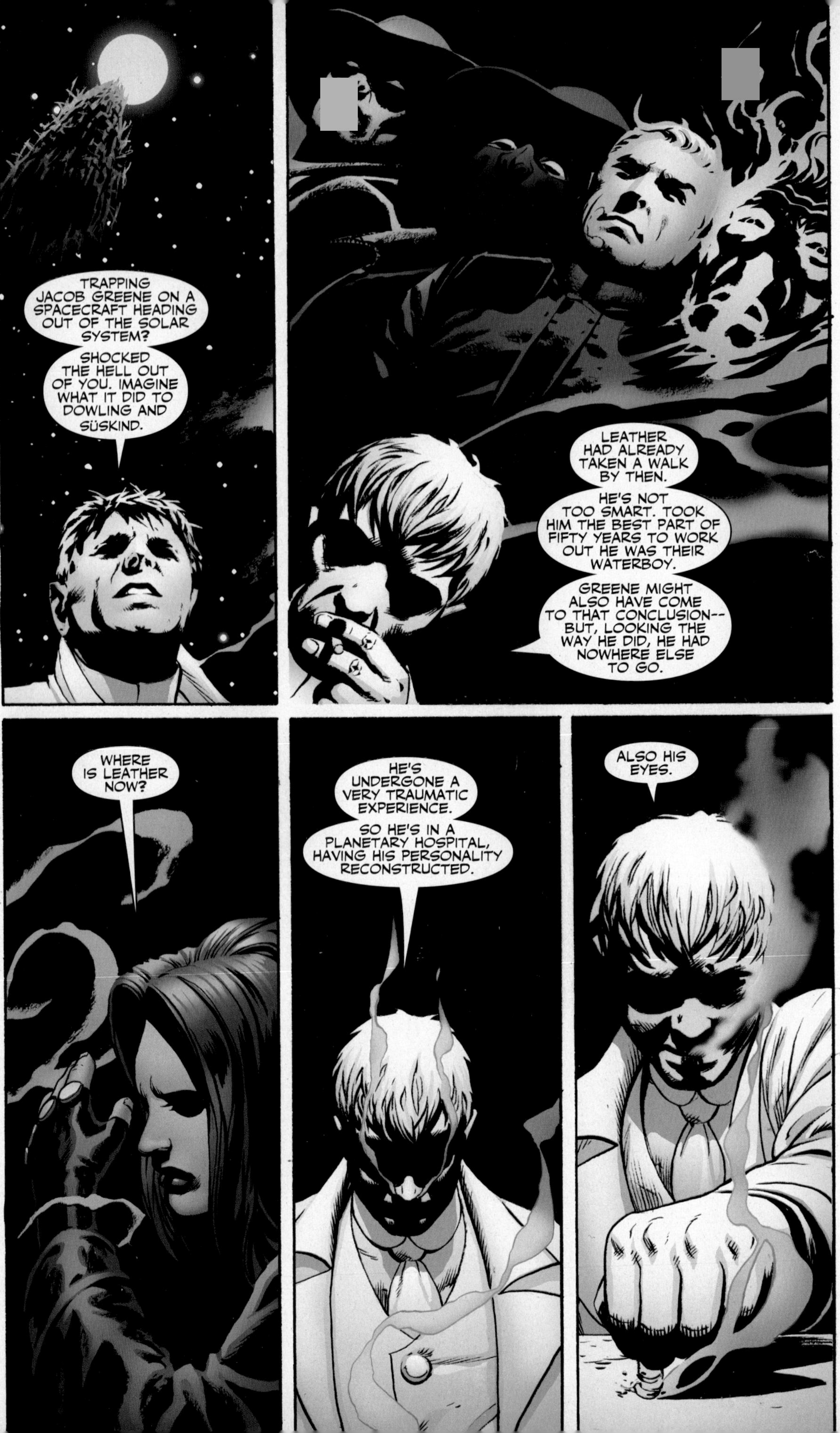
TRAPPING JACOB GREENE ON A SPACECRAFT HEADING OUT OF THE SOLAR SYSTEM?
SHOCKED THE HELL OUT OF YOU. IMAGINE WHAT IT DID TO DOWLING AND SÜSKIND.
LEATHER HAD ALREADY TAKEN A WALK BY THEN.
HE'S NOT TOO SMART. TOOK HIM THE BEST PART OF FIFTY YEARS TO WORK OUT HE WAS THEIR WATERBOY.
GREENE MIGHT ALSO HAVE COME TO THAT CONCLUSION-- BUT, LOOKING THE WAY HE DID, HE HAD NOWHERE ELSE TO GO.
WHERE IS LEATHER NOW?
HE'S UNDERGONE A VERY TRAUMATIC EXPERIENCE.
SO HE'S IN A PLANETARY HOSPITAL, HAVING HIS PERSONALITY RECONSTRUCTED.
ALSO HIS EYES.

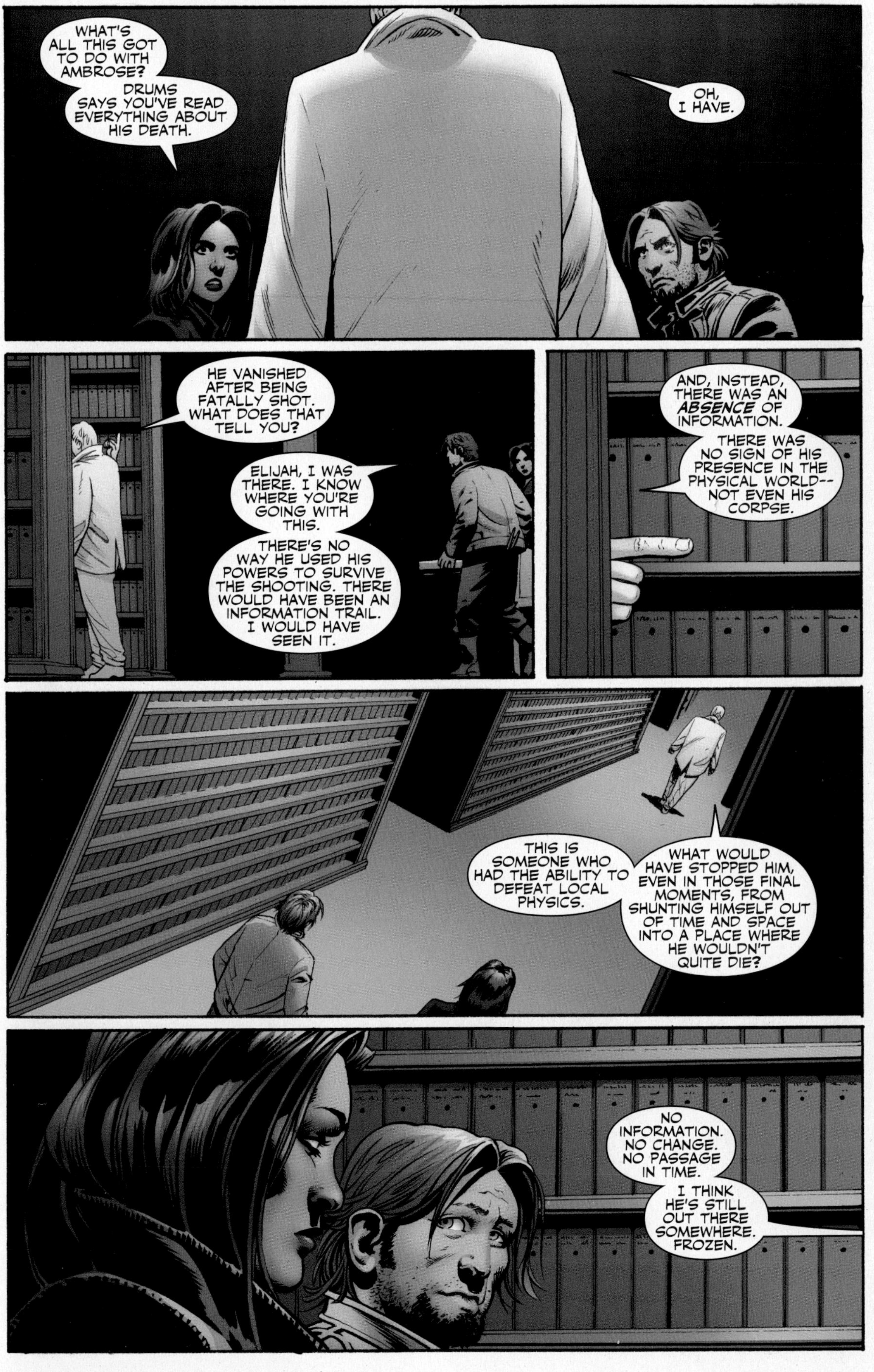
WHAT'S ALL THIS GOT TO DO WITH AMBROSE?
DRUMS SAYS YOU'VE READ EVERYTHING ABOUT HIS DEATH.
OH, I HAVE.
HE VANISHED AFTER BEING FATALLY SHOT. WHAT DOES THAT TELL YOU?
ELIJAH, I WAS THERE. I KNOW WHERE YOU'RE GOING WITH THIS.
THERE'S NO WAY HE USED HIS POWERS TO SURVIVE THE SHOOTING. THERE WOULD HAVE BEEN AN INFORMATION TRAIL. I WOULD HAVE SEEN IT.
AND, INSTEAD, THERE WAS AN ABSENCE OF INFORMATION.
THERE WAS NO SIGN OF HIS PRESENCE IN THE PHYSICAL WORLD--NOT EVEN HIS CORPSE.
THIS IS SOMEONE WHO HAD THE ABILITY TO DEFEAT LOCAL PHYSICS.
WHAT WOULD HAVE STOPPED HIM, EVEN IN THOSE FINAL MOMENTS, FROM SHUNTING HIMSELF OUT OF TIME AND SPACE INTO A PLACE WHERE HE WOULDN'T QUITE DIE?
NO INFORMATION. NO CHANGE. NO PASSAGE IN TIME.
I THINK HE'S STILL OUT THERE SOMEWHERE. FROZEN.

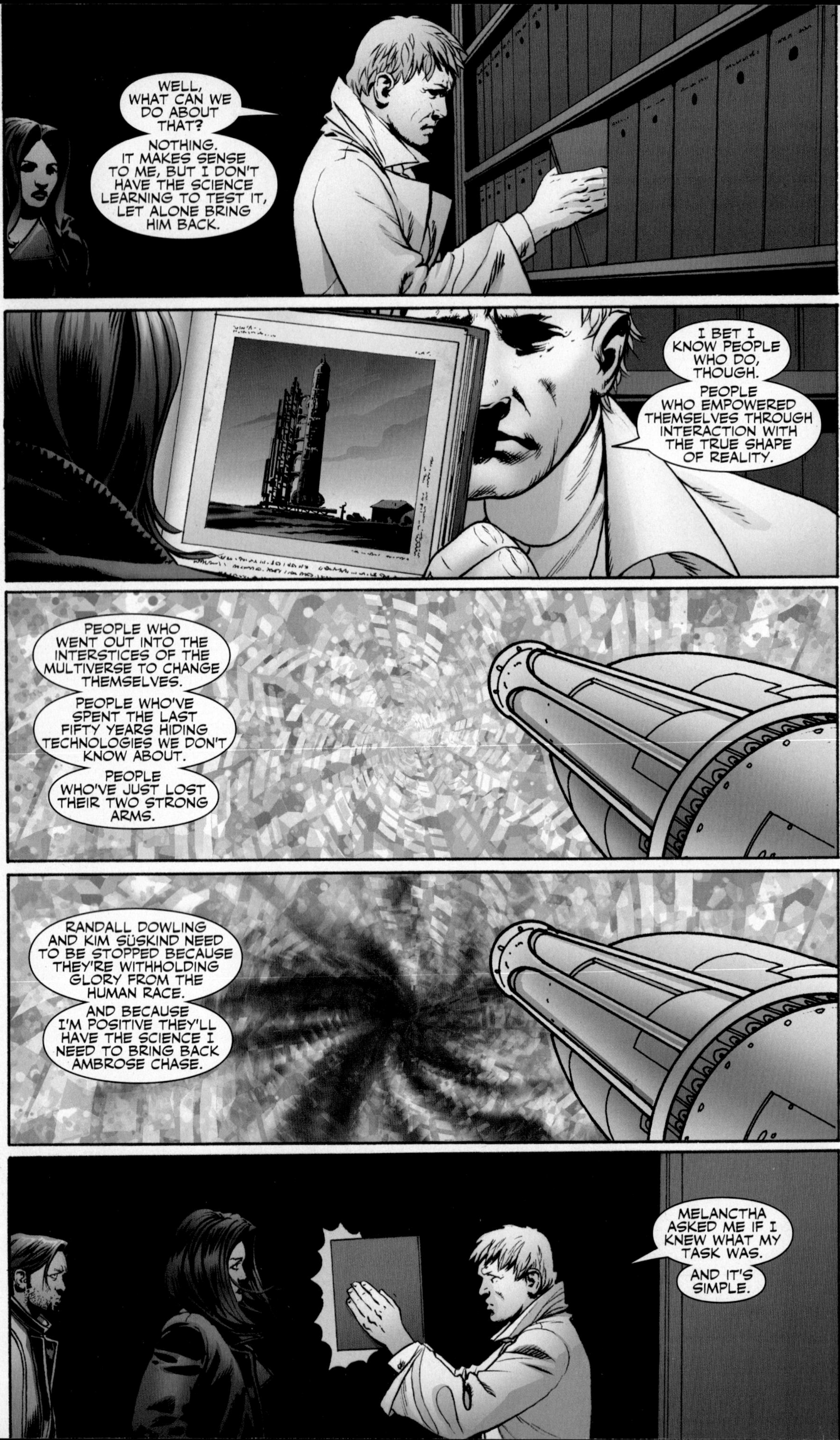
WELL, WHAT CAN WE DO ABOUT THAT?
NOTHING. IT MAKES SENSE TO ME, BUT I DON'T HAVE THE SCIENCE LEARNING TO TEST IT, LET ALONE BRING HIM BACK.
I BET I KNOW PEOPLE WHO DO, THOUGH.
PEOPLE WHO EMPOWERED THEMSELVES THROUGH INTERACTION WITH THE TRUE SHAPE OF REALITY.
PEOPLE WHO WENT OUT INTO THE INTERSTICES OF THE MULTIVERSE TO CHANGE THEMSELVES.
PEOPLE WHO'VE SPENT THE LAST FIFTY YEARS HIDING TECHNOLOGIES WE DON'T KNOW ABOUT.
PEOPLE WHO'VE JUST LOST THEIR TWO STRONG ARMS.
RANDALL DOWLING AND KIM SÜSKIND NEED TO BE STOPPED BECAUSE THEY'RE WITHHOLDING GLORY FROM THE HUMAN RACE.
AND BECAUSE I'M POSITIVE THEY'LL HAVE THE SCIENCE I NEED TO BRING BACK AMBROSE CHASE.
MELANCTHA ASKED ME IF I KNEW WHAT MY TASK WAS.
AND IT'S SIMPLE.

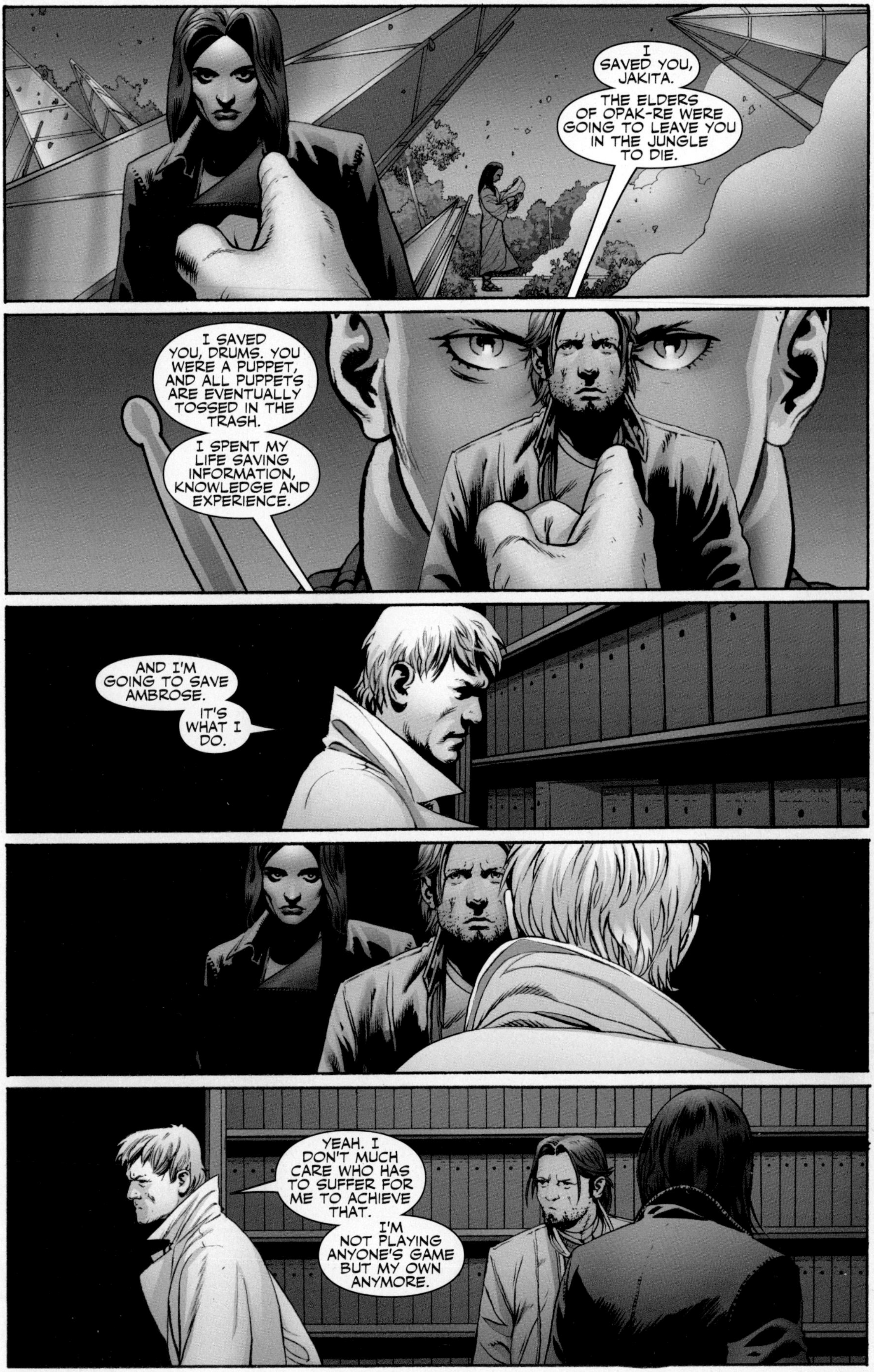
I SAVED YOU, JAKITA.
THE ELDERS OF OPAK-RE WERE GOING TO LEAVE YOU IN THE JUNGLE TO DIE.
I SAVED YOU, DRUMS. YOU WERE A PUPPET, AND ALL PUPPETS ARE EVENTUALLY TOSSED IN THE TRASH.
I SPENT MY LIFE SAVING INFORMATION, KNOWLEDGE AND EXPERIENCE.
AND I'M GOING TO SAVE AMBROSE.
IT'S WHAT I DO.
YEAH. I DON'T MUCH CARE WHO HAS TO SUFFER FOR ME TO ACHIEVE THAT.
I'M NOT PLAYING ANYONE'S GAME BUT MY OWN ANYMORE.

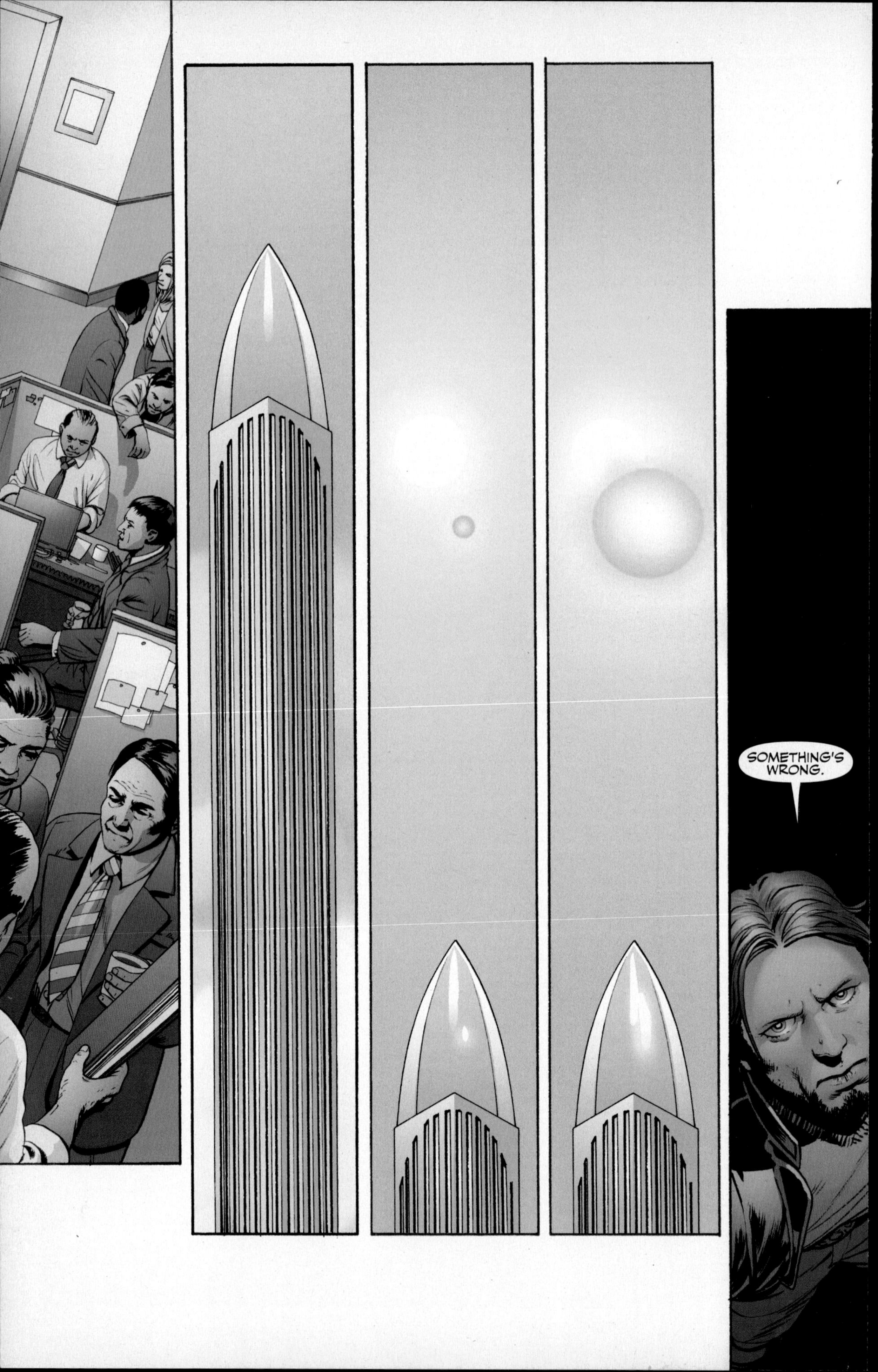
SOMETHING'S WRONG.

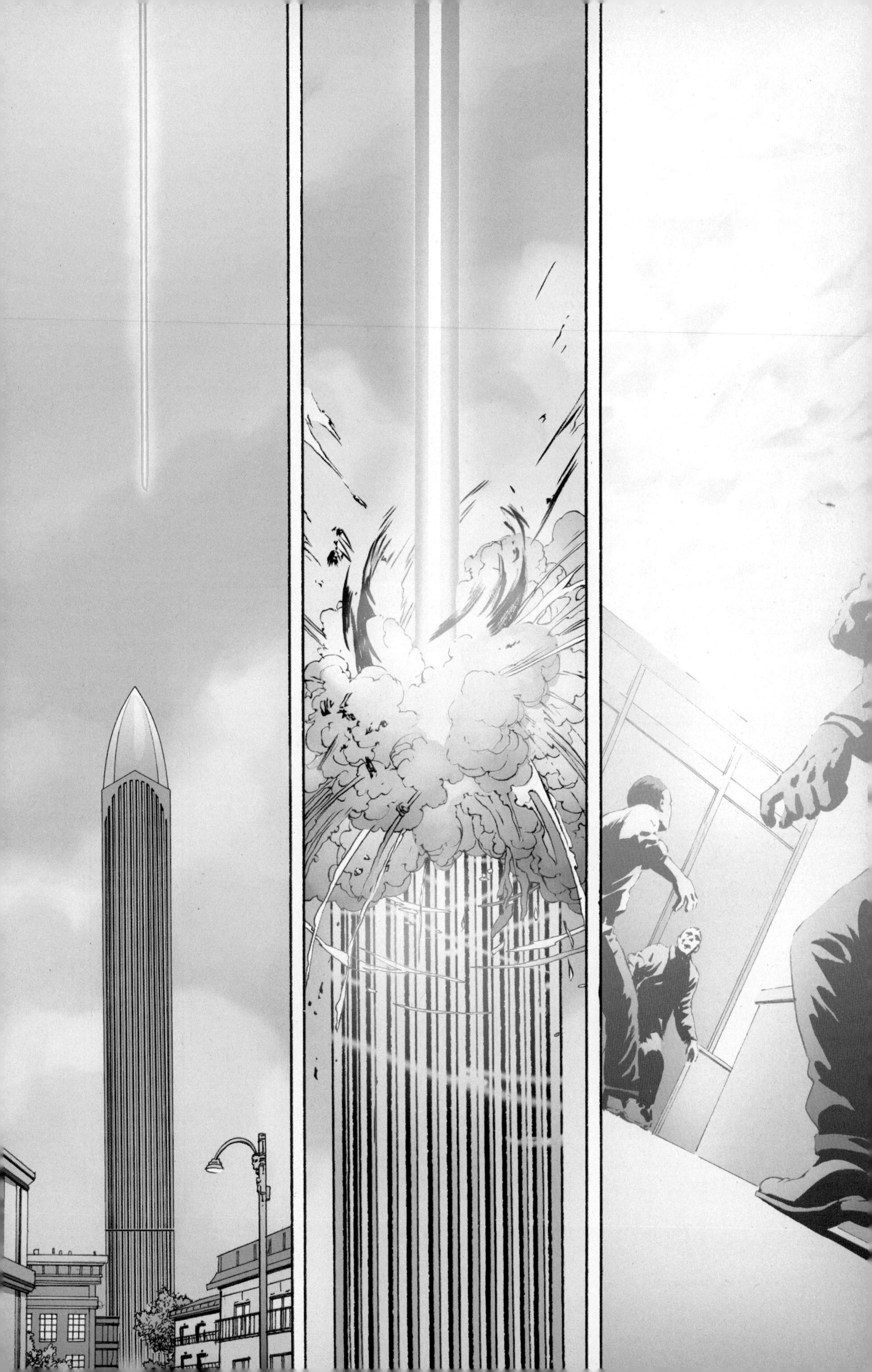

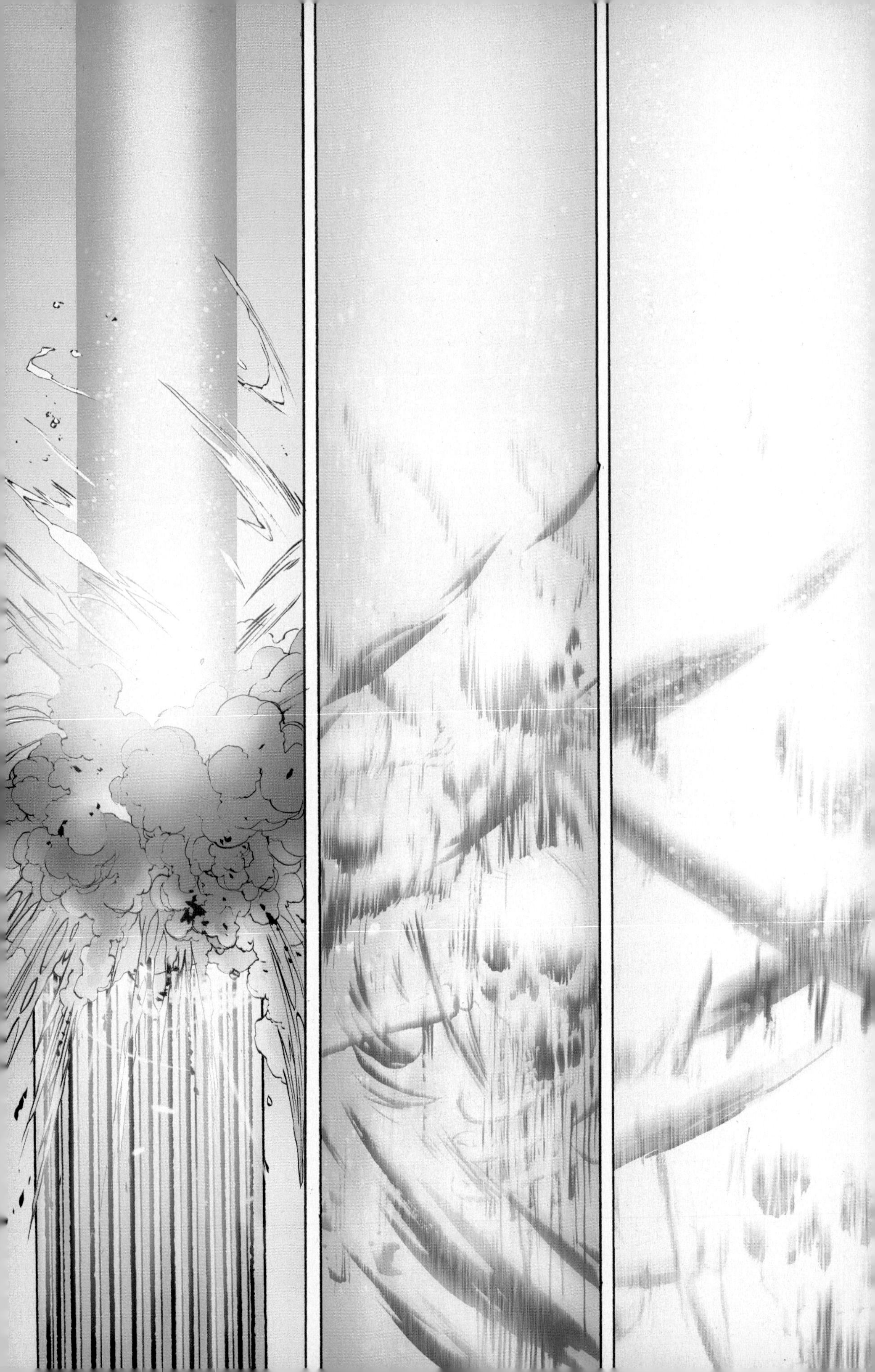

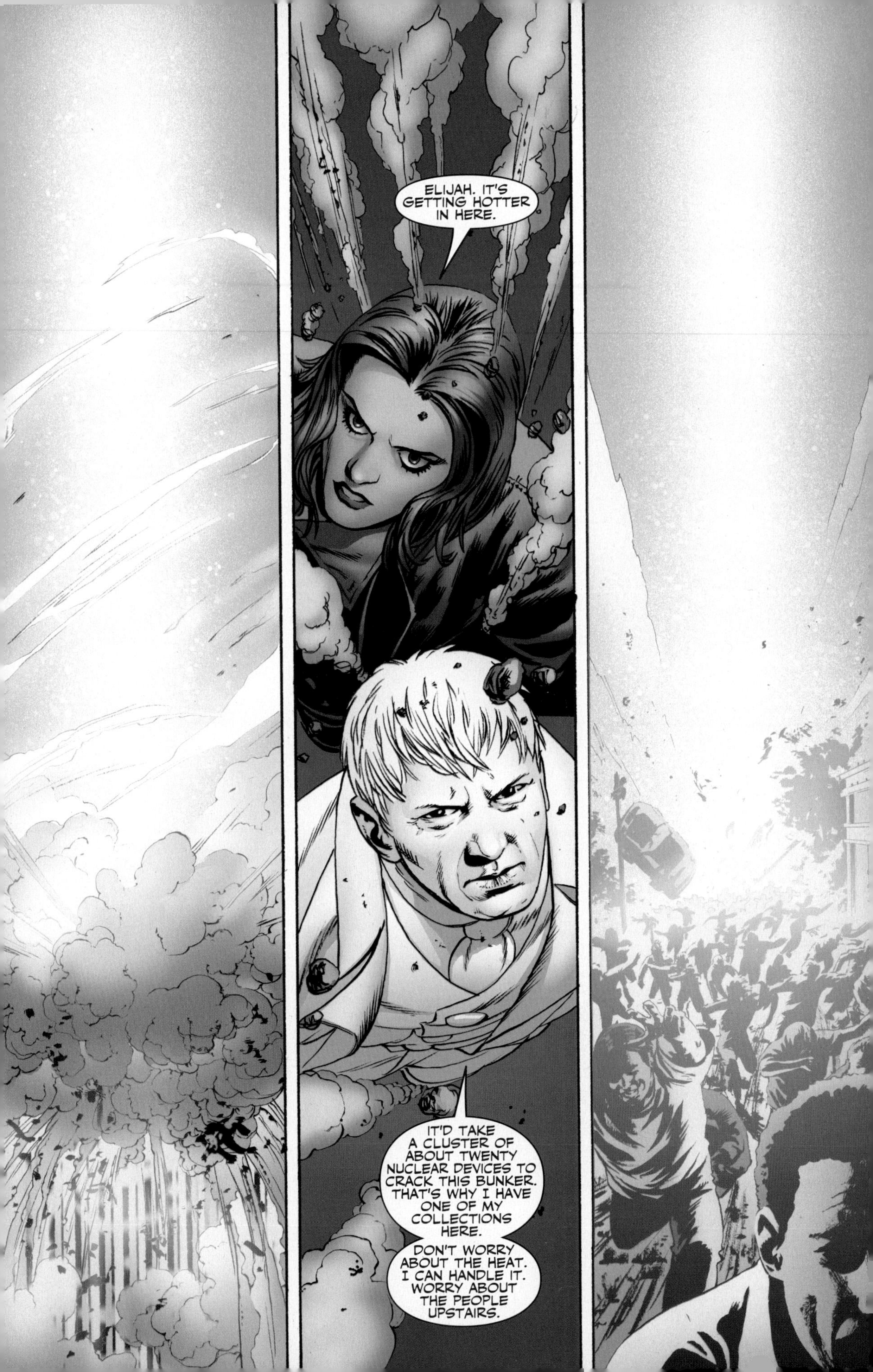
ELIJAH. IT'S GETTING HOTTER IN HERE.
IT'D TAKE A CLUSTER OF ABOUT TWENTY NUCLEAR DEVICES TO CRACK THIS BUNKER. THAT'S WHY I HAVE ONE OF MY COLLECTIONS HERE.
DON'T WORRY ABOUT THE HEAT. I CAN HANDLE IT. WORRY ABOUT THE PEOPLE UPSTAIRS.

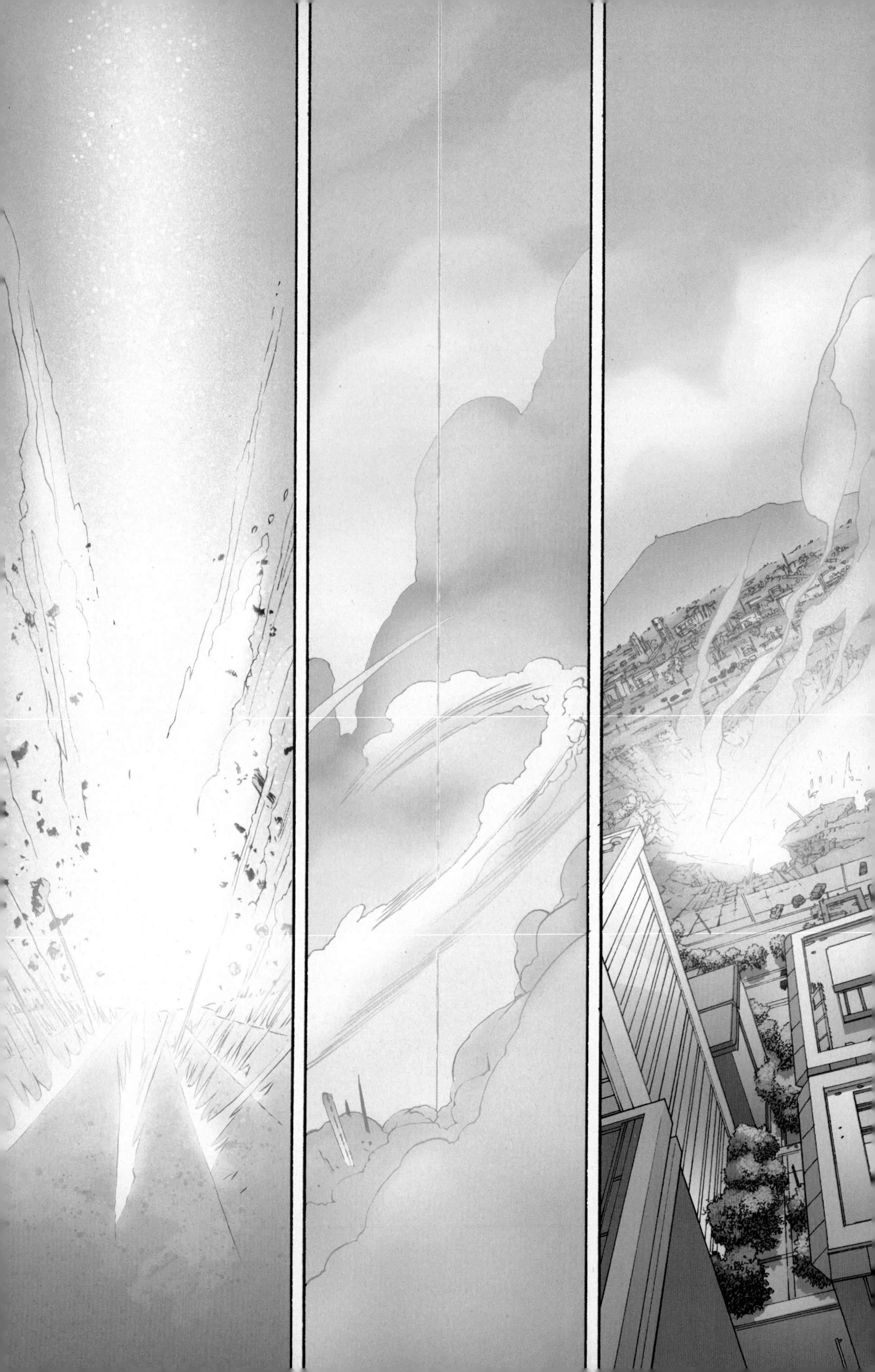

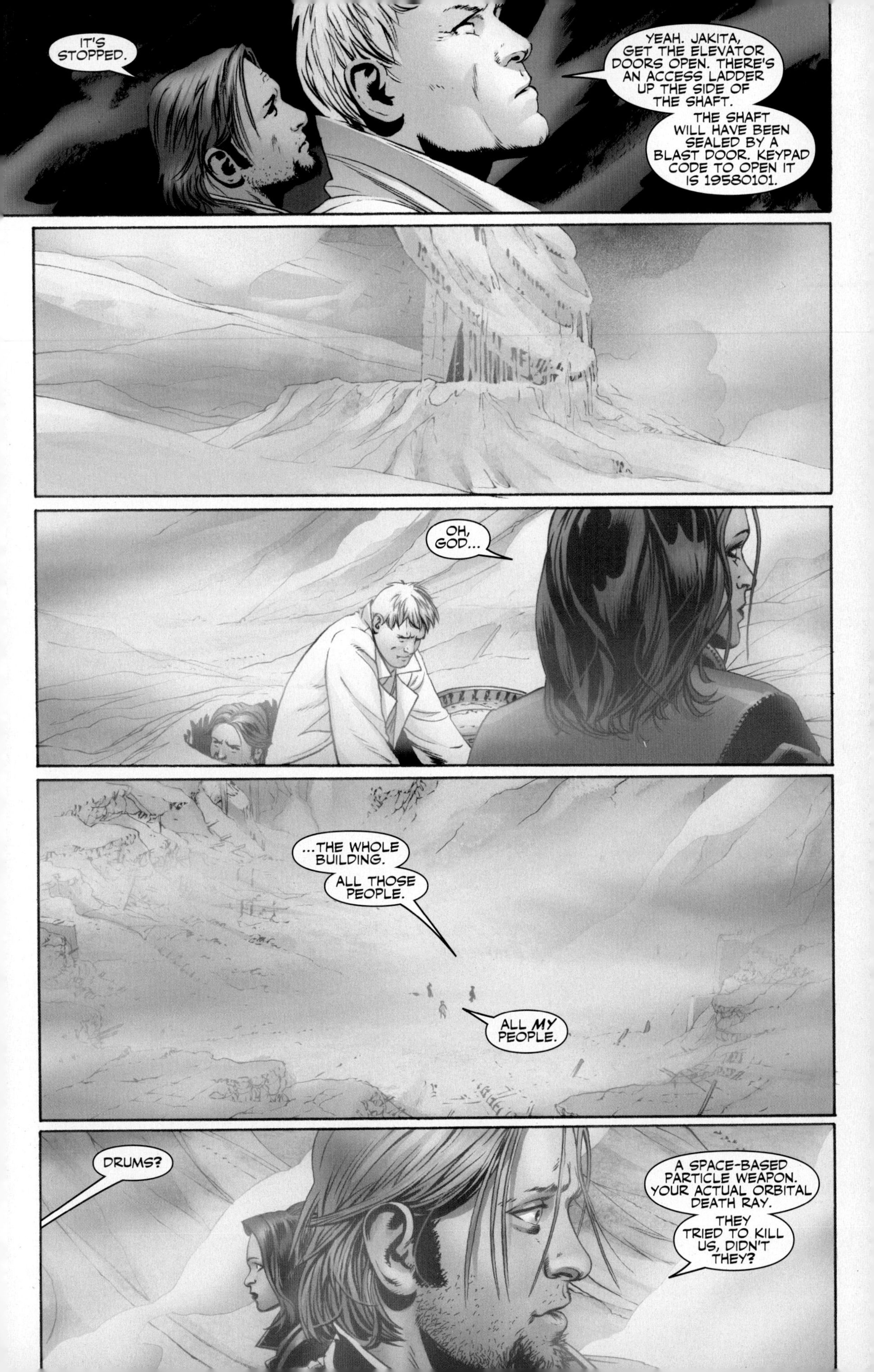
IT'S STOPPED.
YEAH. JAKITA, GET THE ELEVATOR DOORS OPEN. THERE'S AN ACCESS LADDER UP THE SIDE OF THE SHAFT.
THE SHAFT WILL HAVE BEEN SEALED BY A BLAST DOOR. KEYPAD CODE TO OPEN IT IS 19580101.
OH, GOD...
...THE WHOLE BUILDING.
ALL THOSE PEOPLE.
ALL MY PEOPLE.
DRUMS?
A SPACE-BASED PARTICLE WEAPON. YOUR ACTUAL ORBITAL DEATH RAY.
THEY TRIED TO KILL US, DIDN'T THEY?

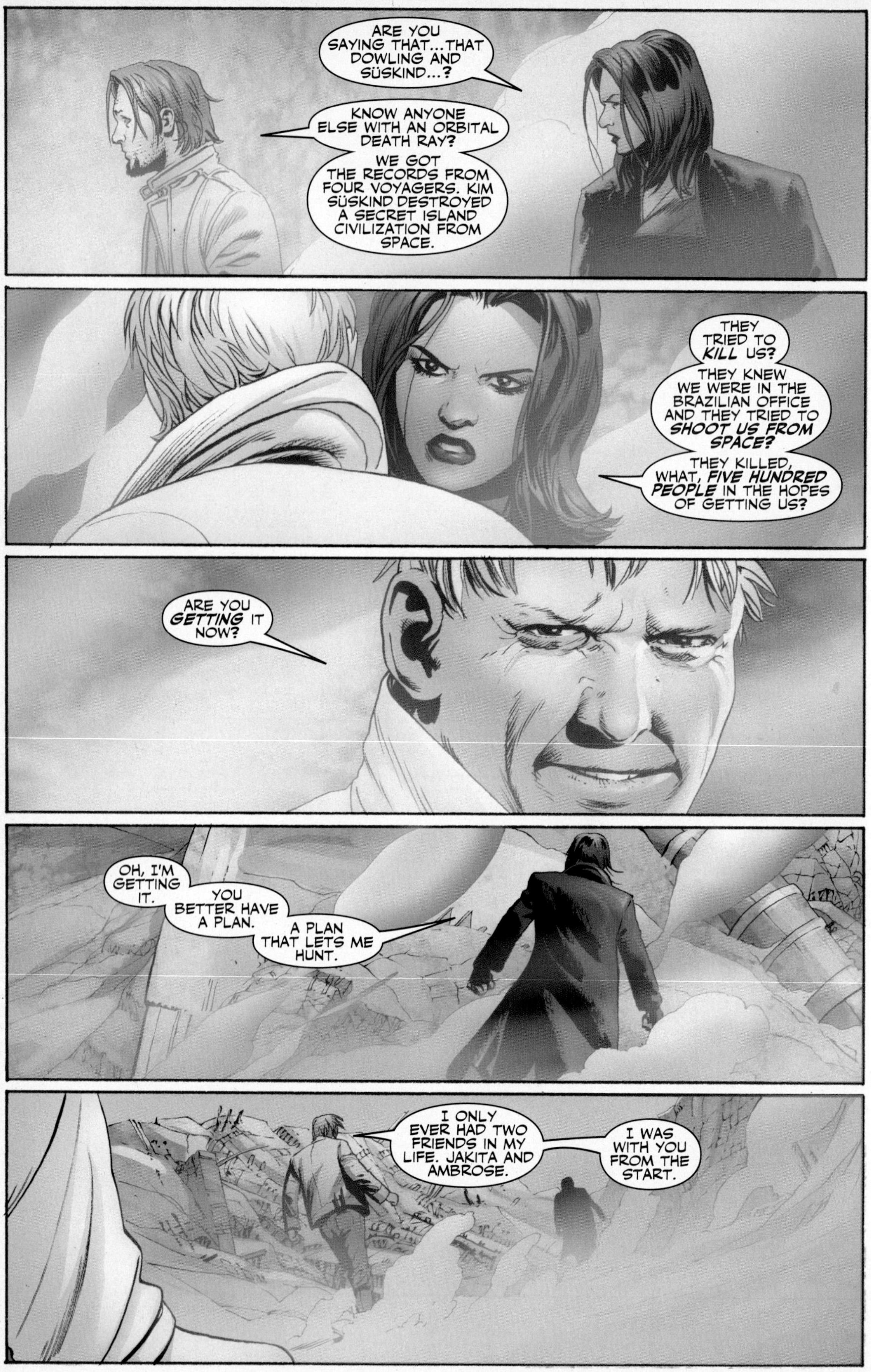
ARE YOU SAYING THAT...THAT DOWLING AND SÜSKIND...?
KNOW ANYONE ELSE WITH AN ORBITAL DEATH RAY?
WE GOT THE RECORDS FROM FOUR VOYAGERS. KIM SÜSKIND DESTROYED A SECRET ISLAND CIVILIZATION FROM SPACE.
THEY TRIED TO KILL US?
THEY KNEW WE WERE IN THE BRAZILIAN OFFICE AND THEY TRIED TO SHOOT US FROM SPACE?
THEY KILLED, WHAT, FIVE HUNDRED PEOPLE IN THE HOPES OF GETTING US?
ARE YOU GETTING IT NOW?
OH, I'M GETTING IT.
YOU BETTER HAVE A PLAN.
A PLAN THAT LETS ME HUNT.
I ONLY EVER HAD TWO FRIENDS IN MY LIFE. JAKITA AND AMBROSE.
I WAS WITH YOU FROM THE START.

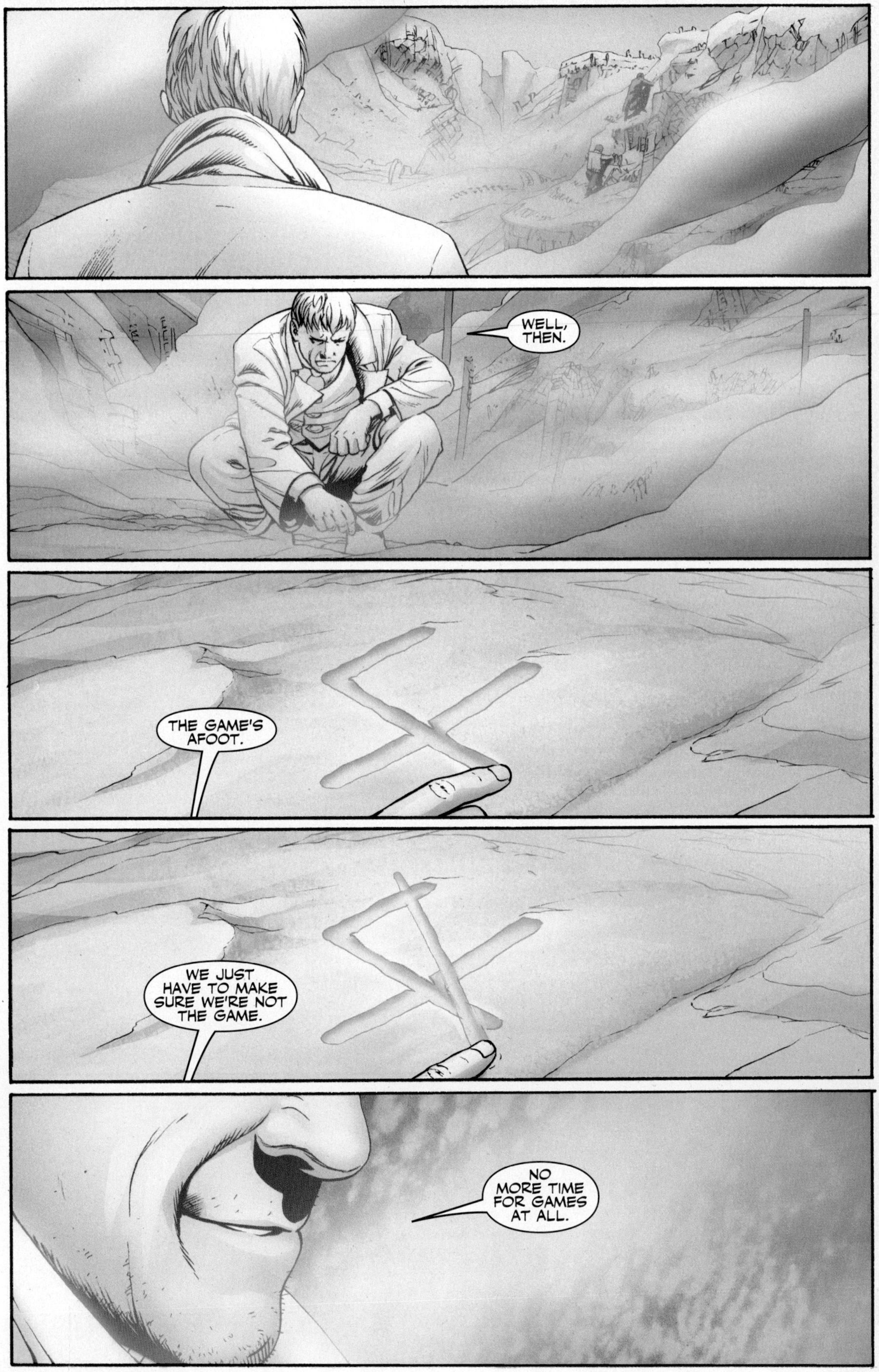
WELL, THEN.
THE GAME'S AFOOT.
WE JUST HAVE TO MAKE SURE WE'RE NOT THE GAME.
NO MORE TIME FOR GAMES AT ALL.

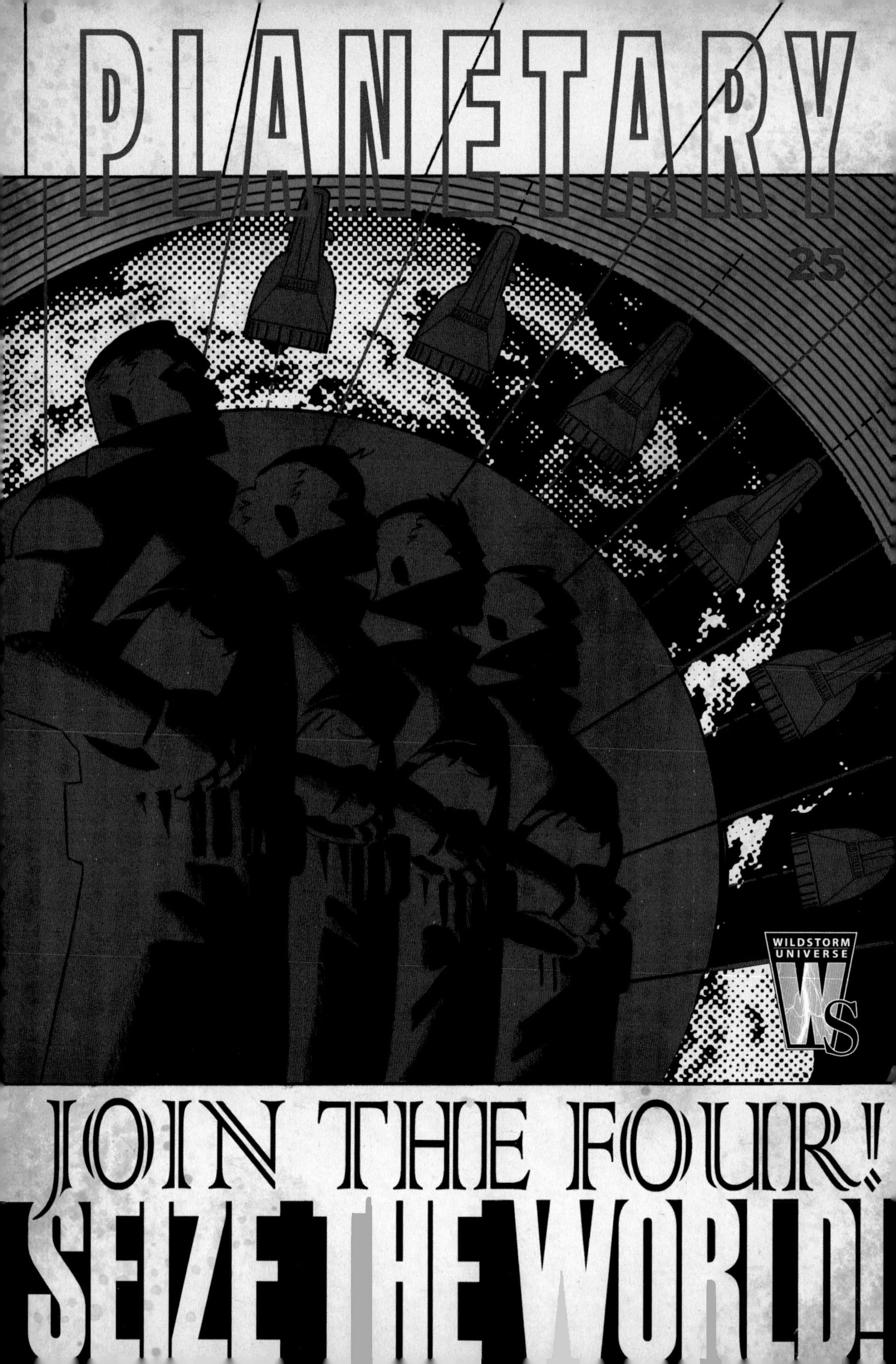
PLANETARY
25
WILDSTORM UNIVERSE
JOIN THE FOUR!
SEIZE THE WORLD!

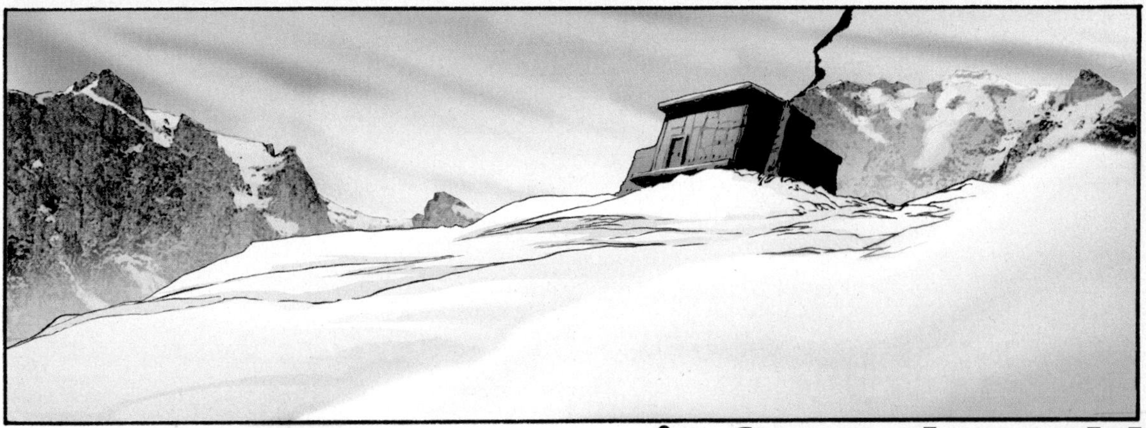

in from the cold

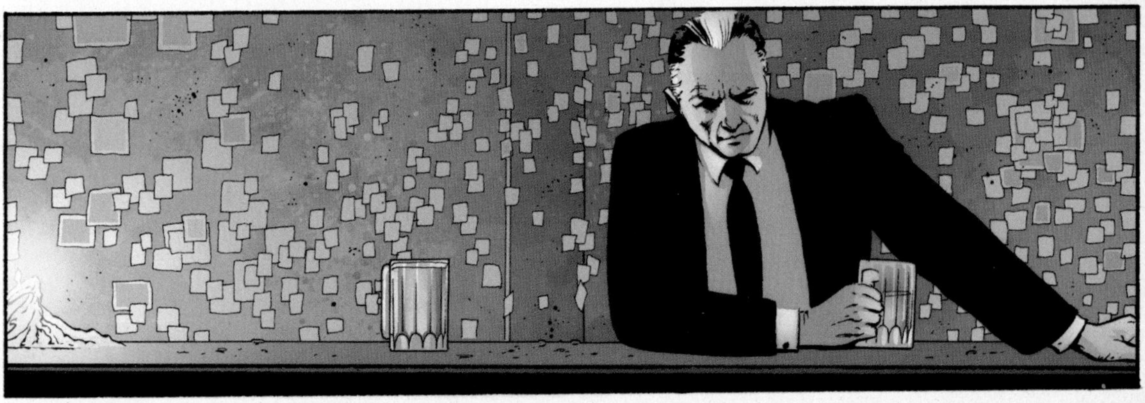

warren ellis   john cassaday

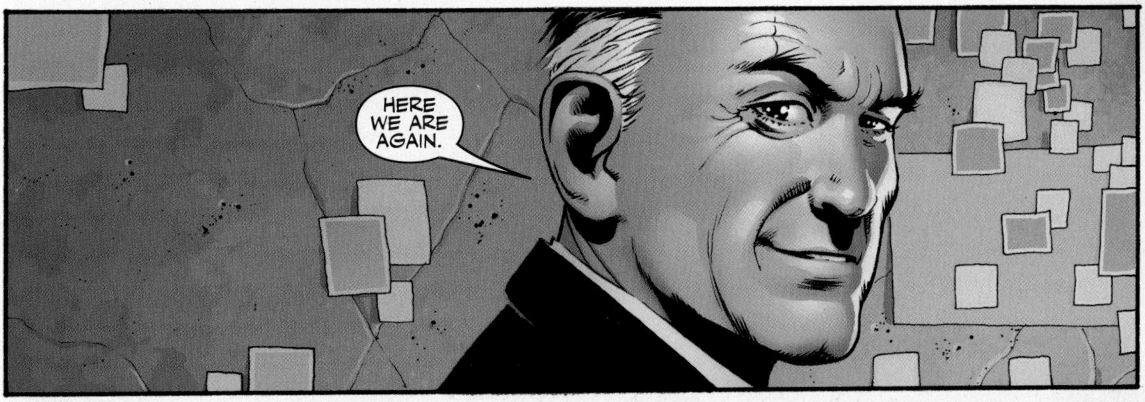
HERE WE ARE AGAIN.

laura martin   starkings   kristy quinn   scott dunbier

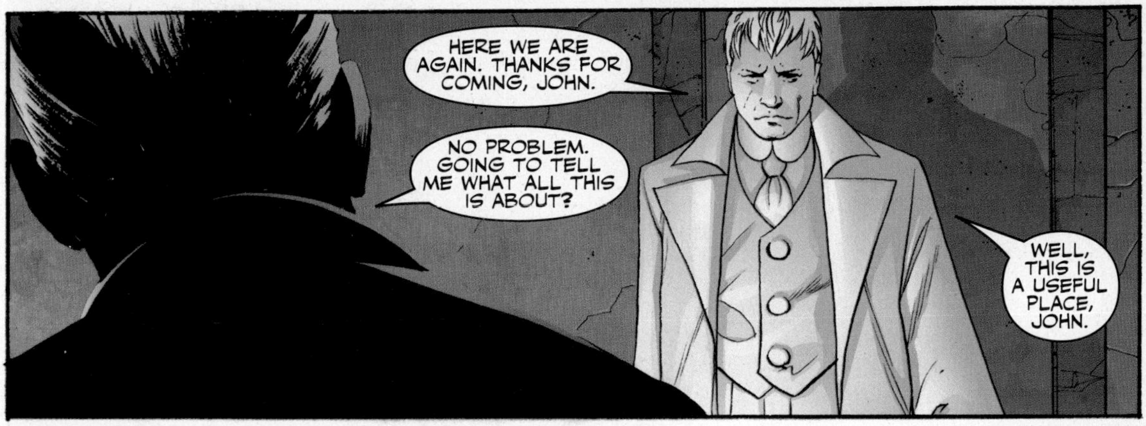
HERE WE ARE AGAIN. THANKS FOR COMING, JOHN.
NO PROBLEM. GOING TO TELL ME WHAT ALL THIS IS ABOUT?
WELL, THIS IS A USEFUL PLACE, JOHN.

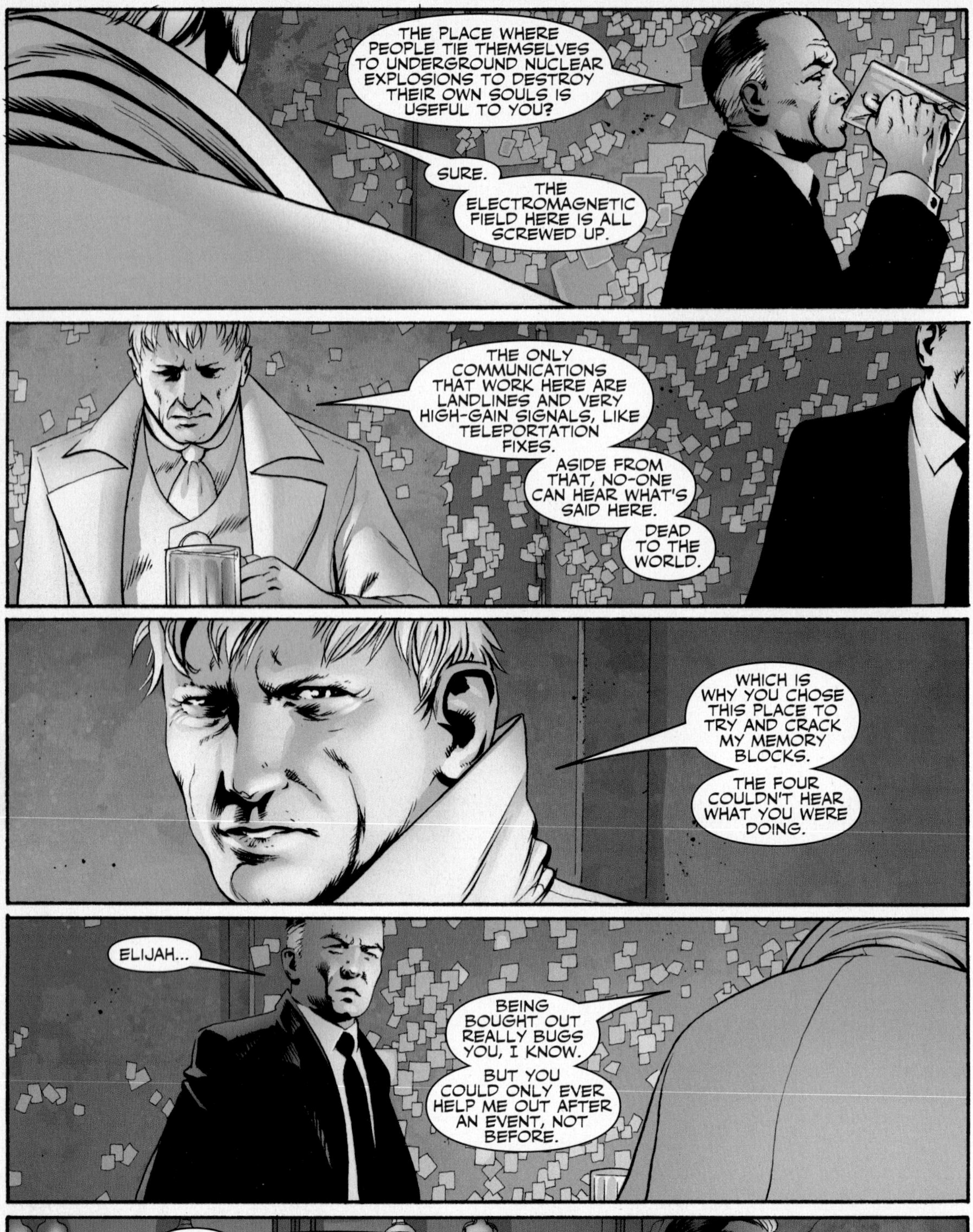

THE PLACE WHERE PEOPLE TIE THEMSELVES TO UNDERGROUND NUCLEAR EXPLOSIONS TO DESTROY THEIR OWN SOULS IS USEFUL TO YOU?
SURE.
THE ELECTROMAGNETIC FIELD HERE IS ALL SCREWED UP.
THE ONLY COMMUNICATIONS THAT WORK HERE ARE LANDLINES AND VERY HIGH-GAIN SIGNALS, LIKE TELEPORTATION FIXES.
ASIDE FROM THAT, NO-ONE CAN HEAR WHAT'S SAID HERE.
DEAD TO THE WORLD.
WHICH IS WHY YOU CHOSE THIS PLACE TO TRY AND CRACK MY MEMORY BLOCKS.
THE FOUR COULDN'T HEAR WHAT YOU WERE DOING.
ELIJAH...
BEING BOUGHT OUT REALLY BUGS YOU, I KNOW.
BUT YOU COULD ONLY EVER HELP ME OUT AFTER AN EVENT, NOT BEFORE.
I NEED TO GO.
YOU DID WHAT YOU COULD, I KNOW. BUT THEY'VE GOT SOMETHING ON YOU.
AND I KNOW YOU'RE MY FRIEND. YOU NEVER DID ANYTHING FOR ANNA HARK, AFTER ALL.

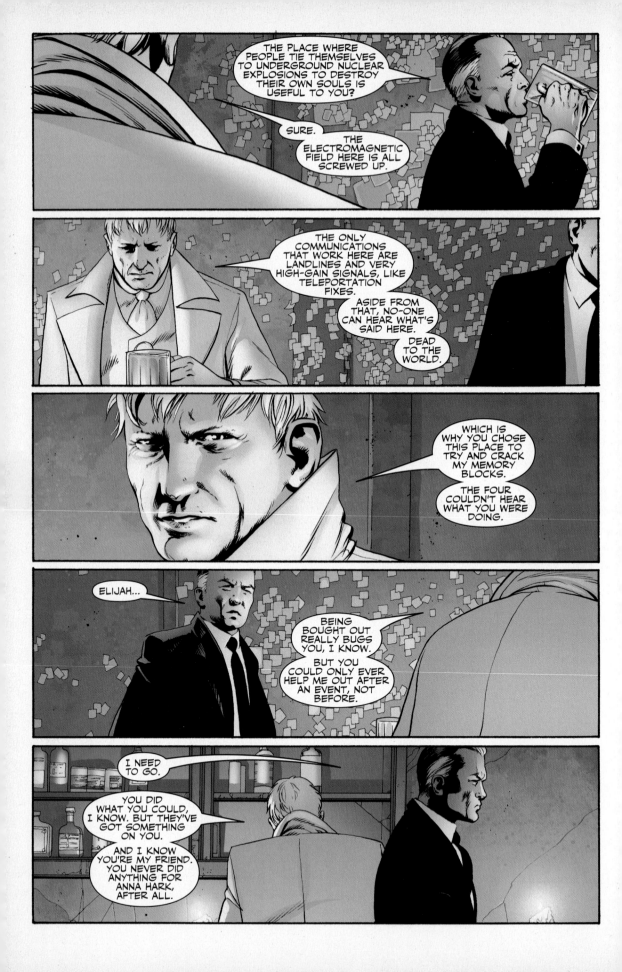

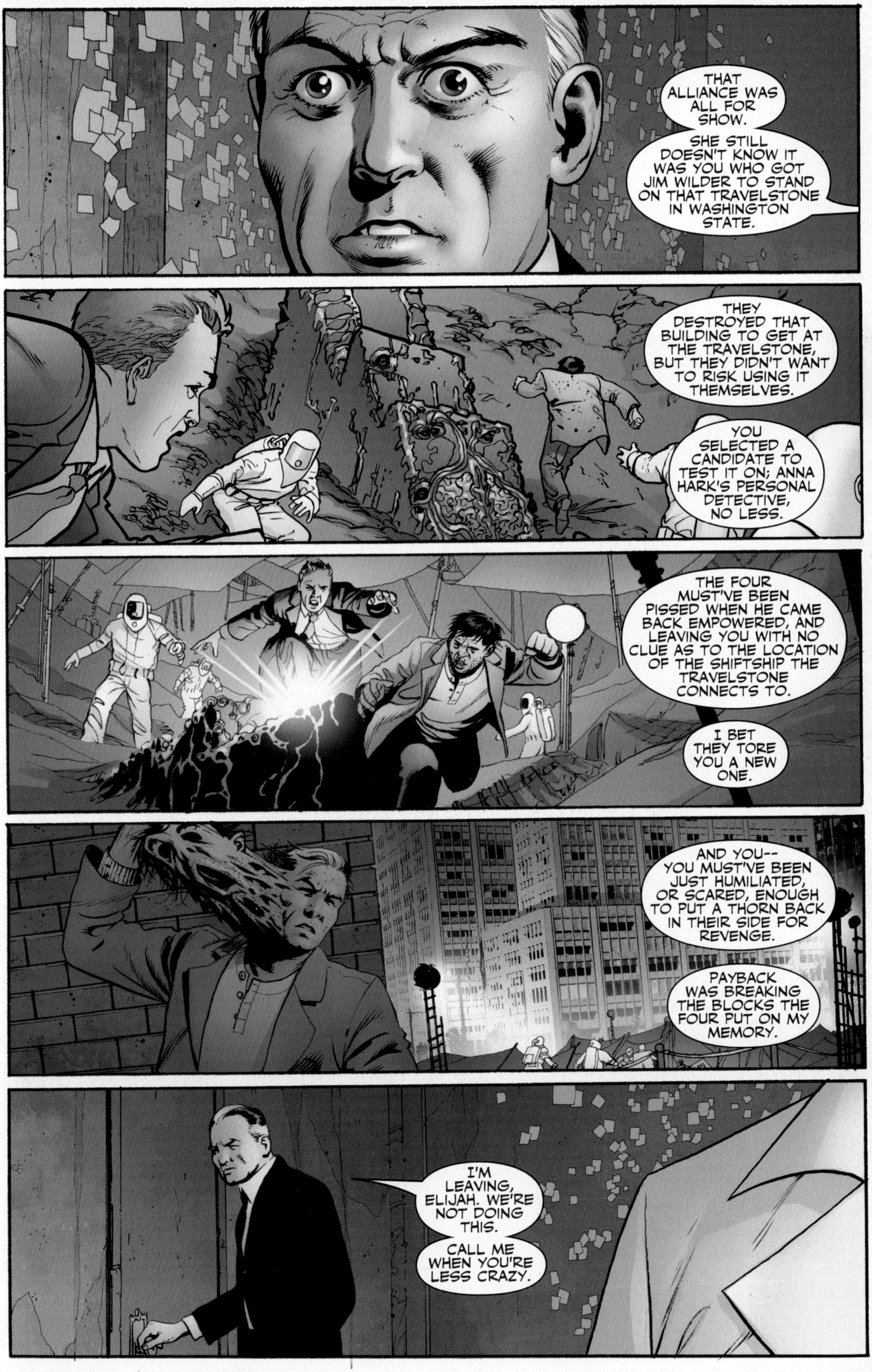

THAT ALLIANCE WAS ALL FOR SHOW.
SHE STILL DOESN'T KNOW IT WAS YOU WHO GOT JIM WILDER TO STAND ON THAT TRAVELSTONE IN WASHINGTON STATE.
THEY DESTROYED THAT BUILDING TO GET AT THE TRAVELSTONE, BUT THEY DIDN'T WANT TO RISK USING IT THEMSELVES.
YOU SELECTED A CANDIDATE TO TEST IT ON; ANNA HARK'S PERSONAL DETECTIVE, NO LESS.
THE FOUR MUST'VE BEEN PISSED WHEN HE CAME BACK EMPOWERED, AND LEAVING YOU WITH NO CLUE AS TO THE LOCATION OF THE SHIFTSHIP THE TRAVELSTONE CONNECTS TO.
I BET THEY TORE YOU A NEW ONE.
AND YOU-- YOU MUST'VE BEEN JUST HUMILIATED, OR SCARED, ENOUGH TO PUT A THORN BACK IN THEIR SIDE FOR REVENGE.
PAYBACK WAS BREAKING THE BLOCKS THE FOUR PUT ON MY MEMORY.
I'M LEAVING, ELIJAH. WE'RE NOT DOING THIS.
CALL ME WHEN YOU'RE LESS CRAZY.

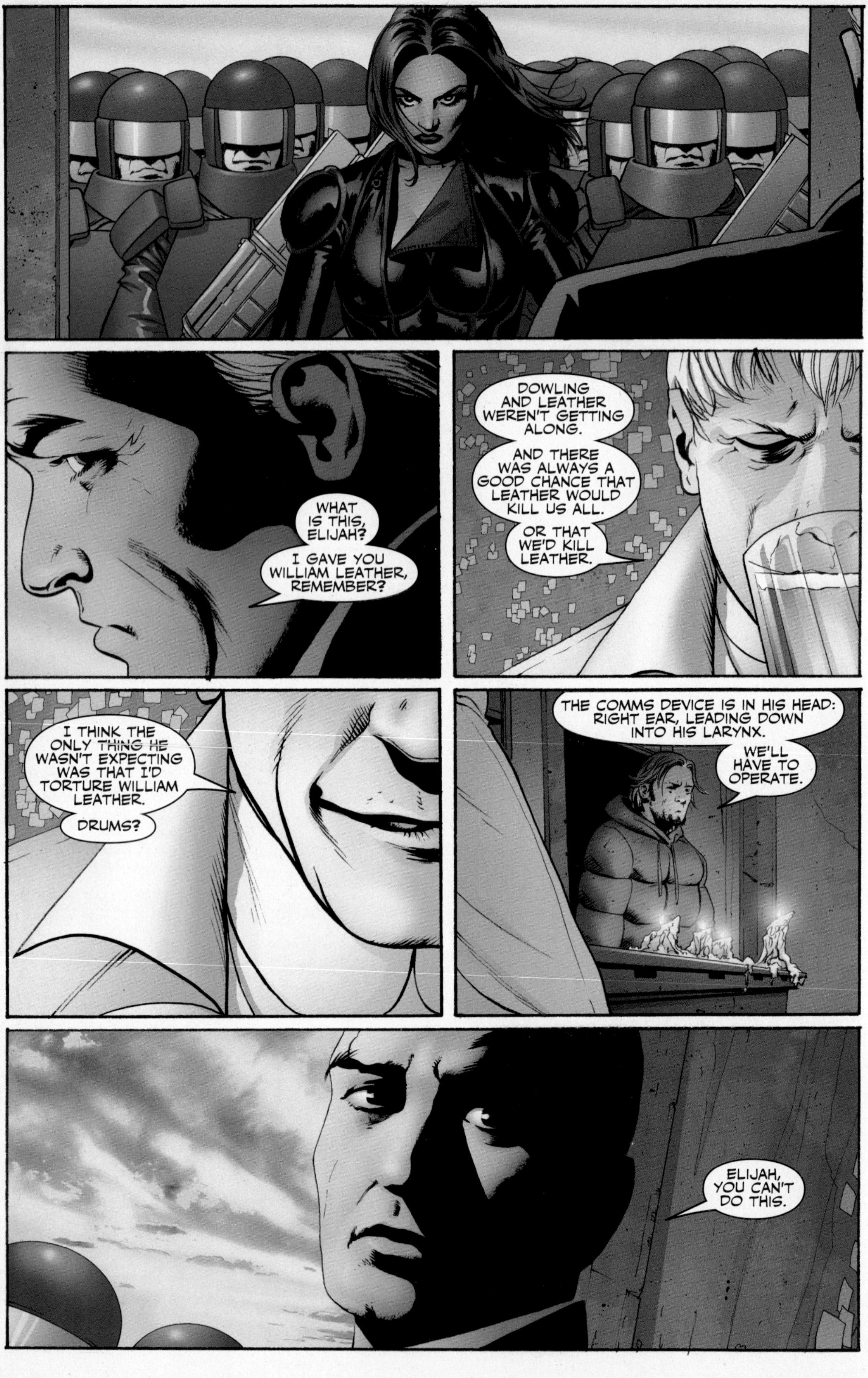
WHAT IS THIS, ELIJAH?
I GAVE YOU WILLIAM LEATHER, REMEMBER?
DOWLING AND LEATHER WEREN'T GETTING ALONG.
AND THERE WAS ALWAYS A GOOD CHANCE THAT LEATHER WOULD KILL US ALL.
OR THAT WE'D KILL LEATHER.
I THINK THE ONLY THING HE WASN'T EXPECTING WAS THAT I'D TORTURE WILLIAM LEATHER.
DRUMS?
THE COMMS DEVICE IS IN HIS HEAD: RIGHT EAR, LEADING DOWN INTO HIS LARYNX.
WE'LL HAVE TO OPERATE.
ELIJAH, YOU CAN'T DO THIS.

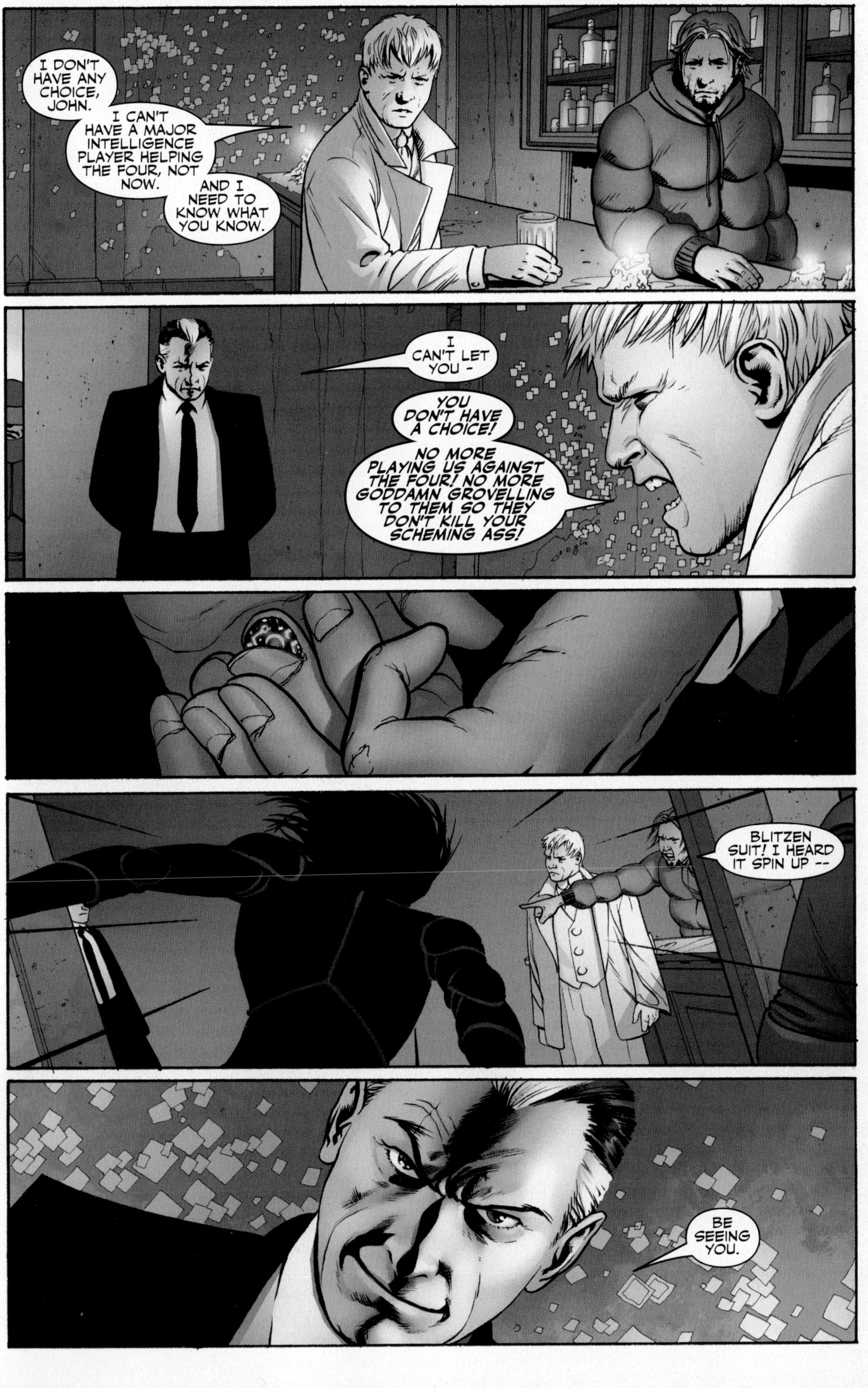
I DON'T HAVE ANY CHOICE, JOHN.
I CAN'T HAVE A MAJOR INTELLIGENCE PLAYER HELPING THE FOUR, NOT NOW.
AND I NEED TO KNOW WHAT YOU KNOW.
I CAN'T LET YOU -
YOU DON'T HAVE A CHOICE!
NO MORE PLAYING US AGAINST THE FOUR! NO MORE GODDAMN GROVELLING TO THEM SO THEY DON'T KILL YOUR SCHEMING ASS!
BLITZEN SUIT! I HEARD IT SPIN UP --
BE SEEING YOU.

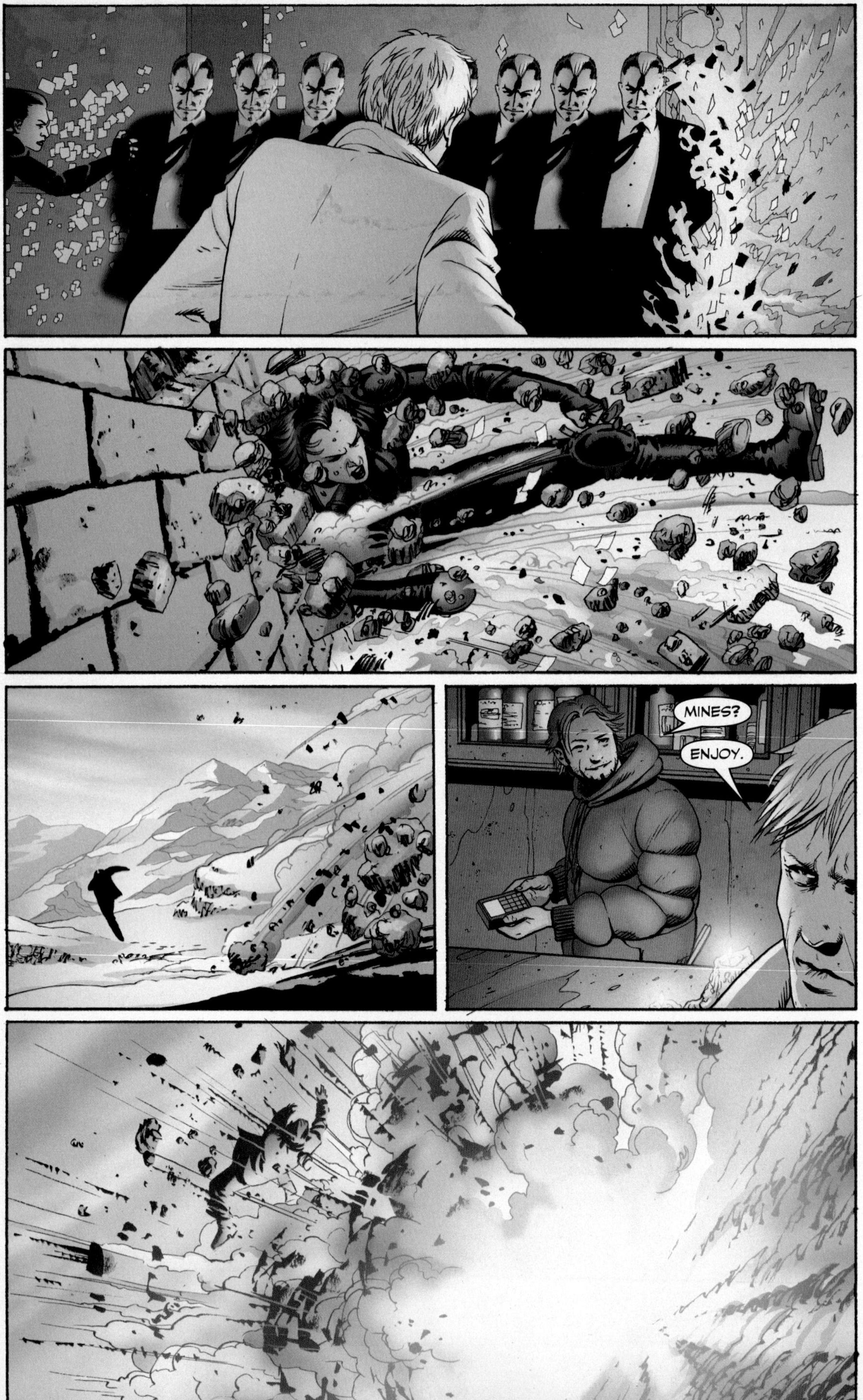
MINES?
ENJOY.

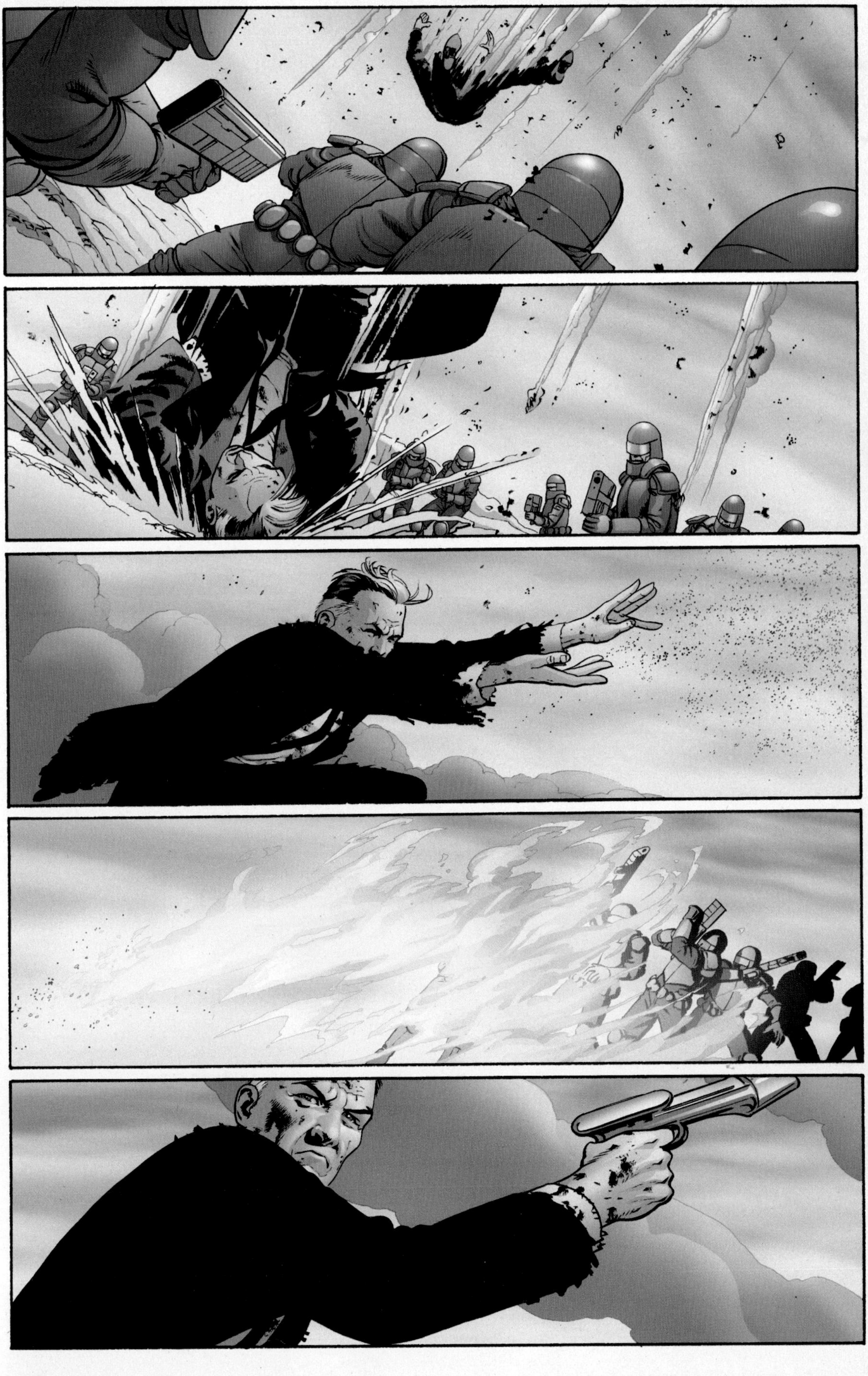

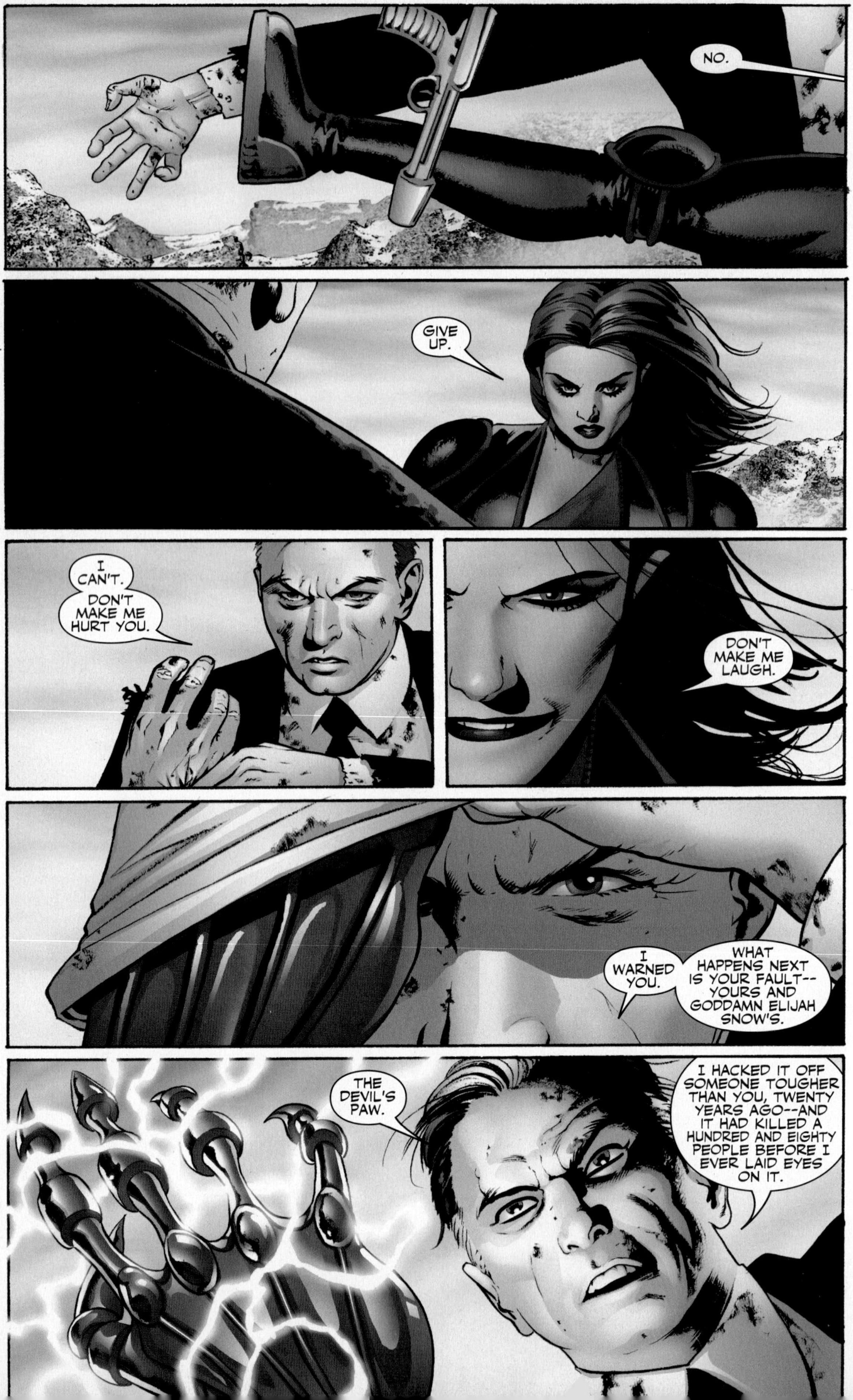
NO.
GIVE UP.
I CAN'T. DON'T MAKE ME HURT YOU.
DON'T MAKE ME LAUGH.
I WARNED YOU.
WHAT HAPPENS NEXT IS YOUR FAULT-- YOURS AND GODDAMN ELIJAH SNOW'S.
THE DEVIL'S PAW.
I HACKED IT OFF SOMEONE TOUGHER THAN YOU, TWENTY YEARS AGO--AND IT HAD KILLED A HUNDRED AND EIGHTY PEOPLE BEFORE I EVER LAID EYES ON IT.

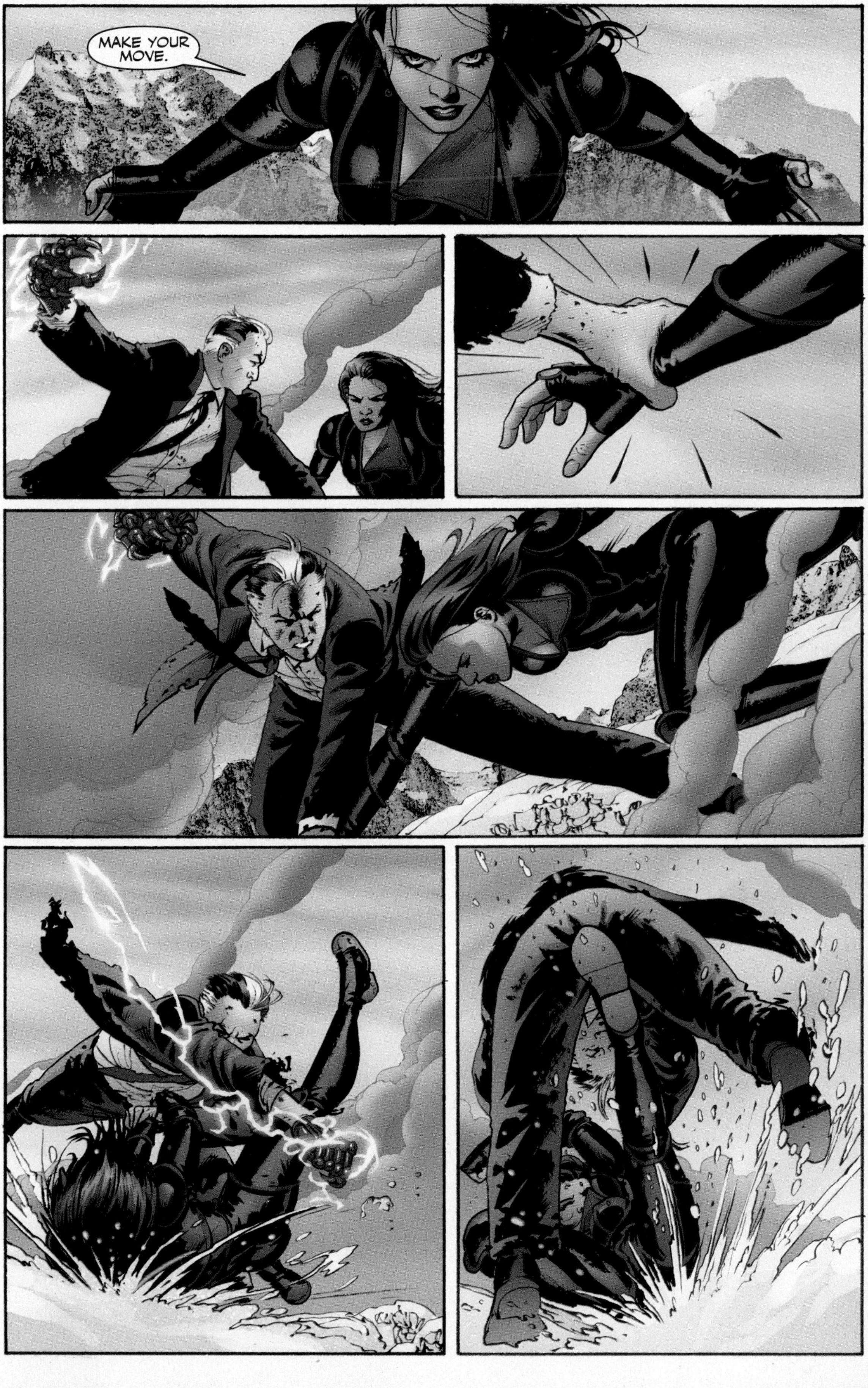
MAKE YOUR MOVE.

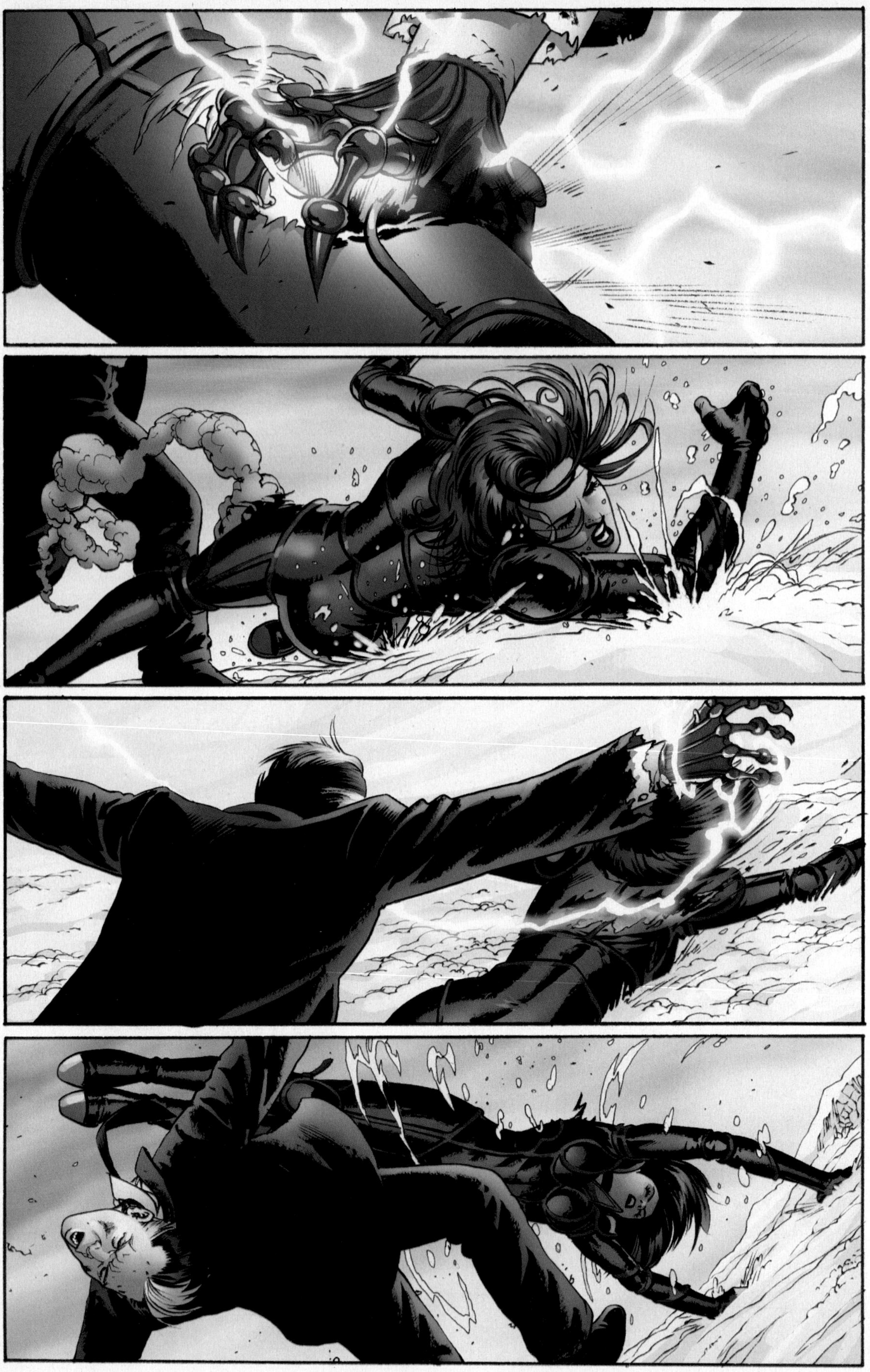

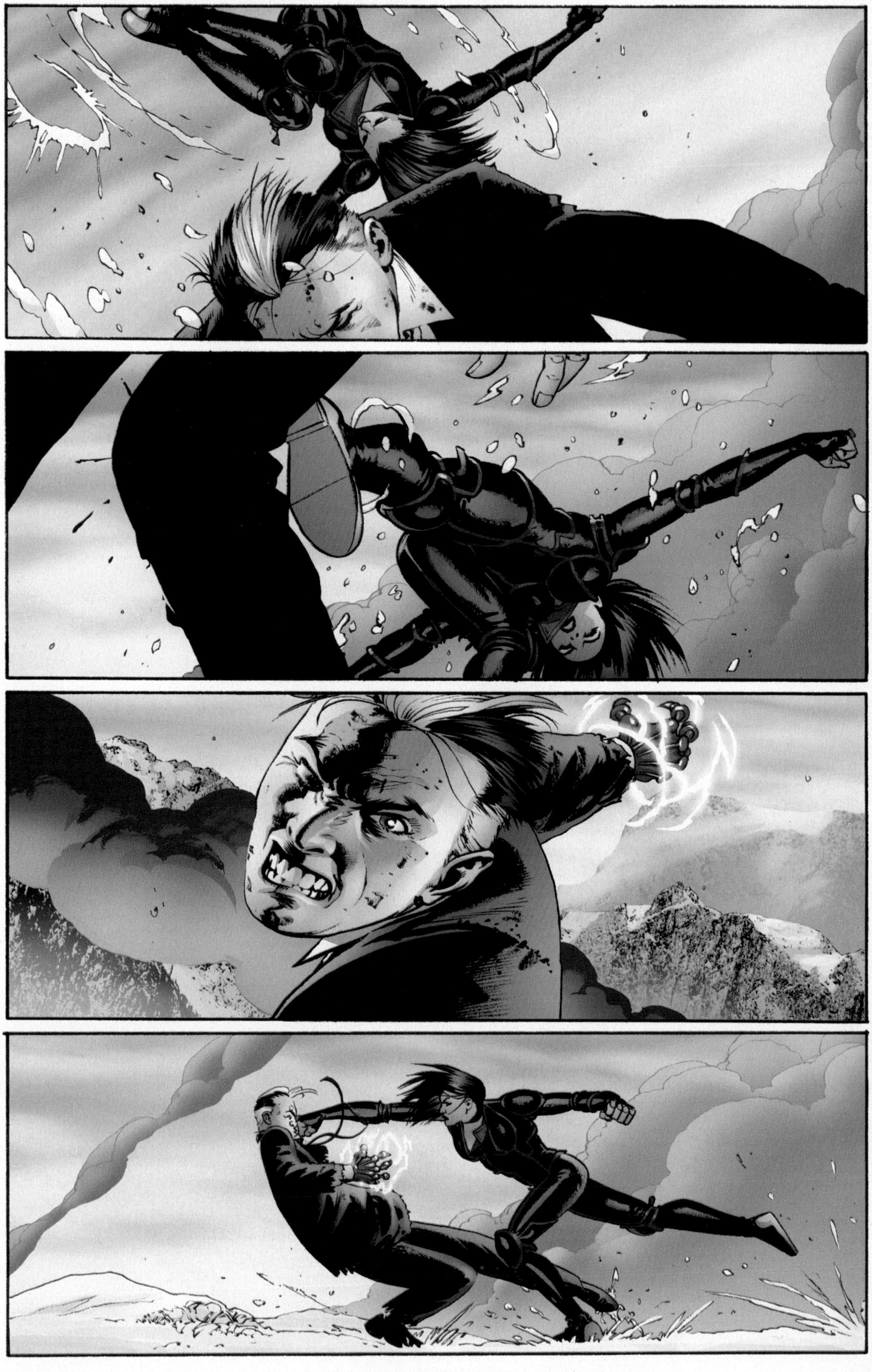

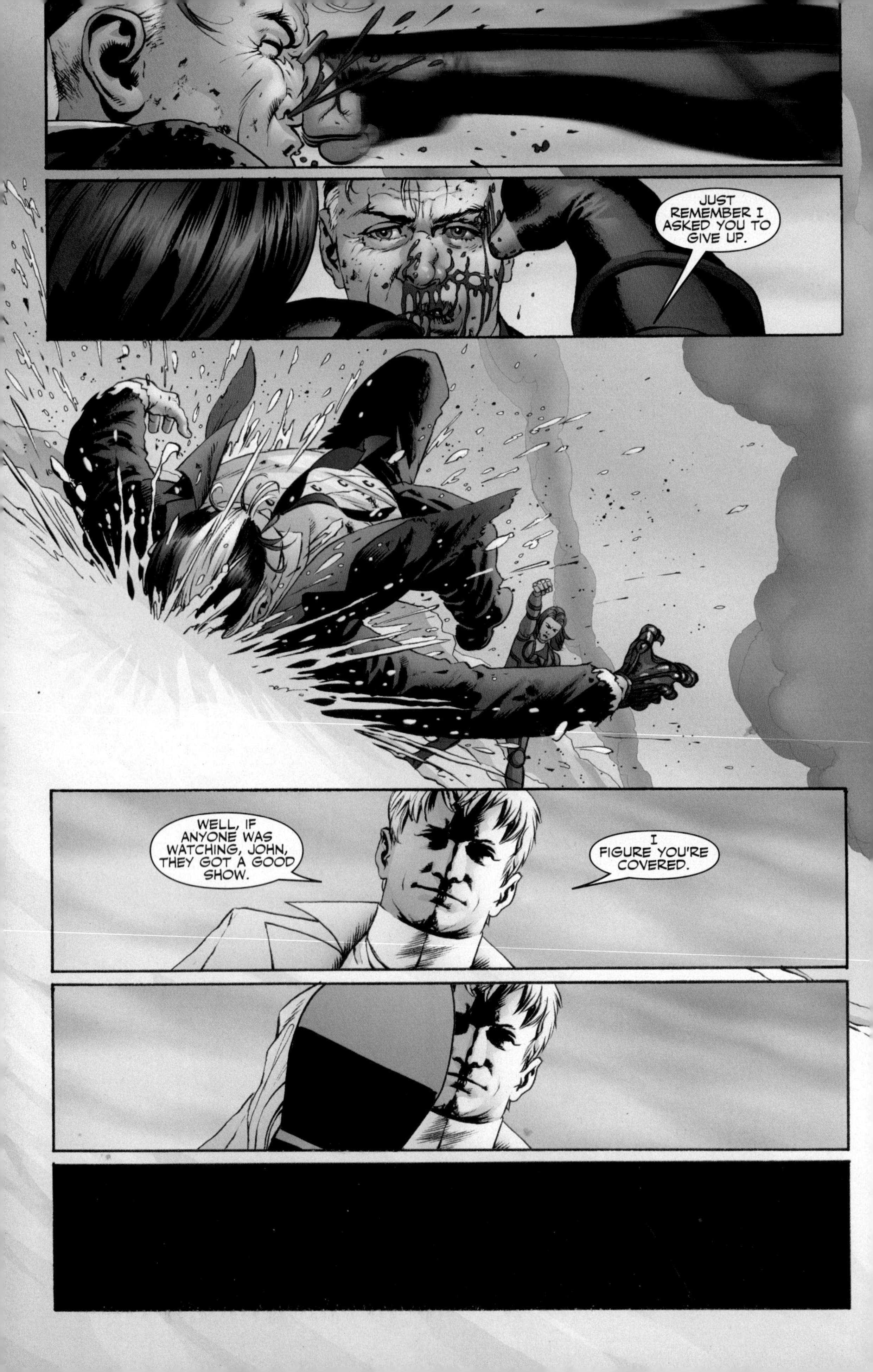
JUST REMEMBER I ASKED YOU TO GIVE UP.
WELL, IF ANYONE WAS WATCHING, JOHN, THEY GOT A GOOD SHOW.
I FIGURE YOU'RE COVERED.

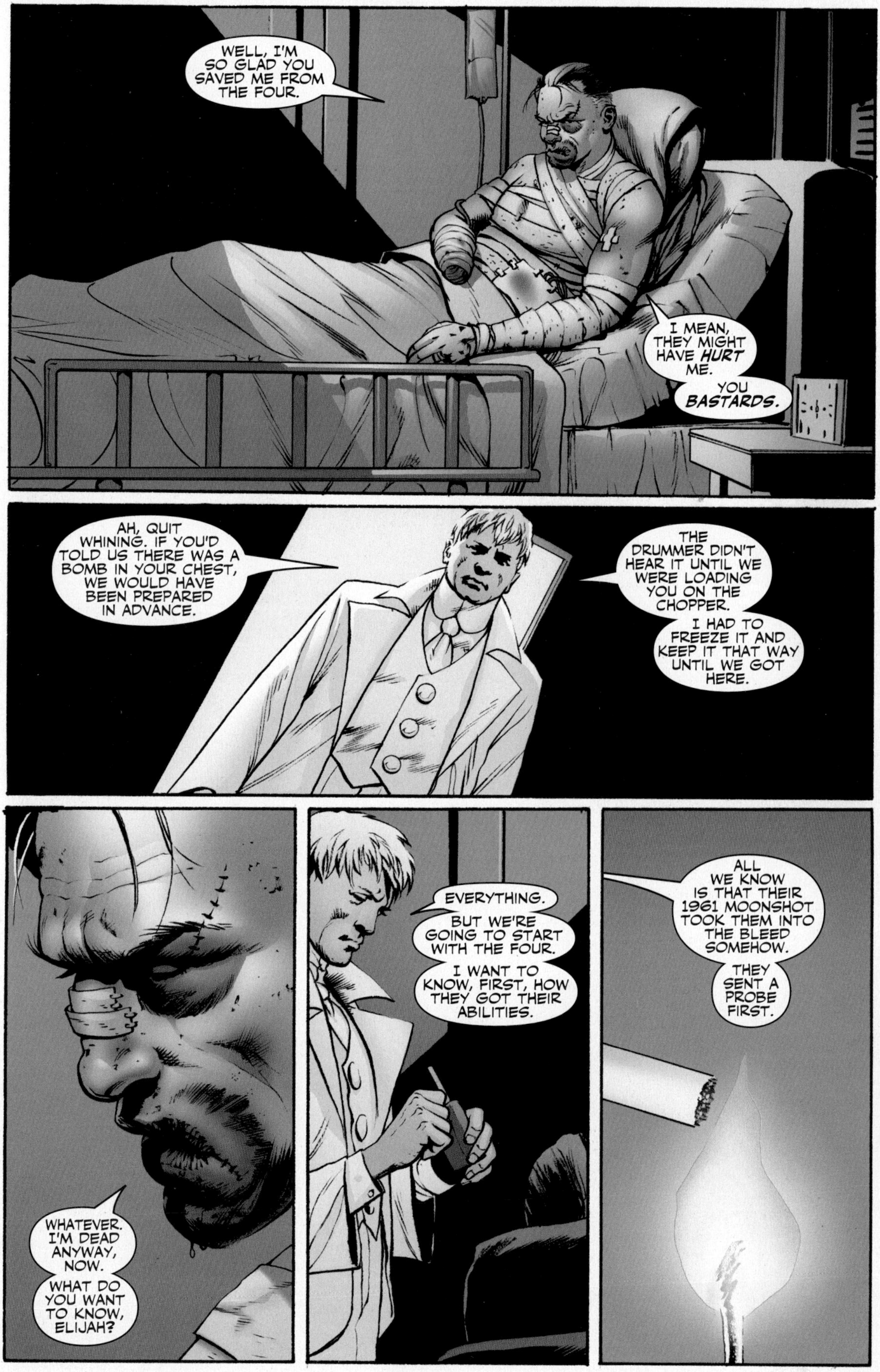
WELL, I'M SO GLAD YOU SAVED ME FROM THE FOUR.
I MEAN, THEY MIGHT HAVE *HURT* ME.
YOU ***BASTARDS.***
AH, QUIT WHINING. IF YOU'D TOLD US THERE WAS A BOMB IN YOUR CHEST, WE WOULD HAVE BEEN PREPARED IN ADVANCE.
THE DRUMMER DIDN'T HEAR IT UNTIL WE WERE LOADING YOU ON THE CHOPPER.
I HAD TO FREEZE IT AND KEEP IT THAT WAY UNTIL WE GOT HERE.
WHATEVER. I'M DEAD ANYWAY, NOW.
WHAT DO YOU WANT TO KNOW, ELIJAH?
EVERYTHING.
BUT WE'RE GOING TO START WITH THE FOUR.
I WANT TO KNOW, FIRST, HOW THEY GOT THEIR ABILITIES.
ALL WE KNOW IS THAT THEIR 1961 MOONSHOT TOOK THEM INTO THE BLEED SOMEHOW.
THEY SENT A PROBE FIRST.

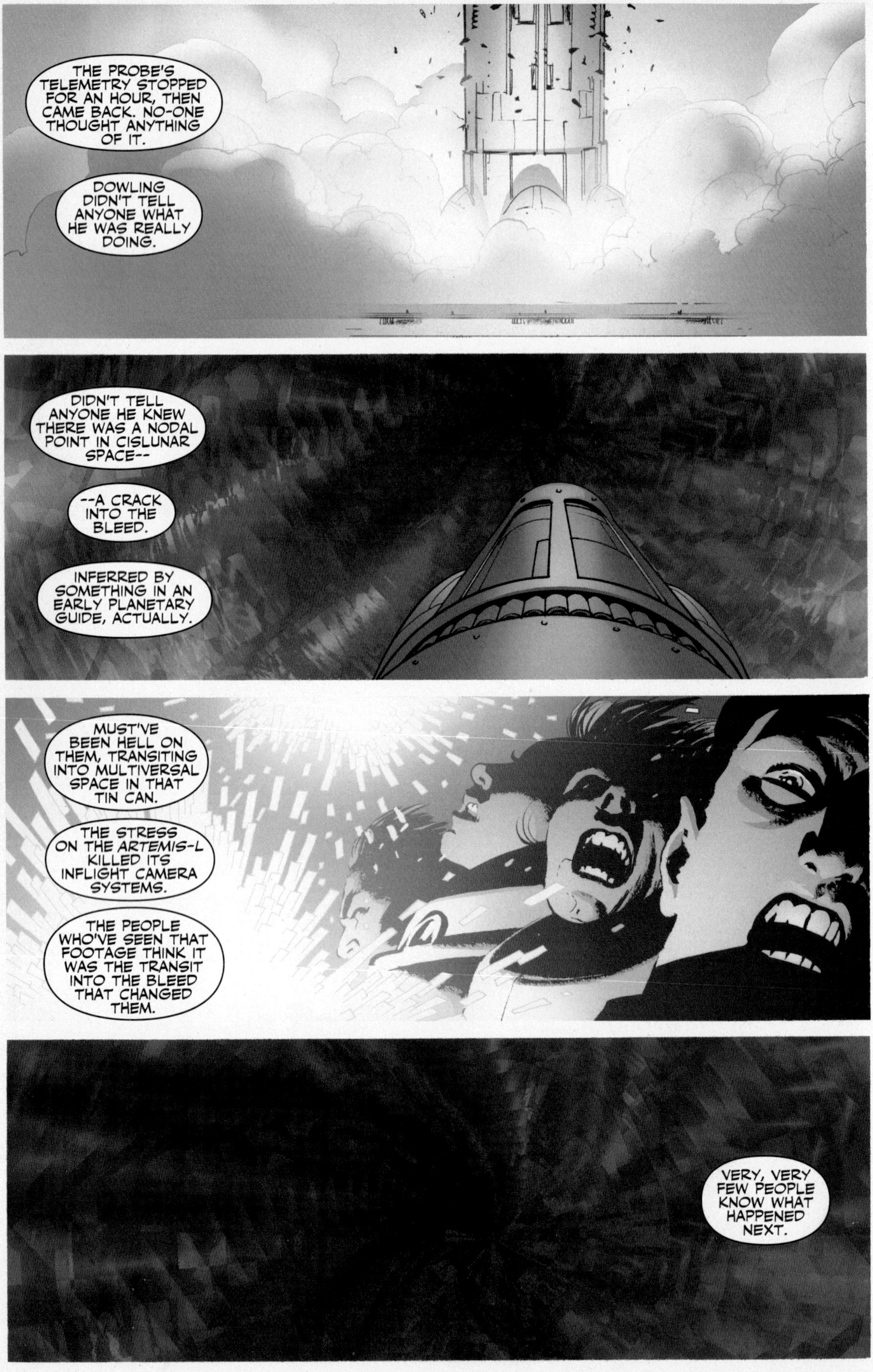
THE PROBE'S TELEMETRY STOPPED FOR AN HOUR, THEN CAME BACK. NO-ONE THOUGHT ANYTHING OF IT.
DOWLING DIDN'T TELL ANYONE WHAT HE WAS REALLY DOING.
DIDN'T TELL ANYONE HE KNEW THERE WAS A NODAL POINT IN CISLUNAR SPACE--
--A CRACK INTO THE BLEED.
INFERRED BY SOMETHING IN AN EARLY PLANETARY GUIDE, ACTUALLY.
MUST'VE BEEN HELL ON THEM, TRANSITING INTO MULTIVERSAL SPACE IN THAT TIN CAN.
THE STRESS ON THE *ARTEMIS-L* KILLED ITS INFLIGHT CAMERA SYSTEMS.
THE PEOPLE WHO'VE SEEN THAT FOOTAGE THINK IT WAS THE TRANSIT INTO THE BLEED THAT CHANGED THEM.
VERY, VERY FEW PEOPLE KNOW WHAT HAPPENED NEXT.

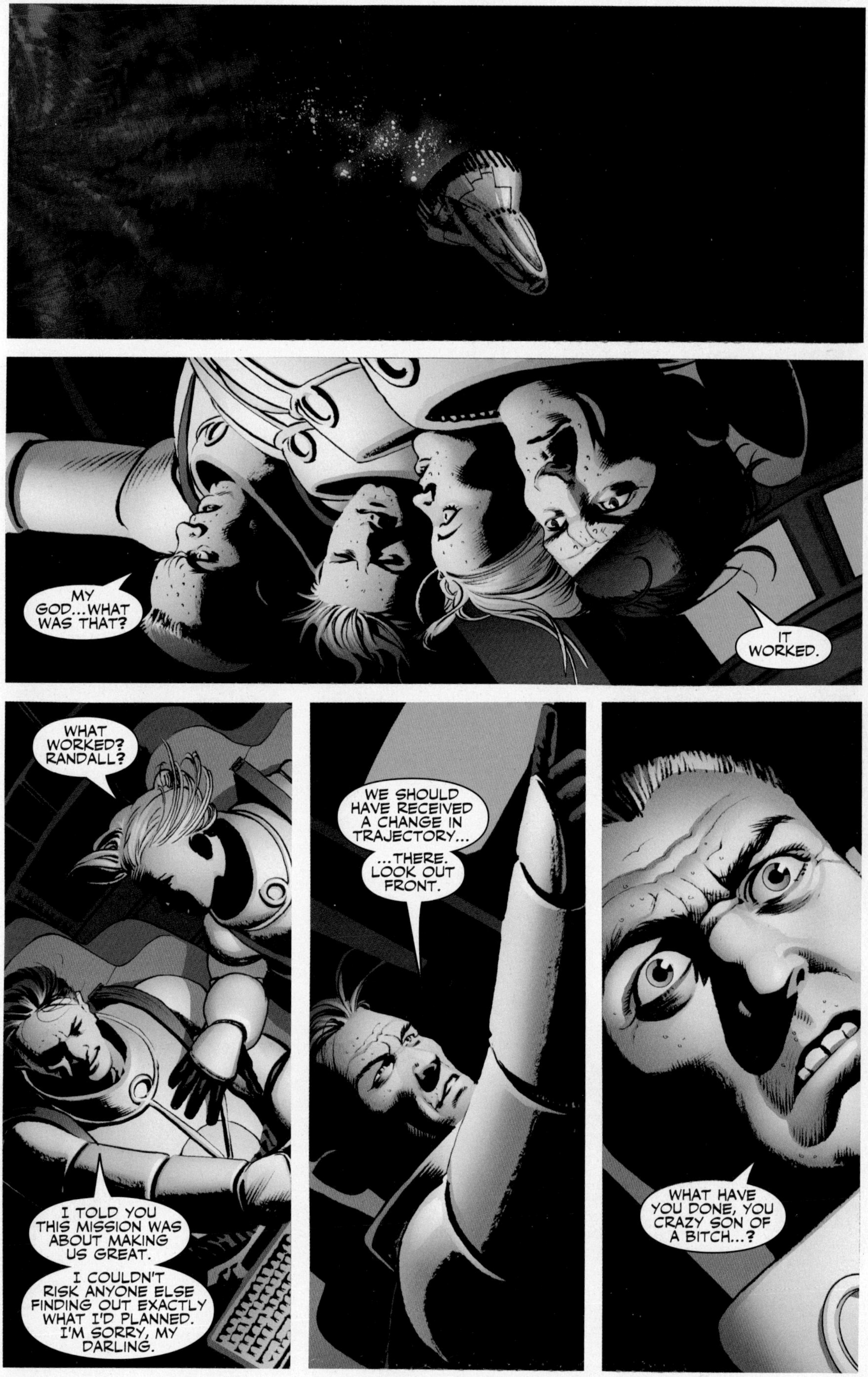
MY GOD...WHAT WAS THAT?
IT WORKED.
WHAT WORKED? RANDALL?
I TOLD YOU THIS MISSION WAS ABOUT MAKING US GREAT.
I COULDN'T RISK ANYONE ELSE FINDING OUT EXACTLY WHAT I'D PLANNED. I'M SORRY, MY DARLING.
WE SHOULD HAVE RECEIVED A CHANGE IN TRAJECTORY...
...THERE. LOOK OUT FRONT.
WHAT HAVE YOU DONE, YOU CRAZY SON OF A BITCH...?

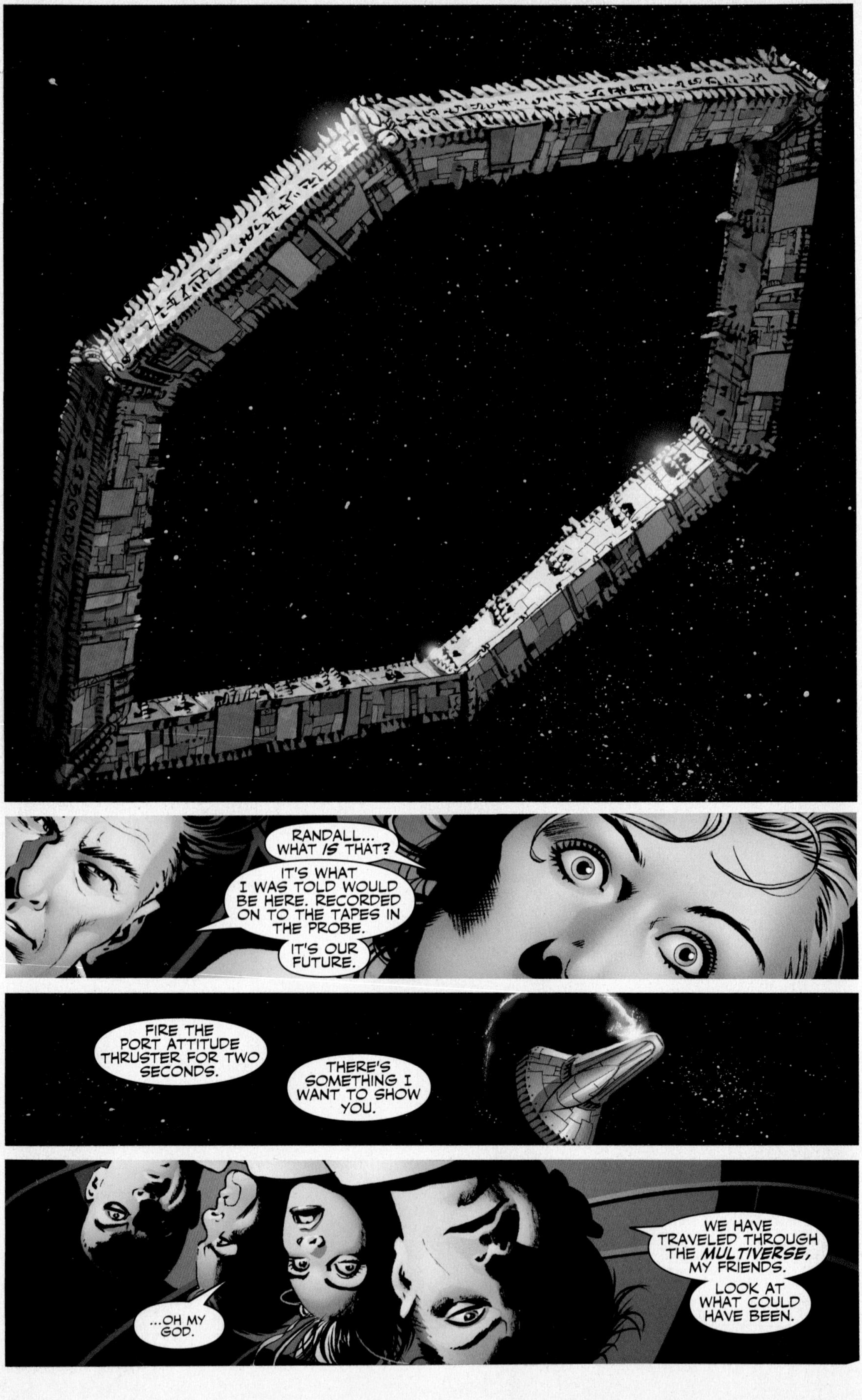
RANDALL... WHAT IS THAT?
IT'S WHAT I WAS TOLD WOULD BE HERE. RECORDED ON TO THE TAPES IN THE PROBE.
IT'S OUR FUTURE.
FIRE THE PORT ATTITUDE THRUSTER FOR TWO SECONDS.
THERE'S SOMETHING I WANT TO SHOW YOU.
WE HAVE TRAVELED THROUGH THE MULTIVERSE, MY FRIENDS.
LOOK AT WHAT COULD HAVE BEEN.
...OH MY GOD.

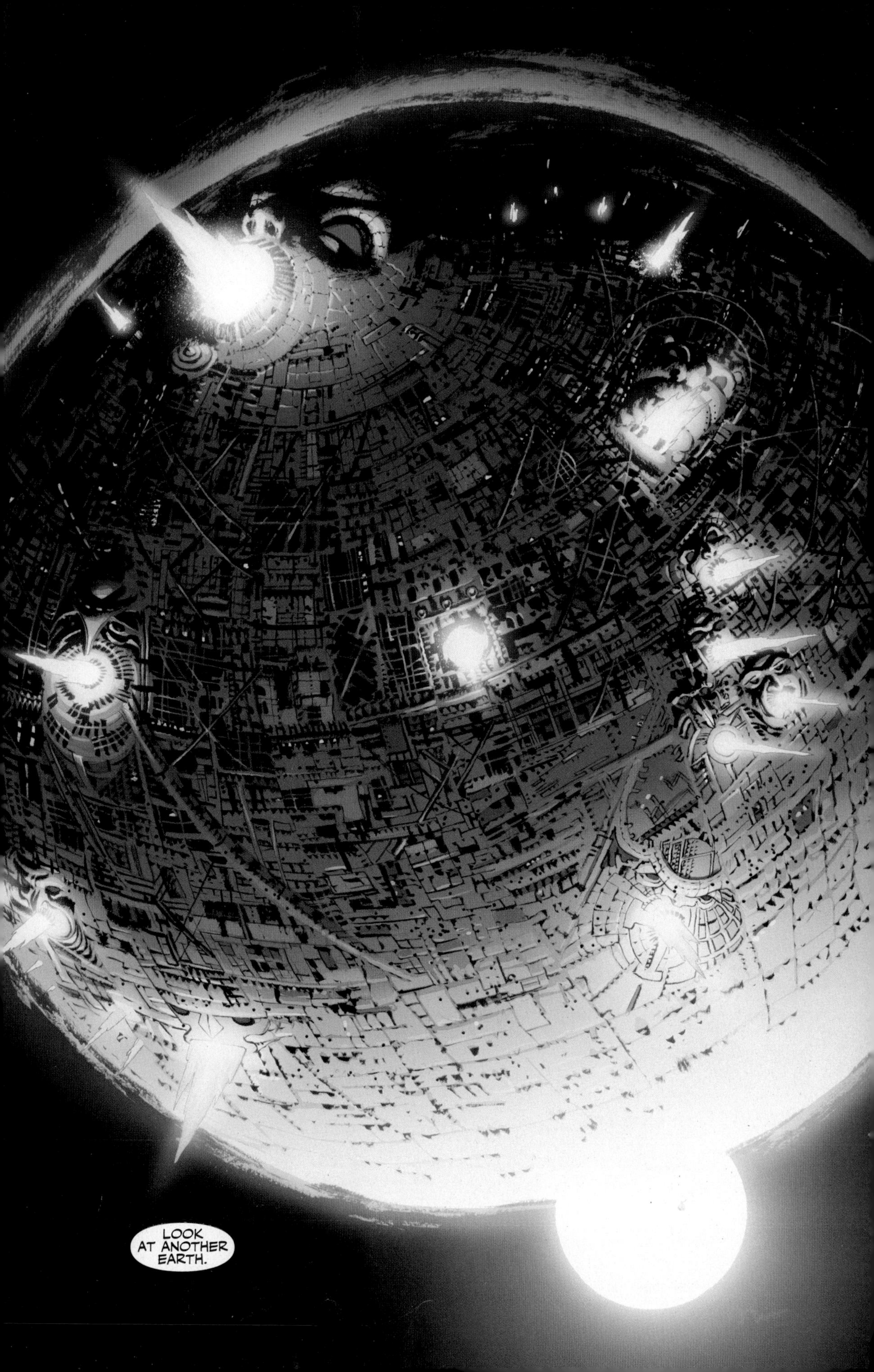
LOOK AT ANOTHER EARTH.

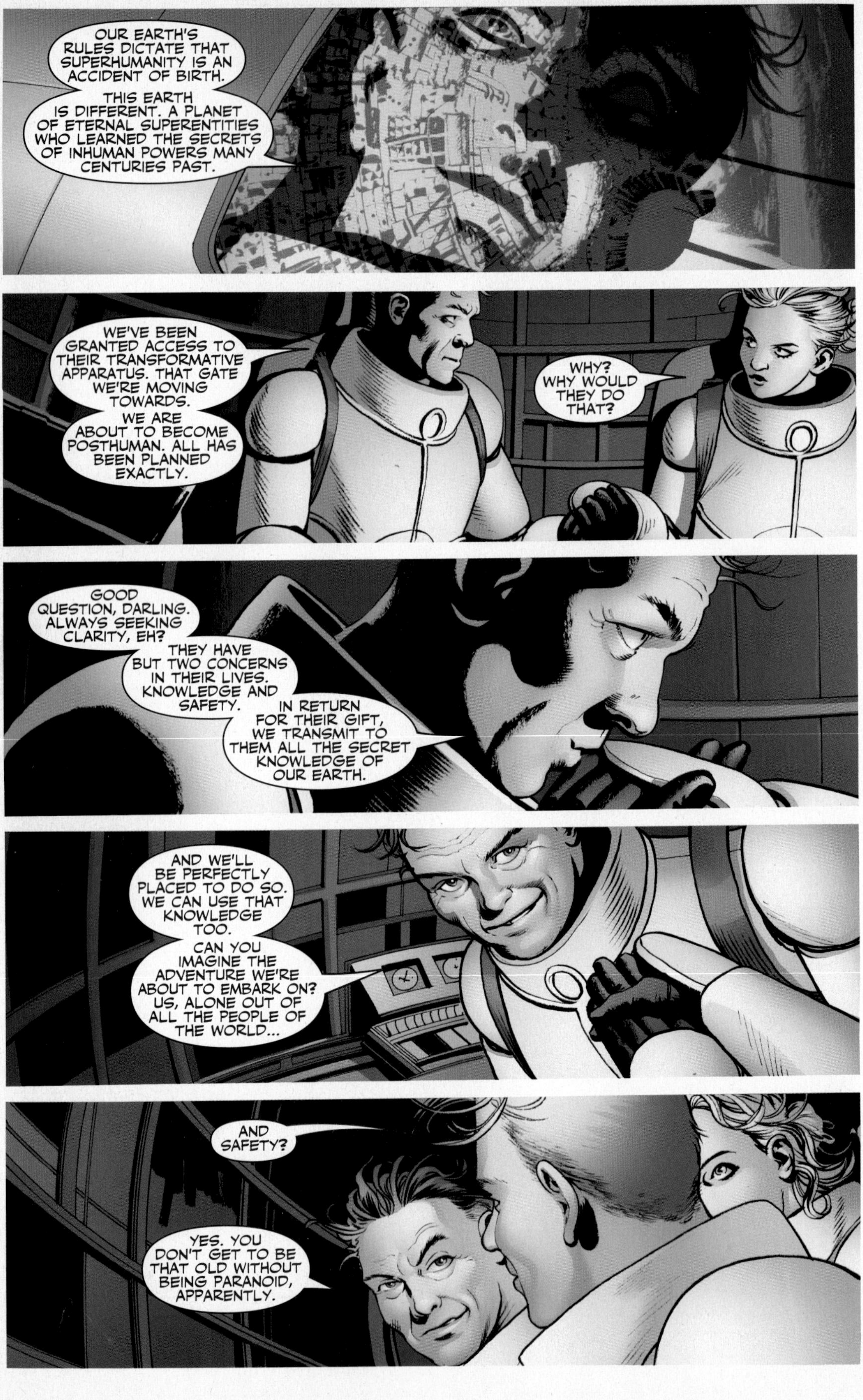
OUR EARTH'S RULES DICTATE THAT SUPERHUMANITY IS AN ACCIDENT OF BIRTH.
THIS EARTH IS DIFFERENT. A PLANET OF ETERNAL SUPERENTITIES WHO LEARNED THE SECRETS OF INHUMAN POWERS MANY CENTURIES PAST.
WE'VE BEEN GRANTED ACCESS TO THEIR TRANSFORMATIVE APPARATUS. THAT GATE WE'RE MOVING TOWARDS.
WE ARE ABOUT TO BECOME POSTHUMAN. ALL HAS BEEN PLANNED EXACTLY.
WHY? WHY WOULD THEY DO THAT?
GOOD QUESTION, DARLING. ALWAYS SEEKING CLARITY, EH?
THEY HAVE BUT TWO CONCERNS IN THEIR LIVES. KNOWLEDGE AND SAFETY.
IN RETURN FOR THEIR GIFT, WE TRANSMIT TO THEM ALL THE SECRET KNOWLEDGE OF OUR EARTH.
AND WE'LL BE PERFECTLY PLACED TO DO SO. WE CAN USE THAT KNOWLEDGE TOO.
CAN YOU IMAGINE THE ADVENTURE WE'RE ABOUT TO EMBARK ON? US, ALONE OUT OF ALL THE PEOPLE OF THE WORLD...
AND SAFETY?
YES. YOU DON'T GET TO BE THAT OLD WITHOUT BEING PARANOID, APPARENTLY.

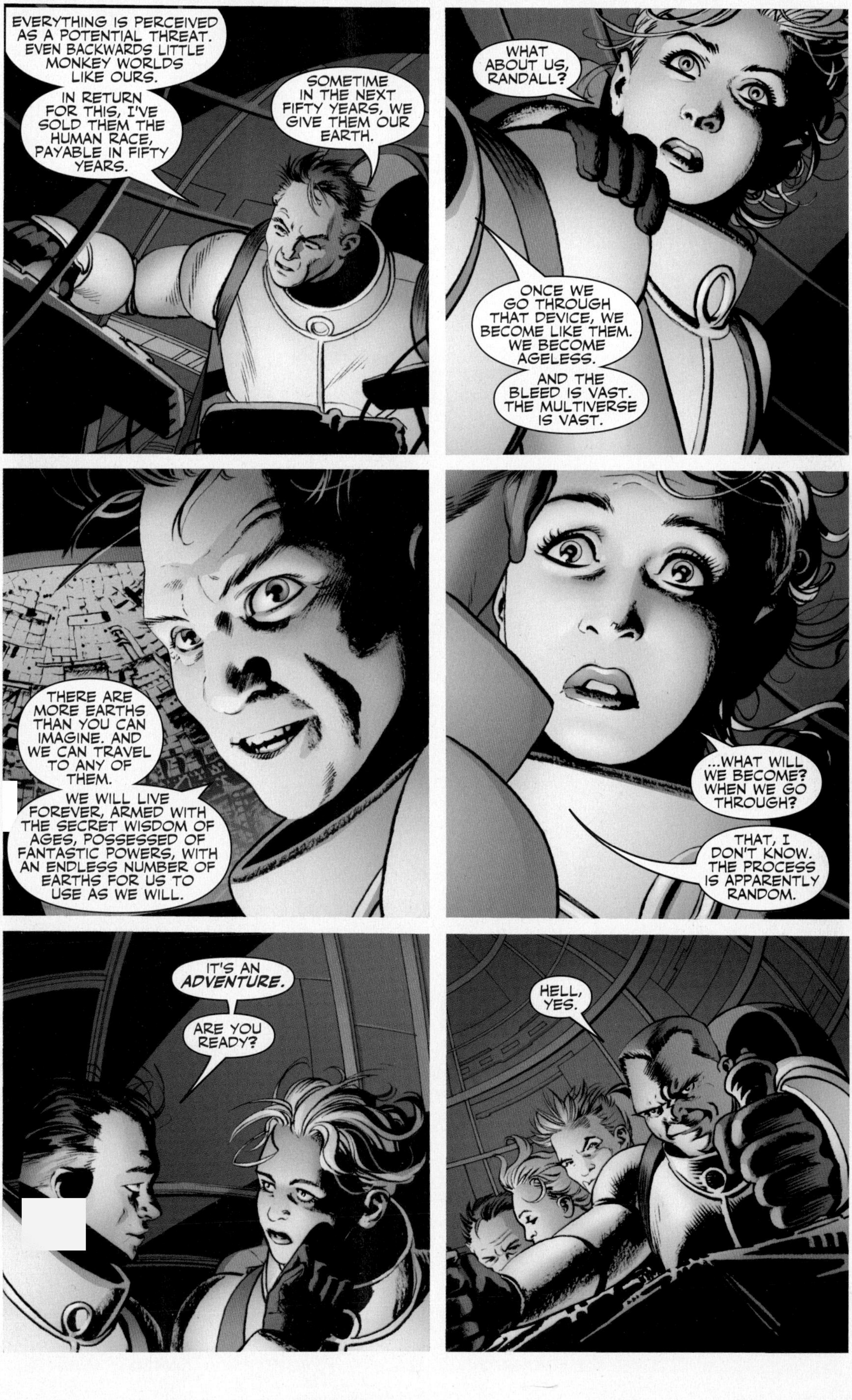
EVERYTHING IS PERCEIVED AS A POTENTIAL THREAT. EVEN BACKWARDS LITTLE MONKEY WORLDS LIKE OURS.
IN RETURN FOR THIS, I'VE SOLD THEM THE HUMAN RACE, PAYABLE IN FIFTY YEARS.
SOMETIME IN THE NEXT FIFTY YEARS, WE GIVE THEM OUR EARTH.
WHAT ABOUT US, RANDALL?
ONCE WE GO THROUGH THAT DEVICE, WE BECOME LIKE THEM. WE BECOME AGELESS.
AND THE BLEED IS VAST. THE MULTIVERSE IS VAST.
THERE ARE MORE EARTHS THAN YOU CAN IMAGINE. AND WE CAN TRAVEL TO ANY OF THEM.
WE WILL LIVE FOREVER, ARMED WITH THE SECRET WISDOM OF AGES, POSSESSED OF FANTASTIC POWERS, WITH AN ENDLESS NUMBER OF EARTHS FOR US TO USE AS WE WILL.
...WHAT WILL WE BECOME? WHEN WE GO THROUGH?
THAT, I DON'T KNOW. THE PROCESS IS APPARENTLY RANDOM.
IT'S AN *ADVENTURE.*
ARE YOU READY?
HELL, YES.

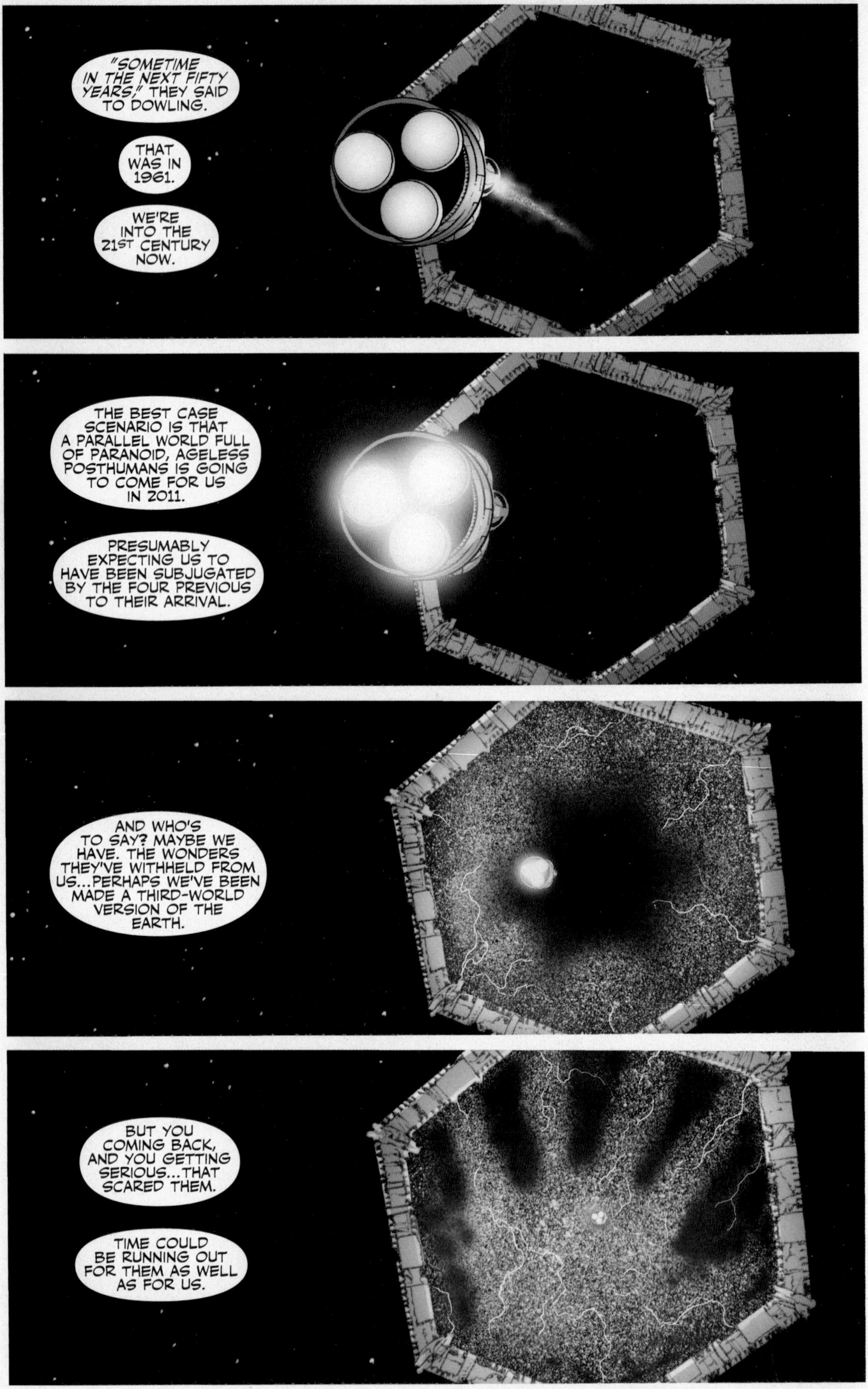
"SOMETIME IN THE NEXT FIFTY YEARS," THEY SAID TO DOWLING.
THAT WAS IN 1961.
WE'RE INTO THE 21ST CENTURY NOW.
THE BEST CASE SCENARIO IS THAT A PARALLEL WORLD FULL OF PARANOID, AGELESS POSTHUMANS IS GOING TO COME FOR US IN 2011.
PRESUMABLY EXPECTING US TO HAVE BEEN SUBJUGATED BY THE FOUR PREVIOUS TO THEIR ARRIVAL.
AND WHO'S TO SAY? MAYBE WE HAVE. THE WONDERS THEY'VE WITHHELD FROM US...PERHAPS WE'VE BEEN MADE A THIRD-WORLD VERSION OF THE EARTH.
BUT YOU COMING BACK, AND YOU GETTING SERIOUS...THAT SCARED THEM.
TIME COULD BE RUNNING OUT FOR THEM AS WELL AS FOR US.

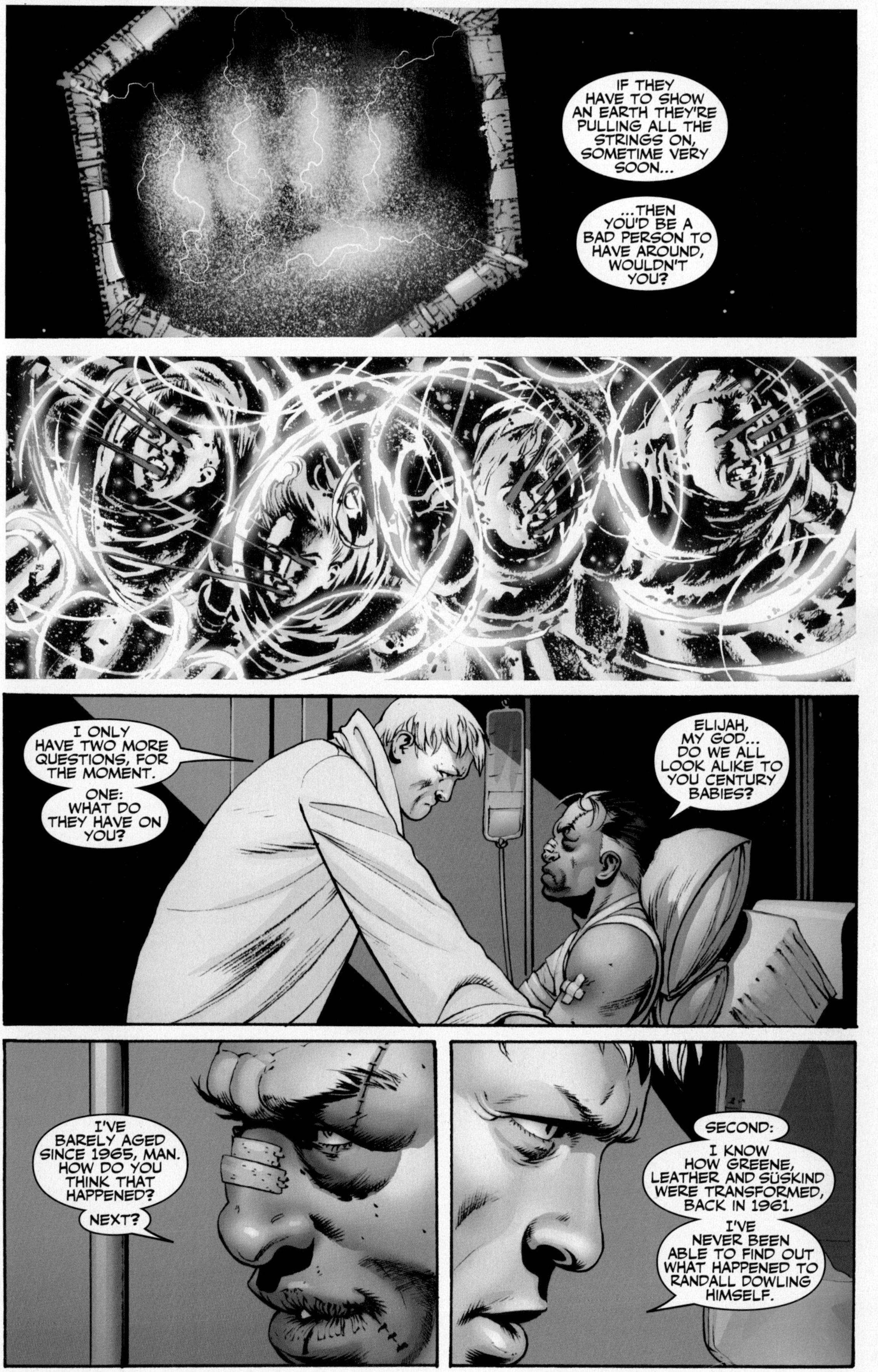
IF THEY HAVE TO SHOW AN EARTH THEY'RE PULLING ALL THE STRINGS ON, SOMETIME VERY SOON...
...THEN YOU'D BE A BAD PERSON TO HAVE AROUND, WOULDN'T YOU?
I ONLY HAVE TWO MORE QUESTIONS, FOR THE MOMENT.
ONE: WHAT DO THEY HAVE ON YOU?
ELIJAH, MY GOD... DO WE ALL LOOK ALIKE TO YOU CENTURY BABIES?
I'VE BARELY AGED SINCE 1965, MAN. HOW DO YOU THINK THAT HAPPENED?
NEXT?
SECOND:
I KNOW HOW GREENE, LEATHER AND SÜSKIND WERE TRANSFORMED, BACK IN 1961.
I'VE NEVER BEEN ABLE TO FIND OUT WHAT HAPPENED TO RANDALL DOWLING HIMSELF.

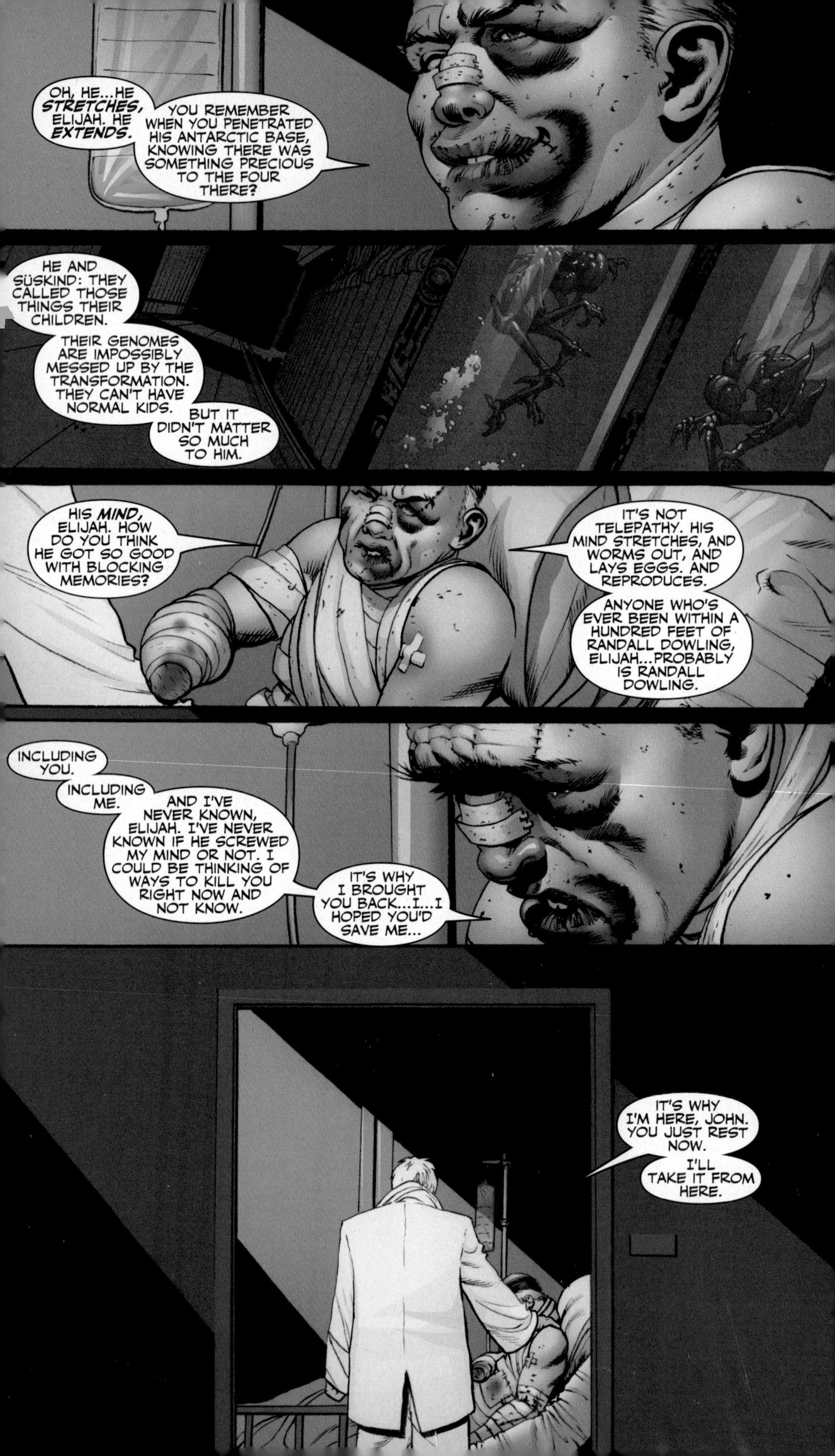
OH, HE...HE STRETCHES, ELIJAH. HE EXTENDS.
YOU REMEMBER WHEN YOU PENETRATED HIS ANTARCTIC BASE, KNOWING THERE WAS SOMETHING PRECIOUS TO THE FOUR THERE?
HE AND SÜSKIND: THEY CALLED THOSE THINGS THEIR CHILDREN.
THEIR GENOMES ARE IMPOSSIBLY MESSED UP BY THE TRANSFORMATION. THEY CAN'T HAVE NORMAL KIDS.
BUT IT DIDN'T MATTER SO MUCH TO HIM.
HIS MIND, ELIJAH. HOW DO YOU THINK HE GOT SO GOOD WITH BLOCKING MEMORIES?
IT'S NOT TELEPATHY. HIS MIND STRETCHES, AND WORMS OUT, AND LAYS EGGS. AND REPRODUCES.
ANYONE WHO'S EVER BEEN WITHIN A HUNDRED FEET OF RANDALL DOWLING, ELIJAH...PROBABLY IS RANDALL DOWLING.
INCLUDING YOU.
INCLUDING ME.
AND I'VE NEVER KNOWN, ELIJAH. I'VE NEVER KNOWN IF HE SCREWED MY MIND OR NOT. I COULD BE THINKING OF WAYS TO KILL YOU RIGHT NOW AND NOT KNOW.
IT'S WHY I BROUGHT YOU BACK...I...I HOPED YOU'D SAVE ME...
IT'S WHY I'M HERE, JOHN. YOU JUST REST NOW.
I'LL TAKE IT FROM HERE.

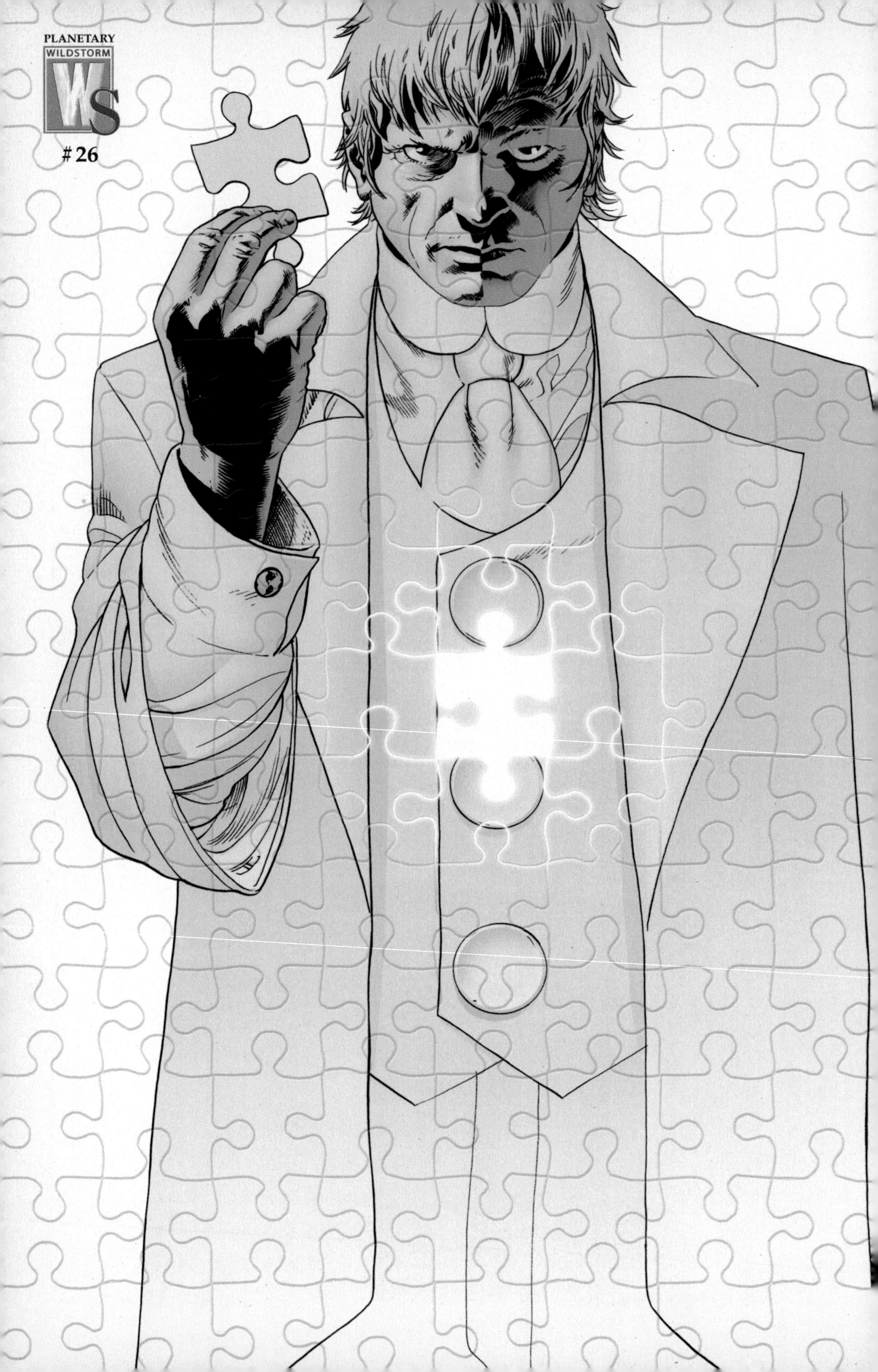
PLANETARY
WILDSTORM
26

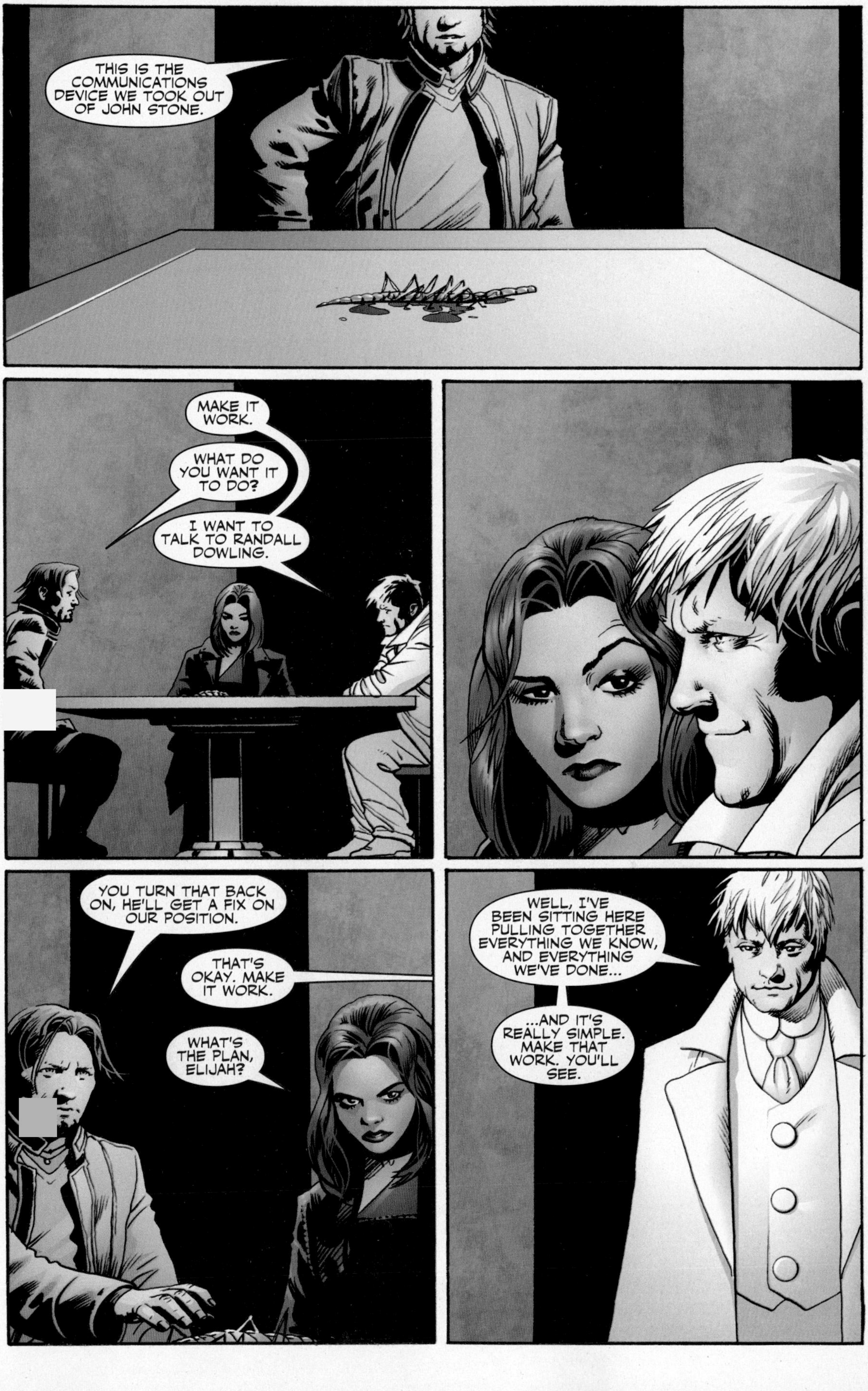
THIS IS THE COMMUNICATIONS DEVICE WE TOOK OUT OF JOHN STONE.
MAKE IT WORK.
WHAT DO YOU WANT IT TO DO?
I WANT TO TALK TO RANDALL DOWLING.
YOU TURN THAT BACK ON, HE'LL GET A FIX ON OUR POSITION.
THAT'S OKAY. MAKE IT WORK.
WHAT'S THE PLAN, ELIJAH?
WELL, I'VE BEEN SITTING HERE PULLING TOGETHER EVERYTHING WE KNOW, AND EVERYTHING WE'VE DONE...
...AND IT'S REALLY SIMPLE. MAKE THAT WORK. YOU'LL SEE.

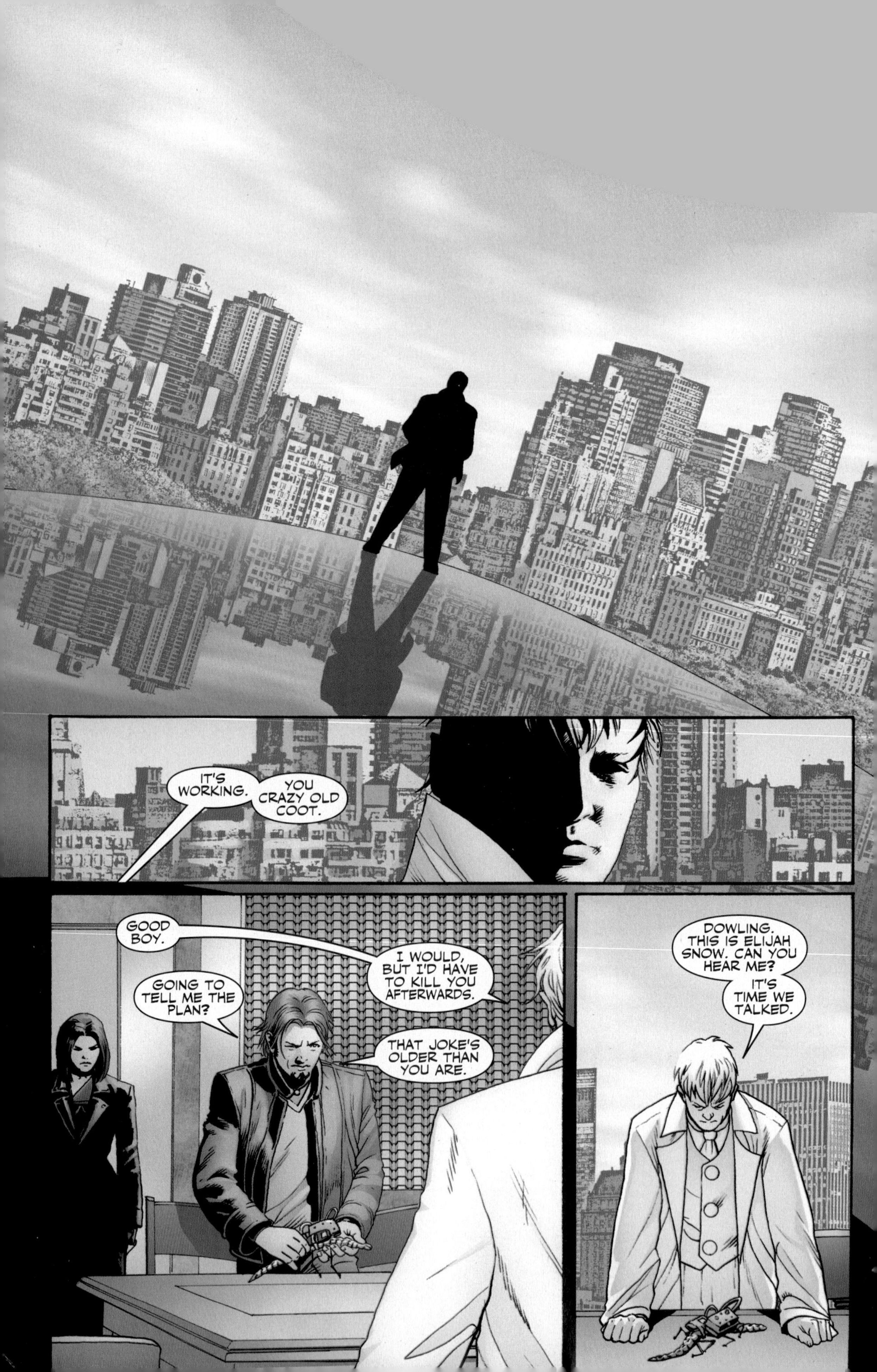
IT'S WORKING.
YOU CRAZY OLD COOT.
GOOD BOY.
GOING TO TELL ME THE PLAN?
I WOULD, BUT I'D HAVE TO KILL YOU AFTERWARDS.
THAT JOKE'S OLDER THAN YOU ARE.
DOWLING. THIS IS ELIJAH SNOW. CAN YOU HEAR ME?
IT'S TIME WE TALKED.

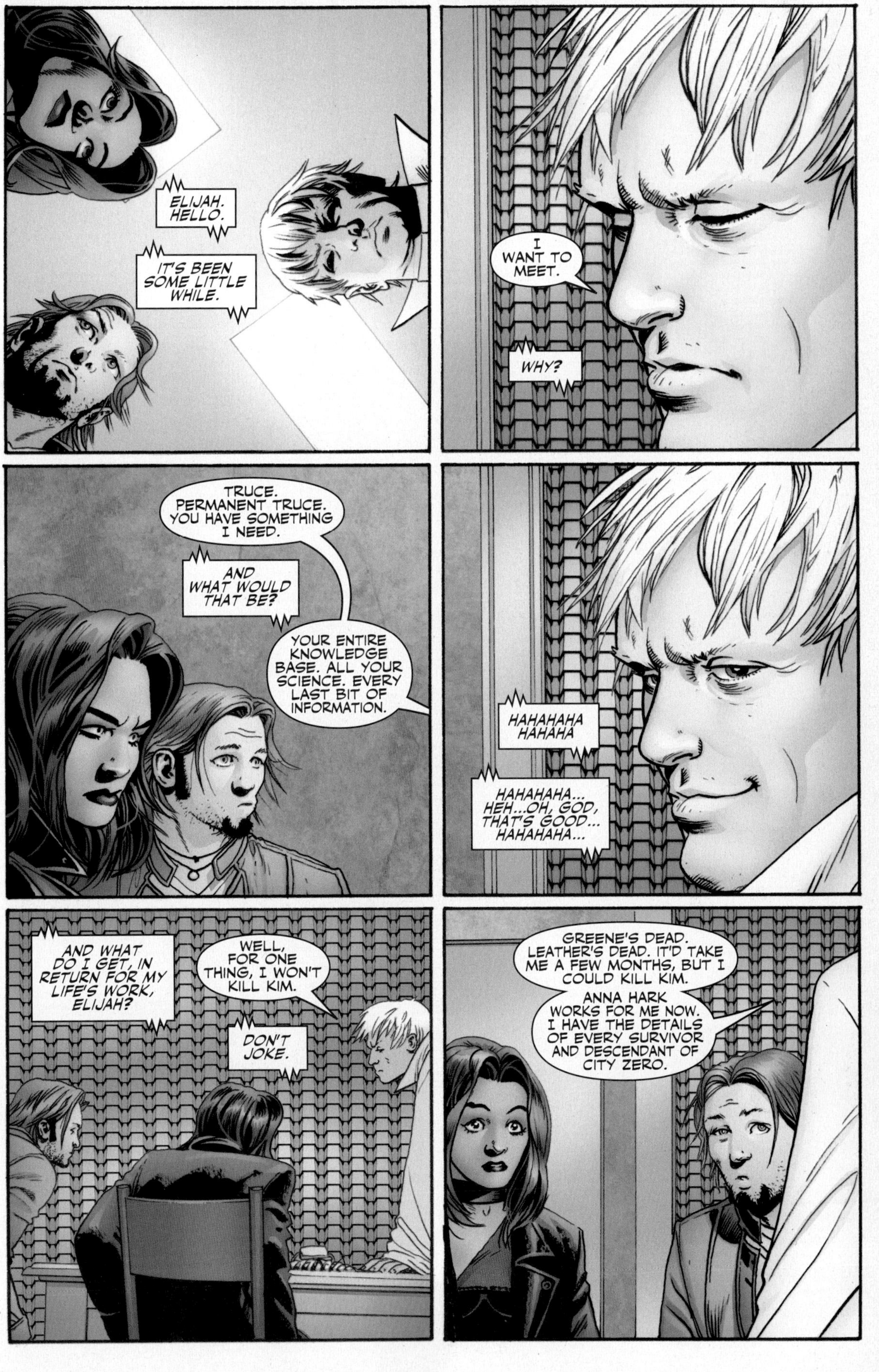
ELIJAH. HELLO.
IT'S BEEN SOME LITTLE WHILE.
I WANT TO MEET.
WHY?
TRUCE. PERMANENT TRUCE. YOU HAVE SOMETHING I NEED.
AND WHAT WOULD THAT BE?
YOUR ENTIRE KNOWLEDGE BASE. ALL YOUR SCIENCE. EVERY LAST BIT OF INFORMATION.
HAHAHAHA HAHAHA
HAHAHAHA... HEH...OH, GOD, THAT'S GOOD... HAHAHAHA...
AND WHAT DO I GET, IN RETURN FOR MY LIFE'S WORK, ELIJAH?
WELL, FOR ONE THING, I WON'T KILL KIM.
DON'T JOKE.
GREENE'S DEAD. LEATHER'S DEAD. IT'D TAKE ME A FEW MONTHS, BUT I COULD KILL KIM.
ANNA HARK WORKS FOR ME NOW. I HAVE THE DETAILS OF EVERY SURVIVOR AND DESCENDANT OF CITY ZERO.

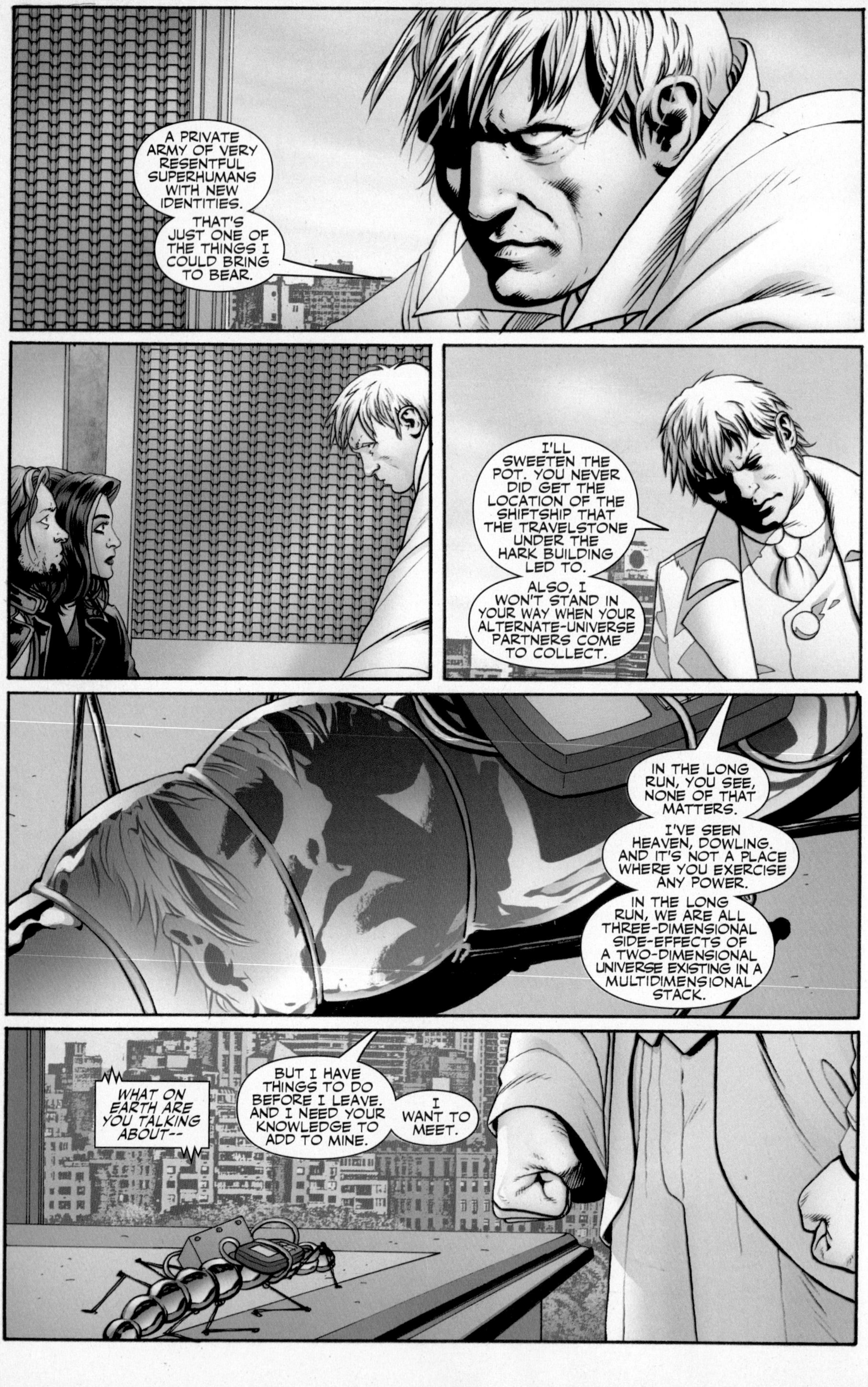
A PRIVATE ARMY OF VERY RESENTFUL SUPERHUMANS WITH NEW IDENTITIES.
THAT'S JUST ONE OF THE THINGS I COULD BRING TO BEAR.
I'LL SWEETEN THE POT. YOU NEVER DID GET THE LOCATION OF THE SHIFTSHIP THAT THE TRAVELSTONE UNDER THE HARK BUILDING LED TO.
ALSO, I WON'T STAND IN YOUR WAY WHEN YOUR ALTERNATE-UNIVERSE PARTNERS COME TO COLLECT.
IN THE LONG RUN, YOU SEE, NONE OF THAT MATTERS.
I'VE SEEN HEAVEN, DOWLING. AND IT'S NOT A PLACE WHERE YOU EXERCISE ANY POWER.
IN THE LONG RUN, WE ARE ALL THREE-DIMENSIONAL SIDE-EFFECTS OF A TWO-DIMENSIONAL UNIVERSE EXISTING IN A MULTIDIMENSIONAL STACK.
WHAT ON EARTH ARE YOU TALKING ABOUT--
BUT I HAVE THINGS TO DO BEFORE I LEAVE. AND I NEED YOUR KNOWLEDGE TO ADD TO MINE.
I WANT TO MEET.

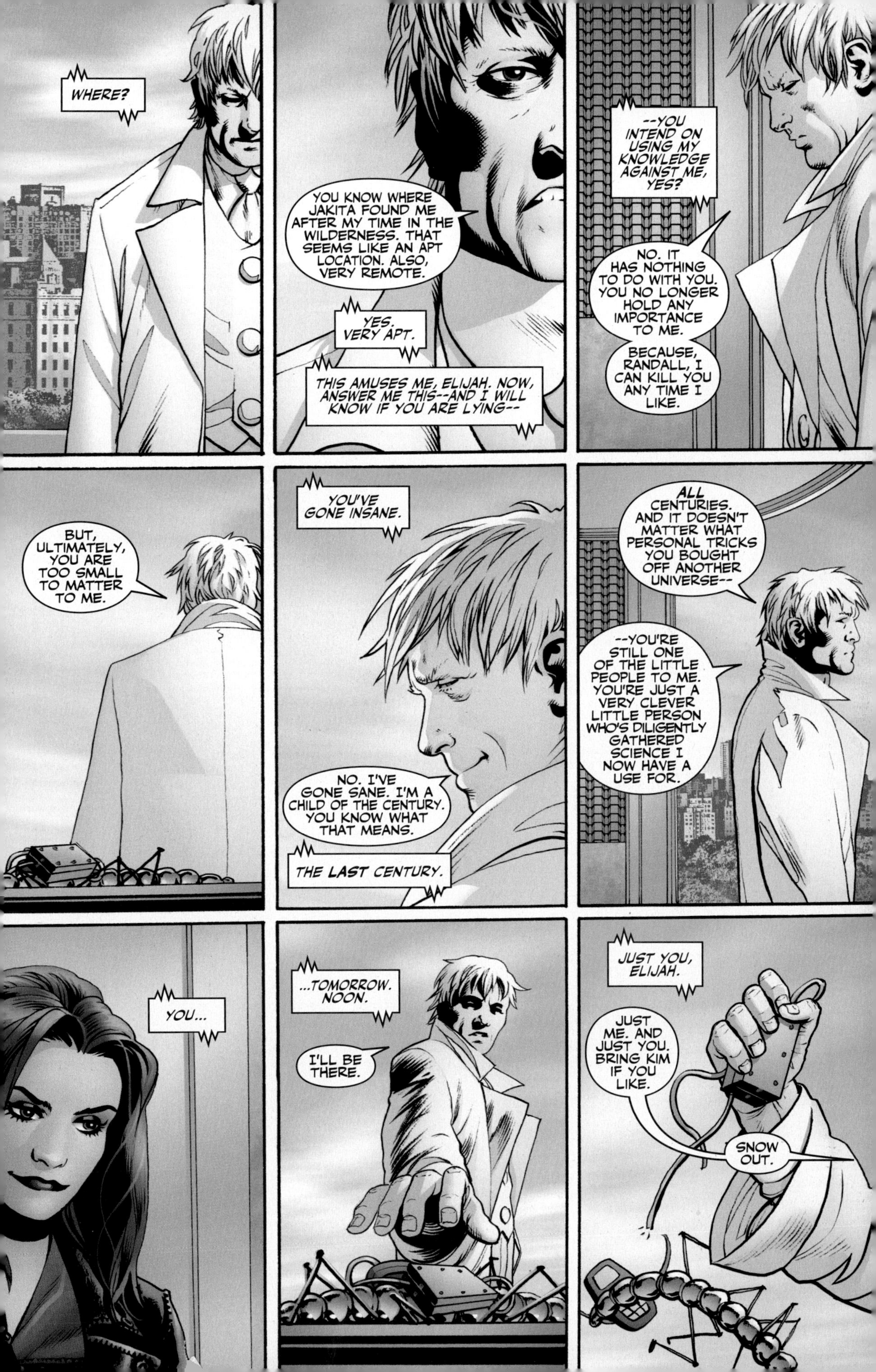
WHERE?
YOU KNOW WHERE JAKITA FOUND ME AFTER MY TIME IN THE WILDERNESS. THAT SEEMS LIKE AN APT LOCATION. ALSO, VERY REMOTE.
YES. VERY APT.
THIS AMUSES ME, ELIJAH. NOW, ANSWER ME THIS--AND I WILL KNOW IF YOU ARE LYING--
--YOU INTEND ON USING MY KNOWLEDGE AGAINST ME, YES?
NO. IT HAS NOTHING TO DO WITH YOU. YOU NO LONGER HOLD ANY IMPORTANCE TO ME.
BECAUSE, RANDALL, I CAN KILL YOU ANY TIME I LIKE.
BUT, ULTIMATELY, YOU ARE TOO SMALL TO MATTER TO ME.
YOU'VE GONE INSANE.
NO. I'VE GONE SANE. I'M A CHILD OF THE CENTURY. YOU KNOW WHAT THAT MEANS.
THE LAST CENTURY.
ALL CENTURIES. AND IT DOESN'T MATTER WHAT PERSONAL TRICKS YOU BOUGHT OFF ANOTHER UNIVERSE--
--YOU'RE STILL ONE OF THE LITTLE PEOPLE TO ME. YOU'RE JUST A VERY CLEVER LITTLE PERSON WHO'S DILIGENTLY GATHERED SCIENCE I NOW HAVE A USE FOR.
YOU...
...TOMORROW. NOON.
I'LL BE THERE.
JUST YOU, ELIJAH.
JUST ME. AND JUST YOU. BRING KIM IF YOU LIKE.
SNOW OUT.

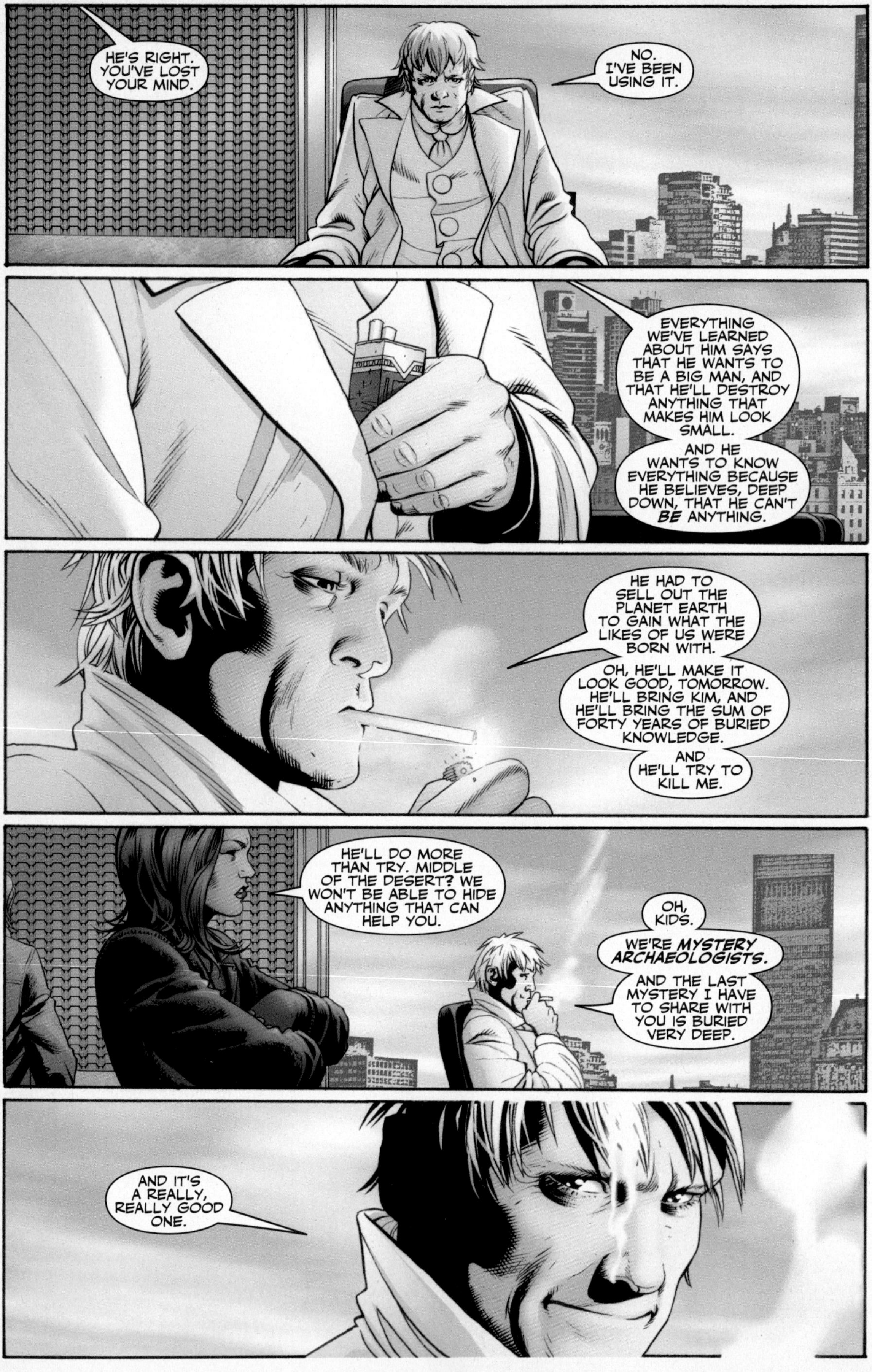
HE'S RIGHT. YOU'VE LOST YOUR MIND.
NO. I'VE BEEN USING IT.
EVERYTHING WE'VE LEARNED ABOUT HIM SAYS THAT HE WANTS TO BE A BIG MAN, AND THAT HE'LL DESTROY ANYTHING THAT MAKES HIM LOOK SMALL.
AND HE WANTS TO KNOW EVERYTHING BECAUSE HE BELIEVES, DEEP DOWN, THAT HE CAN'T *BE* ANYTHING.
HE HAD TO SELL OUT THE PLANET EARTH TO GAIN WHAT THE LIKES OF US WERE BORN WITH.
OH, HE'LL MAKE IT LOOK GOOD, TOMORROW. HE'LL BRING KIM, AND HE'LL BRING THE SUM OF FORTY YEARS OF BURIED KNOWLEDGE.
AND HE'LL TRY TO KILL ME.
HE'LL DO MORE THAN TRY. MIDDLE OF THE DESERT? WE WON'T BE ABLE TO HIDE ANYTHING THAT CAN HELP YOU.
OH, KIDS.
WE'RE *MYSTERY ARCHAEOLOGISTS*.
AND THE LAST MYSTERY I HAVE TO SHARE WITH YOU IS BURIED VERY DEEP.
AND IT'S A REALLY, REALLY GOOD ONE.

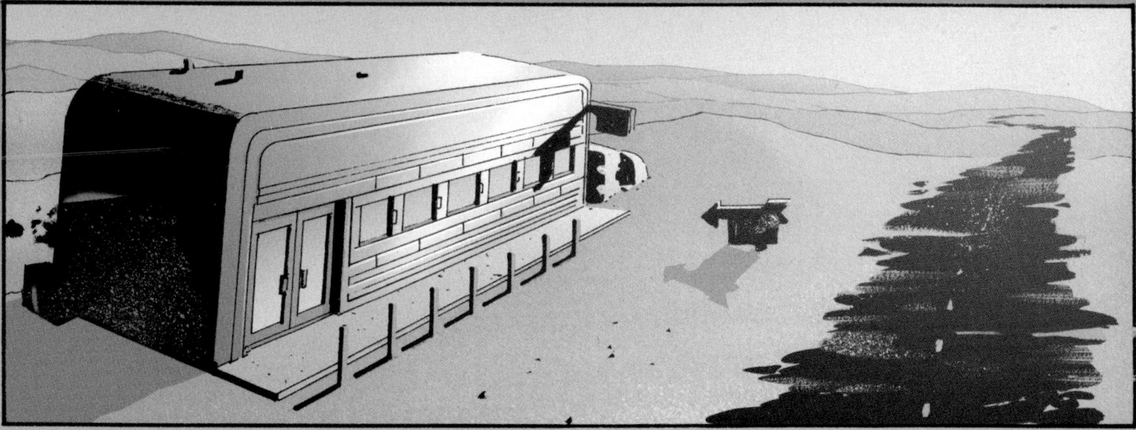
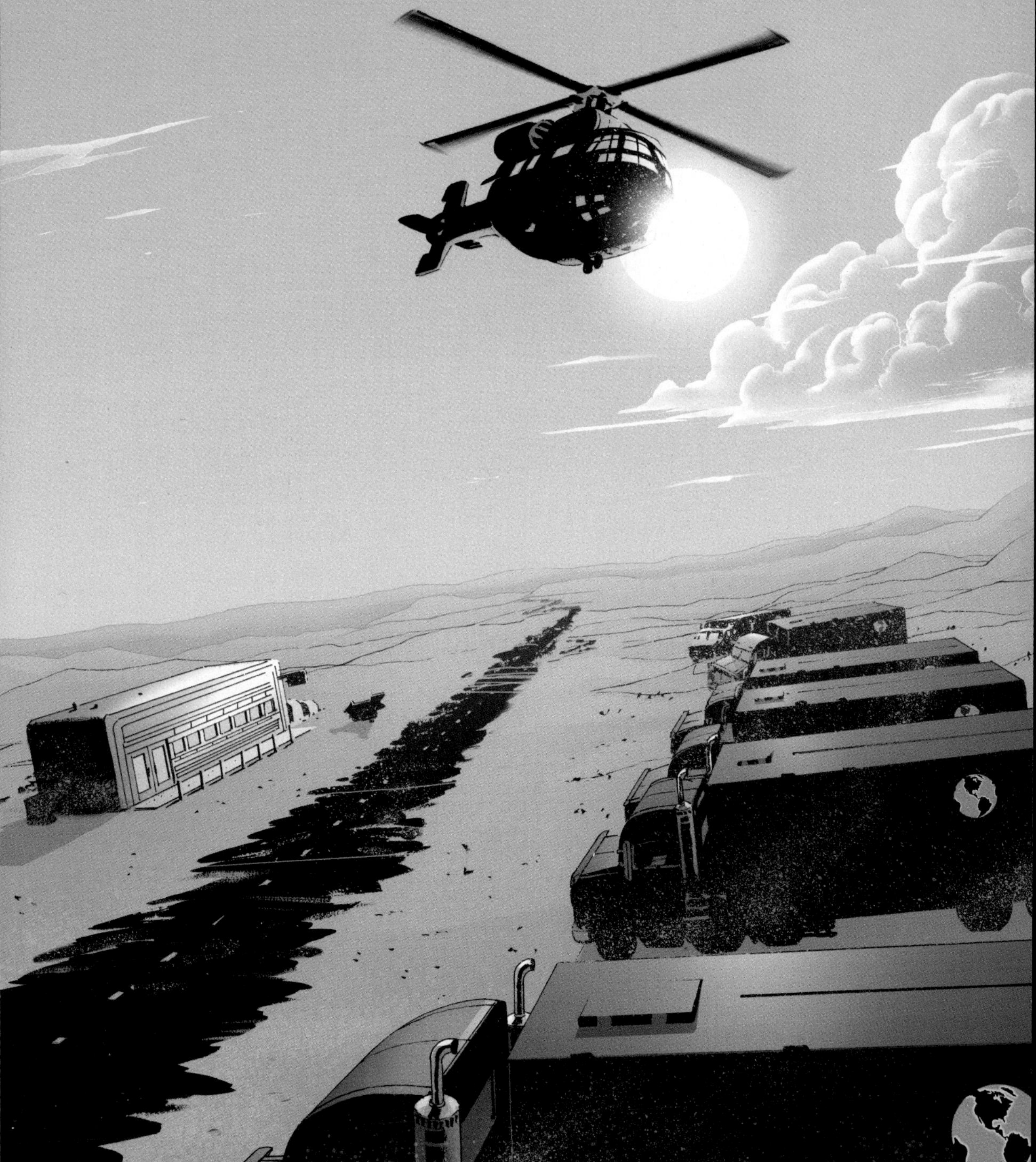

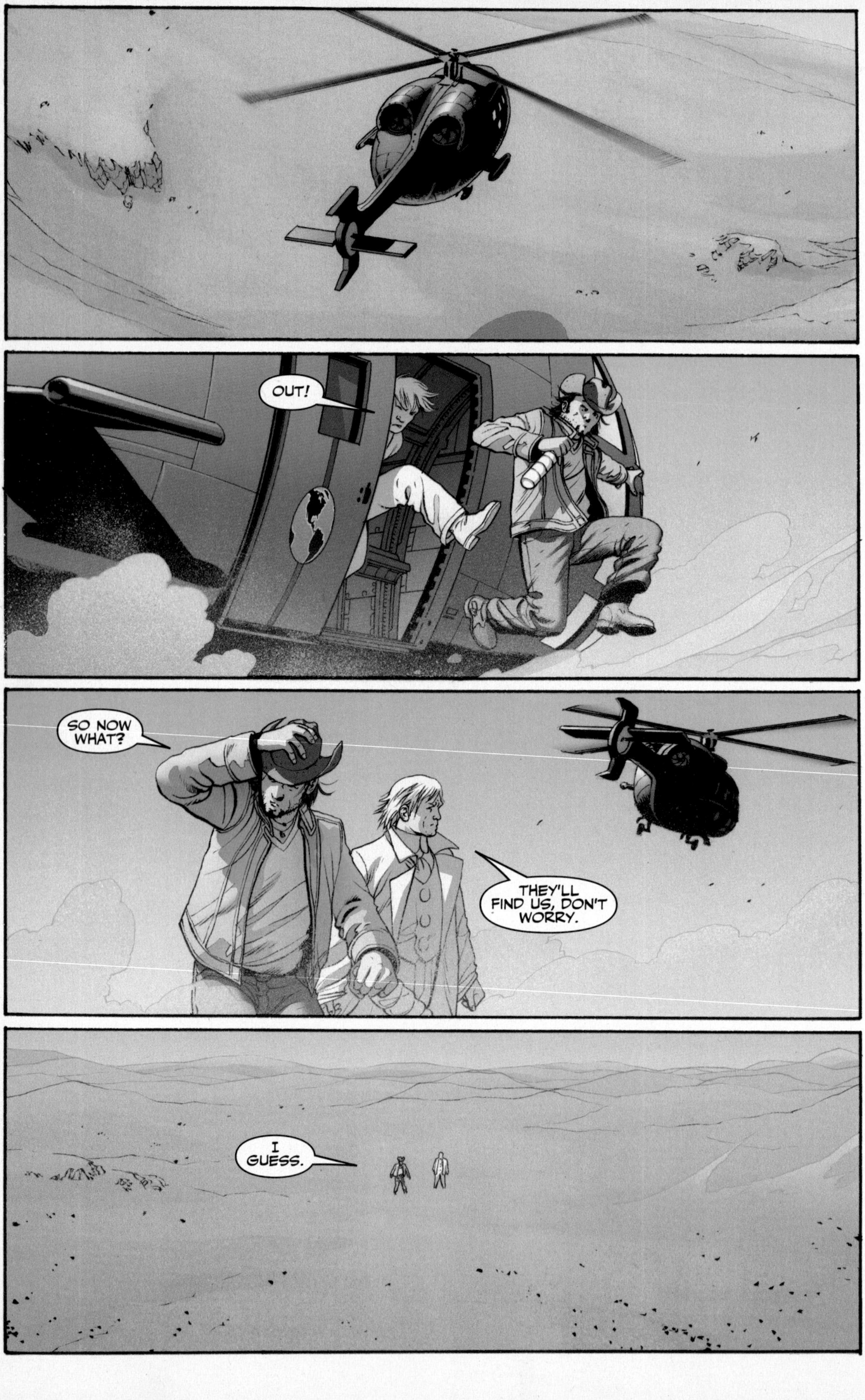
OUT!
SO NOW WHAT?
THEY'LL FIND US, DON'T WORRY.
I GUESS.

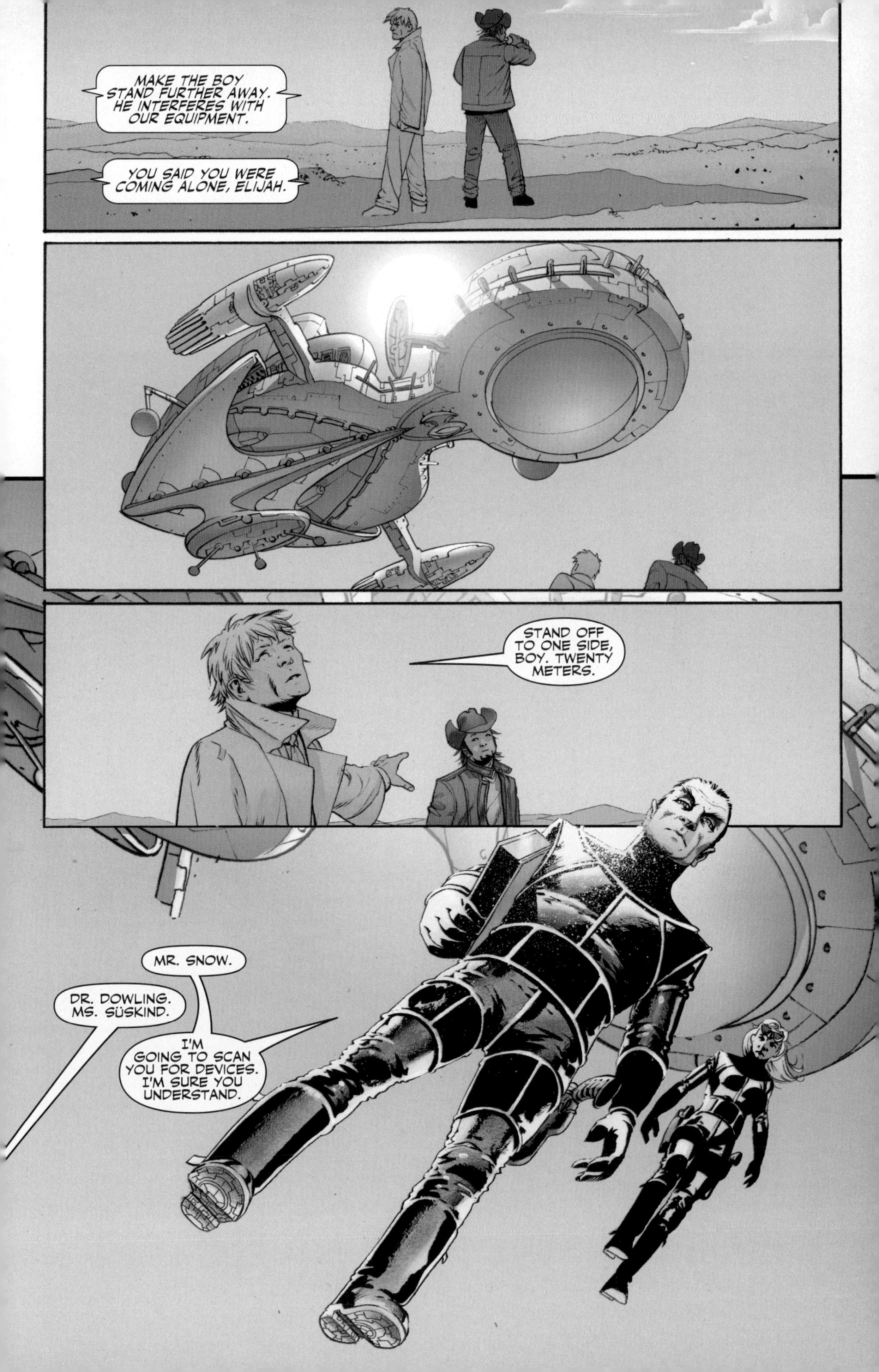
MAKE THE BOY STAND FURTHER AWAY. HE INTERFERES WITH OUR EQUIPMENT.
YOU SAID YOU WERE COMING ALONE, ELIJAH.
STAND OFF TO ONE SIDE, BOY. TWENTY METERS.
MR. SNOW.
DR. DOWLING. MS. SÜSKIND.
I'M GOING TO SCAN YOU FOR DEVICES. I'M SURE YOU UNDERSTAND.

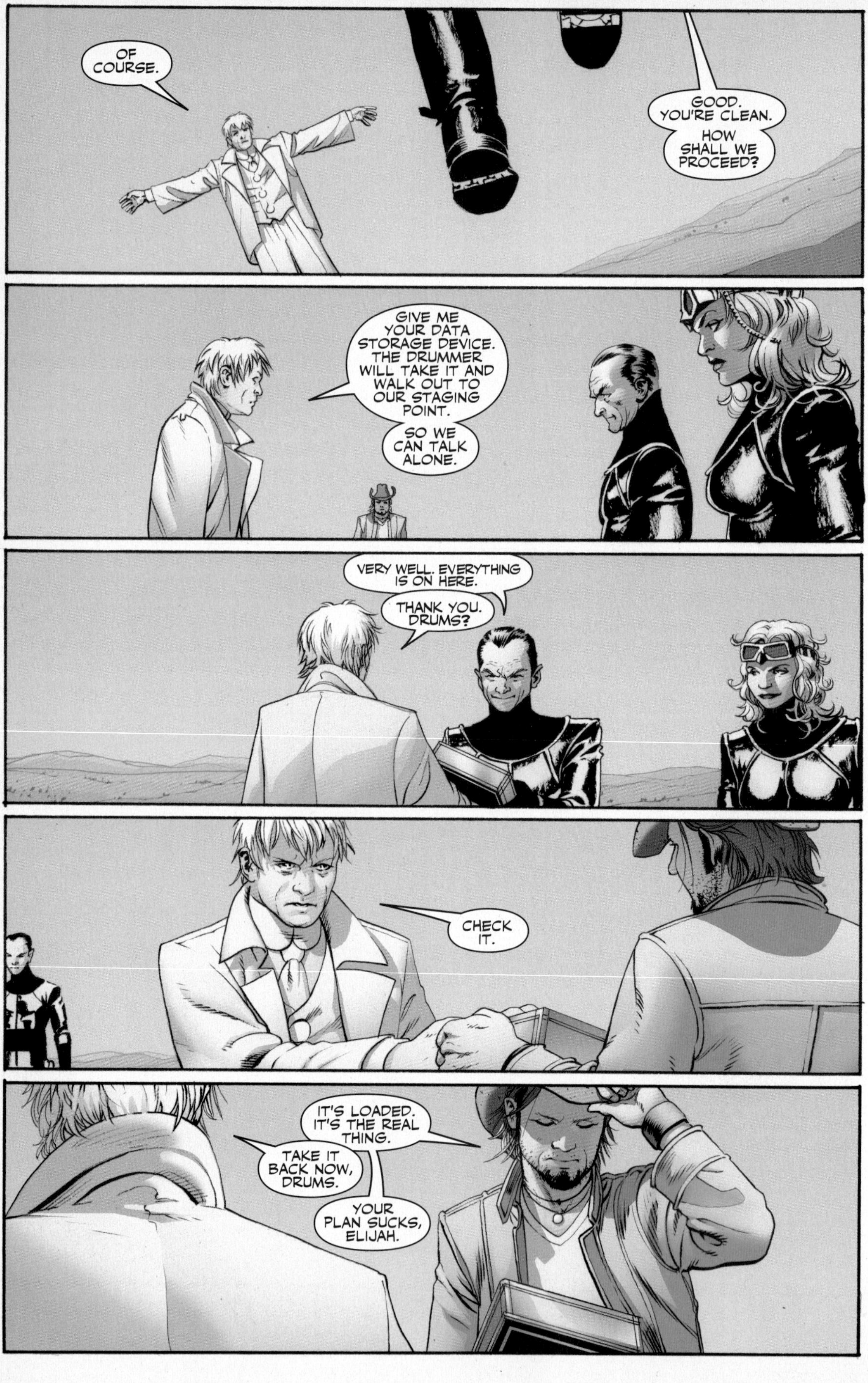
OF COURSE.
GOOD. YOU'RE CLEAN.
HOW SHALL WE PROCEED?
GIVE ME YOUR DATA STORAGE DEVICE. THE DRUMMER WILL TAKE IT AND WALK OUT TO OUR STAGING POINT.
SO WE CAN TALK ALONE.
VERY WELL. EVERYTHING IS ON HERE.
THANK YOU. DRUMS?
CHECK IT.
IT'S LOADED. IT'S THE REAL THING.
TAKE IT BACK NOW, DRUMS.
YOUR PLAN SUCKS, ELIJAH.

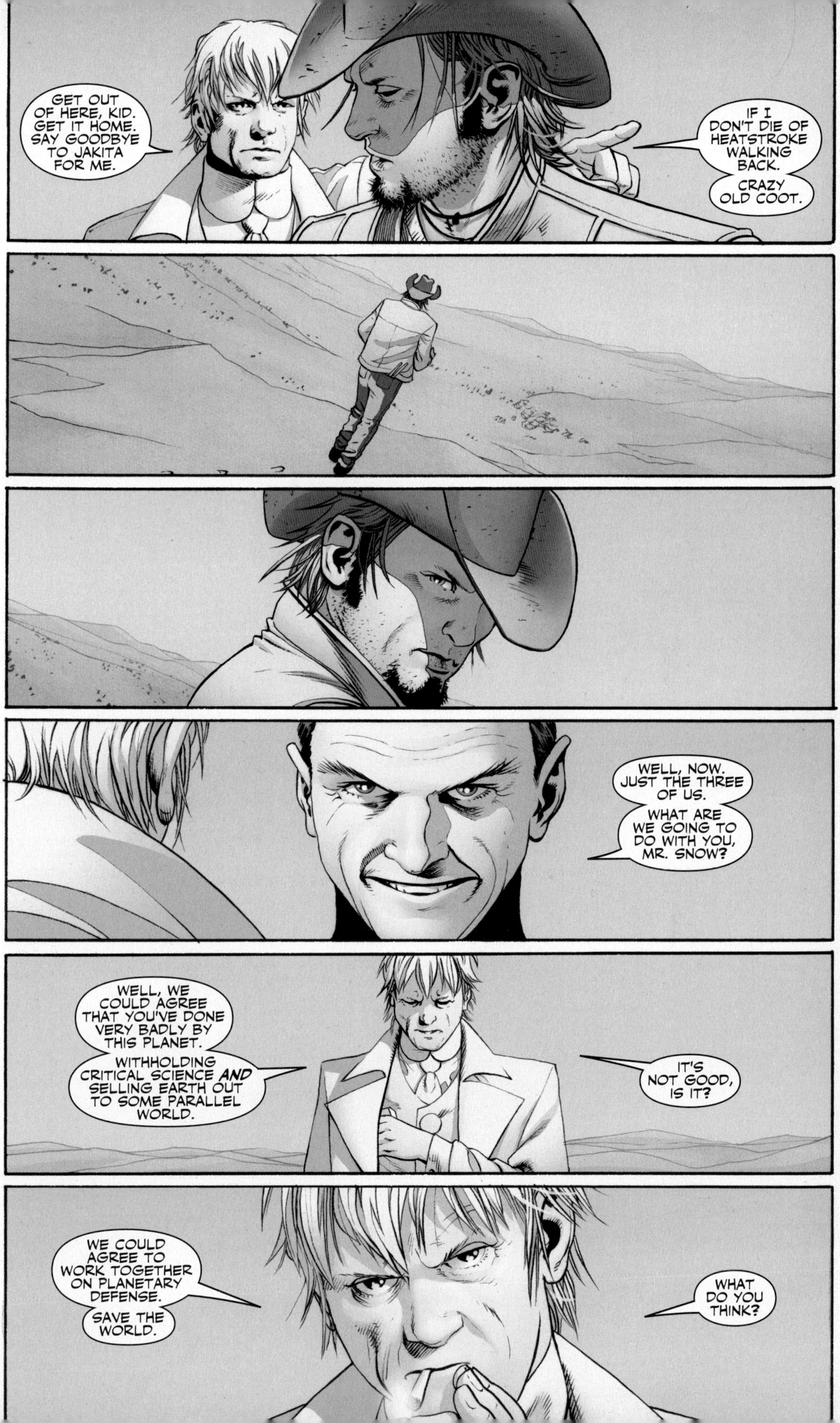
GET OUT OF HERE, KID. GET IT HOME. SAY GOODBYE TO JAKITA FOR ME.
IF I DON'T DIE OF HEATSTROKE WALKING BACK.
CRAZY OLD COOT.
WELL, NOW. JUST THE THREE OF US.
WHAT ARE WE GOING TO DO WITH YOU, MR. SNOW?
WELL, WE COULD AGREE THAT YOU'VE DONE VERY BADLY BY THIS PLANET.
WITHHOLDING CRITICAL SCIENCE **AND** SELLING EARTH OUT TO SOME PARALLEL WORLD.
IT'S NOT GOOD, IS IT?
WE COULD AGREE TO WORK TOGETHER ON PLANETARY DEFENSE.
SAVE THE WORLD.
WHAT DO YOU THINK?

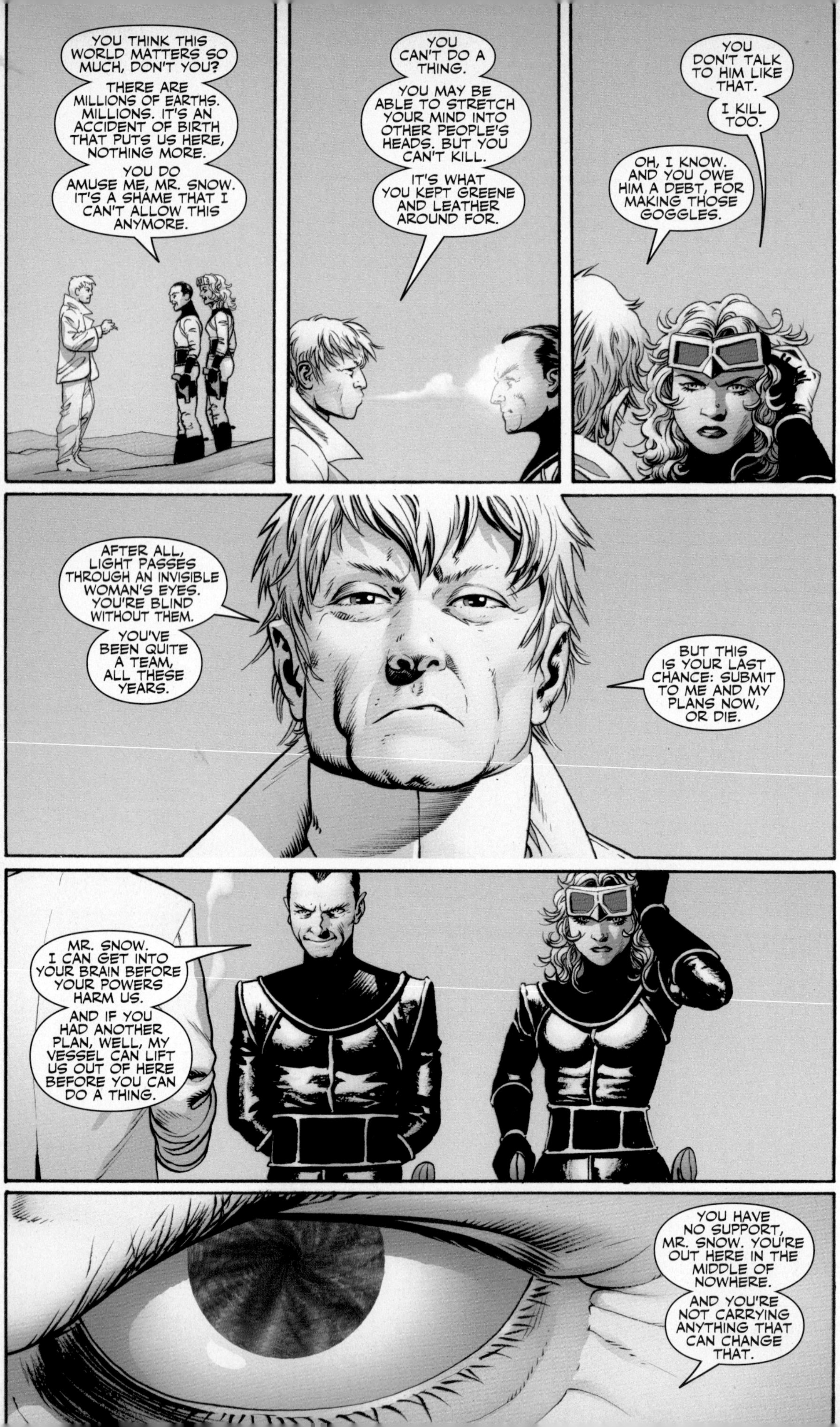
YOU THINK THIS WORLD MATTERS SO MUCH, DON'T YOU?
THERE ARE MILLIONS OF EARTHS. MILLIONS. IT'S AN ACCIDENT OF BIRTH THAT PUTS US HERE, NOTHING MORE.
YOU DO AMUSE ME, MR. SNOW. IT'S A SHAME THAT I CAN'T ALLOW THIS ANYMORE.
YOU CAN'T DO A THING.
YOU MAY BE ABLE TO STRETCH YOUR MIND INTO OTHER PEOPLE'S HEADS. BUT YOU CAN'T KILL.
IT'S WHAT YOU KEPT GREENE AND LEATHER AROUND FOR.
YOU DON'T TALK TO HIM LIKE THAT.
I KILL TOO.
OH, I KNOW. AND YOU OWE HIM A DEBT, FOR MAKING THOSE GOGGLES.
AFTER ALL, LIGHT PASSES THROUGH AN INVISIBLE WOMAN'S EYES. YOU'RE BLIND WITHOUT THEM.
YOU'VE BEEN QUITE A TEAM, ALL THESE YEARS.
BUT THIS IS YOUR LAST CHANCE: SUBMIT TO ME AND MY PLANS NOW, OR DIE.
MR. SNOW. I CAN GET INTO YOUR BRAIN BEFORE YOUR POWERS HARM US.
AND IF YOU HAD ANOTHER PLAN, WELL, MY VESSEL CAN LIFT US OUT OF HERE BEFORE YOU CAN DO A THING.
YOU HAVE NO SUPPORT, MR. SNOW. YOU'RE OUT HERE IN THE MIDDLE OF NOWHERE.
AND YOU'RE NOT CARRYING ANYTHING THAT CAN CHANGE THAT.

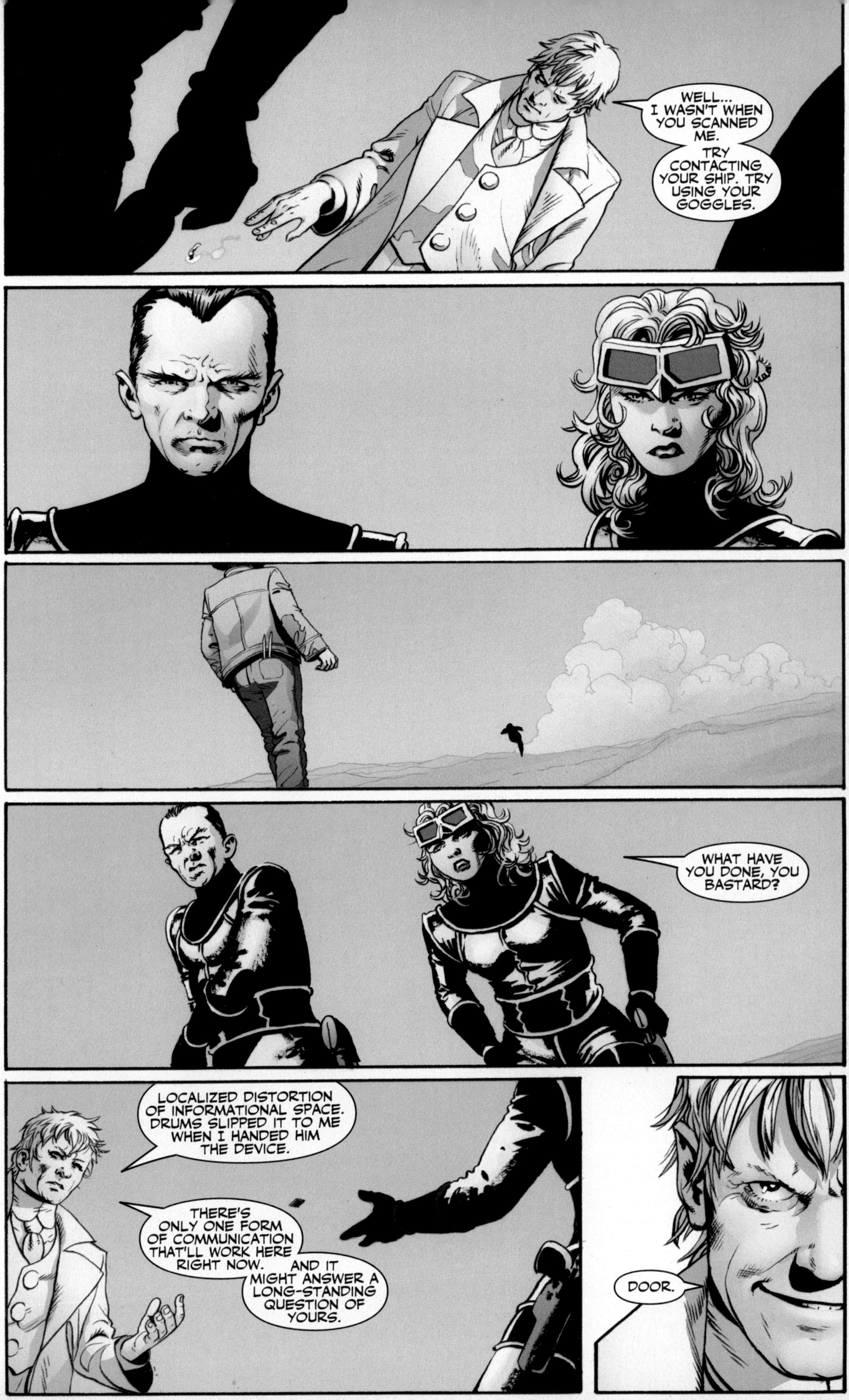
WELL... I WASN'T WHEN YOU SCANNED ME.
TRY CONTACTING YOUR SHIP. TRY USING YOUR GOGGLES.
WHAT HAVE YOU DONE, YOU BASTARD?
LOCALIZED DISTORTION OF INFORMATIONAL SPACE. DRUMS SLIPPED IT TO ME WHEN I HANDED HIM THE DEVICE.
THERE'S ONLY ONE FORM OF COMMUNICATION THAT'LL WORK HERE RIGHT NOW.
AND IT MIGHT ANSWER A LONG-STANDING QUESTION OF YOURS.
DOOR.

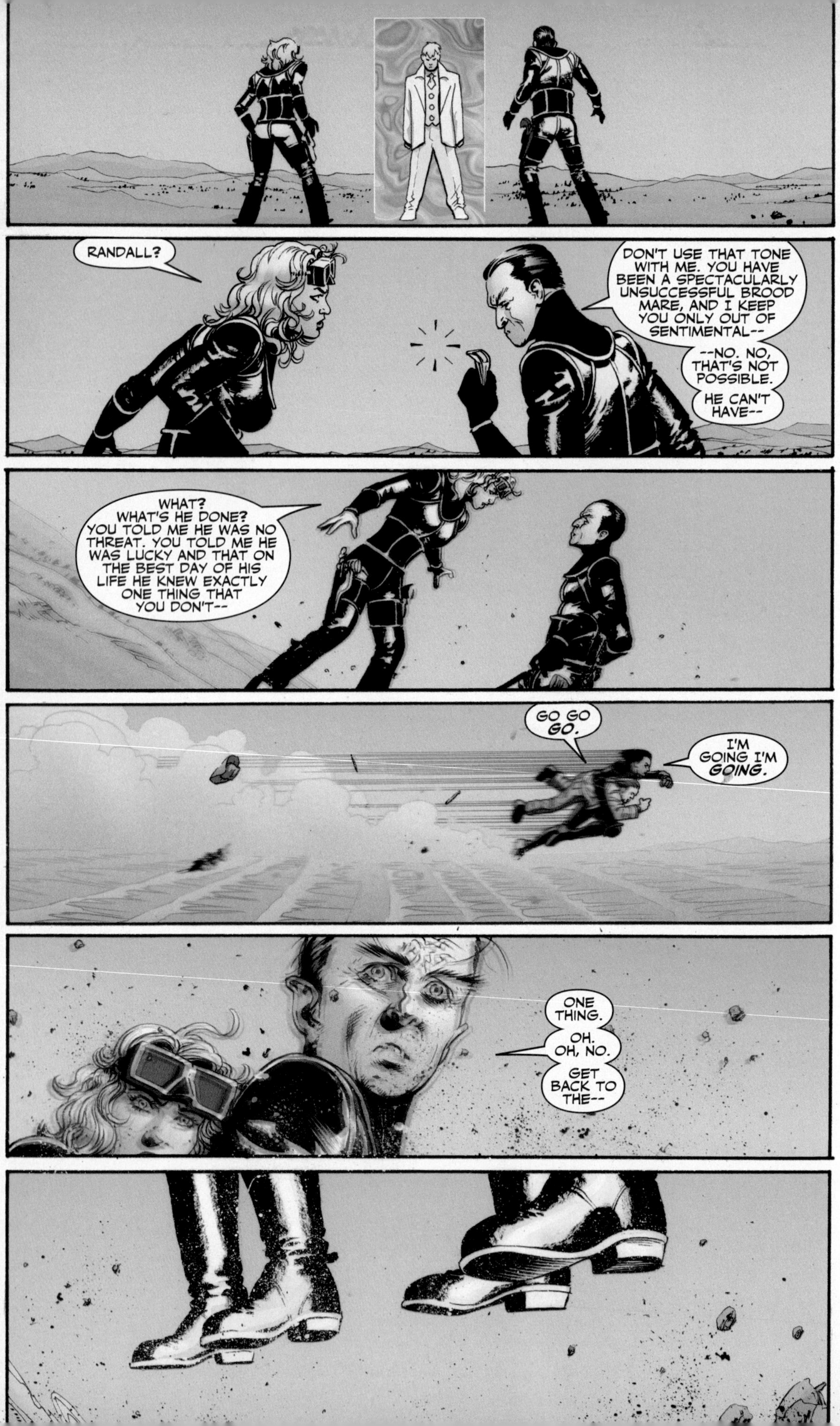
RANDALL?
DON'T USE THAT TONE WITH ME. YOU HAVE BEEN A SPECTACULARLY UNSUCCESSFUL BROOD MARE, AND I KEEP YOU ONLY OUT OF SENTIMENTAL--
--NO. NO, THAT'S NOT POSSIBLE.
HE CAN'T HAVE--
WHAT? WHAT'S HE DONE? YOU TOLD ME HE WAS NO THREAT. YOU TOLD ME HE WAS LUCKY AND THAT ON THE BEST DAY OF HIS LIFE HE KNEW EXACTLY ONE THING THAT YOU DON'T--
GO GO *GO.*
I'M GOING I'M *GOING.*
ONE THING.
OH. OH, NO.
GET BACK TO THE--

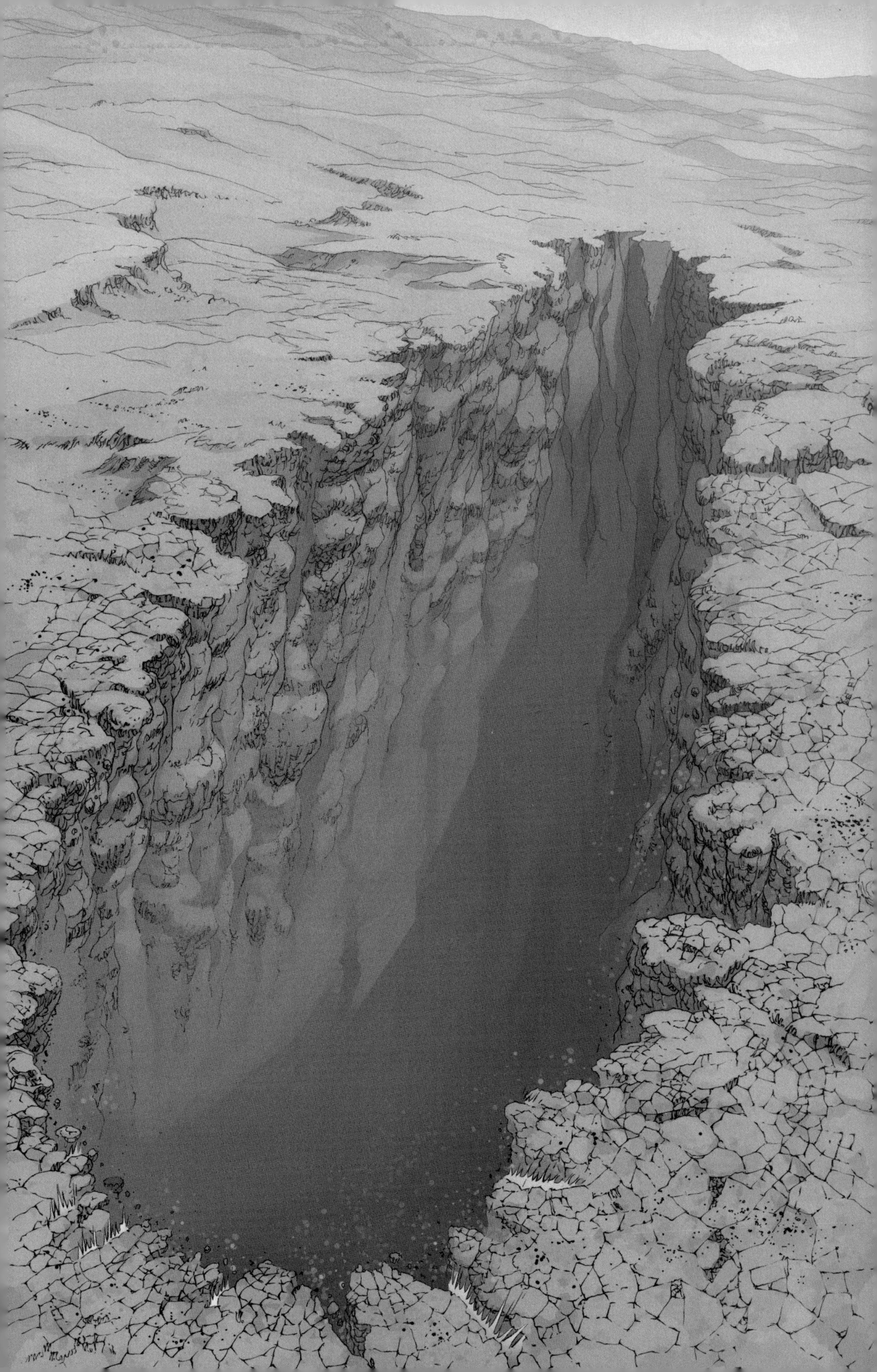

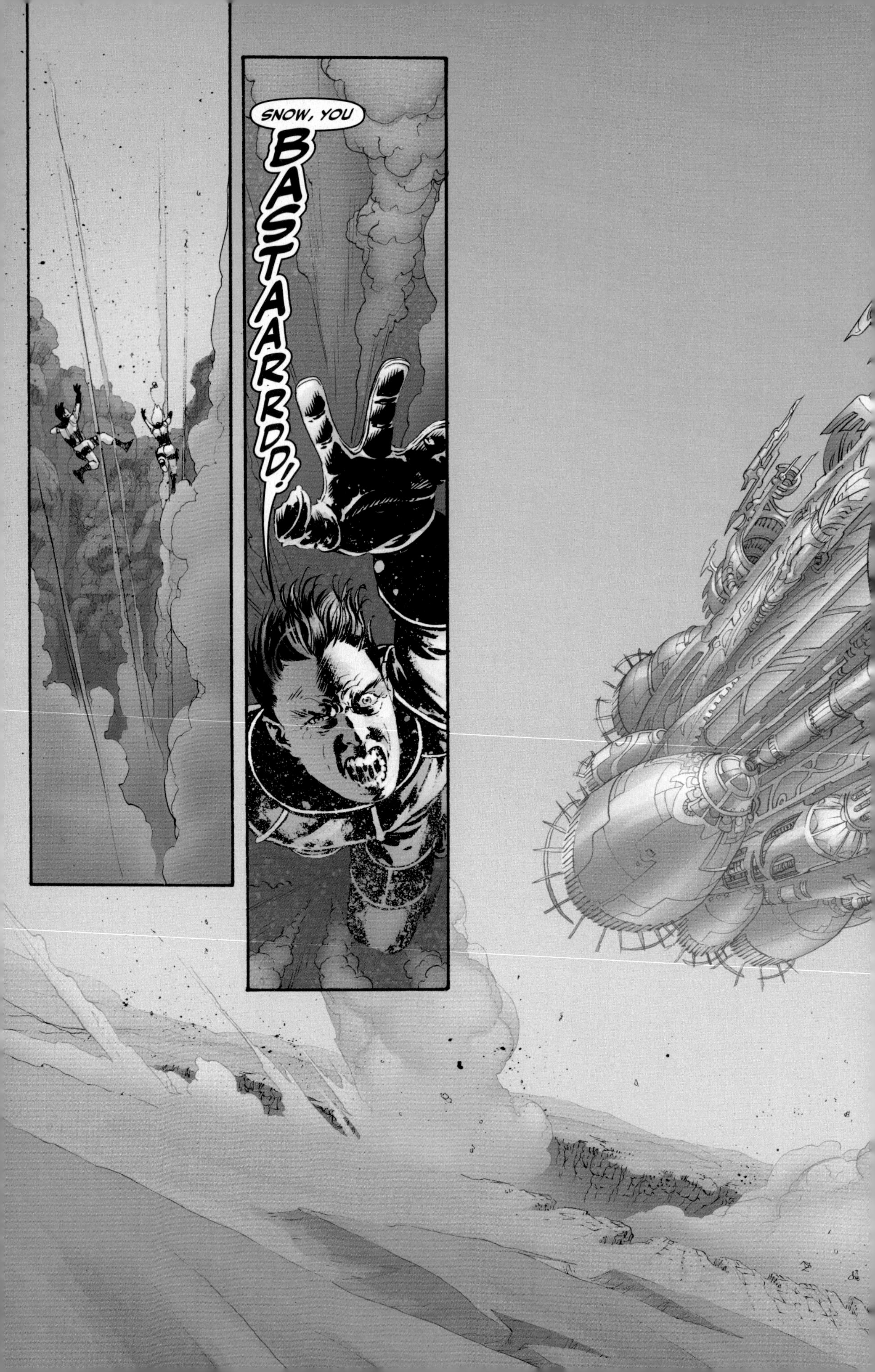
SNOW, YOU
BASTAARRDD!

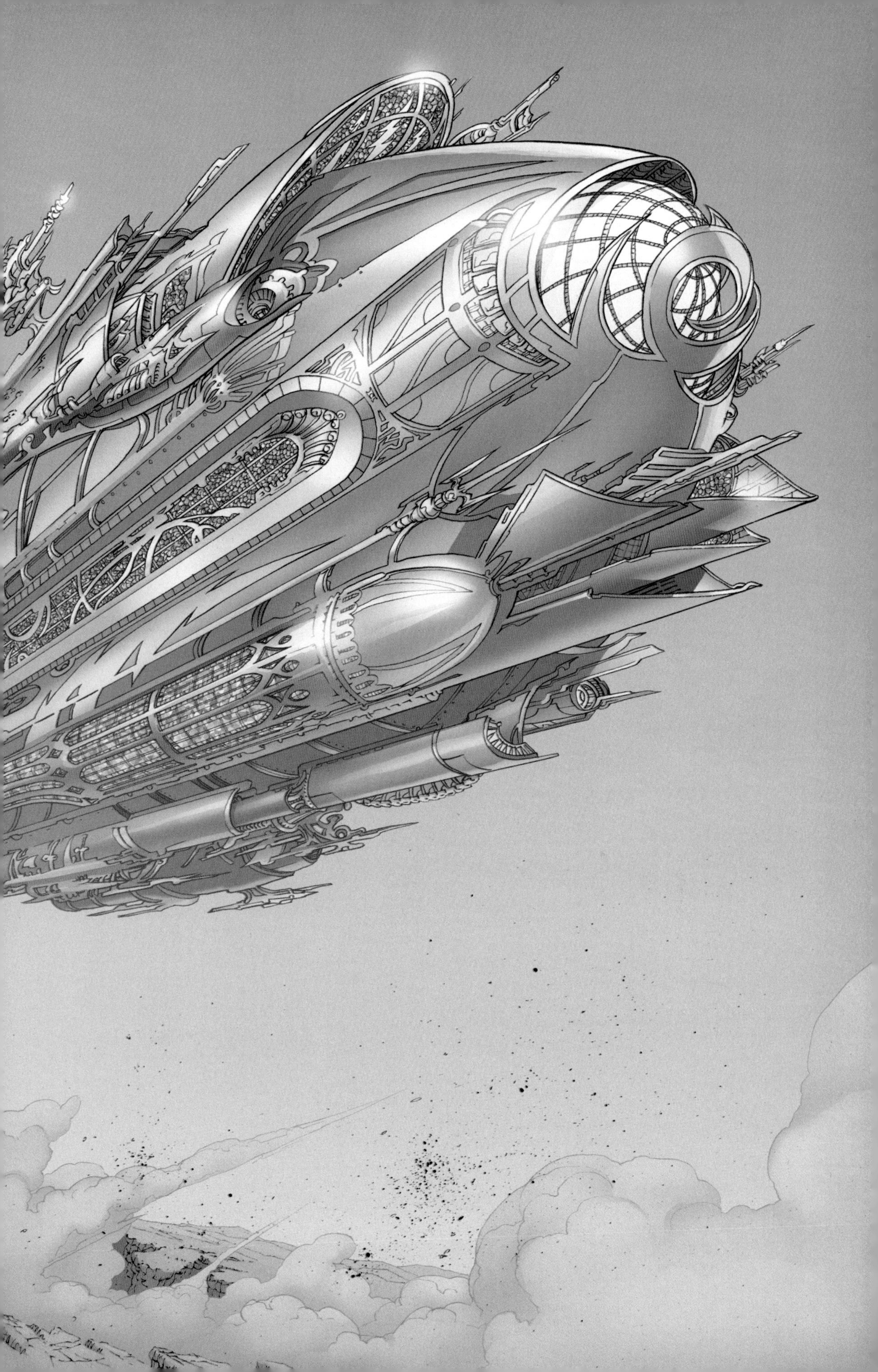

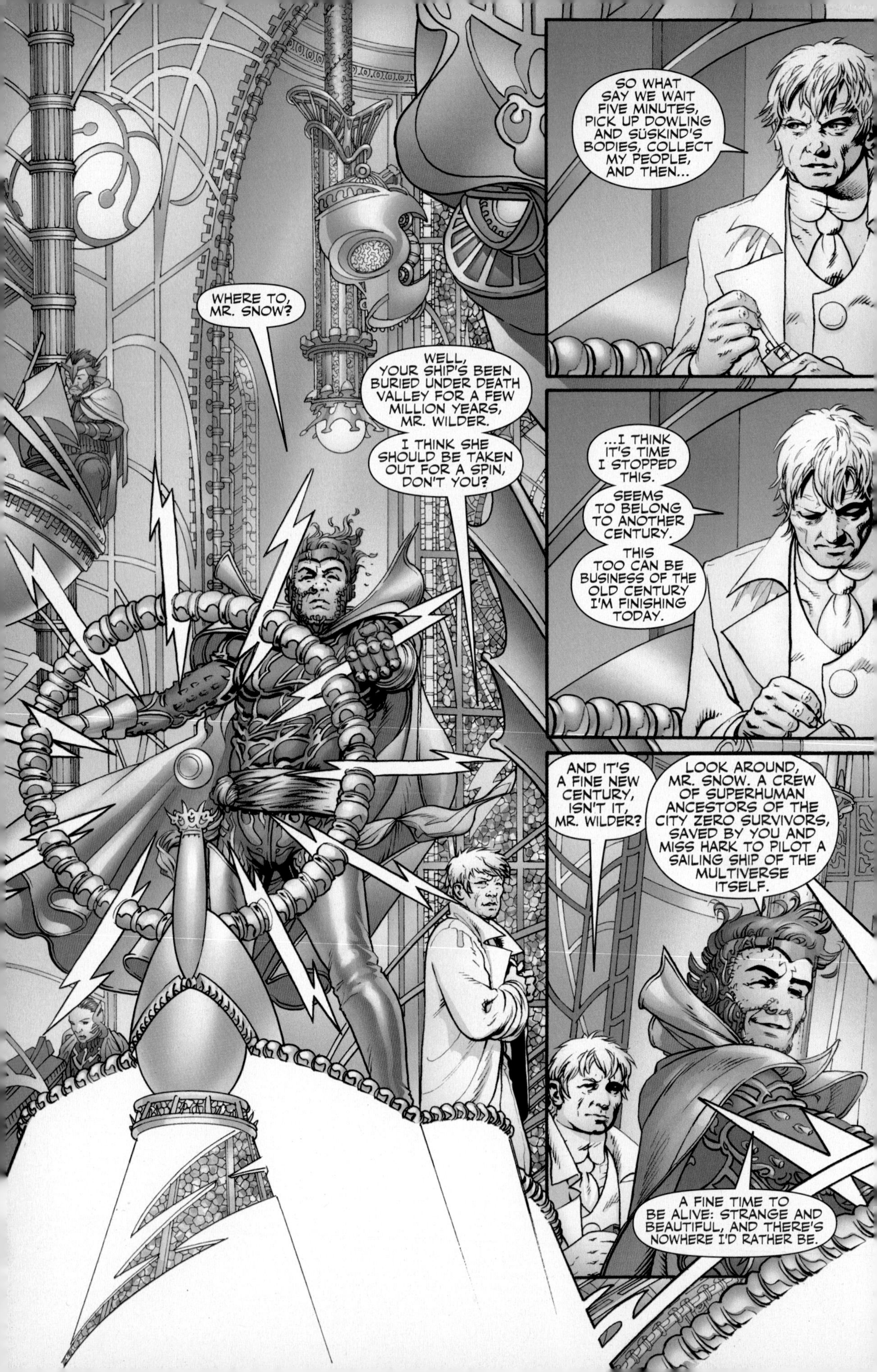
WHERE TO, MR. SNOW?
WELL, YOUR SHIP'S BEEN BURIED UNDER DEATH VALLEY FOR A FEW MILLION YEARS, MR. WILDER.
I THINK SHE SHOULD BE TAKEN OUT FOR A SPIN, DON'T YOU?
SO WHAT SAY WE WAIT FIVE MINUTES, PICK UP DOWLING AND SÜSKIND'S BODIES, COLLECT MY PEOPLE, AND THEN...
...I THINK IT'S TIME I STOPPED THIS.
SEEMS TO BELONG TO ANOTHER CENTURY.
THIS TOO CAN BE BUSINESS OF THE OLD CENTURY I'M FINISHING TODAY.
AND IT'S A FINE NEW CENTURY, ISN'T IT, MR. WILDER?
LOOK AROUND, MR. SNOW. A CREW OF SUPERHUMAN ANCESTORS OF THE CITY ZERO SURVIVORS, SAVED BY YOU AND MISS HARK TO PILOT A SAILING SHIP OF THE MULTIVERSE ITSELF.
A FINE TIME TO BE ALIVE: STRANGE AND BEAUTIFUL, AND THERE'S NOWHERE I'D RATHER BE.

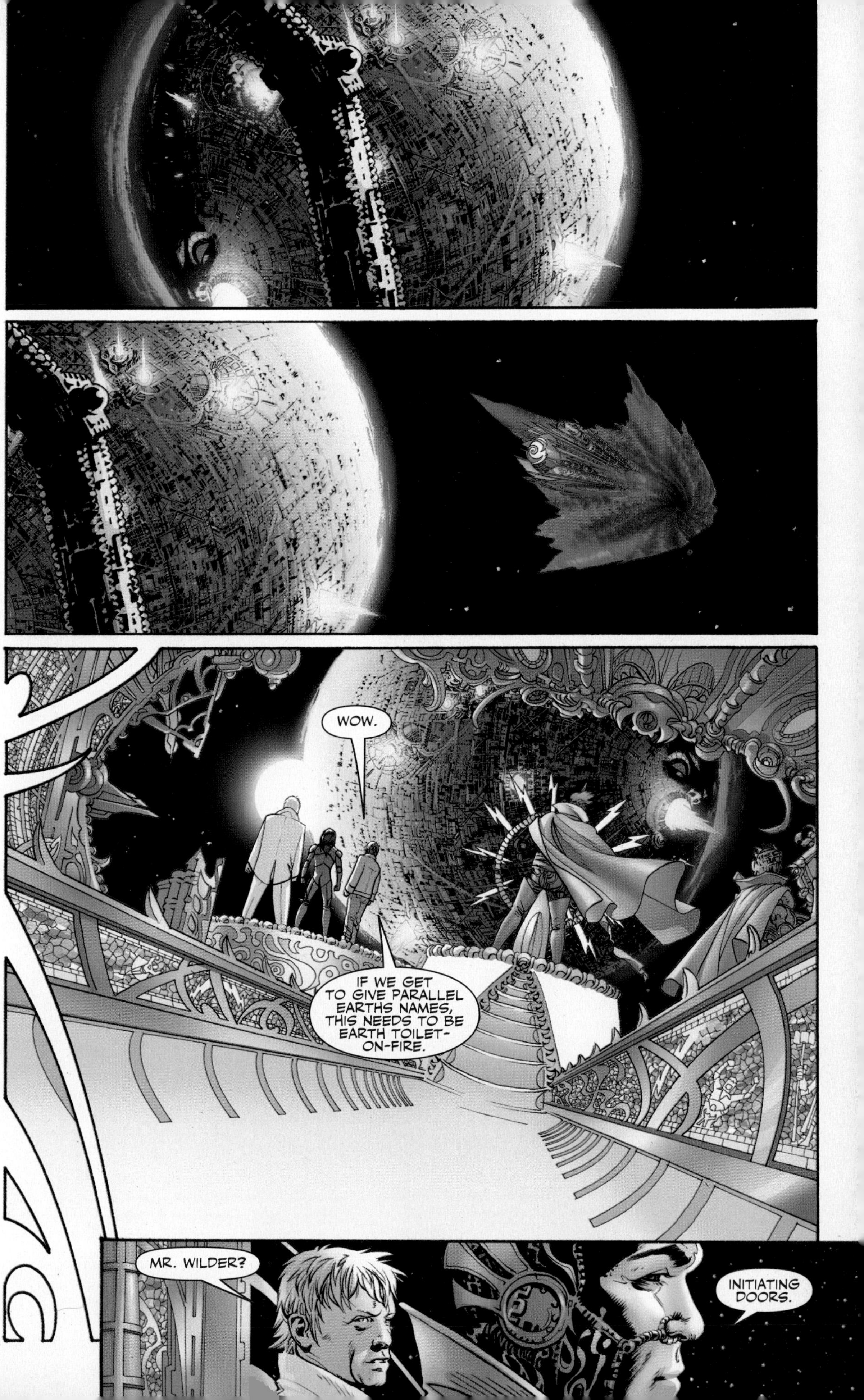
WOW.
IF WE GET TO GIVE PARALLEL EARTHS NAMES, THIS NEEDS TO BE EARTH TOILET-ON-FIRE.
MR. WILDER?
INITIATING DOORS.

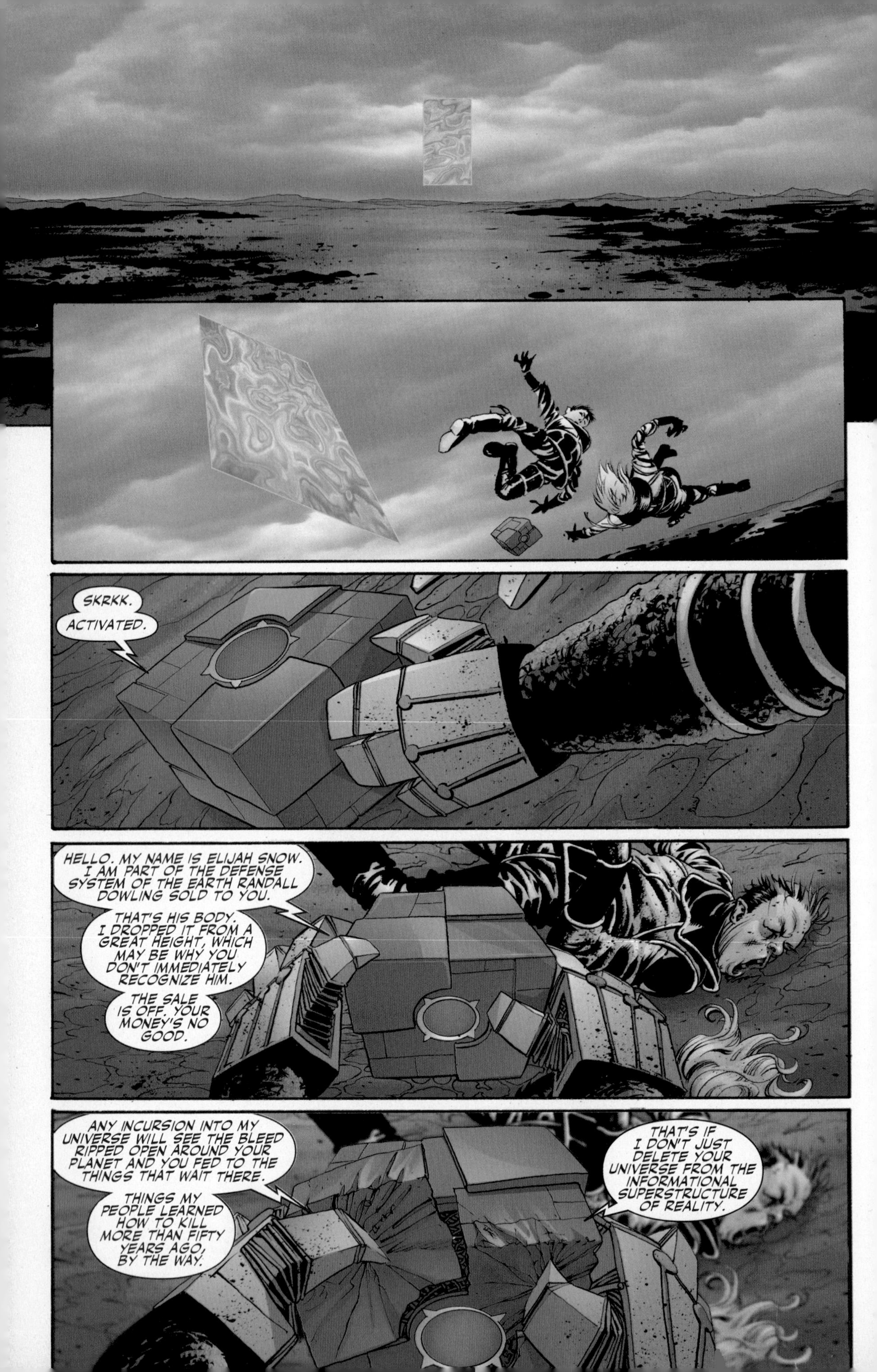
SKRKK.
ACTIVATED.
HELLO. MY NAME IS ELIJAH SNOW. I AM PART OF THE DEFENSE SYSTEM OF THE EARTH RANDALL DOWLING SOLD TO YOU.
THAT'S HIS BODY. I DROPPED IT FROM A GREAT HEIGHT, WHICH MAY BE WHY YOU DON'T IMMEDIATELY RECOGNIZE HIM.
THE SALE IS OFF. YOUR MONEY'S NO GOOD.
ANY INCURSION INTO MY UNIVERSE WILL SEE THE BLEED RIPPED OPEN AROUND YOUR PLANET AND YOU FED TO THE THINGS THAT WAIT THERE.
THINGS MY PEOPLE LEARNED HOW TO KILL MORE THAN FIFTY YEARS AGO, BY THE WAY.
THAT'S IF I DON'T JUST DELETE YOUR UNIVERSE FROM THE INFORMATIONAL SUPERSTRUCTURE OF REALITY.

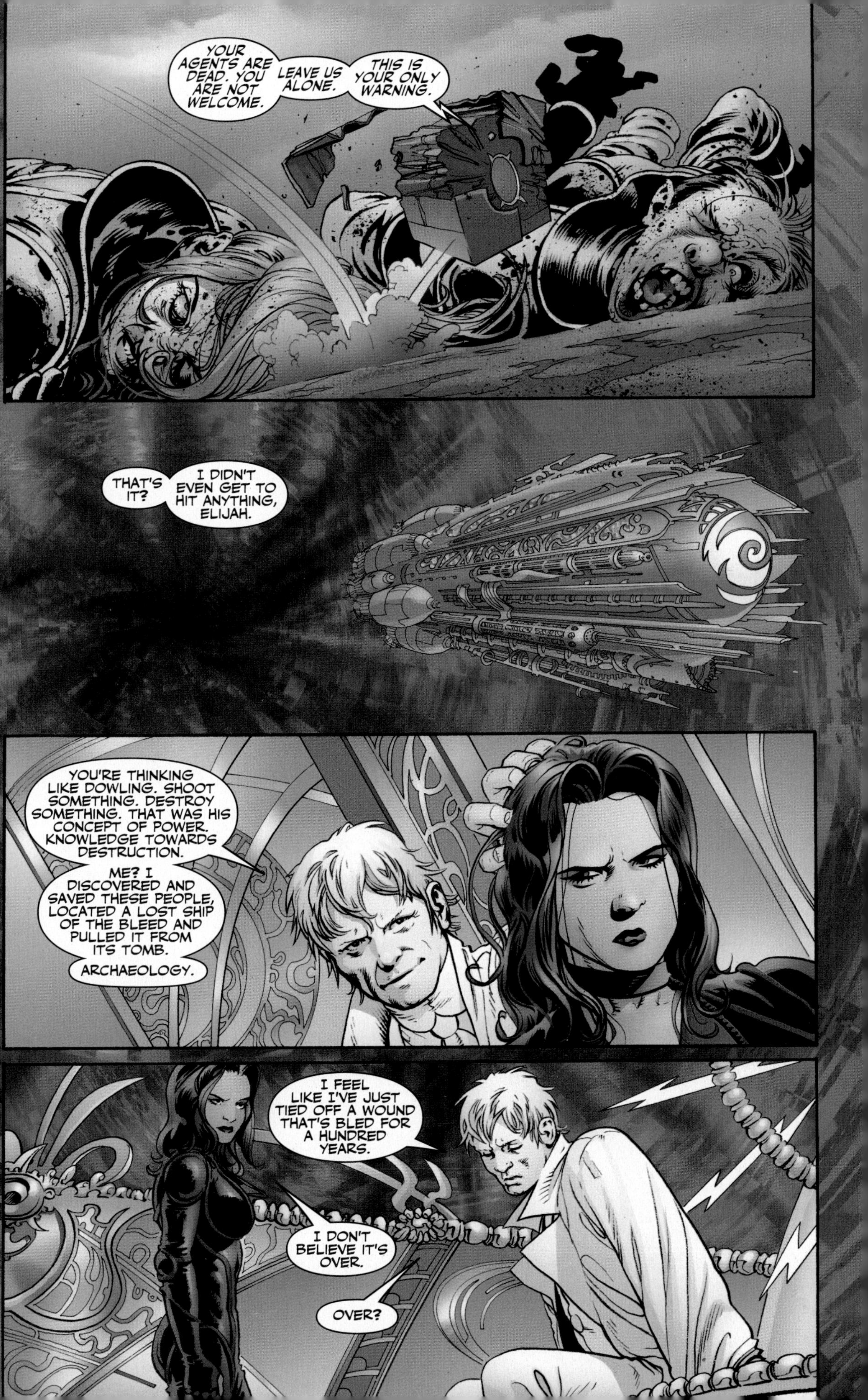
YOUR AGENTS ARE DEAD. YOU ARE NOT WELCOME.
LEAVE US ALONE.
THIS IS YOUR ONLY WARNING.
THAT'S IT?
I DIDN'T EVEN GET TO HIT ANYTHING, ELIJAH.
YOU'RE THINKING LIKE DOWLING. SHOOT SOMETHING. DESTROY SOMETHING. THAT WAS HIS CONCEPT OF POWER. KNOWLEDGE TOWARDS DESTRUCTION.
ME? I DISCOVERED AND SAVED THESE PEOPLE, LOCATED A LOST SHIP OF THE BLEED AND PULLED IT FROM ITS TOMB.
ARCHAEOLOGY.
I FEEL LIKE I'VE JUST TIED OFF A WOUND THAT'S BLED FOR A HUNDRED YEARS.
I DON'T BELIEVE IT'S OVER.
OVER?

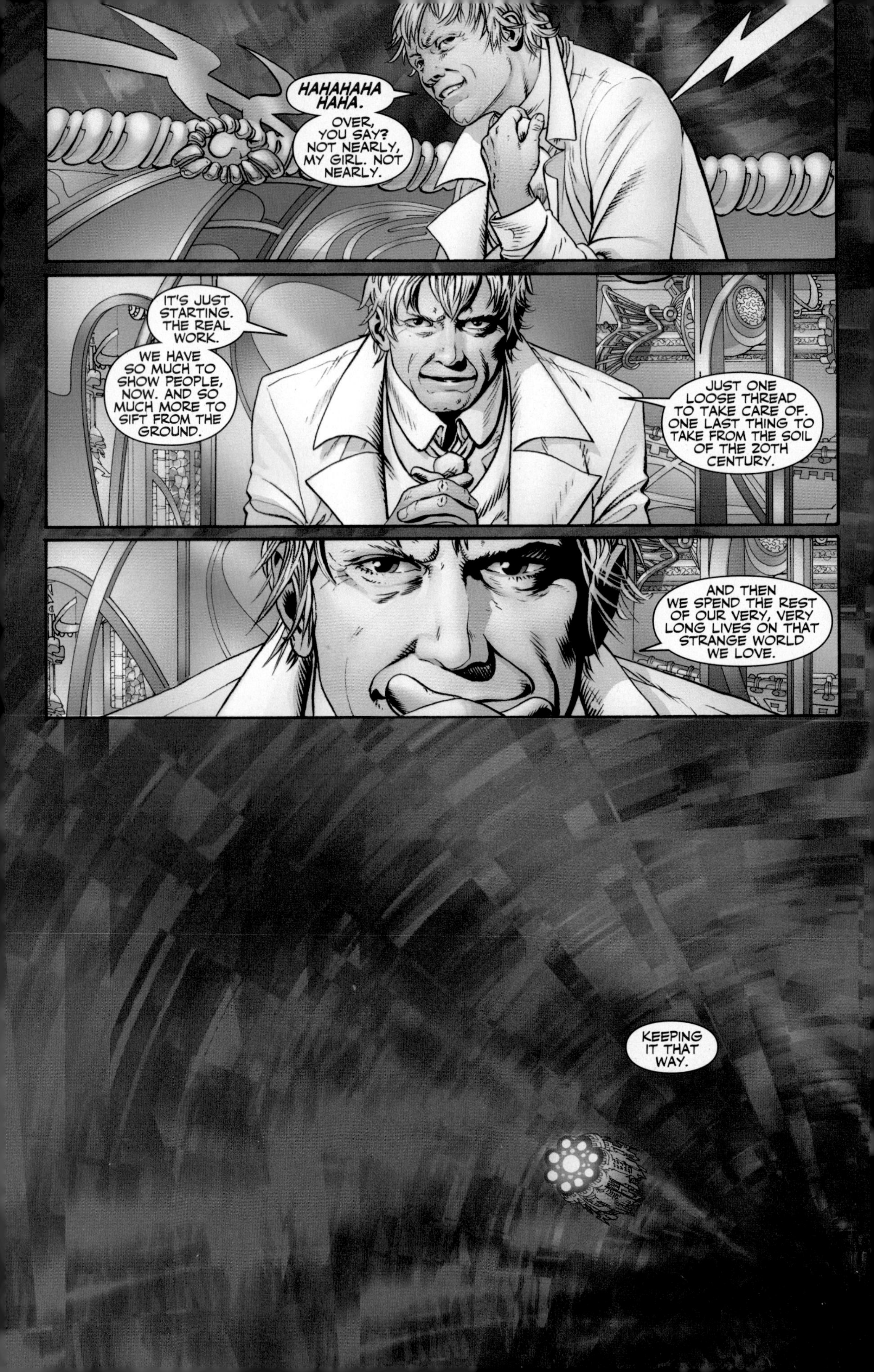
HAHAHAHA HAHA.
OVER, YOU SAY? NOT NEARLY, MY GIRL. NOT NEARLY.
IT'S JUST STARTING. THE REAL WORK.
WE HAVE SO MUCH TO SHOW PEOPLE, NOW. AND SO MUCH MORE TO SIFT FROM THE GROUND.
JUST ONE LOOSE THREAD TO TAKE CARE OF. ONE LAST THING TO TAKE FROM THE SOIL OF THE 20TH CENTURY.
AND THEN WE SPEND THE REST OF OUR VERY, VERY LONG LIVES ON THAT STRANGE WORLD WE LOVE.
KEEPING IT THAT WAY.

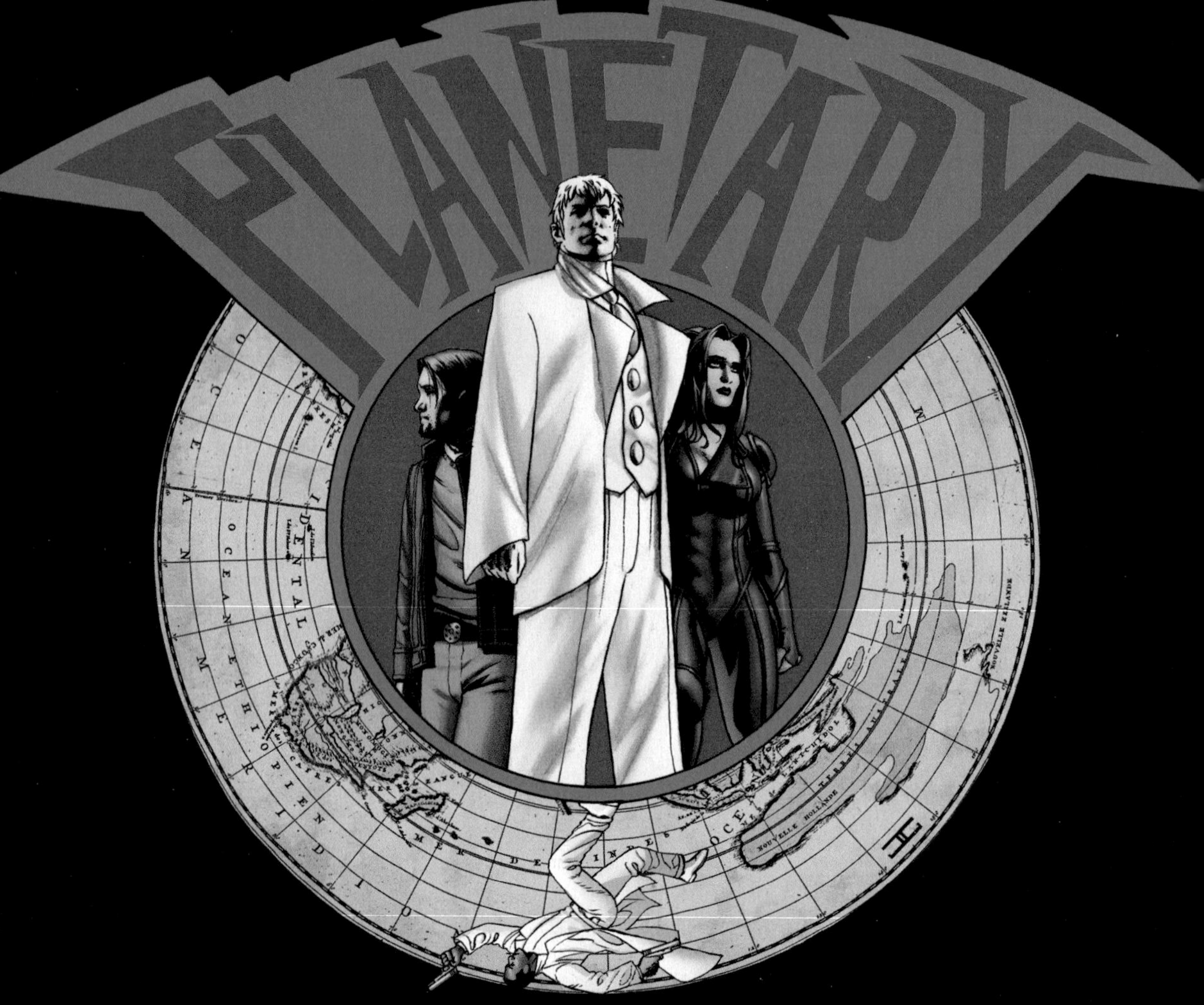
PLANETARY

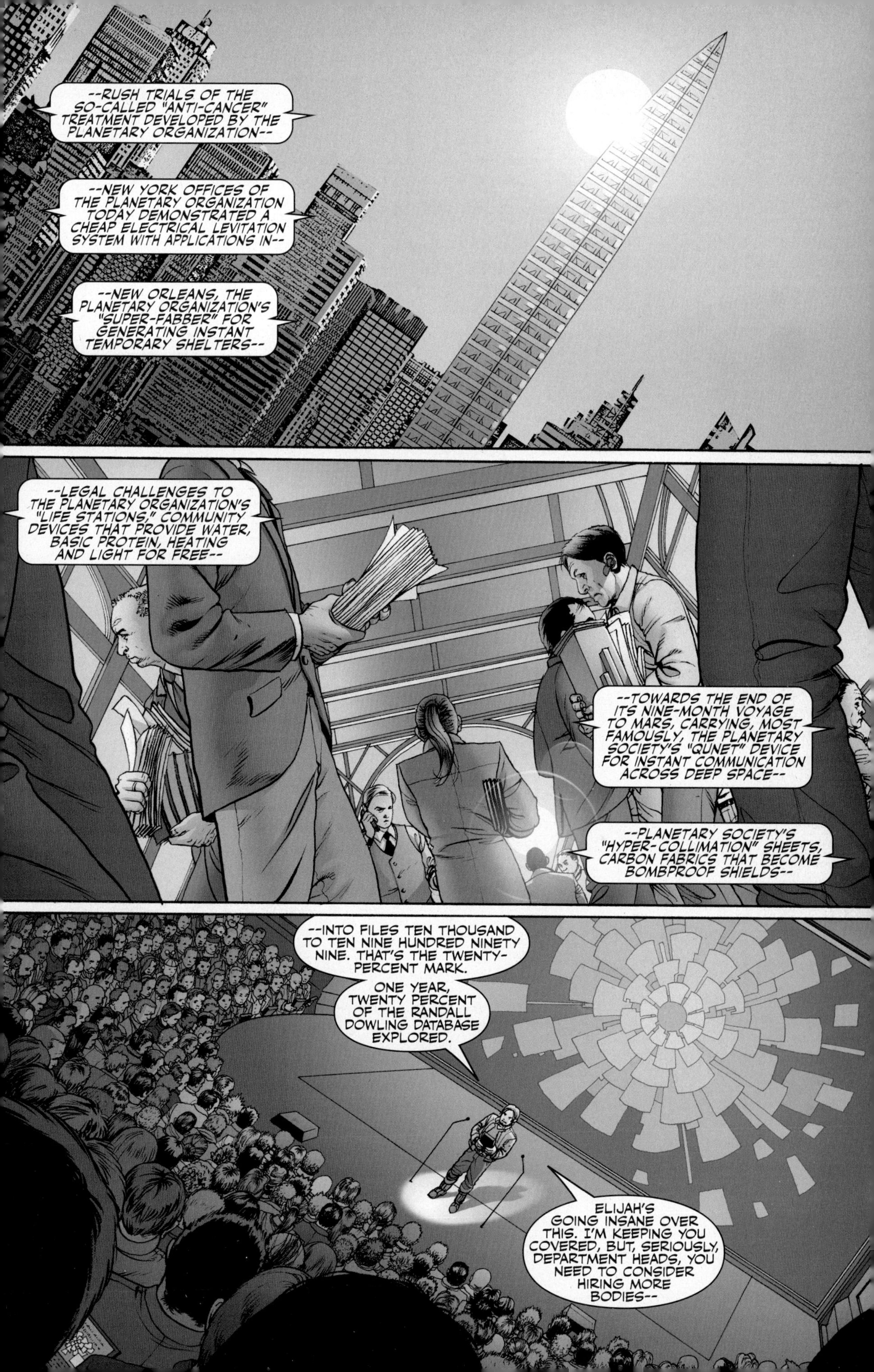
--RUSH TRIALS OF THE SO-CALLED "ANTI-CANCER" TREATMENT DEVELOPED BY THE PLANETARY ORGANIZATION--
--NEW YORK OFFICES OF THE PLANETARY ORGANIZATION TODAY DEMONSTRATED A CHEAP ELECTRICAL LEVITATION SYSTEM WITH APPLICATIONS IN--
--NEW ORLEANS, THE PLANETARY ORGANIZATION'S "SUPER-FABBER" FOR GENERATING INSTANT TEMPORARY SHELTERS--
--LEGAL CHALLENGES TO THE PLANETARY ORGANIZATION'S "LIFE STATIONS," COMMUNITY DEVICES THAT PROVIDE WATER, BASIC PROTEIN, HEATING AND LIGHT FOR FREE--
--TOWARDS THE END OF ITS NINE-MONTH VOYAGE TO MARS, CARRYING, MOST FAMOUSLY, THE PLANETARY SOCIETY'S "QUNET" DEVICE FOR INSTANT COMMUNICATION ACROSS DEEP SPACE--
--PLANETARY SOCIETY'S "HYPER-COLLIMATION" SHEETS, CARBON FABRICS THAT BECOME BOMBPROOF SHIELDS--
--INTO FILES TEN THOUSAND TO TEN NINE HUNDRED NINETY NINE. THAT'S THE TWENTY-PERCENT MARK.
ONE YEAR, TWENTY PERCENT OF THE RANDALL DOWLING DATABASE EXPLORED.
ELIJAH'S GOING INSANE OVER THIS. I'M KEEPING YOU COVERED, BUT, SERIOUSLY, DEPARTMENT HEADS, YOU NEED TO CONSIDER HIRING MORE BODIES--

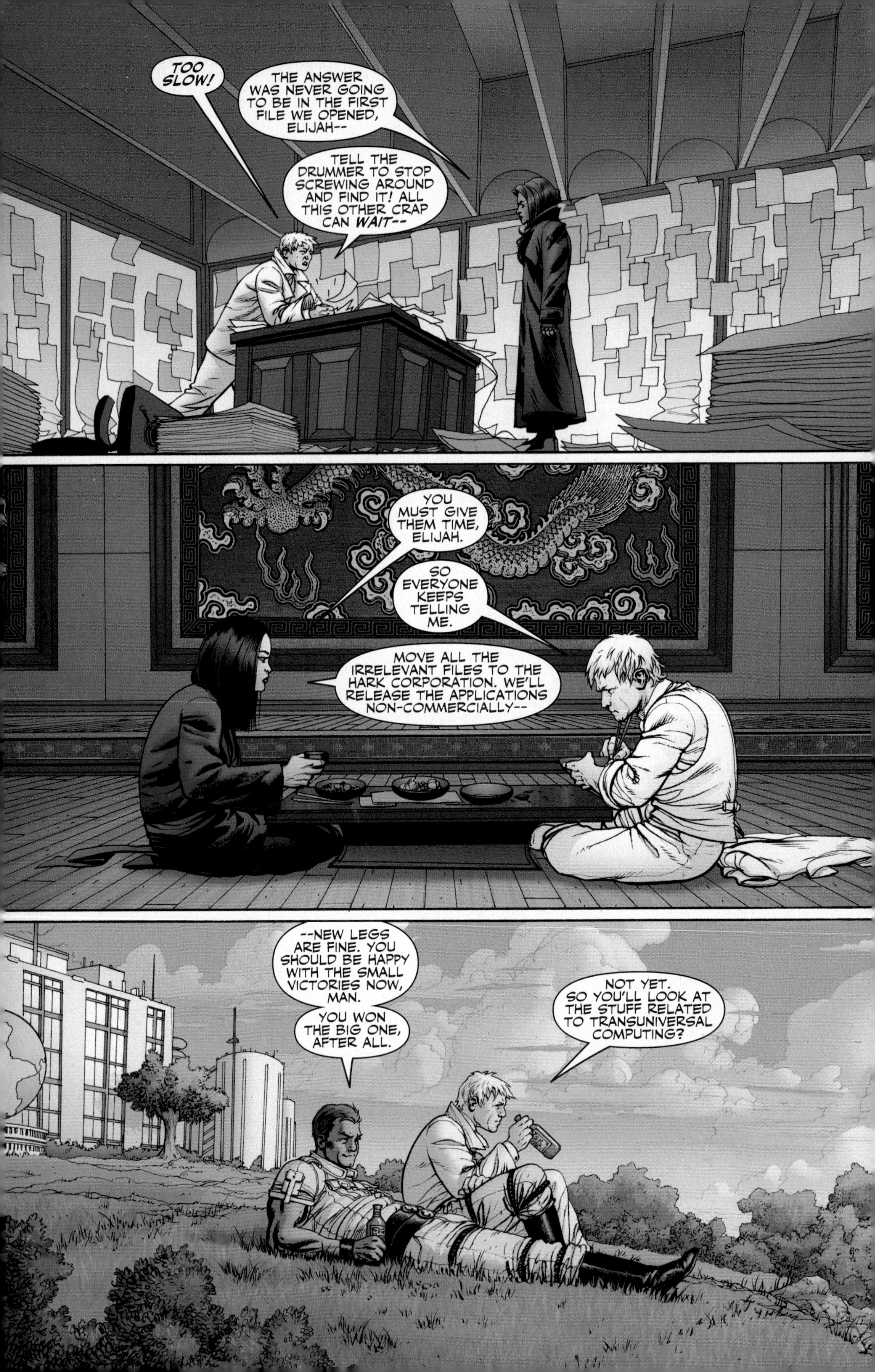
TOO SLOW!
THE ANSWER WAS NEVER GOING TO BE IN THE FIRST FILE WE OPENED, ELIJAH--
TELL THE DRUMMER TO STOP SCREWING AROUND AND FIND IT! ALL THIS OTHER CRAP CAN WAIT--
YOU MUST GIVE THEM TIME, ELIJAH.
SO EVERYONE KEEPS TELLING ME.
MOVE ALL THE IRRELEVANT FILES TO THE HARK CORPORATION. WE'LL RELEASE THE APPLICATIONS NON-COMMERCIALLY--
--NEW LEGS ARE FINE. YOU SHOULD BE HAPPY WITH THE SMALL VICTORIES NOW, MAN.
YOU WON THE BIG ONE, AFTER ALL.
NOT YET. SO YOU'LL LOOK AT THE STUFF RELATED TO TRANSUNIVERSAL COMPUTING?

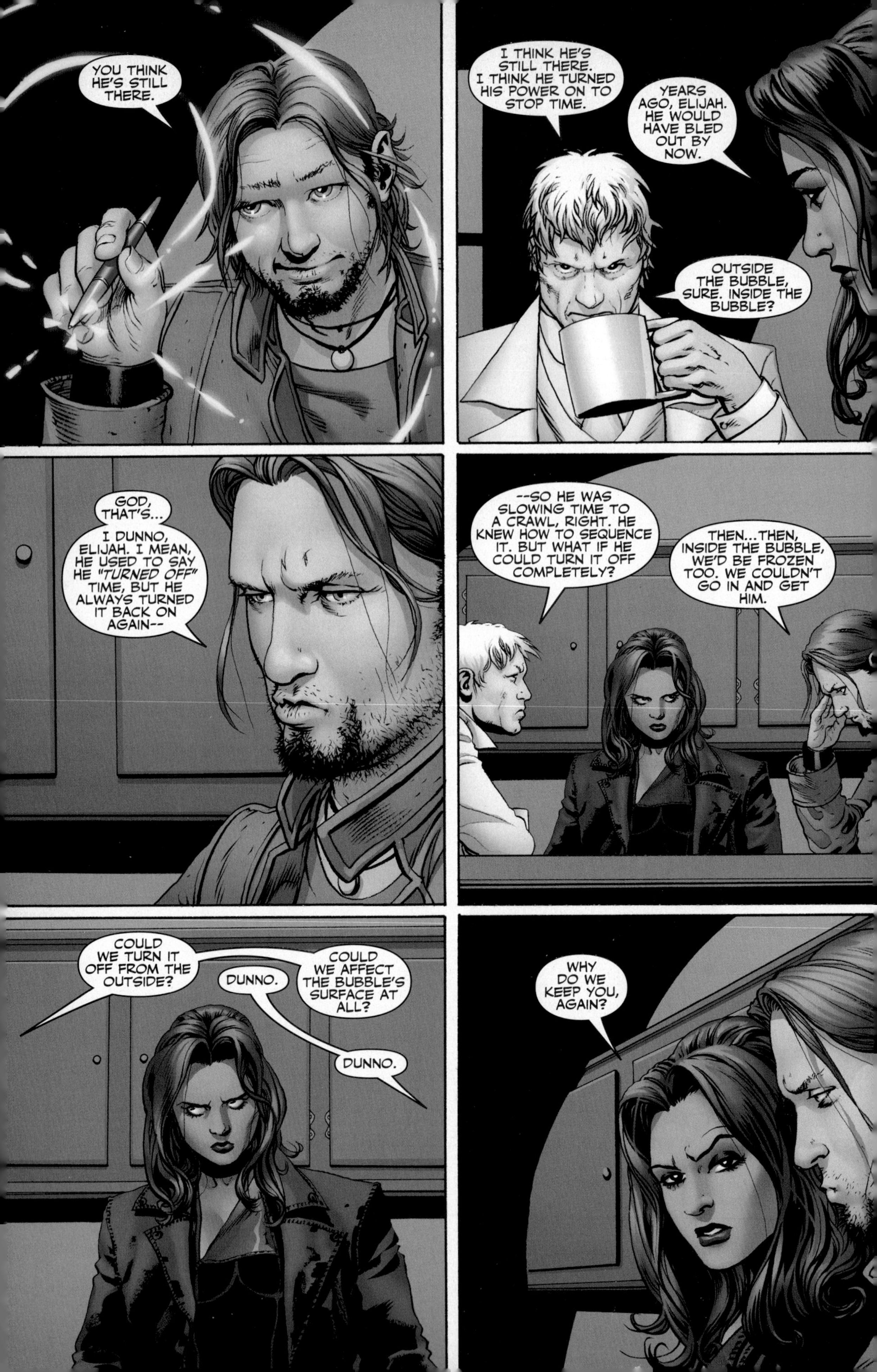
YOU THINK HE'S STILL THERE.
I THINK HE'S STILL THERE. I THINK HE TURNED HIS POWER ON TO STOP TIME.
YEARS AGO, ELIJAH. HE WOULD HAVE BLED OUT BY NOW.
OUTSIDE THE BUBBLE, SURE. INSIDE THE BUBBLE?
GOD, THAT'S...
I DUNNO, ELIJAH. I MEAN, HE USED TO SAY HE *"TURNED OFF"* TIME, BUT HE ALWAYS TURNED IT BACK ON AGAIN--
--SO HE WAS SLOWING TIME TO A CRAWL, RIGHT. HE KNEW HOW TO SEQUENCE IT. BUT WHAT IF HE COULD TURN IT OFF COMPLETELY?
THEN...THEN, INSIDE THE BUBBLE, WE'D BE FROZEN TOO. WE COULDN'T GO IN AND GET HIM.
COULD WE TURN IT OFF FROM THE OUTSIDE?
DUNNO.
COULD WE AFFECT THE BUBBLE'S SURFACE AT ALL?
DUNNO.
WHY DO WE KEEP YOU, AGAIN?

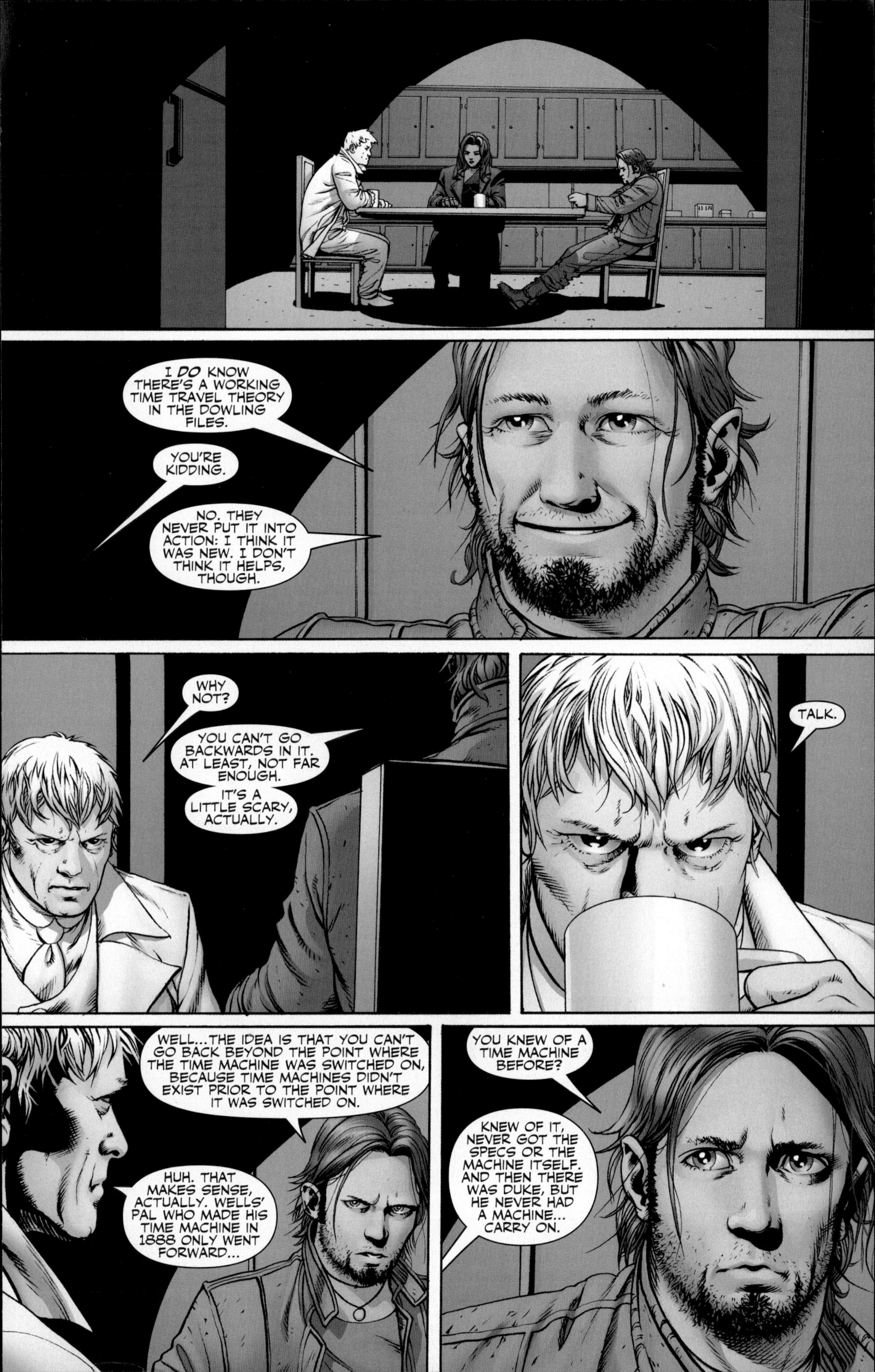
I DO KNOW THERE'S A WORKING TIME TRAVEL THEORY IN THE DOWLING FILES.
YOU'RE KIDDING.
NO. THEY NEVER PUT IT INTO ACTION: I THINK IT WAS NEW. I DON'T THINK IT HELPS, THOUGH.
WHY NOT?
YOU CAN'T GO BACKWARDS IN IT. AT LEAST, NOT FAR ENOUGH.
IT'S A LITTLE SCARY, ACTUALLY.
TALK.
WELL...THE IDEA IS THAT YOU CAN'T GO BACK BEYOND THE POINT WHERE THE TIME MACHINE WAS SWITCHED ON, BECAUSE TIME MACHINES DIDN'T EXIST PRIOR TO THE POINT WHERE IT WAS SWITCHED ON.
HUH. THAT MAKES SENSE, ACTUALLY. WELLS' PAL WHO MADE HIS TIME MACHINE IN 1888 ONLY WENT FORWARD...
YOU KNEW OF A TIME MACHINE BEFORE?
KNEW OF IT, NEVER GOT THE SPECS OR THE MACHINE ITSELF. AND THEN THERE WAS DUKE, BUT HE NEVER HAD A MACHINE... CARRY ON.

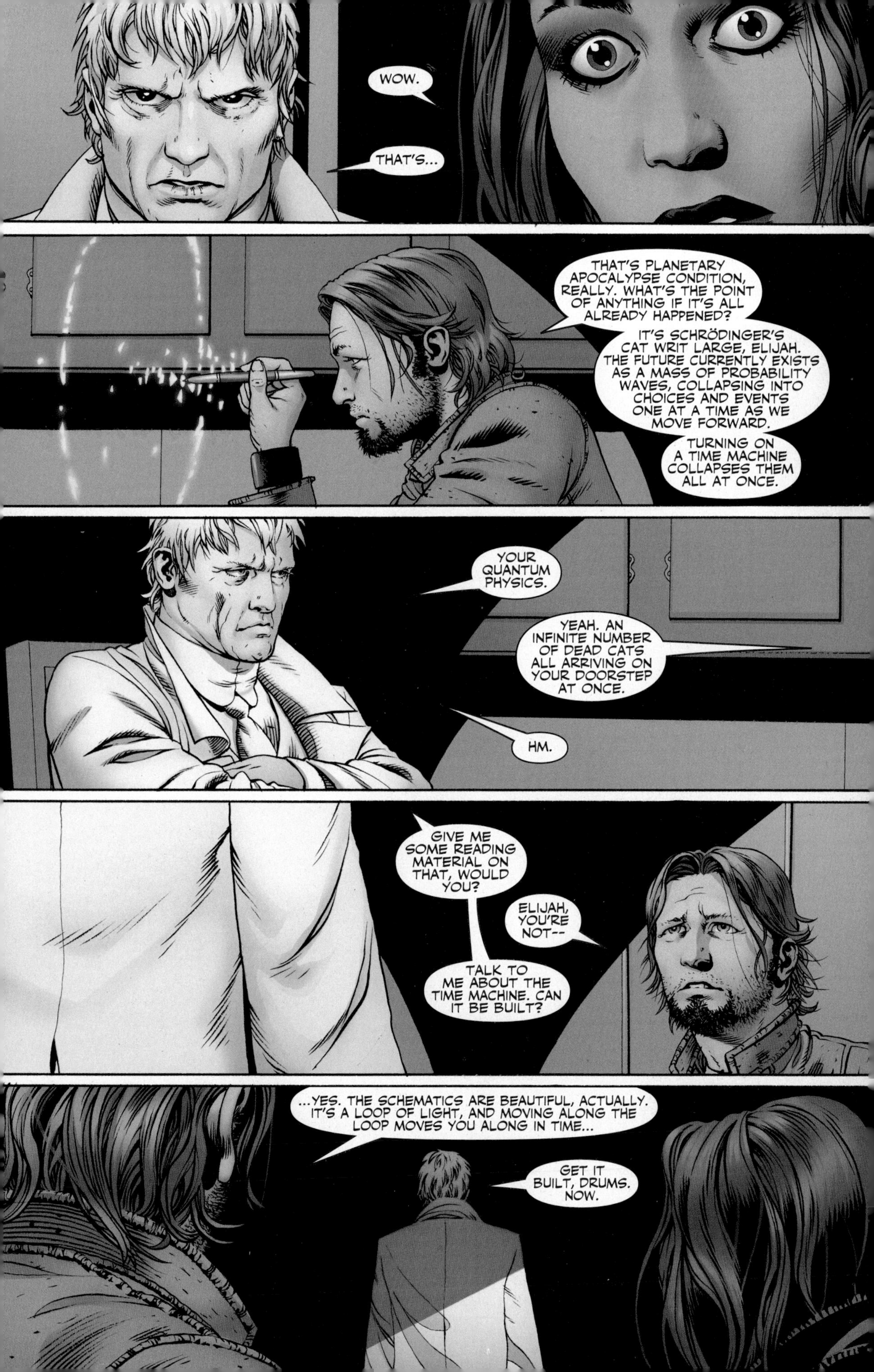
WOW.
THAT'S...
THAT'S PLANETARY APOCALYPSE CONDITION, REALLY. WHAT'S THE POINT OF ANYTHING IF IT'S ALL ALREADY HAPPENED?
IT'S SCHRÖDINGER'S CAT WRIT LARGE, ELIJAH. THE FUTURE CURRENTLY EXISTS AS A MASS OF PROBABILITY WAVES, COLLAPSING INTO CHOICES AND EVENTS ONE AT A TIME AS WE MOVE FORWARD.
TURNING ON A TIME MACHINE COLLAPSES THEM ALL AT ONCE.
YOUR QUANTUM PHYSICS.
YEAH. AN INFINITE NUMBER OF DEAD CATS ALL ARRIVING ON YOUR DOORSTEP AT ONCE.
HM.
GIVE ME SOME READING MATERIAL ON THAT, WOULD YOU?
ELIJAH, YOU'RE NOT--
TALK TO ME ABOUT THE TIME MACHINE. CAN IT BE BUILT?
...YES. THE SCHEMATICS ARE BEAUTIFUL, ACTUALLY. IT'S A LOOP OF LIGHT, AND MOVING ALONG THE LOOP MOVES YOU ALONG IN TIME...
GET IT BUILT, DRUMS. NOW.

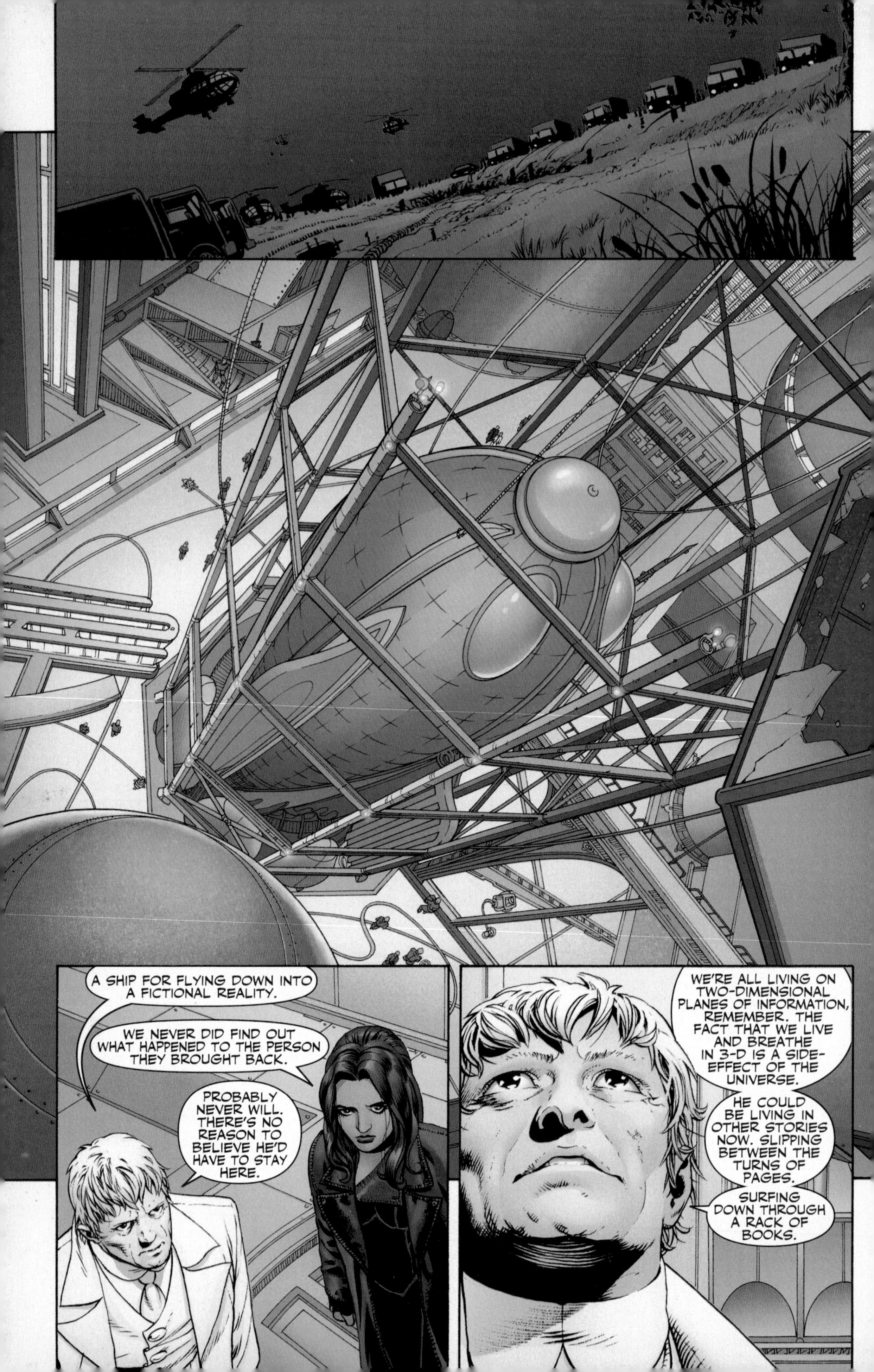
A SHIP FOR FLYING DOWN INTO A FICTIONAL REALITY.
WE NEVER DID FIND OUT WHAT HAPPENED TO THE PERSON THEY BROUGHT BACK.
PROBABLY NEVER WILL. THERE'S NO REASON TO BELIEVE HE'D HAVE TO STAY HERE.
WE'RE ALL LIVING ON TWO-DIMENSIONAL PLANES OF INFORMATION, REMEMBER. THE FACT THAT WE LIVE AND BREATHE IN 3-D IS A SIDE-EFFECT OF THE UNIVERSE.
HE COULD BE LIVING IN OTHER STORIES NOW. SLIPPING BETWEEN THE TURNS OF PAGES.
SURFING DOWN THROUGH A RACK OF BOOKS.

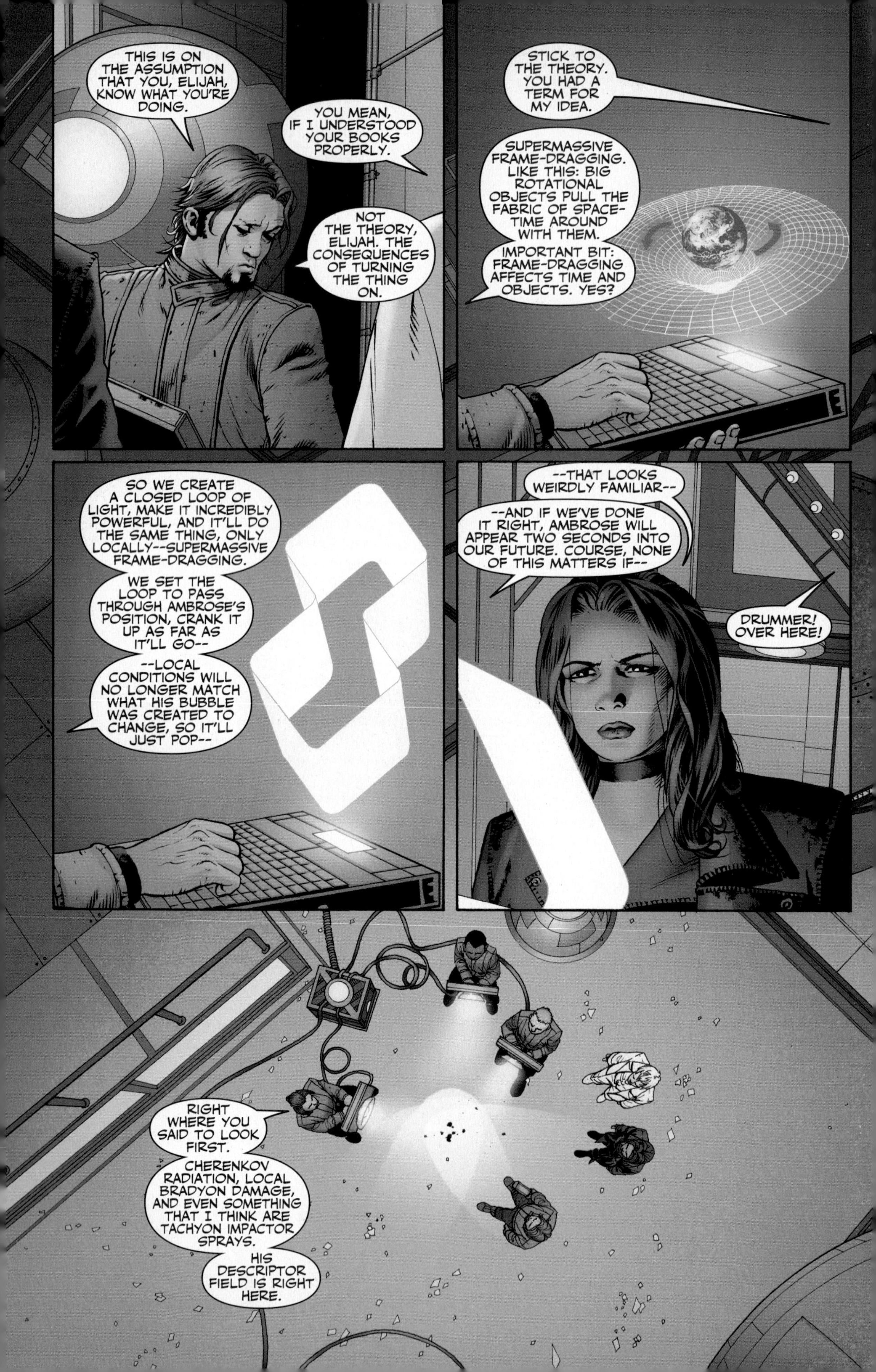
THIS IS ON THE ASSUMPTION THAT YOU, ELIJAH, KNOW WHAT YOU'RE DOING.
YOU MEAN, IF I UNDERSTOOD YOUR BOOKS PROPERLY.
NOT THE THEORY, ELIJAH. THE CONSEQUENCES OF TURNING THE THING ON.
STICK TO THE THEORY. YOU HAD A TERM FOR MY IDEA.
SUPERMASSIVE FRAME-DRAGGING. LIKE THIS: BIG ROTATIONAL OBJECTS PULL THE FABRIC OF SPACE-TIME AROUND WITH THEM.
IMPORTANT BIT: FRAME-DRAGGING AFFECTS TIME AND OBJECTS. YES?
SO WE CREATE A CLOSED LOOP OF LIGHT, MAKE IT INCREDIBLY POWERFUL, AND IT'LL DO THE SAME THING, ONLY LOCALLY--SUPERMASSIVE FRAME-DRAGGING.
WE SET THE LOOP TO PASS THROUGH AMBROSE'S POSITION, CRANK IT UP AS FAR AS IT'LL GO--
--LOCAL CONDITIONS WILL NO LONGER MATCH WHAT HIS BUBBLE WAS CREATED TO CHANGE, SO IT'LL JUST POP--
--THAT LOOKS WEIRDLY FAMILIAR--
--AND IF WE'VE DONE IT RIGHT, AMBROSE WILL APPEAR TWO SECONDS INTO OUR FUTURE. COURSE, NONE OF THIS MATTERS IF--
DRUMMER! OVER HERE!
RIGHT WHERE YOU SAID TO LOOK FIRST.
CHERENKOV RADIATION, LOCAL BRADYON DAMAGE, AND EVEN SOMETHING THAT I THINK ARE TACHYON IMPACTOR SPRAYS.
HIS DESCRIPTOR FIELD IS RIGHT HERE.

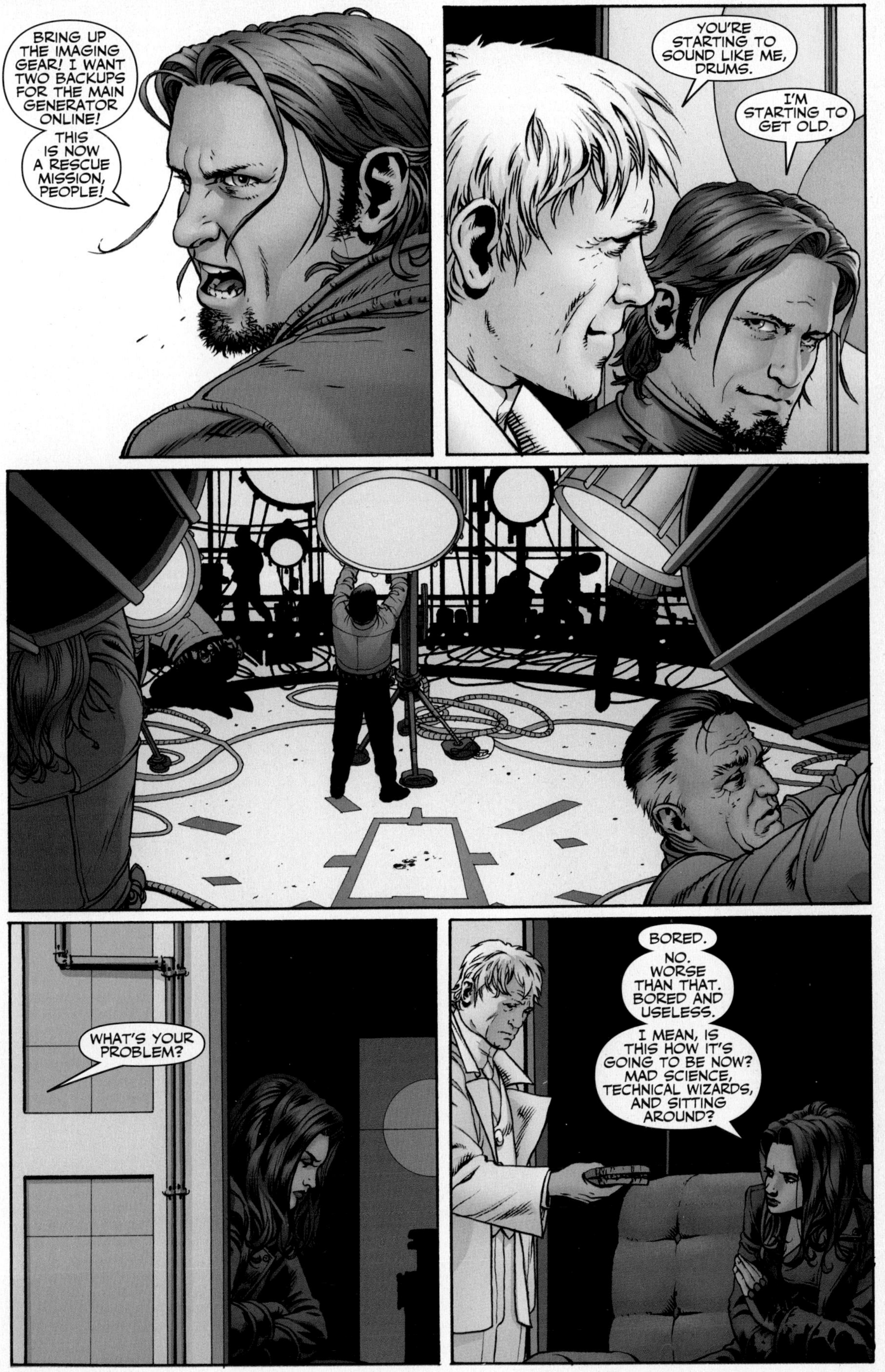
BRING UP THE IMAGING GEAR! I WANT TWO BACKUPS FOR THE MAIN GENERATOR ONLINE!
THIS IS NOW A RESCUE MISSION, PEOPLE!
YOU'RE STARTING TO SOUND LIKE ME, DRUMS.
I'M STARTING TO GET OLD.
WHAT'S YOUR PROBLEM?
BORED.
NO. WORSE THAN THAT. BORED AND USELESS.
I MEAN, IS THIS HOW IT'S GOING TO BE NOW? MAD SCIENCE, TECHNICAL WIZARDS, AND SITTING AROUND?

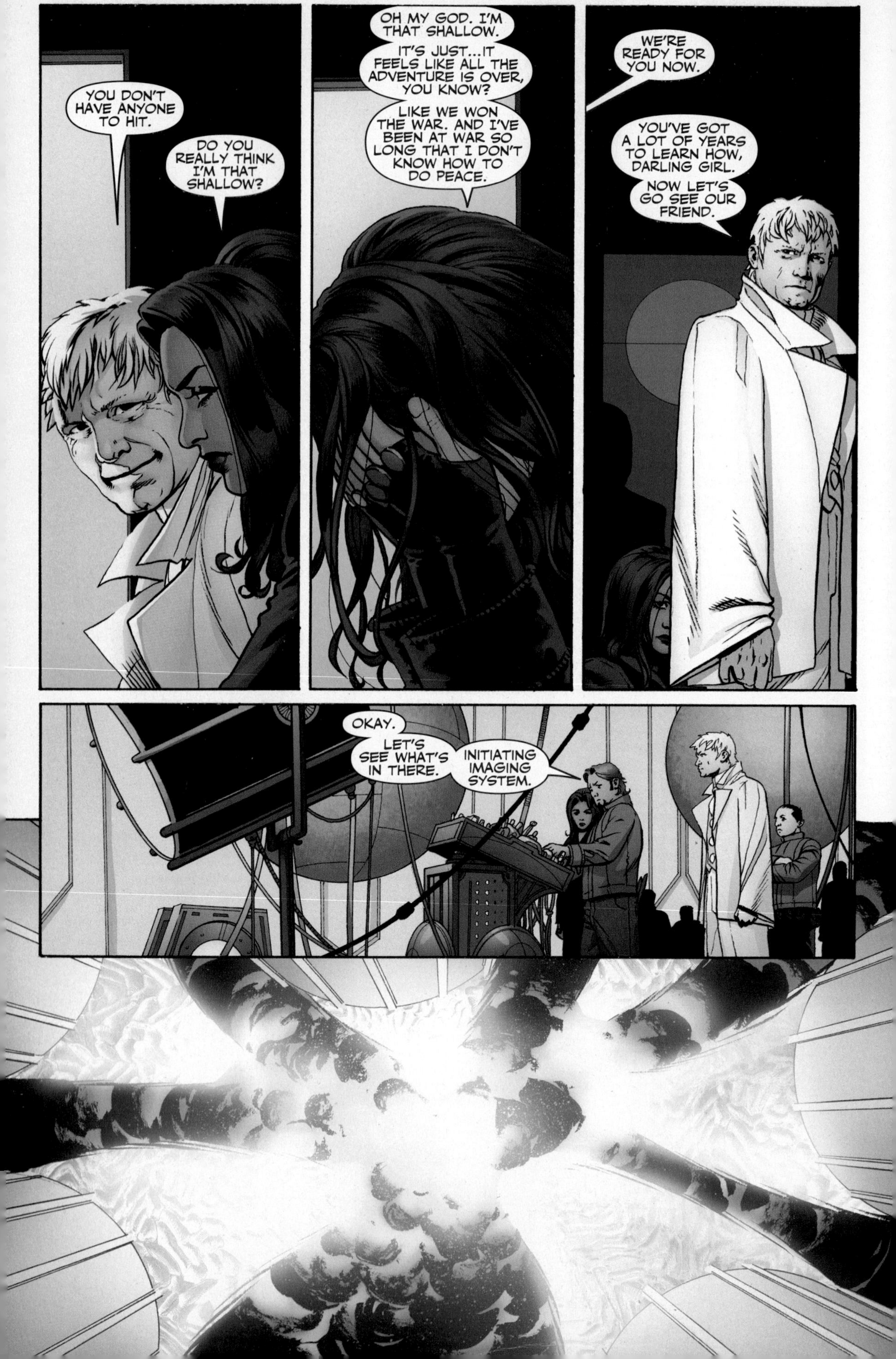
YOU DON'T HAVE ANYONE TO HIT.
DO YOU REALLY THINK I'M THAT SHALLOW?
OH MY GOD. I'M THAT SHALLOW.
IT'S JUST...IT FEELS LIKE ALL THE ADVENTURE IS OVER, YOU KNOW?
LIKE WE WON THE WAR. AND I'VE BEEN AT WAR SO LONG THAT I DON'T KNOW HOW TO DO PEACE.
WE'RE READY FOR YOU NOW.
YOU'VE GOT A LOT OF YEARS TO LEARN HOW, DARLING GIRL.
NOW LET'S GO SEE OUR FRIEND.
OKAY.
LET'S SEE WHAT'S IN THERE.
INITIATING IMAGING SYSTEM.

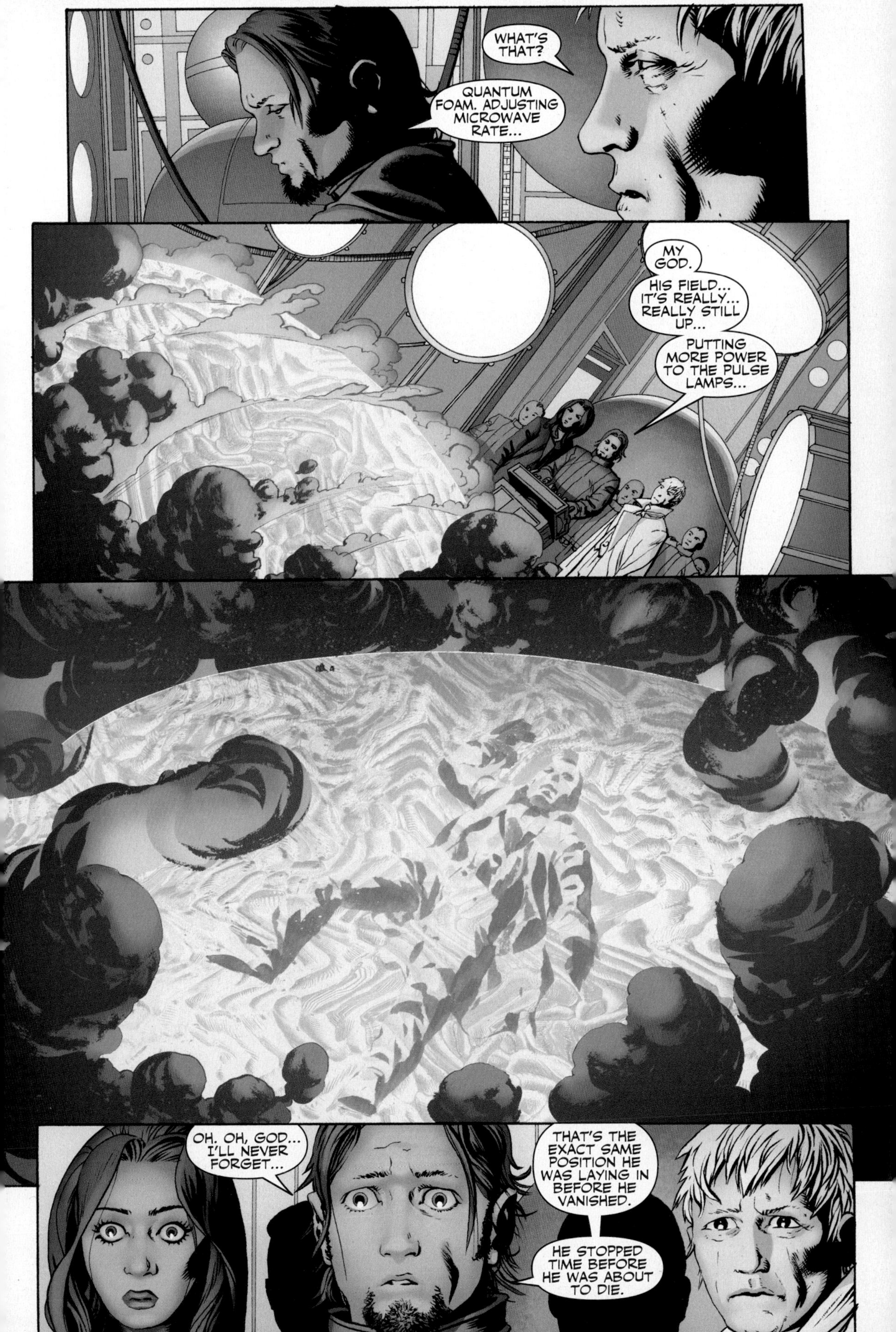
WHAT'S THAT?
QUANTUM FOAM. ADJUSTING MICROWAVE RATE...
MY GOD.
HIS FIELD... IT'S REALLY... REALLY STILL UP...
PUTTING MORE POWER TO THE PULSE LAMPS...
OH. OH, GOD... I'LL NEVER FORGET...
THAT'S THE EXACT SAME POSITION HE WAS LAYING IN BEFORE HE VANISHED.
HE STOPPED TIME BEFORE HE WAS ABOUT TO DIE.

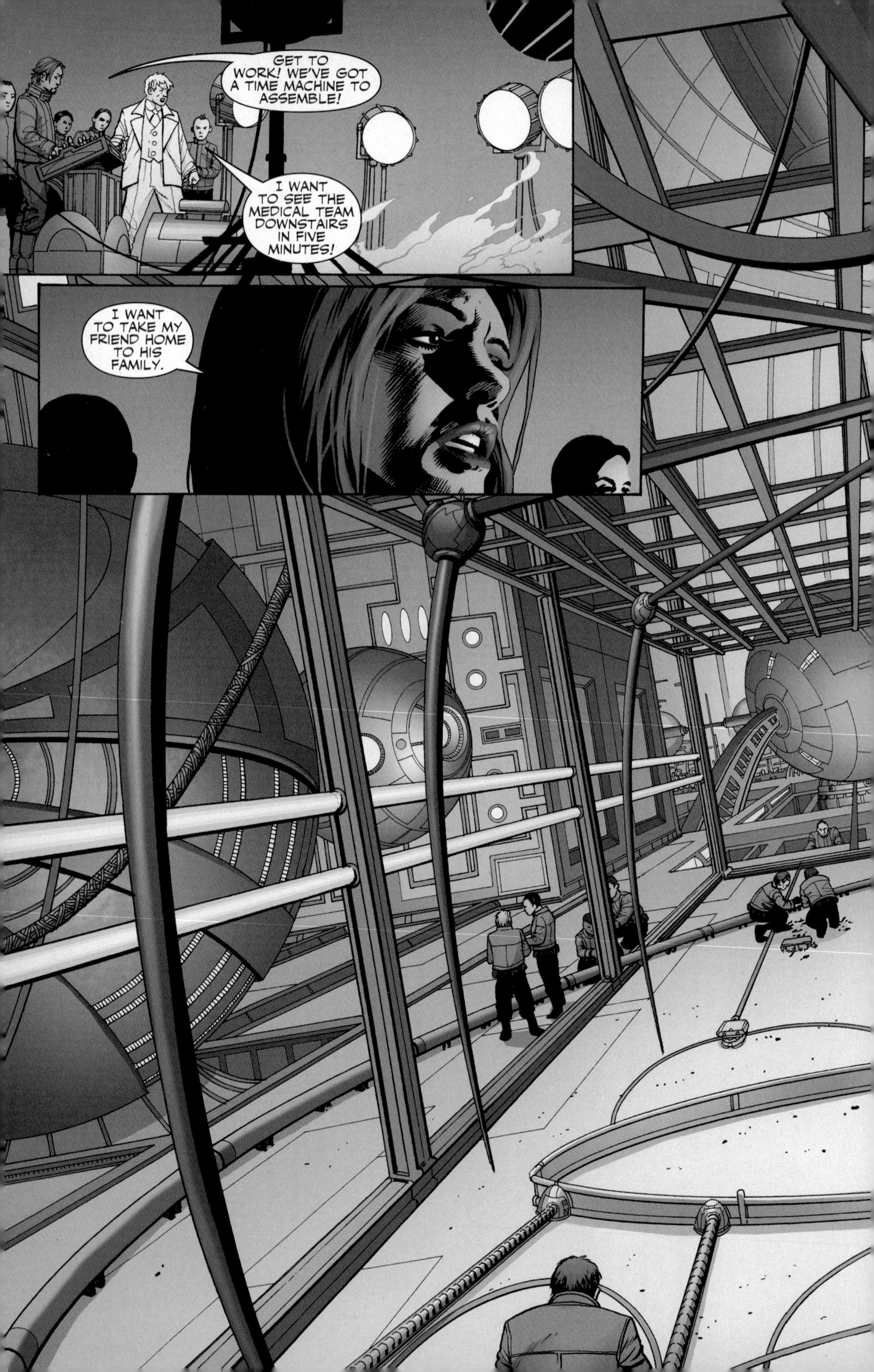
GET TO WORK! WE'VE GOT A TIME MACHINE TO ASSEMBLE!
I WANT TO SEE THE MEDICAL TEAM DOWNSTAIRS IN FIVE MINUTES!
I WANT TO TAKE MY FRIEND HOME TO HIS FAMILY.

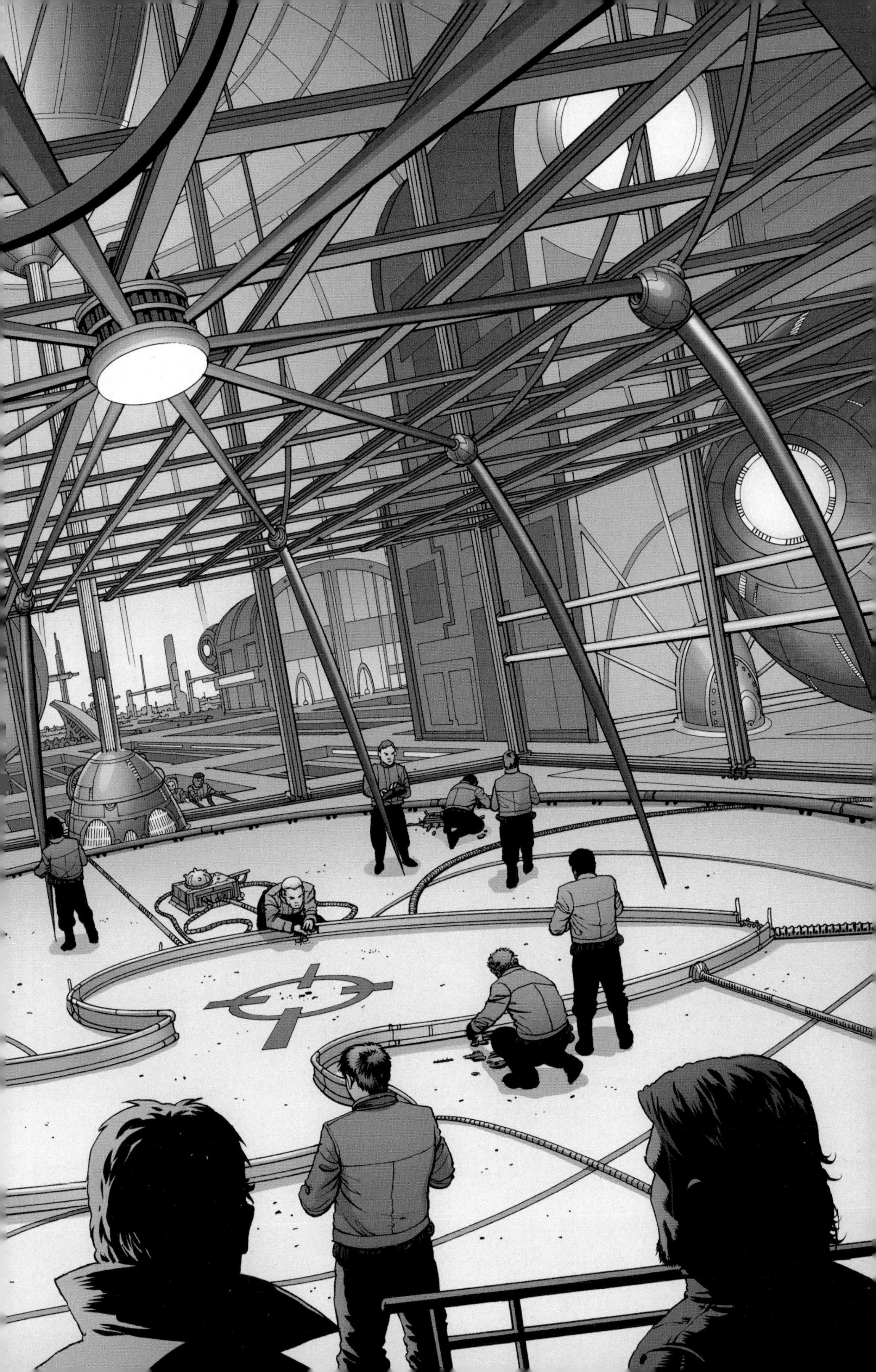

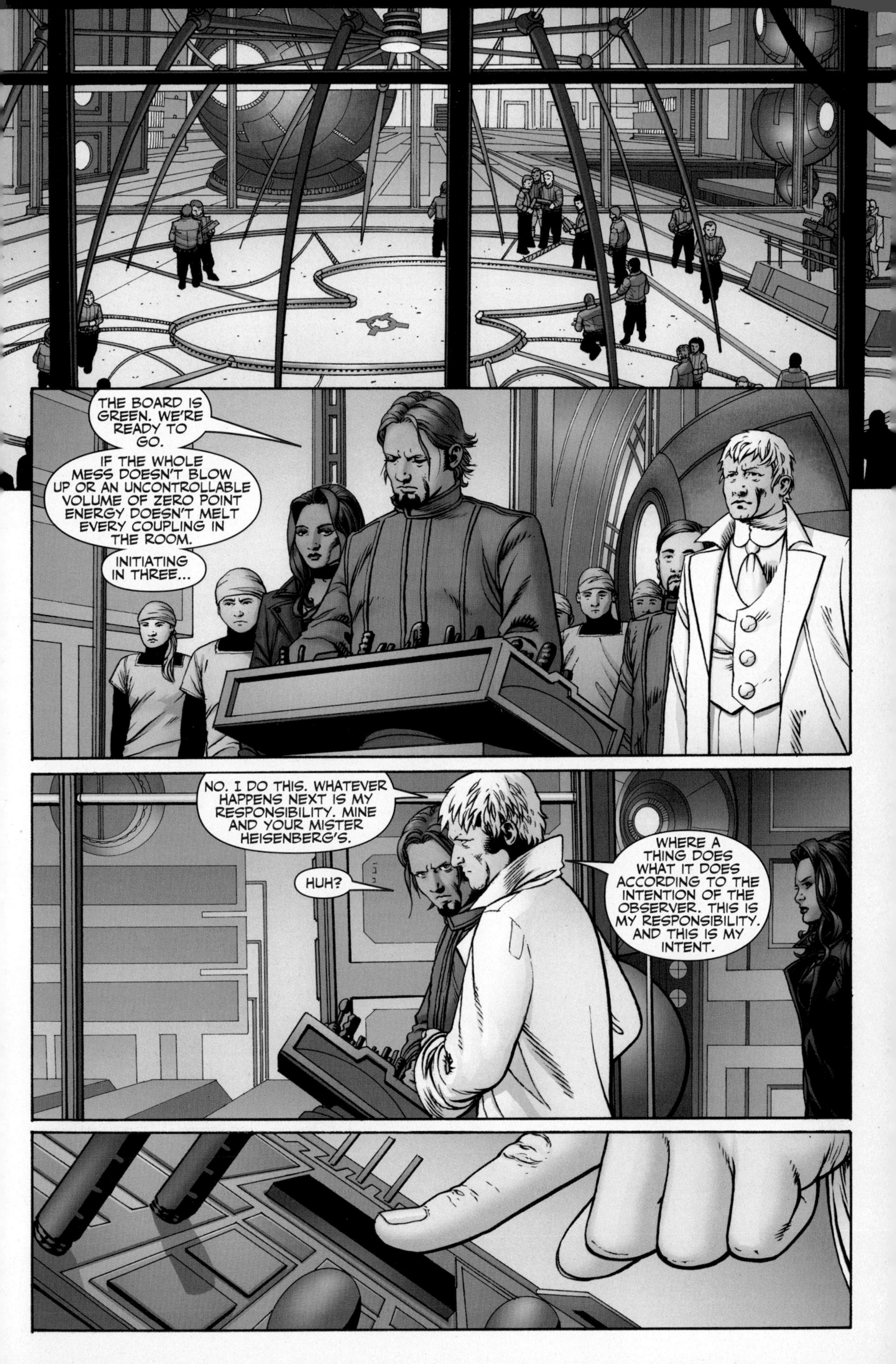
THE BOARD IS GREEN. WE'RE READY TO GO.
IF THE WHOLE MESS DOESN'T BLOW UP OR AN UNCONTROLLABLE VOLUME OF ZERO POINT ENERGY DOESN'T MELT EVERY COUPLING IN THE ROOM.
INITIATING IN THREE...
NO. I DO THIS. WHATEVER HAPPENS NEXT IS MY RESPONSIBILITY. MINE AND YOUR MISTER HEISENBERG'S.
HUH?
WHERE A THING DOES WHAT IT DOES ACCORDING TO THE INTENTION OF THE OBSERVER. THIS IS MY RESPONSIBILITY. AND THIS IS MY INTENT.

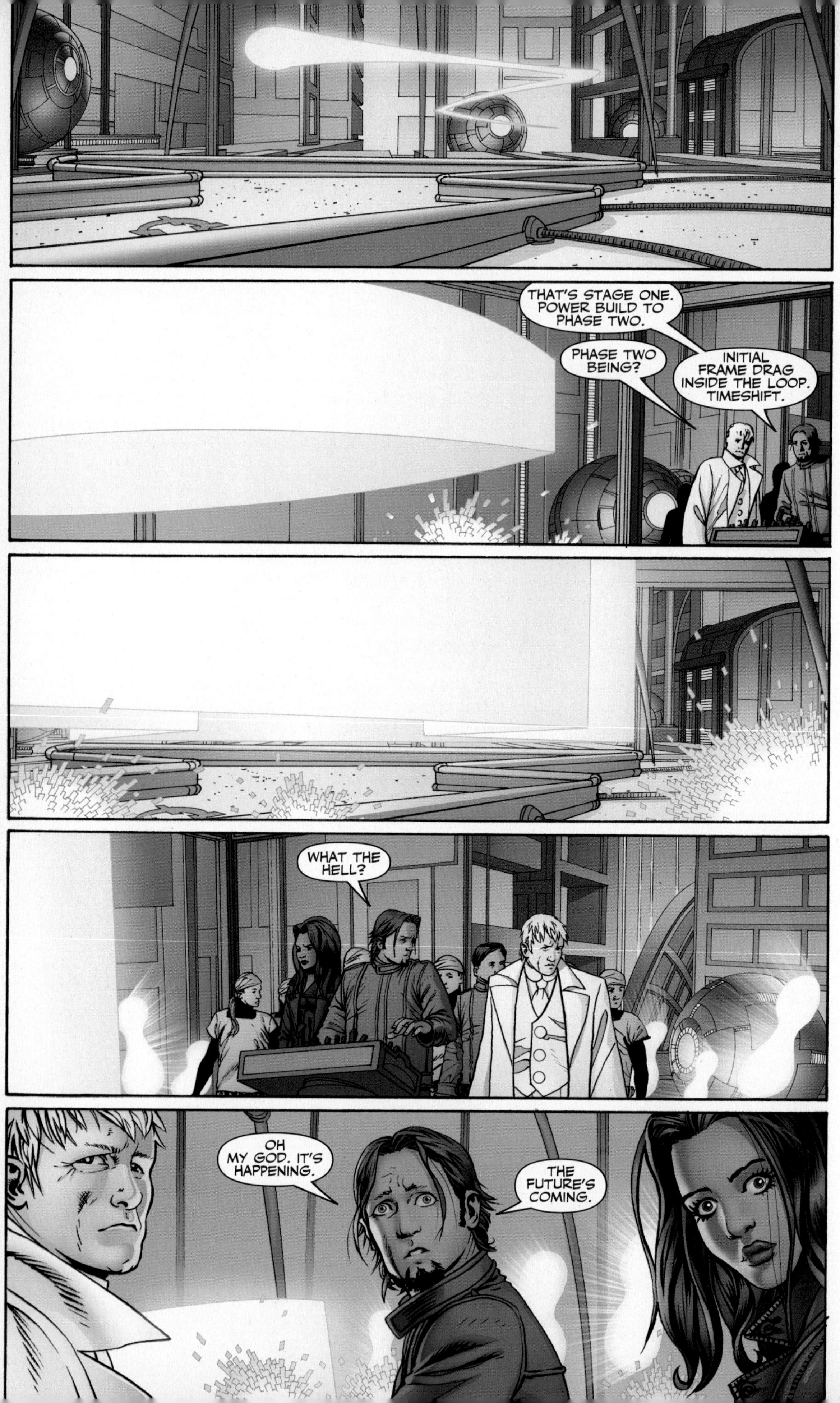
THAT'S STAGE ONE. POWER BUILD TO PHASE TWO.
PHASE TWO BEING?
INITIAL FRAME DRAG INSIDE THE LOOP. TIMESHIFT.
WHAT THE HELL?
OH MY GOD. IT'S HAPPENING.
THE FUTURE'S COMING.

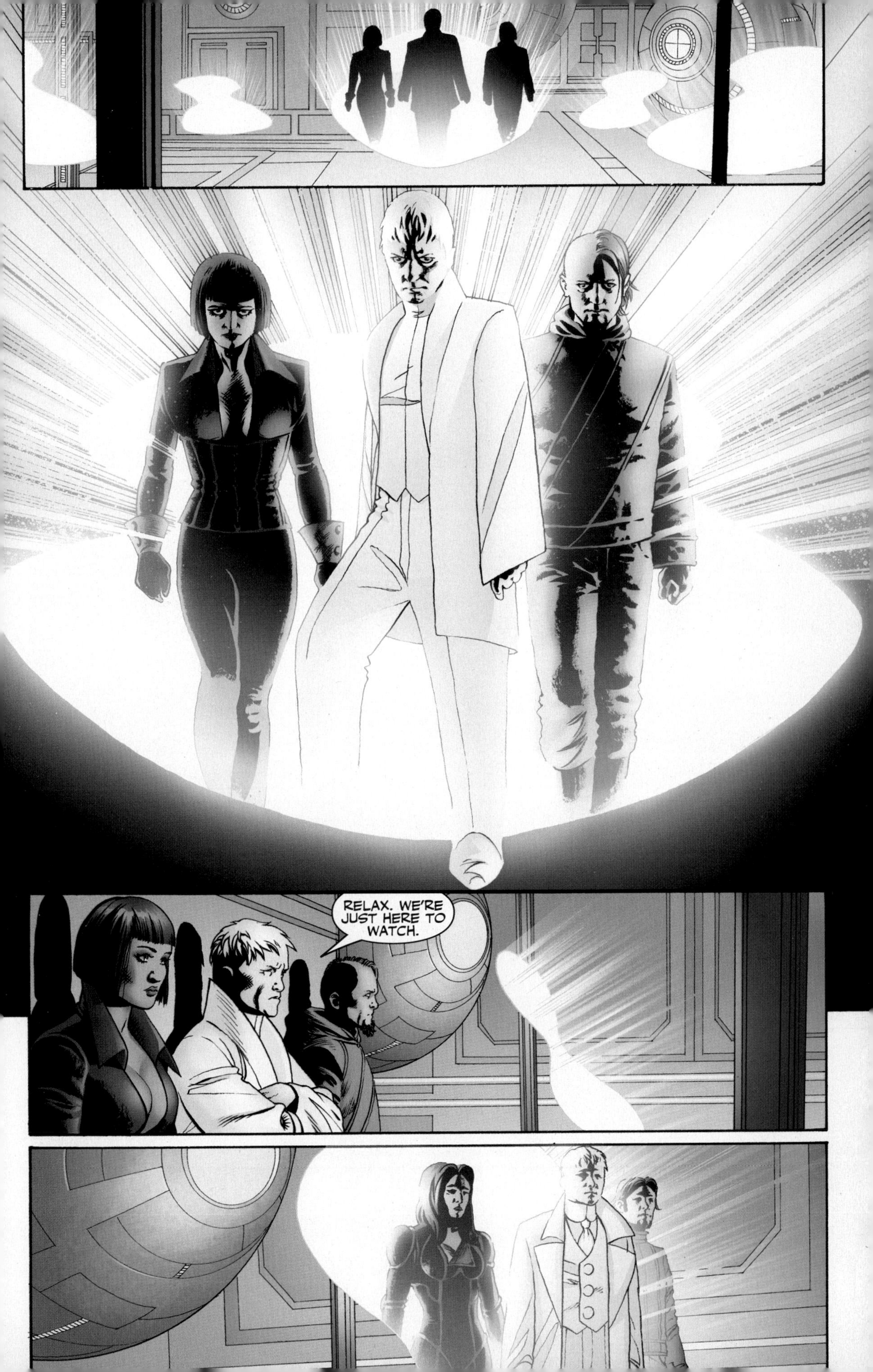
RELAX. WE'RE JUST HERE TO WATCH.

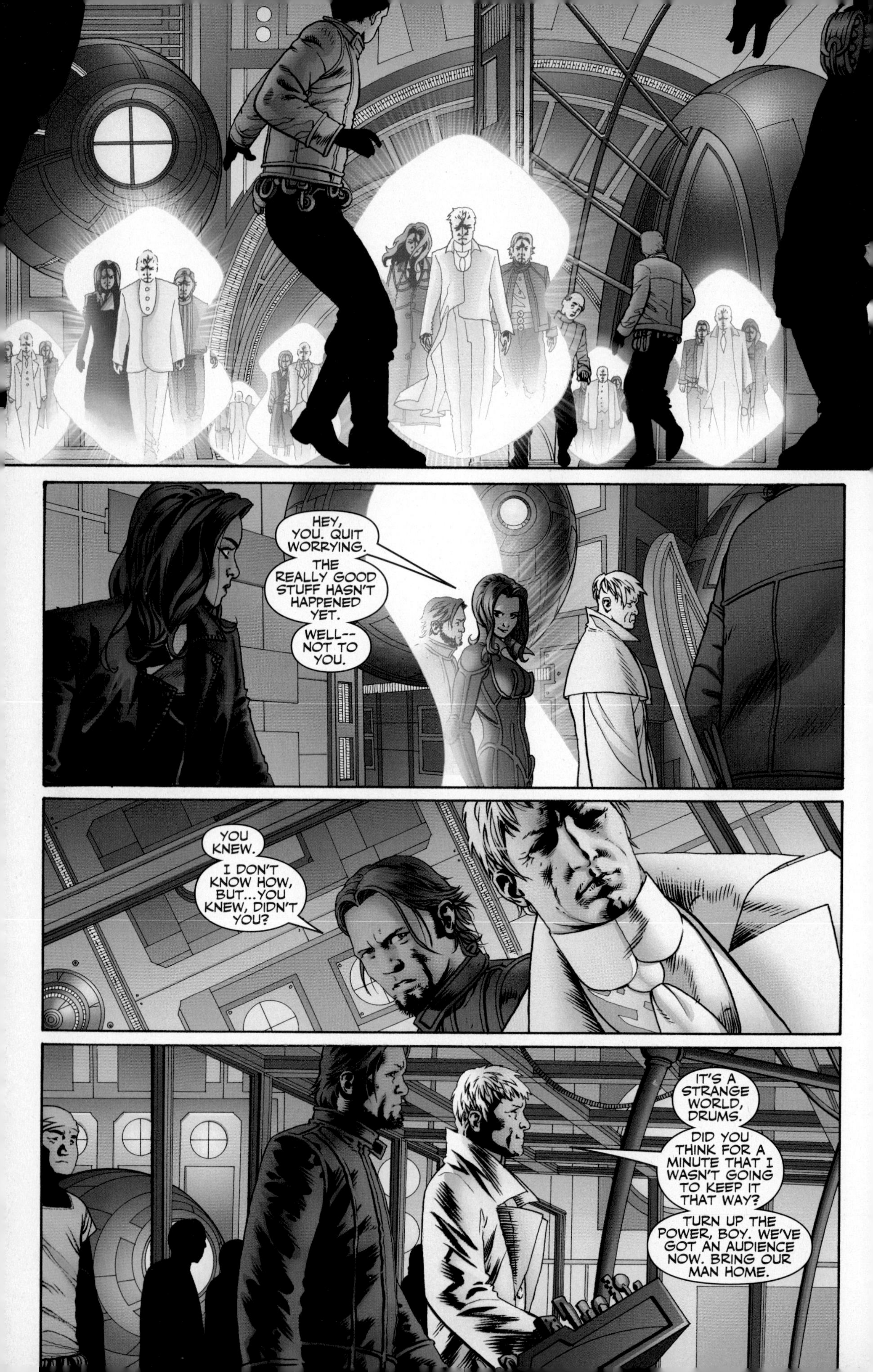
HEY, YOU. QUIT WORRYING.
THE REALLY GOOD STUFF HASN'T HAPPENED YET.
WELL-- NOT TO YOU.
YOU KNEW.
I DON'T KNOW HOW, BUT...YOU KNEW, DIDN'T YOU?
IT'S A STRANGE WORLD, DRUMS.
DID YOU THINK FOR A MINUTE THAT I WASN'T GOING TO KEEP IT THAT WAY?
TURN UP THE POWER, BOY. WE'VE GOT AN AUDIENCE NOW. BRING OUR MAN HOME.

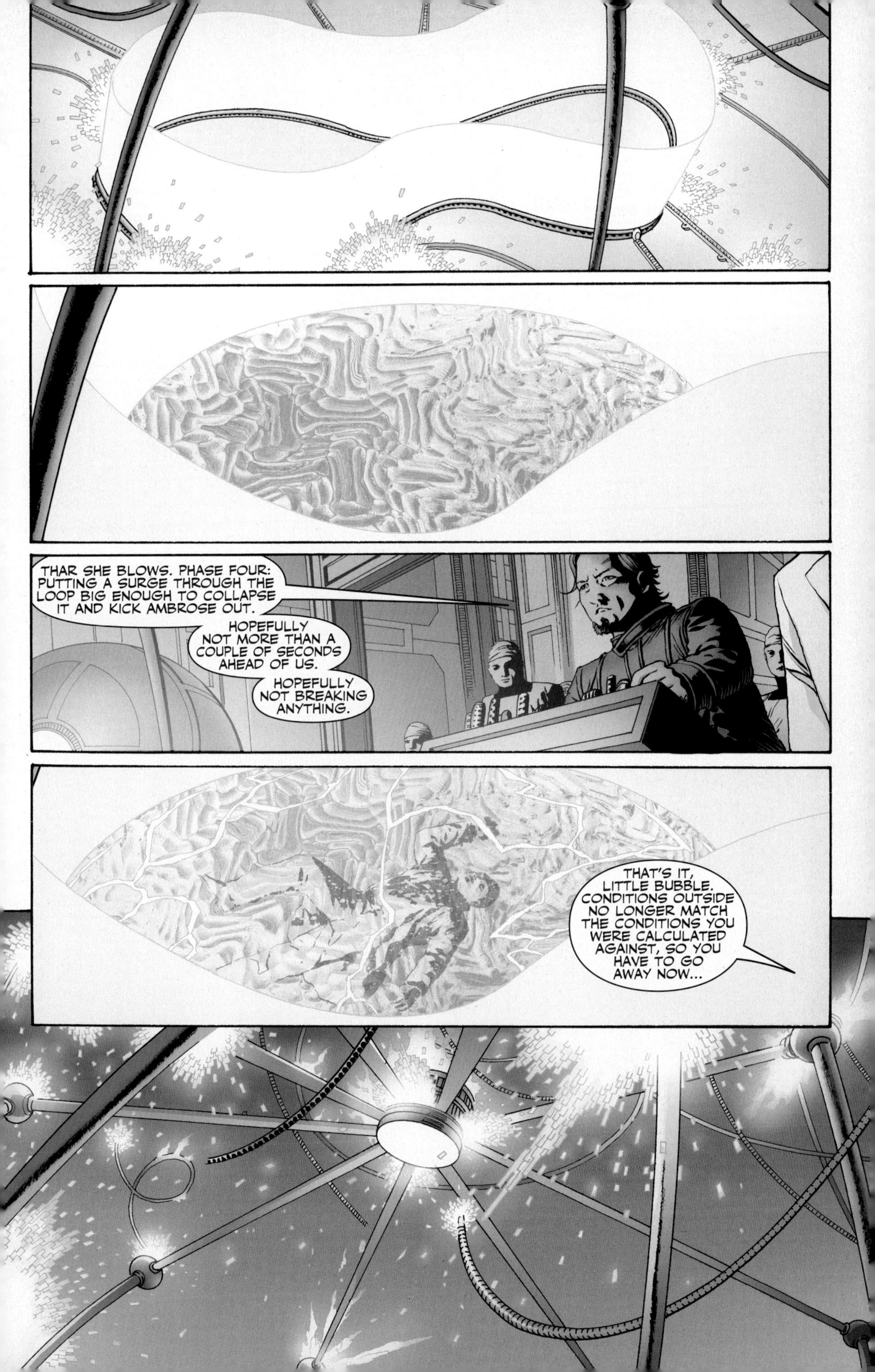
THAR SHE BLOWS. PHASE FOUR: PUTTING A SURGE THROUGH THE LOOP BIG ENOUGH TO COLLAPSE IT AND KICK AMBROSE OUT.
HOPEFULLY NOT MORE THAN A COUPLE OF SECONDS AHEAD OF US.
HOPEFULLY NOT BREAKING ANYTHING.
THAT'S IT, LITTLE BUBBLE. CONDITIONS OUTSIDE NO LONGER MATCH THE CONDITIONS YOU WERE CALCULATED AGAINST, SO YOU HAVE TO GO AWAY NOW...

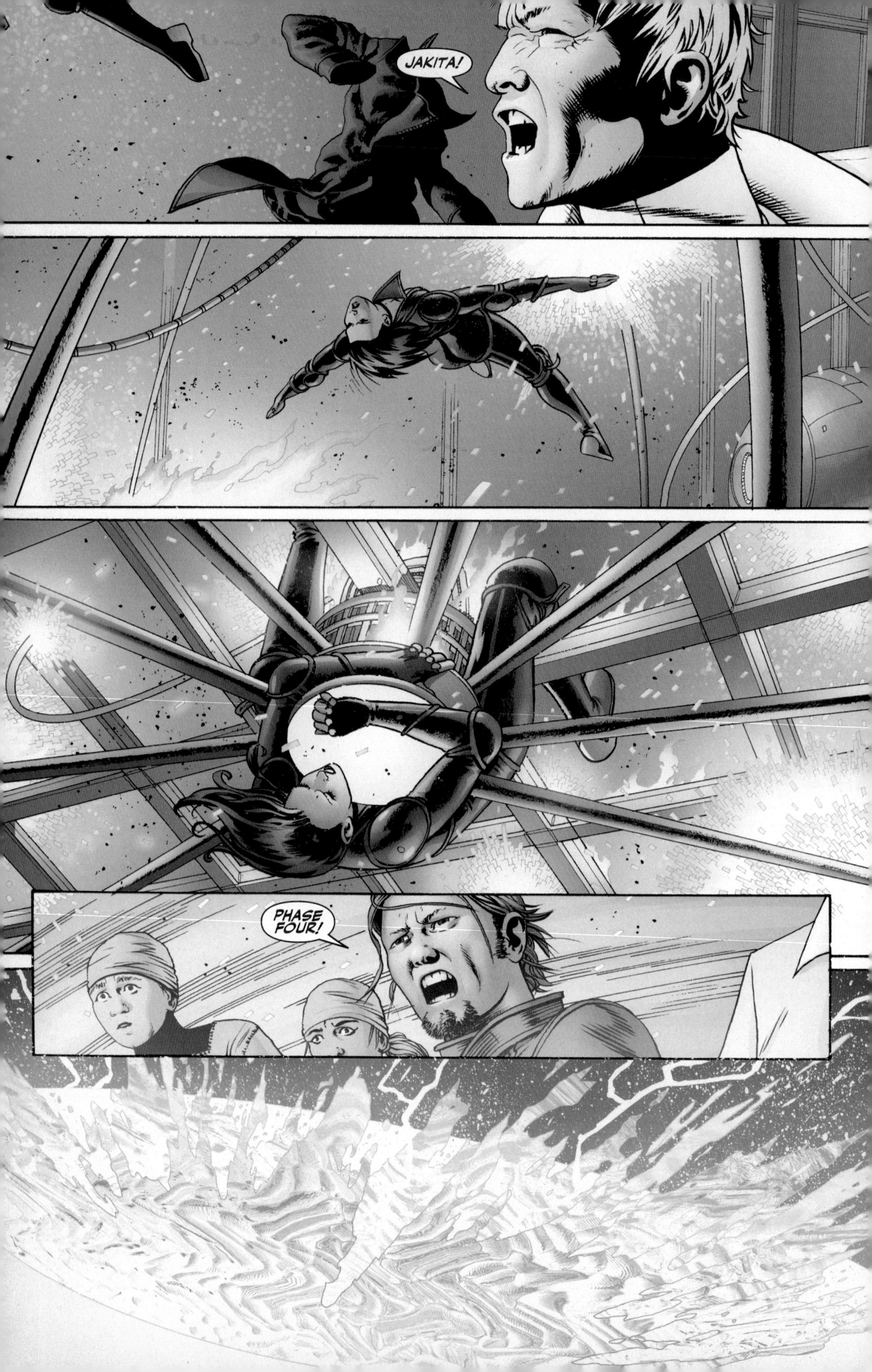
JAKITA!
PHASE FOUR!

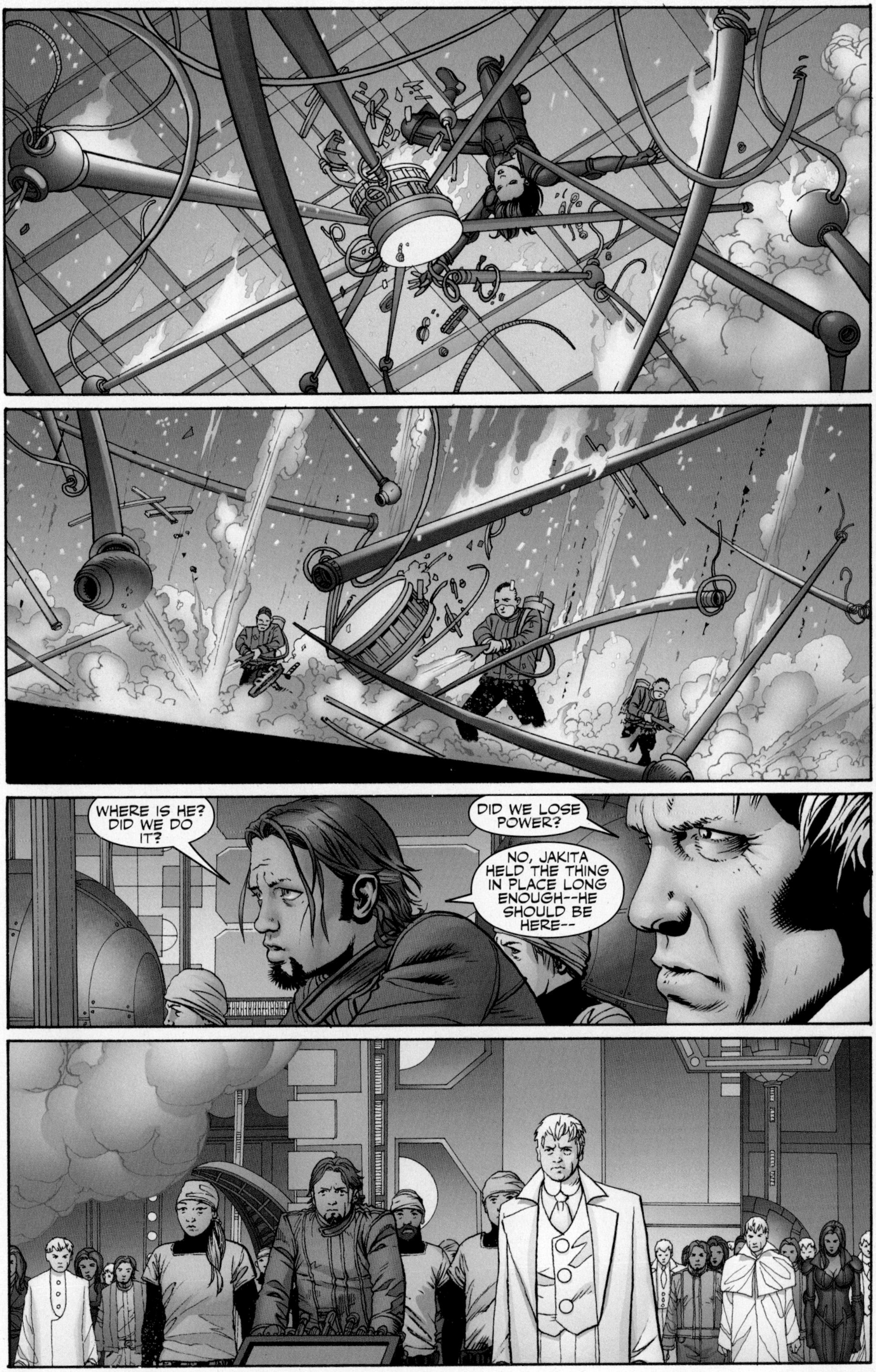
WHERE IS HE? DID WE DO IT?
DID WE LOSE POWER?
NO, JAKITA HELD THE THING IN PLACE LONG ENOUGH--HE SHOULD BE HERE--

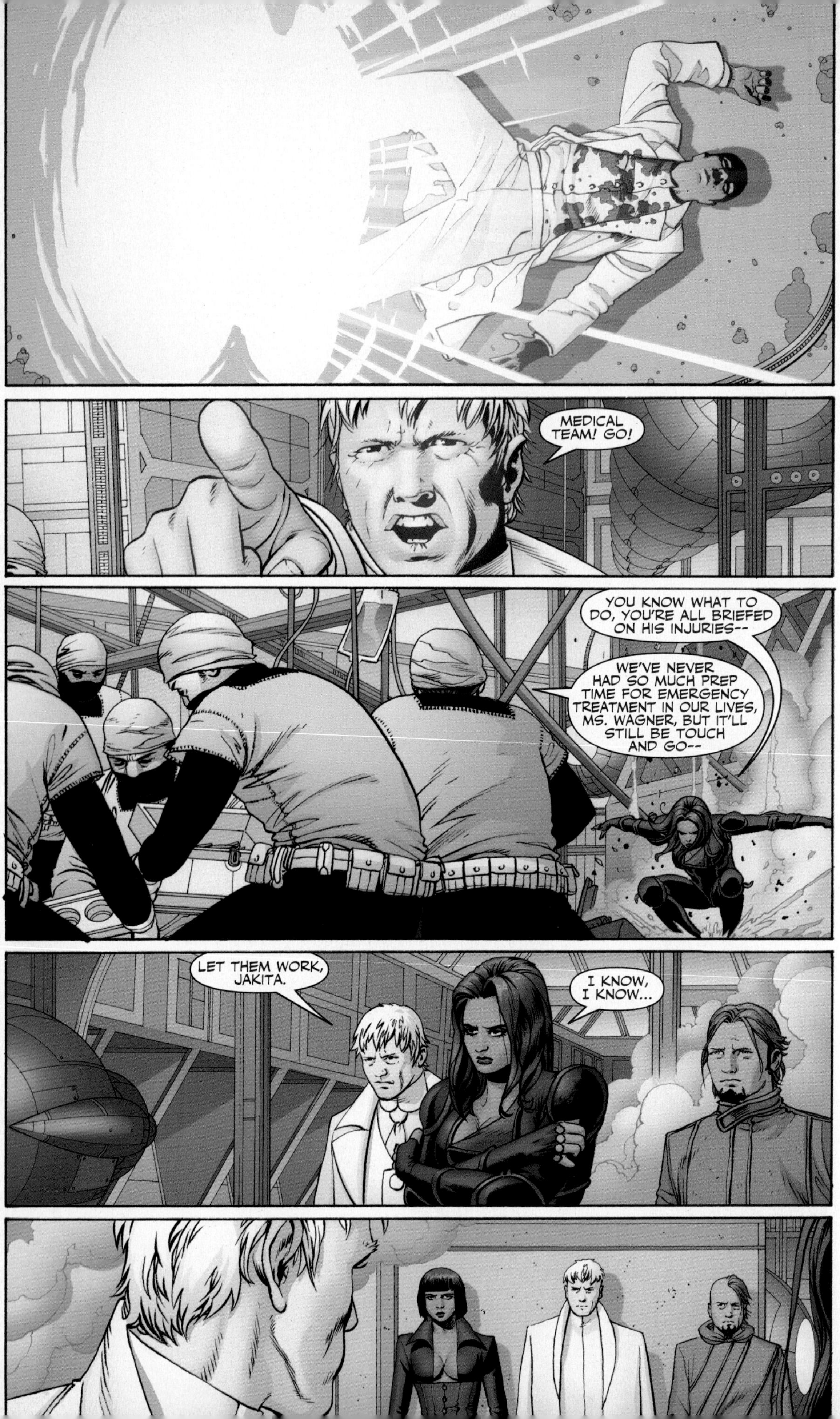
MEDICAL TEAM! GO!
YOU KNOW WHAT TO DO, YOU'RE ALL BRIEFED ON HIS INJURIES--
WE'VE NEVER HAD SO MUCH PREP TIME FOR EMERGENCY TREATMENT IN OUR LIVES, MS. WAGNER, BUT IT'LL STILL BE TOUCH AND GO--
LET THEM WORK, JAKITA.
I KNOW, I KNOW...

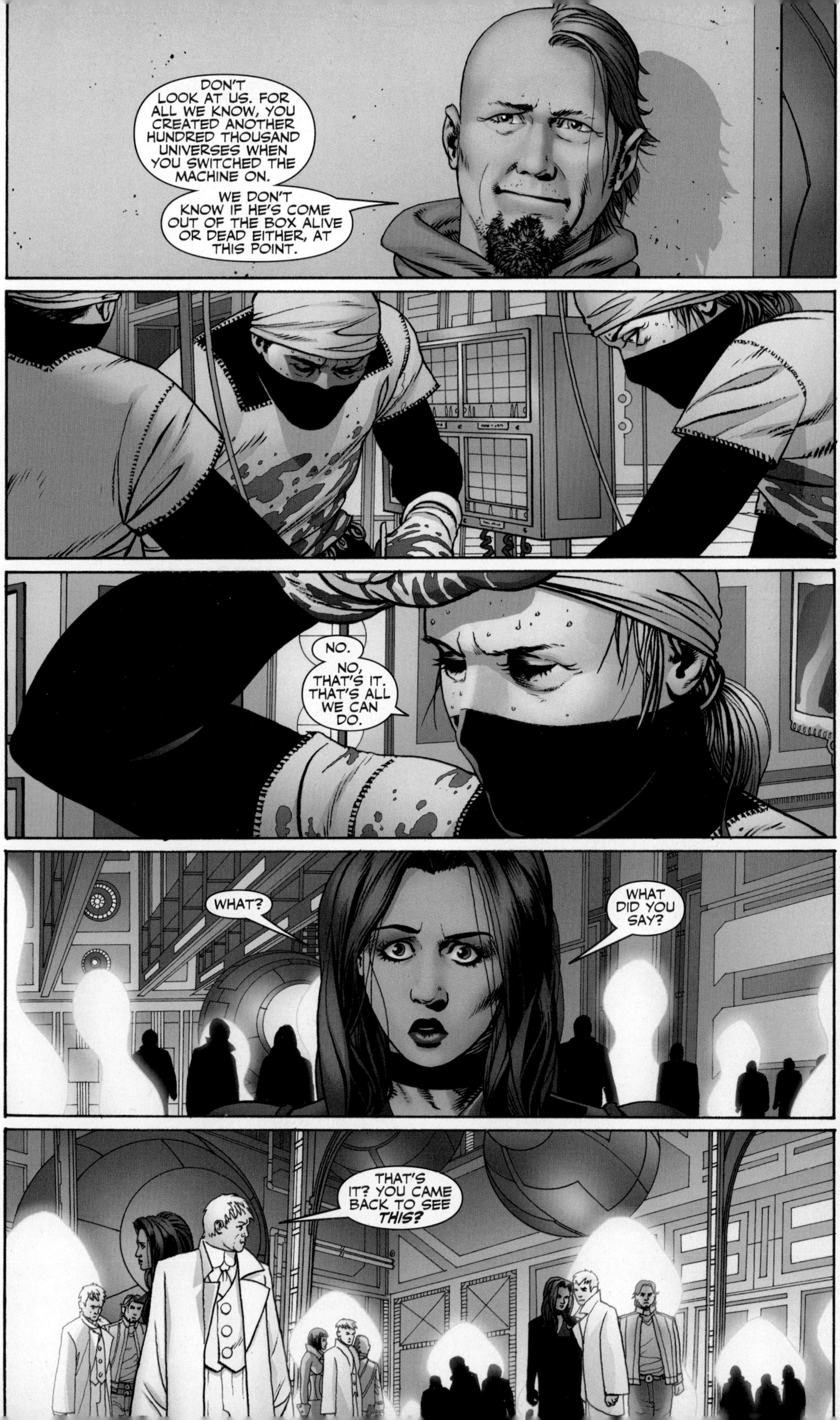
DON'T LOOK AT US. FOR ALL WE KNOW, YOU CREATED ANOTHER HUNDRED THOUSAND UNIVERSES WHEN YOU SWITCHED THE MACHINE ON.
WE DON'T KNOW IF HE'S COME OUT OF THE BOX ALIVE OR DEAD EITHER, AT THIS POINT.
NO.
NO, THAT'S IT. THAT'S ALL WE CAN DO.
WHAT?
WHAT DID YOU SAY?
THAT'S IT? YOU CAME BACK TO SEE *THIS?*

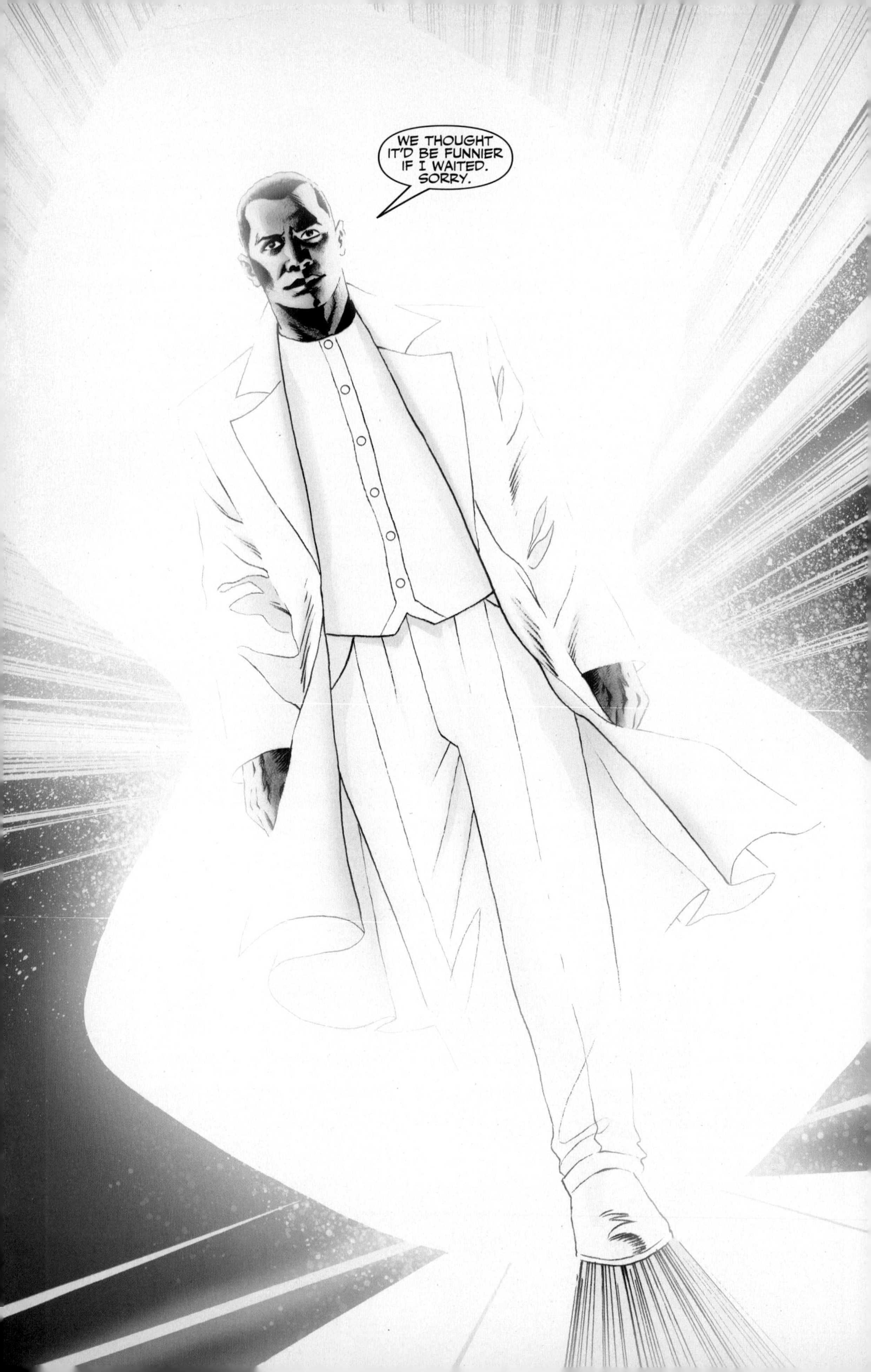
WE THOUGHT IT'D BE FUNNIER IF I WAITED. SORRY.

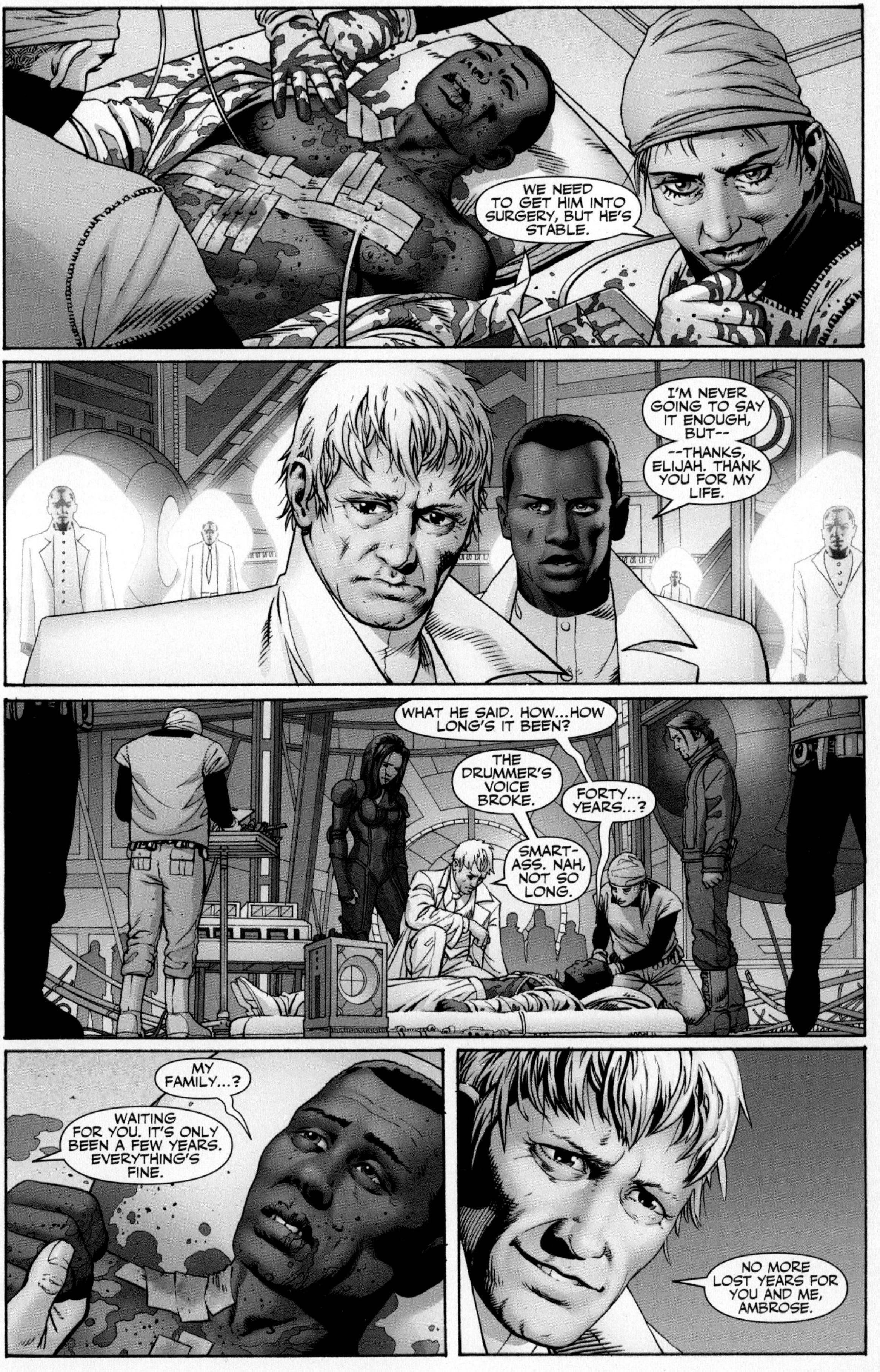
WE NEED TO GET HIM INTO SURGERY, BUT HE'S STABLE.
I'M NEVER GOING TO SAY IT ENOUGH, BUT--
--THANKS, ELIJAH. THANK YOU FOR MY LIFE.
WHAT HE SAID. HOW...HOW LONG'S IT BEEN?
THE DRUMMER'S VOICE BROKE.
FORTY... YEARS...?
SMART-ASS. NAH, NOT SO LONG.
MY FAMILY...?
WAITING FOR YOU. IT'S ONLY BEEN A FEW YEARS. EVERYTHING'S FINE.
NO MORE LOST YEARS FOR YOU AND ME, AMBROSE.

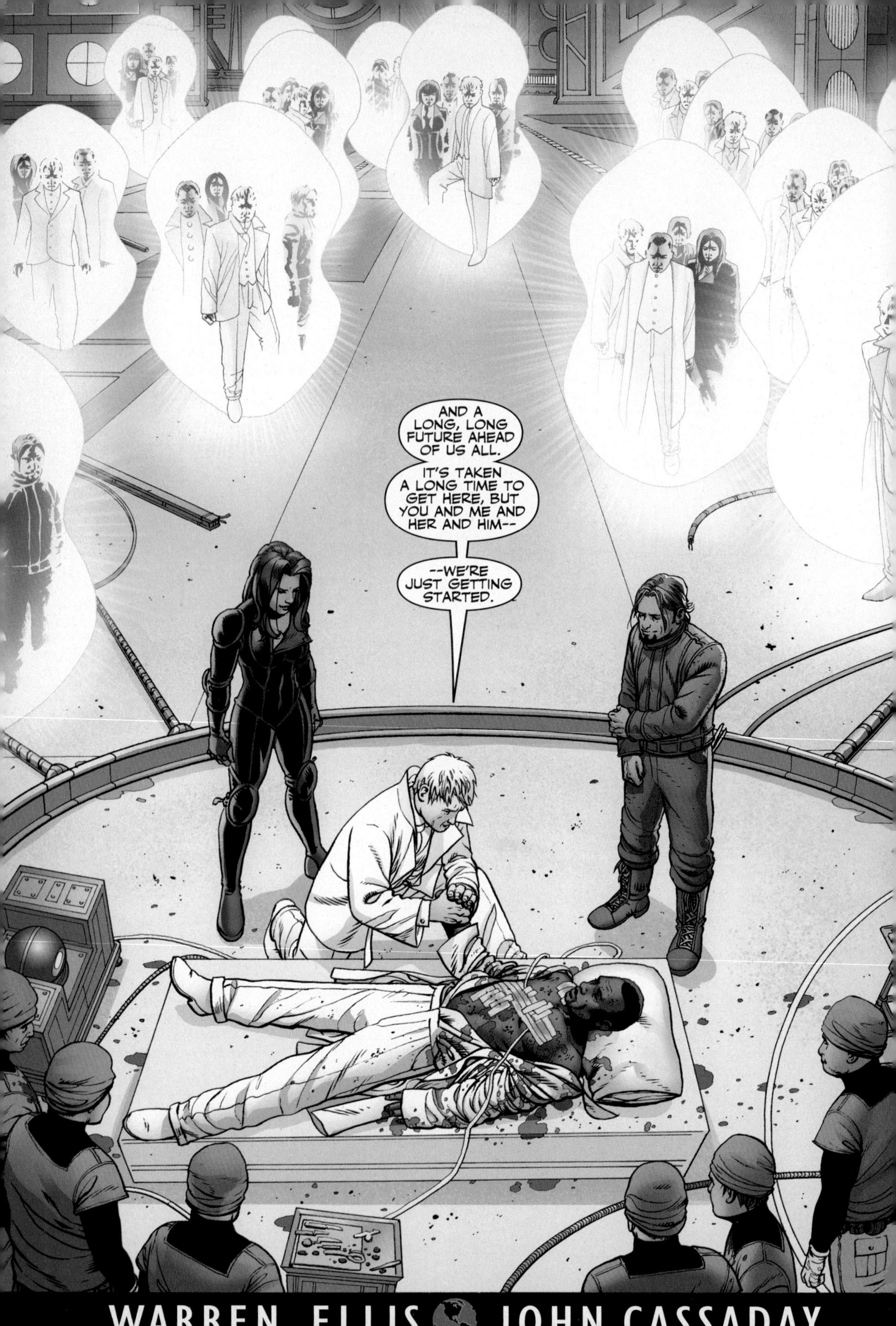

AND A LONG, LONG FUTURE AHEAD OF US ALL.
IT'S TAKEN A LONG TIME TO GET HERE, BUT YOU AND ME AND HER AND HIM--
--WE'RE JUST GETTING STARTED.

WARREN ELLIS JOHN CASSADAY

laura martin colors, comicraft letters, ass't editor kristy quinn, editor ben abernathy

For my father.

- Warren Ellis

To Warren Ellis, for making me a better artist.

- John Cassaday

For my family, and for Randy, my love. For my friends who keep me grounded while challenging my creativity. For all the flatters, colorists, and editors who keep me working. And finally, for Michael James, found and then lost way too soon. Miss you, sweetheart.

- Laura Martin

Warren Ellis is the award-winning creator of graphic novels such as Fell, Ministry Of Space and TRANSMETROPOLITAN, and the author of "underground classic" Crooked Little Vein.

Born in Fort Worth, Texas, **John Cassaday** has called New York City home since 1997, the same year he broke into the comics industry. John co-created the series DESPERADOES and PLANETARY and in 2002 re-launched Captain America. He then collaborated with Joss Whedon (Buffy: The Vampire Slayer, Toy Story) on Marvel's best-selling Astonishing X-Men. John's work on PLANETARY and Astonishing X-Men garnered him an unprecedented three consecutive Eisner Awards for Best Artist.

Cassaday's work has been exhibited in Hong Kong, New York and the Smithsonian Institute in Washington, DC. Aside from his comic projects, John has created designs for Ringling Bros. & Barnum Bailey Circus, Levi's Blue Jeans, and the Watchmen film. In late 2009, John made his directorial debut on Joss Whedon's TV series Dollhouse.

Laura Martin's fourteen-year career started right here at WildStorm FX. Her most recent work includes Astonishing X-Men with John Cassaday, The Ultimates, Stephen King's The Stand, Thor, Secret Invasion, Siege, DETECTIVE COMICS: THE QUESTION, BLACK LIGHTNING, and Dave Stevens' The Rocketeer. She's won two Eisners, three Harveys, and several Eagles and Wizard Fan Awards. She keeps saying she's going to write a book, but so far most people think it's a colorist legend, told around digital campfires by impressionable young flatters.

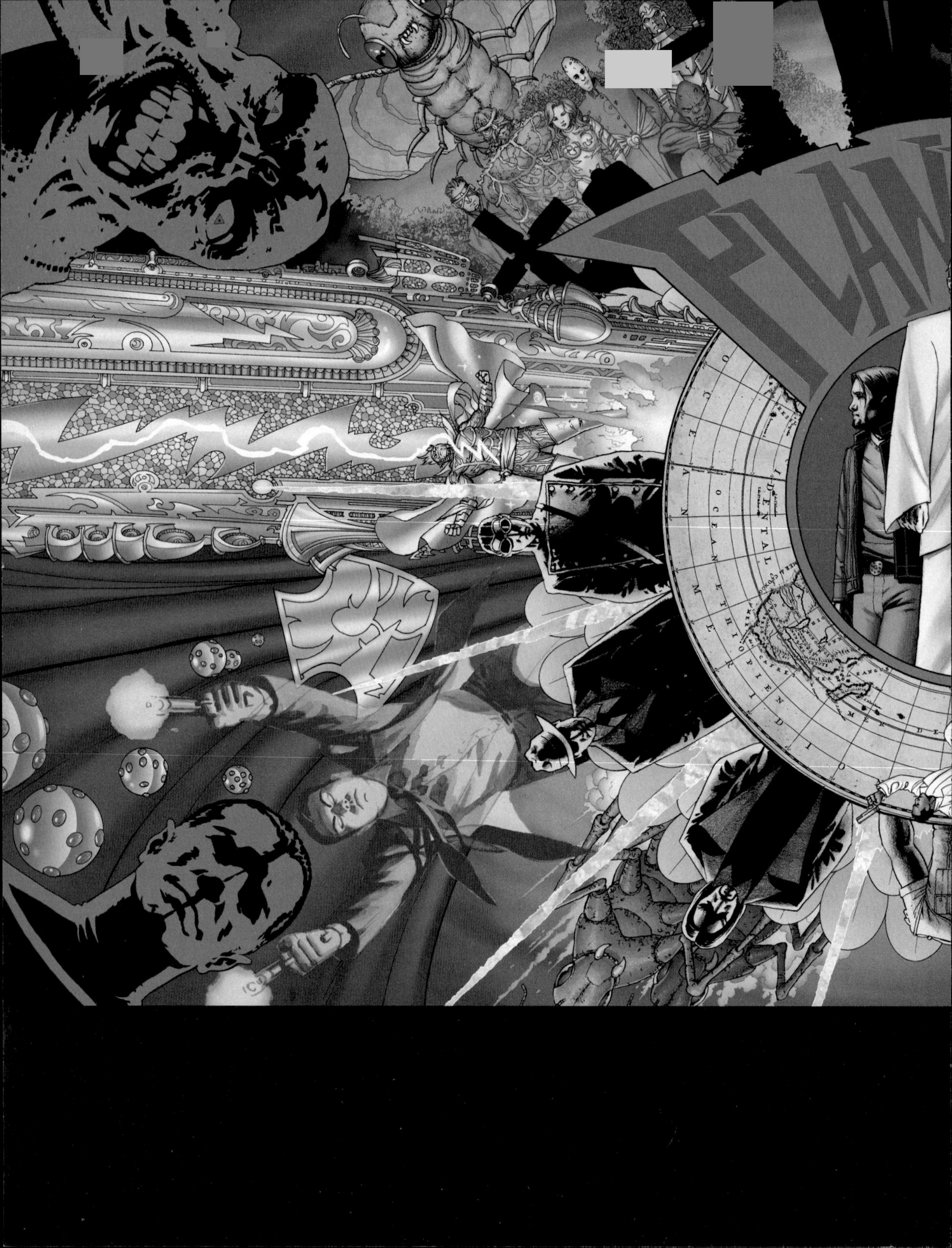

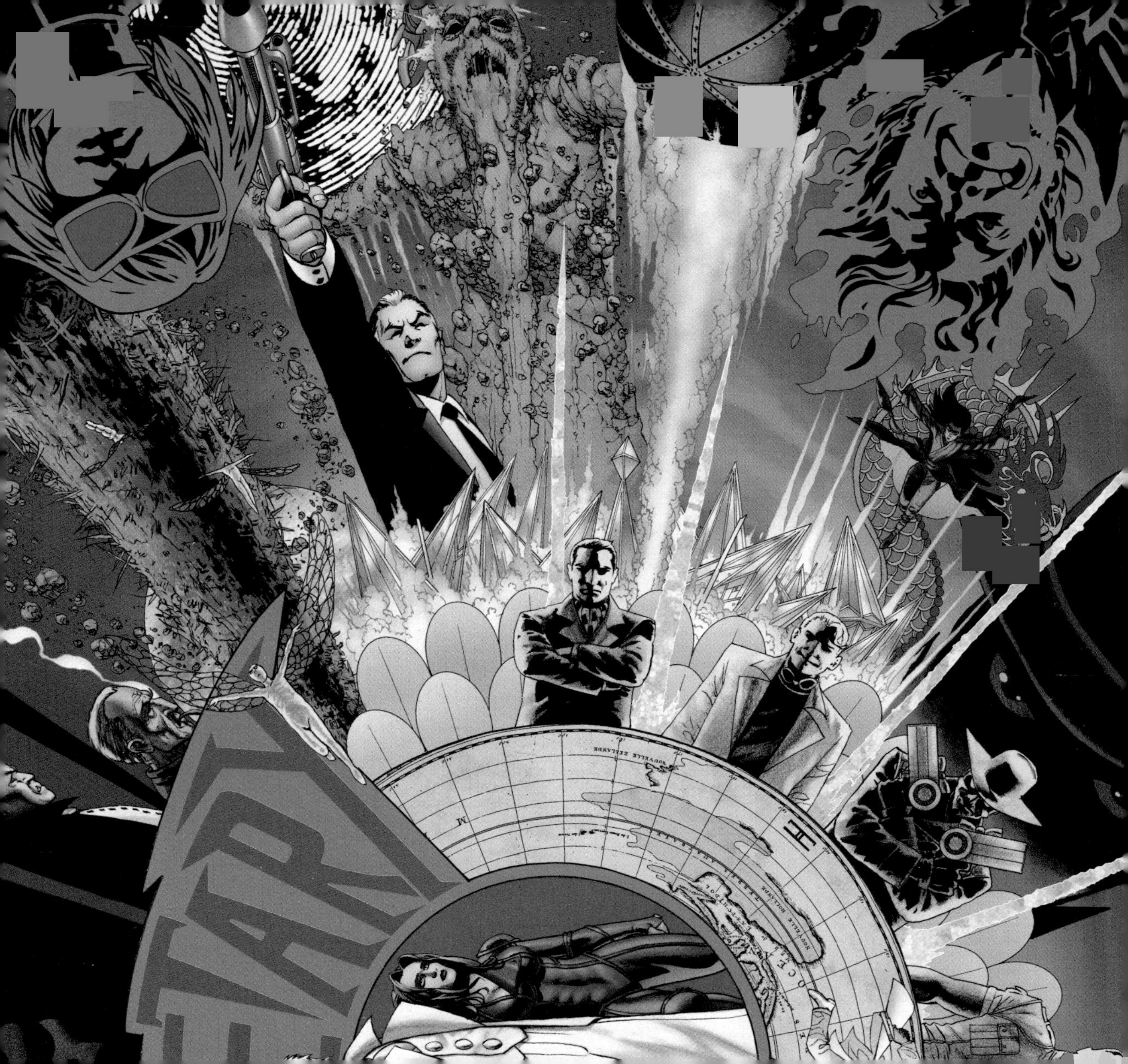

NOUVELLE ZELANDE
NOUVELLE HOLLANDE

PLANETARY
1

PLANETARY
WARREN ELLIS
2

PLANETARY
WARREN ELLIS
3

PLANETARY
CROSSING WORLDS

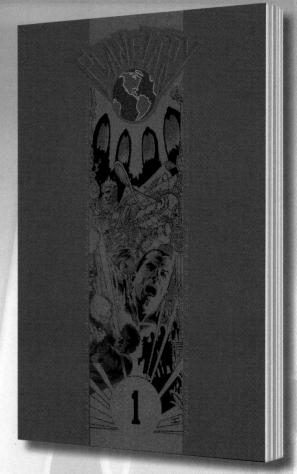

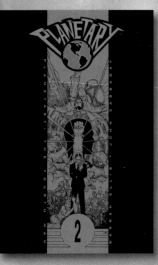

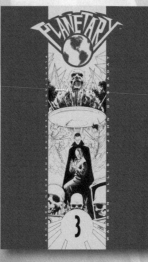

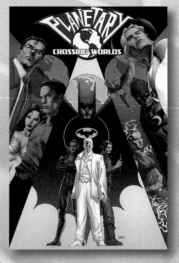

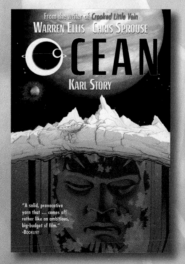

This is how the world ended...

WILDSTORM: ARMAGEDDON

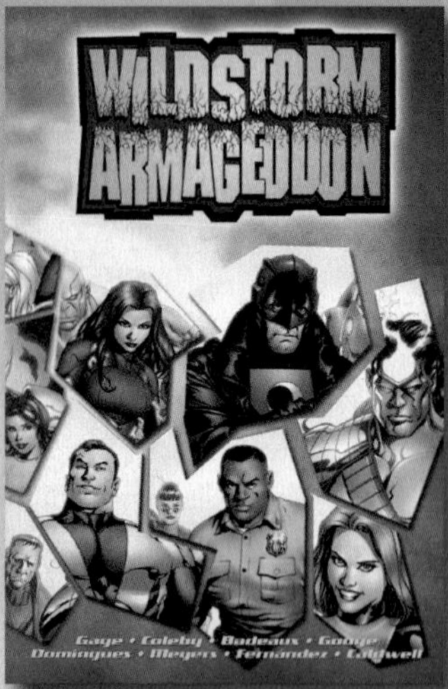
WILDSTORM ARMAGEDDON

Gage • Various

WILDSTORM: REVELATIONS

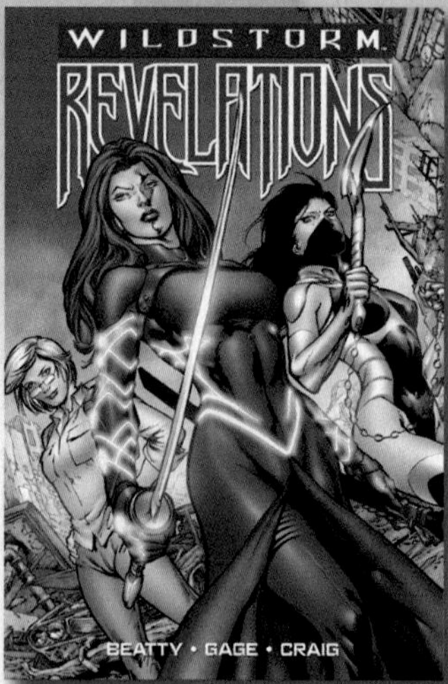
WILDSTORM
REVELATIONS
BEATTY • GAGE • CRAIG

**Gage • Beatty
Craig**

NUMBER OF THE BEAST

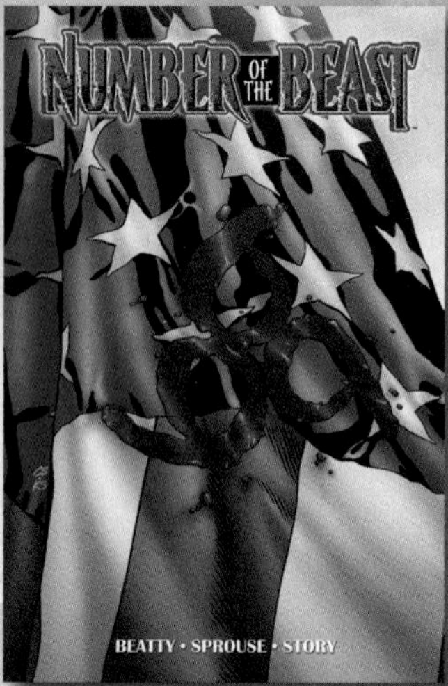
NUMBER OF THE BEAST
BEATTY • SPROUSE • STORY

**Beatty • Sprouse
Story**

THE AUTHORITY: WORLD'S END

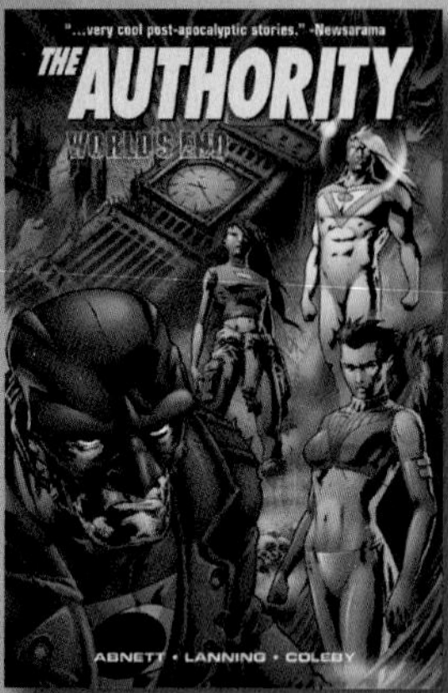
"...very cool post-apocalyptic stories." -Newsarama
THE AUTHORITY
WORLD'S END
ABNETT • LANNING • COLEBY

**Abnett • Lanning
Coleby**

GEN13: WORLD'S END

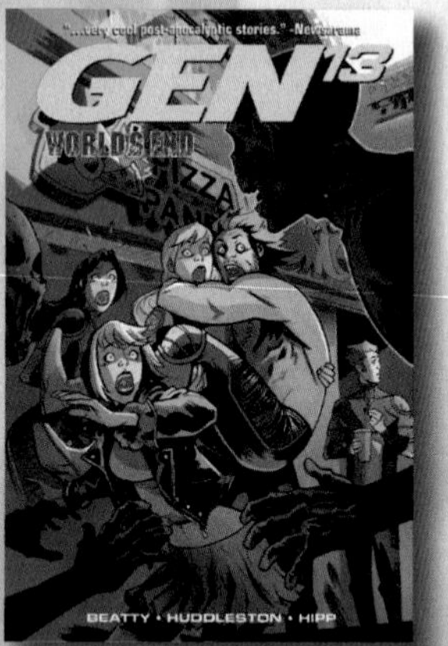
GEN13
WORLD'S END
BEATTY • HUDDLESTON • HIPP

**Beatty
Huddleston**

STORMWATCH: PHD WORLD'S END

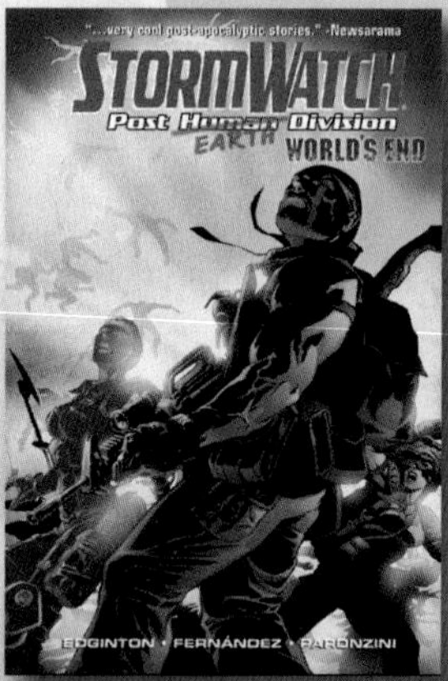
"...very cool post-apocalyptic stories." -Newsarama
STORMWATCH
Post Human Division
EARTH WORLD'S END
EDGINTON • FERNÁNDEZ • PARONZINI

**Edginton • Fernández
Paronzini**

WILDCATS: WORLD'S END

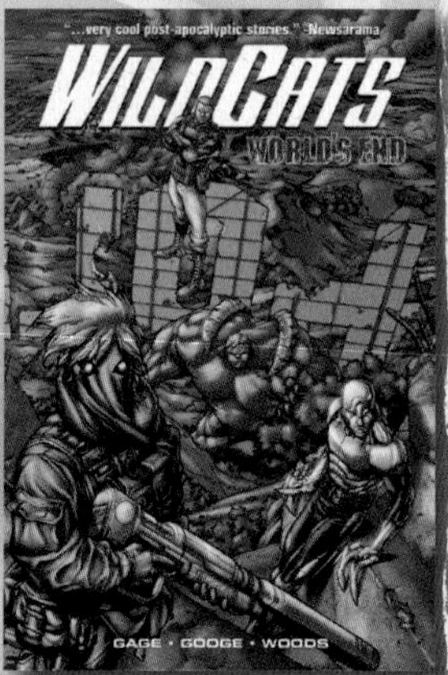
"...very cool post-apocalyptic stories." -Newsarama
WILDCATS
WORLD'S END
GAGE • GOOGE • WOODS

Gage • Googe

TO FIND COLLECTED EDITIONS AND MONTHLY COMICS FROM WILDSTORM AND DC COMICS
CALL 1-888-COMIC-BOOK
FOR THE NEAREST COMICS SHOP, OR GO TO YOUR LOCAL BOOKSTORE

ML

6/10